1993

Testing in American Schools

Asking the Right Questions

**CONGRESS OF THE UNITED STATES
OFFICE OF TECHNOLOGY ASSESSMENT**

Recommended Citation

U.S. Congress, Office of Technology Assessment, *Testing in American Schools: Asking the Right Questions*, OTA-SET-519 (Washington, DC: U.S. Government Printing Office, February 1992).

For sale by the U.S. Government Printing Office
Superintendent of Documents, Mail Stop: SSOP, Washington, DC 20402-9328
ISBN 0-16-036161-3

Foreword

Education is a primary concern for our country, and testing is a primary tool of education. No other country tests its school children with the frequency and seriousness that characterizes the United States. Once the province of classroom teachers, testing has also become an instrument of State and Federal policy. Over the past decade in particular, the desire of the Congress and State Legislatures to improve education and evaluate programs has substantially intensified the amount and importance of testing.

Because of these developments and in light of current research on thinking and learning, Congress asked OTA to provide a comprehensive report on educational testing, with emphasis on new approaches. Changing technology and new understanding of thinking and learning offer avenues for testing in different ways. These new approaches are attractive, but inevitably carry some drawbacks.

Too often, testing is treated narrowly, rather than as a flexible tool to obtain information about important questions. In this report, OTA places testing in its historical and policy context, examines the reasons for testing and the ways it is done, and identifies particular ways Federal policy affects the picture. The report also explores new approaches to testing that derive from modern technology and cognitive research.

The advisory panel, workshop participants, reviewers, and other contributors to this study were instrumental in defining the key issues and providing a range of perspectives on them. OTA thanks them for their commitment of energy and sense of purpose. Their participation does not necessarily represent endorsement of the contents of this report, for which OTA bears sole responsibility.

JOHN H. GIBBONS
Director

Testing in American Schools: Asking the Right Questions
Advisory Panel

---

[1]Formerly, Supervisor, Michigan Educational Assessment Program.

Testing in American Schools: Asking the Right Questions
OTA Project Staff

John Andelin, *Assistant Director, OTA*
Science, Information, and Natural Resources Division

Nancy Carson, *Program Manager*
Science, Education, and Transportation

Michael J. Feuer, *Project Director*

Kathleen Fulton, *Senior Analyst*

Patricia Morison, *Analyst*

David Wye, *Analyst*

Stephen Garcia, *Research Assistant*

George Branyan, *Research Analyst*

Elizabeth Hirsch, *Research Assistant*

Jamie Notter, *Research Assistant*

Caryn Cherlin, *Summer Intern*

Marsha Fenn, *Technical Editor*

Gay Jackson, *PC Specialist*

Tamara Cymanski, *Administrative Secretary*

Contractors

Douglas A. Archbald
University of Delaware

C.V. Bunderson
The Institute for Computer Uses in Education

Paul Burke
Consultant

Alan Collins and Jan Hawkins
Center for Children and Technology
Bank Street College

Larry Cuban
Stanford University

Thomas Kellaghan
St. Patricks College
Dublin, Ireland

Nancy Kober
Consultant

Robert L. Linn
University of Colorado, Boulder

George F. Madaus
Boston College

Gail R. Meister
Research for Better Schools

Ruth Mitchell and Amy Stempel
Council for Basic Education

Nelson L. Noggle
Centers for the Advancement of
    Educational Practices

Andrew C. Porter
University of Wisconsin, Madison

Judah Schwartz and Katherine Viator
Harvard University

Reviewers and Contributors

Judith Alamprese
COSMOS Corp.

Joseph Anzek
Brunswick Acres School
Kendall Park, New Jersey

Pam Aschbacher
University of California at Los Angeles

Walter Askin
California State University, Los Angeles

James Ayrer
Philadelphia School District

Eva Baker
University of California at Los Angeles

Gail Barcelo
New Jersey Board of Education

Walter Bartman
Walt Whitman High School
Bethesda, Maryland

Ernest Bauer
Oakland Michigan School District

Robert Bednarzik
U.S. Department of Labor

Grant Behnke
San Diego City Schools

Randy Bennet
Educational Testing Service

Sue Bennett
California Department of Education

Sue Betka
U.S. Department of Education

Marilyn Binkley
U.S. Department of Education

Diane Bishop
Arizona Department of Education

John Bledsoe
Walter Johnson High School
Bethesda, Maryland

Phyllis Blumenfeld
Center for Research on Learning and
    Schooling

Sigmund Boloz
Ganado Primary School
Ganado, Arizona

Norberto Bottani
Organisation for Economic Cooperation
    and Development

Gene Bottoms
Southern Regional Education Board

Gerald Bracey
Consultant

John Bransford
Learning Technology Center
Vanderbilt University

Alfred Brennan
Riverside Publishing Co.

W. Ross Brewer
Vermont Department of Education

Daniel Broun
Office of Technology Assessment

Diane Brown
American Psychological Association

Wallace Brown
Arizona Department of Education

Clare Burstall
National Foundation for Educational
    Research in England and Wales

Paula Butterfield
School District #7
Bozeman, Montana

Wayne Camara
American Psychological Association

Raymond Campeau
Bozeman Senior High School
Bozeman, Montana

Dale Carlson
California Department of Education

Ruben Carriedo
San Diego City Schools

Linda Carstens
San Diego City Schools

Daryl Chubin
Office of Technology Assessment

Stephen Clyman
National Board of Examiners

Kathleen Connor
Philadelphia Public Schools

John Cradler
Far West Laboratory

Stephanie Craib
Green Brook School

Elaine Craig
Center for Civic Education
Calabasis, California

James Crouse
University of Delaware

William Cummings
Harvard Institute for International
    Development

Susan Davis
San Diego City School Board

Christopher Dede
George Mason University

Richard Devore
Educational Testing Service

Kevin Dopart
Office of Technology Assessment

Nancy Draper
Chinle School District

Steven Dunbar
University of Iowa

E. Alden Dunham
Carnegie Corp. of New York

Mary Duru
District of Columbia Public Schools

Lois Easton
Arizona Department of Education

Max Eckstein
Queens College
City University of New York

Dorinda Edmondson
Office of Technology Assessment

Carol Edwards
Office of Technology Assessment

Donald Eklund
Association of American Publishers

Emerson Elliot
National Center for Education Statistics

Penelope Engel
Educational Testing Service

Thomas Fagan
U.S. Department of Education

Roger Farr
Indiana University

Frederick Finch
Riverside Publishing Co.

Tom Fitzgibbon
Techné Group, Inc.

Dexter Fletcher
Institute for Defense Analyses

Wendell Fletcher
Office of Technology Assessment

Geoffrey Fletcher
Texas Education Agency

Jack Foster
Education and Humanities Cabinet,
  Kentucky

Joy Frechtling
Montgomery County Public Schools,
  Maryland

John Fremer
Educational Testing Service

Susan Fuhrman
Rutgers University

Louis Gappmayer
Bozeman Senior High School
Bozeman, Montana

Howard Gardner
Harvard University

Robert Glaser
University of Pittsburgh

Alan Glenn
University of Washington

Susan Goldman
Learning Technology Center
Vanderbilt University

Steve Gorman
U.S. Department of Education

Jim Greeno
Stanford University

Robert Guion
Consulting Psychologist

Bill Haffey
Marine Corps Combat Development
  Command
Quantico, Virginia

Tom Haladyna
Arizona State University, West Campus

Robert Hample
University of Delaware

Kathi Hanna
Office of Technology Assessment

Walter Haney
Boston College

Walter Hathaway
Portland Public Schools

Lawrence Hecht
The College Board

Bev Hermon
Arizona House of Representatives

Richard Herrnstein
Harvard University

Lianping He
Chinese Embassy
Washington, DC

Steve Heyneman
World Bank

W. John Higham
New York State Education Department

Patricia Holliday
Deans School
Monmouth Junction, New Jersey

Shinichiro Horie
Japanese Embassy
Washington, DC

Jerry Hume
Basic American Foods

Michael Katz
University of Pennsylvania

Michael Kean
CTB MacMillan/McGraw Hill

E.W. Kelly
Cornell University

Jeff Kenney
National Council of Architectural
  Registration Boards

G. Gage Kingsbury
Portland Public Schools, Oregon

David Kirp
University of California, Berkeley

Daniel Koretz
Rand Corp.

Hannah Kruglanski
Maryland State Department of Education

Alan Lesgold
University of Pittsburgh

Mary Jean LeTendre
U.S. Department of Education

Janice Loomis
Alabama Center for Law and
  Civic Education

Esse Lovgren
Swedish National Board of Education

George Madaus
Boston College

Gene Maeroff
Carnegie Foundation for Advancement of
  Teaching

Lois Martin
Consultant

Michael Martinez
Educational Testing Service

Walter McDonald
Educational Testing Service

Michael Meagher
Longfellow Elementary School
Bozeman, Montana

William Mehrens
Michigan State University

Harry Miller
New England Telephone

Chip Moore
Office of Technology Assessment

Richard Murnane
Harvard University

Joseph S. Murphy
City University of New York

V. Nebyvaev
Embassy of the U.S.S.R.

David Niguidula
Brown University

Harold Noah
State University of New York, Buffalo

Nelson Noggle
Arizona State University

Desmond Nuttall
London School of Economics & Political
  Science

John O'Neill
National Computer Systems

James Olsen
WICAT Systems

Christine Onrubia
Office of Technology Assessment

Ralph Patrick
Jostens Learning Corp.

Bridgitte Pierre
French Embassy
Washington, DC

Barbara Plake
University of Nebraska, Lincoln

Neville Postlewaithe
University of Hamburg

James A. Poteet
Ball State University

Robert Radcliffe
British Embassy
Washington, DC

Robert Raines
San Diego City Schools

NOTE: OTA appreciates and is grateful for the valuable assistance and thoughtful critiques provided by the reviewers and contributors. The reviewers and contributors do not, however, necessarily approve, disapprove, or endorse this report. OTA assumes full responsibility for the report and the accuracy of its contents.

Workshop on Examination Systems in Other Countries and Lessons for the United States, March 27 and 28, 1991

Max Eckstein, *Workshop Chair*
Queens College, City University of New York, and
Teachers College, Columbia University

Gordon M. Ambach
Council of Chief State School Officers

Albert Beaton
Educational Testing Service

Sue Berryman
Columbia University

William Cummings
Harvard University

Carol Dahlberg
Richard Montgomery High School

Steve Heyneman
World Bank

Tom Kellaghan
St. Patrick's College, Dublin

George Madaus
Boston College

Gene Maeroff
Carnegie Foundation for Advancement of Teaching

Desmond Nuttall
London School of Economics & Political Science

Sol Pelavin
Pelavin Associates

Gary Phillips
U.S. Department of Education

Daniel Resnick
Carnegie-Mellon University

Edward D. Roeber
Michigan Educational Assessment Program

Sheldon H. White
Harvard University

NOTE: OTA appreciates and is grateful for the valuable assistance and thoughtful critiques provided by the workshop participants. The workshop participants do not, however, necessarily approve, disapprove, or endorse this report. OTA assumes full responsibility for the report and the accuracy of its contents.

Contents

Summary and Policy Options

Contents

Boxes

Figures

CHAPTER 1
Summary and Policy Options

The American educational system is unique. Among the first in the world to establish a commitment to public elementary and secondary schooling for all children, it has achieved an extraordinary record: enrollment rates of school-age children in the United States are among the highest in the world, and over 80 percent finish high school in some form between the ages of 18 and 24.[1] This tradition of education for the masses was nurtured in a system that, by all outward appearances, is complex and fragmented: 40 million children enrolled in some 83,000 schools scattered across some 15,000 school districts. Pluralism, diversity, and local control—hallmarks of American democracy—distinguish the American educational experiment from others in the world.

Student testing has always played a pivotal role in this experiment. Every day millions of school children take tests. Most are devised by teachers to see how well their pupils are learning and to signal to pupils what they should be studying. Surprise quizzes, take-home written assignments, oral presentations, pretests, retests, and end-of-year comprehensive examinations are all in the teacher's toolbox.

It is another category of test, however—originating outside the classroom, usually with standardized rules for scoring and administration—that has garnered the most attention, discussion, and controversy. From the earliest days of the public school movement, American educators, parents, policymakers, and taxpayers have turned to these tests as multipurpose tools: yardstick of individual progress in classrooms, agent of school reform, filter of educational opportunity, and barometer of the national educational condition.

Commonly referred to as "standardized tests,"[2] these instruments usually serve management functions; they are intended to inform decisions made by people other than the classroom teacher. They are used to monitor the achievement of children in school systems and guide decisions, such as students' eligibility for special resources or their qualification for admission to special school programs. Children's scores on such tests are often aggregated to describe the performance of classrooms, schools, districts, or States. With technological advances, these tests have become more reliable and more precise, and their popularity has grown. Today they are a fixture in American schools, as common as books and classrooms; standardized test results have become a major force in shaping public attitudes about the quality of American schools and the capabilities of American students.

Testing at a Crossroads

Tests designed and administered outside the classroom are given less frequently than teacher-made tests, but they are thoroughly entrenched in the American school scene and their use has been on the rise. One indicator of growth is sales of commercially produced standardized tests. Revenues from sales of tests used in elementary and secondary schools more than doubled (in constant dollars) between 1960 and 1989 (see figure 1-1), a period during which student enrollments grew by only 15 percent.[3] The rise in testing reflects a heightened demand from legislators at all levels—and their constituents—for evidence that education dollars

---

[1]For current data comparing primary and secondary school enrollment rates in the United States and other countries, see U.S. Department of Education, National Center for Education Statistics, *Digest of Education Statistics, 1990* (Washington, DC: February 1991), p. 380; and George Madaus, Boston College, and Thomas Kellaghan, St. Patricks College, Dublin, "Student Examination Systems in the European Community: Lessons for the United States," OTA contractor report, June 1991. For a thorough analysis of completion and dropout data, see U.S. Department of Education, National Center for Education Statistics, *Dropout Rates in the US: 1989* (Washington, DC: September 1990). With respect to postsecondary education, as well, participation rates of American high school graduates are the highest in the world: close to 60 percent of persons of college-going age were enrolled in postsecondary institutions in 1985, compared to 30 percent in France, Germany, and Japan, 21 percent in the United Kingdom, and 55 percent in Canada. For details see Kenneth Redd and Wayne Riddle, Congressional Research Service, "Comparative Education: Statistics on Education in the U.S. and Selected Foreign Nations," 88-764 EPW, Nov. 14, 1988.

[2]Testing terms have both technical and common meanings, and often cause confusion. Box 1-A is a glossary of words used in this report, and will help the reader understand the precise meanings of these words.

[3]U.S. Department of Education, *Digest of Education Statistics, 1990*, op. cit., footnote 1, p. 12. The fact that testing grew proportionally more rapidly than the student population suggests that policymakers may have responded to increased enrollments by attempting to institute greater administrative efficiency in the schools. As discussed in ch. 4, this is a familiar historical trend.

Figure 1-1—Growth in Revenues From Test Sales and in Public School Enrollments, 1960-89

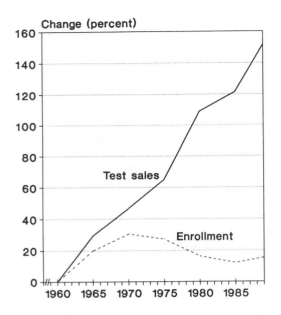

NOTE: Revenues from test sales are in constant 1982 dollars. Tests are commercially produced standardized tests for grades K-12. Enrollments are total students in public schools, grades K-12. Percent change is computed over 1960 base year (not over prior year level).

SOURCE: Office of Technology Assessment, 1992. Test sales data from Filomena Simora (ed.), *The Bowker Annual* (New York, NY: Reed Publishing, 1970-1990). Enrollment data from U.S. Department of Education, National Center for Educational Statistics, *Digest of Education Statistics, 1990* (Washington, DC: February 1991), p. 12.

Figure 1-2—Shifts in Federal, State, and Local Funding Patterns for Public Elementary and Secondary Schools, Selected Years

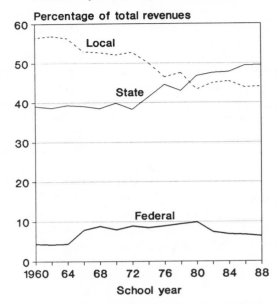

SOURCE: U.S. Department of Education, National Center for Education Statistics, *Digest of Educational Statistics 1990* (Washington, DC: February 1991).

are spent effectively. Holding schools and teachers "accountable" has increasingly become synonymous with increased standardized testing.

State and local governments have traditionally assumed the greatest share of elementary and secondary education funding, as shown in figure 1-2. State funding began to exceed local funding as a percentage of the total starting in the mid-1970s, and State-mandated testing grew accordingly; 46 States had mandated testing programs in 1990 as compared to 29 in 1980.[4] Similarly, increases in Federal education spending during the 1960s and 1970s spurred increases in testing as Congress sought data to evaluate Federal programs and monitor national educational progress. The Federal Government currently spends over $20 billion per year on elementary and secondary education in programs administered by over a dozen Federal agencies.[5]

Outcome-based measures of the effectiveness of educational programs—generally achievement test scores—have become key elements in the congressional appropriations and authorization process.

Contradictory demands for reevaluation of testing have been caught up in recent school reform initiatives. On the one hand, many teachers, administrators, and others attempting to redesign curricula, reform instruction, and improve learning feel stymied by tests that do not accurately reflect new educational goals. On the other hand, most leading educational measurement experts emphasize that conventional standardized tests are useful tools in gauging the strengths, weaknesses, and progress of American students.

Motivated in part by changing visions of classroom learning and by frustration with tests that many critics claim can hinder children's progress toward higher levels of achievement, many educators are turning to changed methods of testing. Some of these methods are modifications of conventional written tests; others are bolder innovations, requiring stu-

---

[4]OTA data on State testing practices, 1985 and 1991.

[5]U.S. Department of Education, *Digest of Education Statistics, 1990*, op. cit., footnote 1, p. 337.

Box 1-A—A Glossary of Testing Terminology

A test score is an estimate. It is based on sampling what the test taker knows or can do. For example, by asking a sample of questions (drawn from all the material that has been taught), a biology test is used to estimate how much biology the student has learned. Tests can provide valuable information about an individual's competence, knowledge, skills, or behavior. *Achievement tests* are intended to estimate what a student knows and can do in a specific subject as a result of schooling. Achievement tests and *aptitude tests* are both instruments that estimate aspects of an individual's developed abilities; they exist on a continuum, with the former being more closely tied to specific curricula and school programs and the latter intended to capture knowledge acquired both in and out of school.

Standardized tests are administered and scored under conditions uniform to all students. Although most people associate standardized tests with the multiple-choice format, it is important to emphasize that standardization is a generic concept that can apply to any testing format—from written essays to oral examinations to producing a portfolio. Standardization is needed to make test scores comparable and to assure as much as possible that test takers have equal chances to demonstrate what they know.

The word *standards* applied to tests has at least two different meanings. In the more general context it denotes goals, desirable behaviors, or models to which students, teachers, or schools should aspire. Such standards describe what optimal performance looks like and what is desirable for students to know. For example, the National Council of Teachers of Mathematics has determined that a standard for mathematics instruction is to emphasize mathematics as problem solving. The word standards, in its more technical meaning, denotes the specific levels of *proficiency* that students are expected to attain. Thus, setting a passing score for a test is equivalent to setting a standard of performance on that test.

Because they are based on samples of behavior, tests are necessarily imprecise: scores can vary for reasons unrelated to the individual's actual achievement. Test scores can only *describe* what skills have been mastered, but they cannot, alone, *explain* why learning has occurred, or prescribe ways to improve it. The fact that achievement is affected by schools, parents, home background, and other factors constrains the inferences that can be drawn about schools and programs. Test scores must be interpreted carefully.

Reliability refers to the consistency and generalizability of test data. Will a student's score today be close (if not identical) to her score tomorrow? Do the questions covering a subset of skills generalize to the broader universe of skills? If tests are scored by human judges, to what extent do different judges agree in their estimations of student achievement? A test needs to demonstrate a high degree of reliability before it is used to make decisions, particularly those with high stakes attached.

Validity refers to whether or not a test measures what it is supposed to measure, and whether appropriate inferences can be drawn from test results. Validity is judged from many types of evidence, including, in the views of some experts, the consequences of translating test-based inferences into decisions or policies that can affect individuals or institutions. An acceptable level of validity must be demonstrated before a test is used to make decisions.

There are two basic ways of interpreting student performance on tests. One is to describe a student's test performance as it compares to that of other students (e.g., he typed better than 90 percent of his classmates). *Norm-referenced tests* are designed to make this type of comparison. The other method is to describe the skills or performance that the student demonstrates (e.g., he typed 45 words per minute without errors). *Criterion-referenced tests* are designed to compare a student's test performance to clearly defined learning tasks or skill levels.

Performance assessment refers to testing methods that require students to create an answer or product that demonstrates their knowledge or skills. Performance assessment can take many different forms including writing short answers, doing mathematical computations, writing an extended essay, conducting an experiment, presenting an oral argument, or assembling a portfolio of representative work.

Constructed-response items are one kind of performance assessment consisting of open-ended written items on a conventional test. However, they require students to produce the solution to a question rather than to select from an array of possible answers (as multiple-choice items do).

Computer-administered testing is a generic term covering any test that is taken by a student seated at a computer. A special type of computer-administered testing is *computer-adaptive testing*, which applies the computer's memory and branching capabilities in order to adapt the test to the skill levels shown by the individual test taker as the test is taken.

SOURCE: Office of Technology Assessment, 1992.

Photo credit: Bob Daemmrich

Most children in the United States take standardized achievement tests several times during elementary and secondary school. Standardized test results have become a major force in shaping public attitudes about the quality of American schools and the capabilities of American students.

dents to demonstrate their knowledge and skills through methods known as "performance assessment." Computer technologies, video, and integrated multimedia systems add capabilities and richness not usually attainable from conventional tests, and are gaining ground in assessment as well as instruction.

These new approaches to testing have been fueled by some cognitive scientists who claim that complex thinking involves processes not easily reduced to the routinized tasks required on conventional tests. A

recent report on science education, for example, argued that:

> Rather than mastering concepts, students believe that recognizing terms in a multiple-choice format is the appropriate educational goal. In the long run the impact of current modes of testing on enduring skills and strategies for learning will be inimical to reform.[6]

In contrast, many testing professionals maintain that school improvement efforts must be constructed on a solid foundation of information about what

[6]National Research Council, *Fulfilling the Promise: Biology Education in the Nation's Schools* (Washington, DC: 1990), p. 44. Another recent report concluded that: ". . . to direct testing along a more constructive course, we must draw on richer direct evidence of knowledge and skill from information sources beyond multiple choice tests." See National Commission on Testing and Public Policy, *From Gatekeeper to Gateway: Transforming Testing in America* (Chestnut Hill, MA: Boston College, 1990), p. xi; also Walter Haney and George Madaus, "Searching for Alternatives to Standardized Tests: Whys, Whats, and Whithers," *Phi Delta Kappan*, vol. 70, No. 9, May 1989.

students are learning; well-designed tests, they say, if used and interpreted properly, can provide invaluable information in a reliable, consistent, and efficient fashion. For example, standardized tests can inform policymakers by supplying trend data on the skill levels of American students. Recent analysis of data from the Iowa Tests of Basic Skills revealed that student performance improved between 1979 and 1985, even on test items designed to assess certain higher order skills, contradicting findings from other test data that improvements were limited to mechanical tasks.[7]

Measurement experts contend that these standardized tests are also useful to teachers, as tools to calibrate classroom impressions of student progress; they are viewed as one relatively efficient, albeit inexact indicator of how a given child or school system is progressing relative to students nationwide. One test author expressed a view shared by many others in the testing community:

> . . . comprehensive, survey-type standardized achievement tests have served a useful function in monitoring the achievement levels of individual pupils and the aggregate groupings of these students in terms of classrooms, buildings, and the district. . . .[8]

Common Ground

To outsiders listening in on this debate, it may appear that proponents of conventional and new forms of assessment are adversaries locked in an intractable stalemate. Closer inspection, however, reveals that testing policy is not a zero-sum game in which either existing testing or new methods win, but an arena with multiple and mutually compatible choices.

The trick is using the kind of test that is best suited to providing the desired type of information. Thus, although some activists in the debate have carved out extreme positions, most others agree on at least these two fundamental points:

- **different forms of testing can, if used correctly, enrich our understanding of student achievement; and**

- **tests of any kind should be used only to serve the functions for which they were designed and validated.**

On this common ground it may be possible to build genuine reform. One prominent psychologist and long-time participant in the politics and science of testing, commenting on what appears to be a rare opportunity, observed that: ''. . . our testing ecology is entirely manmade; what we made we can change.''[9]

Lessons of History

But history tempers the optimism. Since the birth of mass public education in America some 150 years ago, innovation in tests and testing has been most attractive during periods of heightened public anxiety about the state of the schools. During these periods, however, legislators and school officials feel the greatest pressure to act, and are most prone to rely on *existing* tests as levers of policy. Thus, researchers and policymakers involved in the painstaking process of curricular reform and new test design often find themselves at odds with those who demand quicker and more immediately noticeable action. Hence (as described in detail in ch. 4), tests have too often been used to serve functions for which they were not designed or adequately validated. Within the education policy and research community, therefore, there is an undercurrent of concern that new tests will, as in the past, be implemented before they have been validated and before their effects on learning can be understood.

For some educators the principal concern is that new tests will raise new barriers—to women, people of color, other minorities, and the economically disadvantaged. On these issues, too, caution flags are up: precisely because testing has historically been viewed as a means to achieve educational equity, tests themselves have always been scrutinized on the question of whether they do more to alleviate or exacerbate social, economic, and educational disparities (see box 1-B).

---

[7]See Elizabeth Witt, Myunghee Han, and H.D. Hoover, ''Recent Trends in Achievement Tests Scores: Which Students are Improving and on What Levels of Skill Complexity?'' paper presented at the annual meeting of the National Council on Measurement in Education, Boston, MA, 1990. See also Robert Linn and Stephen Dunbar, ''The Nation's Report Card Goes Home: Good News and Bad About Trends in Achievement,'' *Phi Delta Kappan*, vol. 72, No. 2, October 1990, p. 132. For a thorough analysis of trends in achievement that illustrates the importance of using multiple measures of performance, see Daniel Koretz, *Trends in Educational Achievement* (Washington, DC: Congressional Budget Office, 1986).

[8]Herbert Rudman, ''The Future of Testing is Now,'' *Educational Measurement: Issues and Practice*, vol. 6, No. 3, fall 1987, p. 6.

[9]Sheldon White, professor of psychology, Harvard University, personal communication, June 1991.

Box 1-B—Equity, Fairness, and Educational Testing

Steven Jay Gould's seminal treatise on the history of intelligence testing is dedicated to ". . . the memory of Grammy and Papa Joe, who came, struggled, and prospered, Mr. Goddard notwithstanding."[1] From his very first pages, then, Gould telegraphs the deeply emotional chords struck by concepts of psychological measurement and testing. As Gould explains midway through the book, Goddard had been one of a handful of prominent American psychologists who used test data to advance racist, xenophobic, and eugenicist ideologies. Although Goddard himself later recanted,[2] in one of the more impressive turnarounds in the history of science, the atmosphere of the 1920s and 1930s gave tests ". . . the rather happy property of being a conservative social innovation. They could be perceived as justifying the richness of the rich and the poverty of the poor; they legitimized the existing social order."[3]

The historical misuse of intelligence tests and their achievement test cousins—to bolster support for restrictive immigration laws, to limit college admissions, and to label children as uneducable—has left an indelible stain on the "science" of mental measurement.[4] It is no wonder that testing policy arouses the passions of Americans concerned with equal opportunity and social mobility. As in the past, those passions run in both directions: everyone may agree that testing can be a wedge, but some see the wedge forcing open the gates of opportunity while others see it as the doorstop keeping the gates tightly shut.

Consider, for example, the following excerpts, both from individuals deeply concerned with opportunities for minority and disadvantaged children:

> . . . minority youngsters who . . . are disproportionately among the poor, tend to be relegated to poor schools, or tracked out of academic courses, just as young women are not encouraged to take math and science. Therefore, the differences in the "group" scores [on the Scholastic Aptitude Test]. . . represent anything but "bias." Rather, the score is a faithful messenger of the unequal distribution in our country of educational resources and encouragement.[5]

> Test makers claim that the lower test scores of racial and ethnic minorities and of students from low-income families simply reflect the biases and inequities that exist in American schools and American society. Biases and inequities certainly exist—but standardized tests do not merely reflect their impact; they compound them.[6]

---

[1]Steven Jay Gould, *The Mismeasure of Man* (New York, NY: Norton, 1981), dedication, p. 7.

[2]See, e.g., Carl Degler, *In Search of Human Nature* (London, England: Oxford University Press, 1991).

[3]Sheldon White, "Social Implications of IQ," *The Myth of Measurability*, Paul Houts (ed.) (New York, NY: Hart Publishing Co., 1977), p. 38. See also Clarence Karier, "Testing for Order and Control in the Liberal Corporate State," *The IQ Controversy*, N. Block and G. Dworkin (eds.) (New York, NY: Random House, 1976), pp. 339-373. Karier's basic argument, as summarized by another historian of testing, was ". . . the tests . . . were biased in terms of social class, economic, cultural, and racial background. Their use in schools served to block opportunity for the lower classes and immigrants . . . [and fashion] a system of tracking in the schools that reinforced social inequality. . . ." Paul Chapman, *Schools as Sorters* (New York, NY: New York University Press, 1988), p. 8. For opposing viewpoints see, e.g., Mark Snyderman and Stanley Rothman, *The IQ Controversy* (New Brunswick, NJ: Transaction Books, 1988); Arthur Jensen, *Bias in Mental Testing* (New York, NY: Free Press, 1980); or Richard Herrnstein, "IQ," *Atlantic Monthly*, vol. 228, September 1971, pp. 43-64.

[4]For details on the history of achievement and intelligence testing, see ch. 4 of this report.

[5]Donald Stewart, president, College Entrance Examination Board, "Thinking the Unthinkable: Standardized Testing and the Future of American Education," speech before the Columbus Metropolitan Club, Columbus, OH, Feb. 22, 1989.

[6]Monty Neill and Noe Medina, "Standardized Testing: Harmful to Educational Health," *Phi Delta Kappan*, vol. 70, No. 9, May 1989, p. 691.

The Purpose of This Report

Federal policymakers are caught in an unenviable dilemma. On the one hand they must satisfy the growing demand for accountability, which is often expressed in terms of simple questions: Do the schools work? Are students learning? On the other hand, they must also be responsive to growing disaffection with the quality of data on which administrators rely for evaluations of programs: achievement scores are rough indicators, at best, of progress in attaining the many goals of federally funded programs. Not surprisingly, Federal evaluation requirements that place additional testing burdens on grantees and program participants often spur an interest in revising those very requirements.[10] As the Federal Government has become a more prominent player in elementary and secondary education,

---

[10]For example, the Department of Education recently formed a task force to look into problems of testing and evaluation for the Chapter 1/Title I compensatory education program. See ch. 3 of this report.

These excerpts make clear the need to specify and control the functions of testing. Both sides appear to agree that tests can be used to identify inequalities in educational opportunities.[7] But the question becomes how to use that information. Advocates of testing as a ''gatekeeper'' argue that ability and achievement, rather than family background, class, or the specific advantages that might accrue to students in wealthy school districts, should govern the distribution of opportunities and rewards in society. Moreover, they add, this system of distribution creates incentives for school systems to provide their students with the best possible chances for success.

On the other hand, opponents contend that ability and achievement scores are highly correlated with socioeconomic background factors[8] and with the quality of schooling children receive[9]; under these circumstances, ''. . . no assessment can be considered equitable for students if there has been differential opportunity to access the material upon which the assessment is based.''[10]

This debate will not be resolved easily or quickly; nor will it become moot with the advent of alternative methods of assessment. On the contrary, it could very well become even more heated and complex.[11] Educational testing policy in the United States is at a crossroads, and if history supplies any clues, the future of assessment will depend in large part on basic issues of equity, fairness, and the improvement of opportunities for minorities and the disadvantaged. The core questions are well summarized in a recent book on science assessment:

> Are we better off with the flawed system now in place or with an unknown examination system that could bring even greater problems? What differences in opportunity to learn and achieve will flow from assessment? Will it help students, teachers, or parents do something different to promote learning, for example, by moving the best teachers to the neediest students or providing summer instruction for students not at grade level at the end of the school year? And does better assessment increase our responsibility for intervention, as better technology in medicine has increased the demand and the ethical dilemmas we face in determining the use of that technology in treatment? If we are prepared to *do* more, once we know more, perhaps the dangers of inequity possible in new assessment are worth the risk. But absent the resolve to intervene, one could argue that assessment becomes little more than voyeurism.[12]

---

[7]For discussion of test bias and the effects of testing on minority students, see, e.g., Walter Haney, Boston College, ''Testing and Minorities,'' draft monograph, January 1991, p. 24.

[8]See, e.g., Christopher Jencks et al., *Inequality* (New York, NY: Basic Books, 1972).

[9]See, e.g., Ronald Ferguson, ''Paying for Public Education: New Evidence on How and Why Money Matters,'' *Harvard Journal on Legislation*, vol. 28, No. 2, summer 1991, pp. 465-498.

[10]Shirley Malcom, ''Equity and Excellence Through Authentic Science Assessment,'' *Science Assessment in the Service of Reform*, Gerald Kulm and Shirley Malcom (eds.) (Washington, DC: American Association for the Advancement of Science, 1991), p. 316. It is interesting to note that standardized test scores, viewed by some critics as blocking entry to education and work opportunities, have been used to justify major public programs to help minority and disadvantaged children: ''. . . the preeminent example . . . was in the 1960s, when lower performance of minority and inner city children was used to bolster arguments for the war on poverty and to help propel passage of the landmark Elementary and Secondary Education Act of 1965. . . .'' (Haney, op. cit., footnote 7, p. 22.)

[11]Some minority educators, for example, fear that new assessment methods will stifle opportunities for minority students who have recently begun to do better on conventional tests. There is also uncertainty over whether or not tests should be used for placing children in remedial programs. Parents in California sued recently, not because their children were being tested but, on the contrary, because the State had followed the precedent set in the landmark *Hobson* v. *Hansen* case, and banned testing as a basis for diagnosing learning difficulties and placing children in remedial tracks. For further discussion of this and other legal issues, see ch. 2.

[12]Malcom, op. cit., footnote 10, p. 320.

and as the public's attitudes toward concepts of national educational goals and standards have evolved, Congress has become more involved in the testing debate.[11]

Congress has a stake in U.S. testing policy for three main reasons:

- to ensure that accurate and reliable data about American educational achievement are provided to lawmakers, program administrators, parents, teachers, test takers, and the general public;

- to ensure that the tests used to evaluate Federal education programs do not, in themselves,

---

[11]A 1989 Gallup poll found that the majority of respondents supported the idea of national achievement standards and goals, but few supported either State or Federal intervention in the definition of those standards and goals. For discussion see George Madaus, Boston College, and Thomas Kellaghan, St. Patricks College, Dublin, ''Examination Systems in the European Community: Implications for a National Examination System in the United States,'' OTA contractor report, April 1991.

impede progress toward program goals; and

- to ensure that tests are used fairly and do not infringe on individual rights or impose unacceptable social costs.

Congress faces a variety of decisions that could have significant and long-term effects on the scope, quantity, and quality of testing in the United States. Issues related to national testing and the role of tests in Federal education programs are already on the congressional agenda; issues regarding the rights of test takers may emerge, as they have in previous times, if new national and State tests are mandated or if the stakes attached to existing tests are raised.

This report is aimed at helping Congress:

- better understand the functions, history, capabilities, limitations, uses, and misuses of educational tests;
- learn more about the promises and pitfalls of new assessment methods and technologies; and
- identify and weigh policy options affecting educational testing.

To unravel the complexities of these topics, OTA examined technological and institutional aspects of educational testing. This summary and policy chapter synthesizes OTA's findings on tests and testing, and outlines options for congressional action. Chapter 2 examines recent changes in the uses of testing as an instrument of policy, chapter 3 covers current issues affecting the role of the Federal Government in educational testing, chapter 4 reviews the history of testing in the United States, and chapter 5 considers lessons from testing in selected European and Asian countries. The final three chapters focus on the tests themselves. Chapter 6 explains characteristics and purposes of existing educational tests, and examines the reasons new test designs seem warranted. Chapter 7 explores various approaches to performance assessment and how these methods are being implemented in schools, and chapter 8 examines the current and future roles of computers and other information technologies in assessment.

In this report, the analysis and discussion are framed in terms of the functions of testing. OTA concludes that examining the capability of various tests to meet specific objectives is the necessary first step in abating the seemingly endless controversy over the quantity and format of testing in American schools, and in laying the groundwork for new approaches.

The Functions of Testing

Educational tests have traditionally served many purposes that can be grouped into three basic functions:

- to aid teachers and students in the conduct of classroom learning;
- to monitor systemwide educational outcomes; and
- to inform decisions about the selection, placement, and credentialing of individual students.

These three functions have a common feature: they provide information to support decisionmaking. However, they differ in the kinds of information they seek and the types of decisions they can support, and test results appropriate for some decisions may be inappropriate for others.

Classroom Feedback for Students and Teachers

Teachers must constantly adapt to the behaviors, learning styles, and progress of the students in their classrooms.[12] Tests can help them organize and process the steady stream of data arising from classroom interactions. Just as physicians use body temperature, blood pressure, heart rate, x rays, and other data to form an image of the patient's health and to determine appropriate treatments, teachers can use data of various types to better manage their classes and, in some circumstances, to tailor lessons to the specific needs of individual students. Students can use information to gain sharper understanding of their strengths and weaknesses in different subjects and can adjust their study time accordingly.

Tests that can aid classroom instruction and learning need to:

- provide detailed information about specific skills, rather than global or general scores;
- be linked to content that is taught in the classroom;
- be administered frequently;
- give feedback to students and teachers as quickly as possible;

---

[12]For a recent analysis of the internal workings of classrooms and implications for education policy, see Edward Pauly, *The Classroom Crucible: What Really Works, What Doesn't, and Why* (New York, NY: Basic Books, 1991), especially ch. 4.

Photo credit: Library of Congress

A student in 1943 takes her oral spelling examination after completing a written examination on the blackboard. Teachers have always used a variety of tests to help them manage their classes and evaluate student progress.

ing systematic and informed answers about the learning that takes place in schools. In an educational system as decentralized and diverse as the American one, there is a nearly insatiable appetite for evidence that all schools are providing children with a decent education. Since the mid-19th century, tests have been used to determine how much students in different schools or school districts were learning. Recent increases in Federal expenditures have stimulated new demands for system accountability.

Test scores alone cannot reveal how or why learning has occurred, or the degree to which schools, parents, the child's home background, or other factors have affected learning. When combined appropriately with other data, however, such as prior test results and children's socioeconomic status, test results can help explain—as well as describe—the outcomes of schooling.[13]

For tests to yield meaningful comparisons across schools and districts, they must:

- be uniformly and impartially administered and scored; and
- meet reasonable standards of consistency, fairness, and validity.

In addition, to be useful system monitoring tools, these tests:

- should provide general information about achievement, rather than detailed information on specific skills;
- should describe the performance of groups of students—classrooms, schools, districts, or States—rather than individuals (thereby allowing the use of sampling methods that yield the desired information without the costly testing of every student); and
- can be administered infrequently (once or twice a year at the most).

- be scored or graded to help students learn from their errors and misunderstandings, and help teachers intervene when students get stuck; and
- be based on clear and open criteria for scoring so that students know what to study and how they are being evaluated.

System Monitoring

How well is a school or school system performing? This is a question often posed from the outside, by parents, legislators, and others with particularly high stakes in the answer. As shown in chapters 2 and 4, the question is usually posed with more urgency when the impression is that the answer will be ''not very well.''

Educational tests of various sorts have long been viewed as objective instruments capable of provid-

Selection, Placement, Credentialing[14]

Tests designed to provide data about *individual* students' current achievement or predicted perform-

---

[13]For example, recent analysis of data from close to 1,000 school districts in Texas found significant differences in student achievement scores that could be explained by variations in measures of teacher quality and other inputs. See Ronald Ferguson, ''Paying for Public Education: New Evidence on How and Why Money Matters,'' *Harvard Journal on Legislation*, vol. 28, No. 2, summer 1991, pp. 465-498; and Richard Murnane, ''Interpreting the Evidence on 'Does Money Matter?' '' *Harvard Journal on Legislation*, vol. 28, No. 2, summer 1991, pp. 457-464.

[14]These three terms overlap. However, selection refers primarily to decisions about a student's qualifications for admission to schools; placement refers to decisions about qualifications of students to participate in programs within schools they attend; and credentialing (or certification) refers to decisions regarding proficiencies reached by students who have participated in programs or completed courses of study.

ance can be used for individual selection, placement, or credentialing decisions. This function of testing has a long historical tradition: the earliest recorded examples are Chinese civil service qualifying tests given in the 2nd century B.C. As discussed in greater detail in chapter 5, many European and Asian countries continue to use examinations primarily for professional and educational ''gatekeeping'' functions, such as certifying students as qualified to attend specialized or elite public education programs.

Placement and certification decisions are still quite commonly based on tests, even in elementary and secondary education. Minimum competency examinations are required in many States for high school graduation, for promotion from one grade to the next, or for placement in remedial or gifted programs;[15] Advanced Placement examinations are used to determine whether high school students will be given college credit and placed in advanced courses when they arrive at college; and the National Teacher's Examination is necessary for teacher licensing in 35 States.

In the United States, however, the use of tests for selective admissions decisions has been more limited than in most other countries.[16] It is rather at the end of high school, when students compete for admission to colleges and universities, that selection tests play a critical role.[17]

Some recent proposals to initiate new tests at the national level include provisions for placement and certification. One such proposal calls for a ''certificate of initial mastery,'' to be issued to graduating high school students who perform at prescribed levels on the test, and for examinations as certification criteria for completion of fourth and eighth grades.[18]

In contrast with tests used for system monitoring, tests used for selection, placement, or certification decisions must:

- provide individual student scores;
- meet particularly high standards of comparability, consistency, fairness, and validity;
- provide information that is demonstrably relevant to successful performance in future school or work situations (in the case of selection tests); and
- provide information that is demonstrably relevant to the identification of children with special needs (in the case of placement tests used for gifted and talented programs, remedial education, or other special K-12 situations).

These tests are similar to system monitoring tests with respect to the need for impartial scoring, standardized administration, generality of information, and frequency of testing.

Some proposals for a new national test or system of examinations have selection or certification as a principal function. Good tests for these purposes must undergo intensive and time-consuming development as well as careful empirical evaluation. They must be carefully and clearly validated for these intended purposes. Historically, tests used for these purposes have been the most subject to legal challenges and scrutiny (see chs. 2 and 4).

[15]There is widespread concern about tests being used as the principal basis for placement of children into special programs, such as ''gifted and talented'' or remedial. ''A major problem is getting students who obviously need it into either gifted or remedial programs when they do not meet the 'required' minimum or maximum score on the tests [to qualify for State funding],'' said Jack Webber, a sixth grade teacher in Redmond, WA (personal communication, September 1991). Precise data on the numbers of schools or districts that rely on tests for these purposes, and on exactly how test data enter into those decisions, are difficult to find. Recently the New York State Commissioner of Education struck down the use of achievement tests as the sole screening criteria for placement of students in ''enriched'' programs. See also discussion in ch. 2.

[16]The situation has changed since the turn of the century, when, e.g., ''. . . a student could not be admitted to Central [High School] without demonstrating academic competence on an entrance exam. . . .'' See David Labaree, *The Making of an American High School: The Credentials Market and the Central High School of Philadelphia, 1838-1939* (New Haven, CT: Yale University Press, 1988), p. 50. This was not a phenomenon limited to the East Coast: rural students in Michigan and elsewhere in the Midwest needed to pass entrance examinations to gain admissions into urban high schools. Since that time, however, policies of selective admissions into public high schools have disappeared in all but a handful of special institutions, such as the Bronx High School of Science in New York.

[17]Over 3,000 colleges and universities use the Scholastic Aptitude Test (SAT) or American College Test (ACT) to aid in their selection from vast numbers of applicants, and recruits take the Armed Services Vocational Aptitude Battery (ASVAB) for placement within the military. Many private elementary and secondary schools use tests as a criterion for admission.

[18]For a summary of national testing proposals as of early 1991, see James Stedman, Congressional Research Service, ''Selected National Organizations Concerned With Educational Testing Policy,'' memorandum, Feb. 8, 1991. For a more recent update and discussion of the central issues, see ''National Testing: An Overview,'' *Youth Policy*, vol. 13, Nos. 4-5, special issue, September 1991, pp. 29-35. For a critique of these proposals see also Madaus and Kellaghan, op. cit., footnote 11.

Photo credit: Panoramic Visions

The United States ranks high in the world in terms of the percentage of the population graduating from high school. These students were photographed during their 1991 graduation ceremony at Woodrow Wilson High School, a large public high school in the District of Columbia. During the 1970s and 1980s many States instituted minimum competency testing as a criterion for graduation.

Raising the Stakes

In theory, educational tests are unobtrusive instruments of estimation. A major sticking point in any discussion of testing, however, is whether, in practice, testing affects the behavior it is intended to measure. In the current debate, advocates of new ways to test often argue that since tests can play a powerful role in influencing learning, they must be designed to support desired educational goals. These advocates disparage ''teaching to the test'' when a test calls for isolated facts from a multiple-choice format, but endorse the concept when the test consists of ''authentic'' tasks. For these educators, one of the main criteria for a ''good'' test is whether it consists of tasks that students should practice.

More traditional measurement theorists, on the other hand, are skeptical about the value of teaching to the test because of the need to obtain valid and reliable information about the whole domain of knowledge, not just the sample of tasks that appears on the test. Thus, they argue that, regardless of a test's format, test scores are meaningless if students have practiced the tasks.

The core of the often shrill debate reflects positions on two central questions:

- Do conventional standardized tests designed to estimate student achievement negatively influence instruction and learning?
- Do new testing methods designed to guide instruction and learning accurately estimate student achievement?

Tests and Consequences

As the Nation's use of standardized tests has increased, the consequences attached to test results have become more serious. All but four States have standardized testing programs. Test scores are applied to a wide array of decisions affecting individual children, schools, and school systems. Students who have taken college entrance examinations, high school juniors who have failed State minimum competency tests, schools that have become lures in real estate advertisements, and States that have found themselves ranked in the national media by their average test scores are likely to remember the event—and its consequences—long afterwards.

Many educators, extrapolating from their experiences in classrooms as students or as teachers, contend that tests influence students and teachers only if they perceive that important consequences are linked to test results.[19] But a fundamental problem arises when important consequences, or high stakes, are attached to test results; and not surprisingly, the increase in high-stakes testing over the past two decades has brought a concomitant rise in controversy. To understand the problems that can arise from high-stakes testing it is useful to consider a familiar medical metaphor.

Fever thermometers are used to measure body temperature without influencing that temperature; they provide information that could lead to treatment of the underlying conditions suspected of causing the fever. Similarly, well-designed educational tests can provide useful information to help students, teachers, or even school systems. Teachers can use tests to gauge their students' progress and decide how to "treat" children who are not doing well; students (in the upper grades especially) can review their test results to see whether they are learning the material and to determine how they might learn it more effectively; and State funding authorities can use information on the relative progress of students in different schools to develop responsive educational strategies. Thus, the information from tests can be used to choose appropriate educational "treatments."

Suppose, however, that patients were punished for running a high fever (or rewarded for a low one), or that doctors were rewarded for bringing down their patients' fever (or penalized if the fever remained high). They could easily take actions—cold showers, aspirin, a glass of cold beer—to "cure" the symptom but not necessarily the underlying illness. More comprehensive and appropriate treatment could be delayed or skipped. Just as temporary drops in body temperature could give misleading indications of changes in health status, fluctuations in scores from high-stakes educational tests may not reflect genuine changes in achievement. When stakes are high, a heavy emphasis is sometimes placed on specific test results, and especially on increasing scores. The symptom—low test scores— is treated without affecting the underlying condition— low achievement.

An instructive lesson about the mixed effects of high-stakes testing comes from the minimum competency testing (MCT) movement of the 1970s and 1980s (see box 1-C). As described also in greater detail in chapter 2, many State legislatures pegged promotion, placement, and graduation requirements to performance on criterion-referenced tests. The underlying rationale was that extrinsic rewards and sanctions would induce students to learn the relevant material more diligently and heighten teachers' motivation to ensure that all students learned the basics before moving them ahead. It now appears that the use of these tests misled policymakers and the public about the progress of students, and in many places hindered the implementation of genuine school reforms.

More recent research seems to confirm that high-stakes testing can mislead policymakers.[20] Complicating this picture, however, is other preliminary research evidence suggesting that students may underperform on tests that bear no individual consequences at all.[21] If such distortions are occurring, they may be misleading policymakers and the general public into believing the schools are in worse shape than they really are (and into blaming the school system for a long list of social and economic problems[22]). The fine-tuning knob that could adjust tests to provide just the right degree of incentive to students—enough to elicit their best *genuine* performance—has not been invented.

Test Use

One of the most vexing problems in testing policy is how to prevent test misuse, principally the

---

[19]See, for example, Lauren Resnick, professor, University of Pittsburgh, testimony before the U.S. Congress, Senate Committee on Labor and Human Resources, Subcommittee on Education, Arts, and Humanities, Mar. 7, 1990.

[20]See, e.g., Daniel Koretz, Robert Linn, Stephen Dunbar, and Lorrie Shepard, "The Effects of High Stakes Testing on Achievement: Preliminary Findings About Generalization Across Tests," paper presented at the annual meeting of the American Educational Research Association, Chicago, IL, April 1991; and Thomas Haladyna, Susan B. Nolan, and Nancy S. Hass, "Raising Standardized Achievement Test Scores and the Origins of Test Score Pollution," *Educational Researcher*, vol. 20, No. 5, June-July 1991.

[21]See, e.g., Steven Brown and Herbert Walberg, University of Illinois at Chicago, "Motivational Effects on Test Scores of Elementary School Students," monograph, n.d.; and Paul Burke, "You Can Lead Adolescents to a Test But You Can't Make Them Try," OTA contractor report, Aug. 14, 1991.

[22]See, e.g., Clark Kerr, "Is Education Really All That Guilty?" *Education Week*, vol. 10, No. 3, Feb. 27, 1991, p. 30.

Box 1-C—The Minimum Competency Debate

The American public school system is often accused of being resistant to change. It is common to hear rhetoric accusing classrooms of being virtually indistinguishable from those of 50 years ago. In fact, though, American schools have been changing since the very inception of the common school in the early 19th century.[1] One education historian and policy analyst, citing the multiple waves of reform of curriculum, instructional methods, and classroom technology, argues that American schools are "awash with innovation."[2] But he questions whether these technological and institutional innovations affect the ". . . core technology of the enterprise—processes of teaching and learning in classrooms and schools."[3]

The question of whether innovation is always a good thing for schools helps frame a discussion of minimum competency testing (MCT), clearly an institutional innovation of major proportion. Its "key demand," as one commentator has written, ". . . was that no student be given a high school diploma without first passing a test showing that he could read everyday English and do simple arithmetic."[4] From its beginnings in a handful of school districts in the late 1970s (Denver's program actually began in 1962), MCT spread rapidly, with the biggest expansion occurring between 1975 and 1979. By 1980, 29 States had implemented legislation that required students to pass criterion-referenced examinations, and 8 more had such legislation pending.[5] Some States used the examinations to determine eligibility for remedial programs and promotions and some required it for graduation. By 1985, growth in such programs had leveled off, although 33 States were still mandating statewide MCT; 11 of these States required the test as a prerequisite for graduation.[6]

Although there is vehement debate about the effects of MCT (and of high-stakes testing in general), there is general agreement on the origins of MCT. As one of its more ardent proponents has written:

> . . . this movement . . . was, in essence, a popular uprising . . . demand[ed] mainly by parents who were anguished about the fact that millions of their children were graduating from high school without the competence to go to the grocery store with a shopping list and come back with the right items and the right change. They were determined to change that, and convinced that a required exit test would produce the result they demanded.[7]

---

[1]The transition of the school system from one servicing the elites to one aspiring to universal access is described in many histories of American education. See, e.g., Ira Katznelson and Margaret Weir, *Schooling for All* (New York, NY: Basic Books, 1985); David Tyack, *The One Best System: A History of American Urban Education* (Cambridge, MA: Harvard University Press, 1975); Michael B. Katz, *The Irony of Early School Reform* (Cambridge, MA: Harvard University Press, 1968); or Lawrence Cremin, *The Transformation of the School: Progressivism in American Education, 1876-1957* (New York, NY: Vintage Books, 1964).

[2]Richard Elmore, "Paradox of Innovation in Education: Cycles of Reform and the Resilience of Teaching," paper presented at the Conference on Fundamental Questions of Innovation, Governors Center, Duke University, May 1991.

[3]Ibid. Other analysts have also addressed the innovation question in education. See, e.g., Richard Nelson and Richard Murnane, "Production and Innovation When Techniques are Tacit: The Case of Education," *Journal of Economic Behavior and Organization*, vol. 5, 1984, pp. 353-373; or Larry Cuban, *Teachers and Machines: The Classroom Use of Technology Since 1920* (New York, NY: Teachers College Press, 1986).

[4]Barbara Lerner, "Good News About American Education," *Commentary*, vol. 91, No. 3, March 1991, p. 21.

[5]Ronald A. Berk, "Minimum Competency Testing: Status and Potential," *The Future of Testing*, Barbara S. Plake and Joseph C. Witt (eds.) (Hillsdale, NJ: L. Erlbaum Associates, 1986), pp. 88-144.

[6]U.S. Congress, Office of Technology Assessment, "State Educational Testing Practices," background paper of the Science, Education and Transportation Program, December 1987.

[7]Lerner, op. cit., footnote 4, p. 21. See also Douglas A. Archbald, University of Delaware, and Andrew C. Porter, University of Wisconsin, Madison, "A Retrospective and an Analysis of the Roles of Mandated Testing in Education Reform," OTA contractor report, Jan. 6, 1990.

Continued on next page

application of a test to purposes for which it was not designed.[23] A familiar case of test misuse is the ranking of State school systems on a "wall chart" displaying average scores on the Scholastic Aptitude Test (SAT) along with other data.[24] Why was this a case of test misuse? First, the SAT is designed to rank applicants from diverse educational backgrounds with respect to their likely individual performance as college freshmen. It is designed specifically to override differences in curricula,

---

[23]See also Burke, op. cit., footnote 21; Larry Cuban, "The Misuse of Tests in Education," OTA contractor report, Sept. 9, 1991; Robert L. Linn, "Test Misuse: Why is it so Prevalent," OTA contractor report, September 1991; and Nelson L. Noggle, "The Misuses of Educational Achievement Tests for Grades K-12: A Perspective," OTA contractor report, October 1991.

[24]The wall chart, now defunct, was initiated in 1984 by then Secretary of Education Terrell Bell.

Box 1-C—The Minimum Competency Debate—Continued

As with every other surge of testing in American education history,[8] MCT was quickly shrouded in controversy. Educators and measurement specialists warned against the quick-fix mentality that exit tests could solve the problems stemming from a complex web of home, school, and societal decay; teachers lamented this new intrusion in their classrooms; and minority advocates challenged the legal and ethical basis for what appeared to be the latest obstacle to the educational and economic well-being of their children.

What have been the effects of MCT? The research community remains divided: there is common ground that MCT influenced education, but disagreement over whether it influenced education for the better.

Challenged to show that MCT worked, its supporters like to point to trends in achievement test scores: the apparent improvement in literacy and numeracy among students generally, the shrinking of the gap between white and minority students, and the upturn in Scholastic Aptitude Test (SAT) scores that began in 1979. Although MCT had its most direct effects on high school juniors and seniors, proponents claim that the effect trickled down to the lower grades too, where students heard the message that they would need to work harder in order to be promoted and eventually graduate. Thus, they credit MCT even with the upturn in standardized test scores in the elementary grades.

Other analysts dismiss these conclusions. First, test scores went up even in States without MCT programs, undermining the causal relation between MCT and achievement.[9] Second, even in States with MCT where scores did go up, the timing of these events raises important questions. A 1987 congressional study noted that: ''. . . most of the increase in competency testing occurred . . . several years after the upturn in achievement first became apparent in the lower grades.''[10] The report showed that achievement scores probably began to climb beginning with fifth graders in 1975. Thus, unless one is willing to believe that tests can have virtually instantaneous effects on achievement, the timing of the rise in scores cannot be attributed to MCT. Third, the change in SAT scores beginning in 1979 reflects the general improvement in performance recorded by that cohort of test takers all through their school years, and not the advent of MCT. As one analyst put it: ''. . . the higher scores rolled through the grades like a rippling wave as the elementary schoolchildren got older.''[11]

Finally, what about the observed improvements in National Assessment of Educational Progress (NAEP) scores? First, NAEP scores did rise in the 1970s and 1980s, but the rise actually began as early as the 1974 assessment, well before MCT was in operation in all but one or two States. Second, analysts point out that while test performance among Black and Hispanic 17-year-olds improved markedly during the 1970s and 1980s, it would be misleading to infer that the gap between white and Black students had disappeared: ''. . . white students constituted the great majority of students in the two highest categories [suggesting] that there is still a substantial

---

[8]See ch. 4.

[9]See Gerald Bracey, rejoinder to Barbara Lerner, *Commentary*, vol. 92, No. 2, August 1991, p. 10.

[10]Daniel Koretz, *Educational Achievement: Explanations and Implications of Recent Trends* (Washington, DC: Congressional Budget Office, August 1987), p. 84.

[11]Bracey, op. cit., footnote 9.

---

instruction, and academic rigor that may exist in the thousands of high schools from which applicants have graduated; by design, therefore, it does not measure a student's mastery of any given curriculum, and therefore should not be used to gauge a school's effectiveness at delivering its curriculum. Second, the SAT is taken only by about one-third of all students nationwide (with considerable regional variation), so it provides a very inadequate measure of the quality of education offered to *all* the students in a State.[25]

There is considerable professional agreement about a number of principles of good test development and appropriate test use. The primary vehicle for enforcing these principles is self-regulation by

---

[25]For discussion of these and other problems in using the Scholastic Aptitude Test as an indicator of State educational programs, see Cuban, op. cit., footnote 23; and Harold Hodgkinson, ''Schools are Awful—Aren't They?'' *Education Week*, vol. 11, No. 9, Oct. 30, 1991, p. A32.

gap between the reading proficiency of the average Black or Hispanic 17-year-old and the average white 17-year-old.''[12] Third, there is a widespread fear that with its emphasis on basic skills, MCT forced many schools to cut back on instruction in so-called ''higher order'' skills.[13]

But the debate over the effects of MCT goes well beyond trends in test scores, which are always difficult to attribute to any single policy or intervention. Proponents look at the test scores and see a glass half full: it is, to them, a reform policy that worked for basic skills and could now be successfully applied toward the goal of teaching more children higher order skills. By and large, though, there is considerable agreement that State-mandated testing, and MCT in particular, had unintended effects on classroom behavior of teachers and students, and that these effects should serve as a warning for any future anticipated uses of high-stakes tests.

For example, one study combined analysis of survey data and intensive interviews with teachers and school administrators, and concluded that the testing reinforced an excessive emphasis on basic skills and stymied local efforts to upgrade the content of education being delivered to all students.[14] Other studies have bemoaned the narrowing effect that MCT seems to have had on instructional strategies, content coverage, and course offerings.[15] Still other studies focus on the potentially misleading information derived from high-stakes tests: recent research suggests that improvements on high-stakes tests do not generalize well to other measures of achievement in the same domain;[16] and studies that focus in particular on teachers in districts with high-stakes testing conditions—such as minimum competency tests, school evaluation tests, or externally developed course-end tests—demonstrate a greater influence of testing on curriculum and instruction.[17]

In the end, then, there appears to be consensus that innovation in school testing policies can have profound effects—the disagreement is over the desirability of those effects. Although some of the evidence is contradictory, at times even confusing, one thing is clear: *test-based accountability is no panacea.* Specific proposals for tests intended to catalyze school improvement must be scrutinized on their individual merits.

---

[12]Robert Linn and Stephen Dunbar, ''The Nation's Report Card Goes Home: Good News and Bad About Trends in Achievement,'' *Phi Delta Kappan*, vol. 72, No. 2, October 1990, p. 130. For discussion of trends in reading scores, see also John Carroll, ''The National Assessments in Reading: Are We Misreading the Findings?'' *Phi Delta Kappan*, vol. 68, No. 6, February 1987, pp. 424-430.

[13]It should be noted, however, that the empirical data on this issue are ambiguous. While the National Assessment of Educational Progress reports generally conclude that American students' higher order abilities have remained stagnant, other studies have challenged that finding. See, e.g., Elizabeth Witt, Myunghee Han, and H.D. Hoover, ''Recent Trends in Achievement Tests Scores: Which Students are Improving and on What Levels of Skill Complexity?'' paper presented at the annual meeting of the National Council on Measurement in Education, Boston, MA, 1990.

[14]H. D. Corbett and B. Wilson, ''Unintended and Unwelcome: The Local Impact of State Testing,'' paper presented at the annual meeting of the American Educational Research Association, Boston, MA, April 1990.

[15]For review and discussion, see Archbald and Porter, op. cit., footnote 7.

[16]Daniel Koretz, Robert Linn, Stephen Dunbar, and Lorrie Shepard, ''The Effects of High Stakes Testing on Achievement: Preliminary Findings About Generalization Across Tests,'' paper presented at the annual meeting of the American Educational Research Association, Chicago, IL, April 1991, p. 20.

[17]Claire Rottenberg and Mary Lee Smith, ''Unintended Effects of External Testing in Elementary Schools,'' paper presented at the annual meeting of the American Educational Research Association, Boston, MA, April 1990.

---

test developers and other trained professionals.[26] Standards and codes developed by professional associations, critical reviews of tests, and individual professional codes of ethics all contribute to better testing. But, in general, few safeguards exist to prevent misuse and misinterpretation of scores, especially once they reach the public domain. Many professionals in the testing community also believe the codes lack enforcement mechanisms. Moreover, there has recently been heightened concern among test authors and publishers that market forces may interfere with good testing practice. As one test

---

[26]An example of self regulation often cited in the testing community is a decision taken by the Educational Testing Service (ETS) concerning the National Teachers Examination (NTE), which is designed to certify new teachers. When the Governor of Arkansas signed a bill in 1983 requiring teachers to pass the test in order to keep their jobs, ETS President Gregory Anrig protested: ''It is morally and educationally wrong to tell someone who has been judged a satisfactory teacher for many years that passing a certain test on a certain day is necessary to keep his or her job.'' ETS announced it would no longer sell the NTE to States or school boards that used it to determine the futures of practicing teachers. See Edward Fiske, ''Test Misuse is Charged,'' *The New York Times*, Nov. 29, 1983, p. C1; also David Owen, *None of the Above* (Boston, MA: Houghton Mifflin, 1985), pp. 243-260.

author has warned: ''. . . new corporate managers . . . [are] rushing to produce tests that will ostensibly meet purposes for which the tests have never been intended.''[27]

New Testing Technologies

Educators dedicated to the proposition that testing can be an integral part of instruction and a tool for assessing the full range of knowledge and skills have given impetus to new efforts to expand the technologies, modes, formats, and content of testing. Test developers and educators are experimenting with:

- performance assessment, a broad category of testing methods that require students to create answers or products that demonstrate what they are learning, and
- computer and video technologies for developing test items, administering tests, and structuring whole new modes of content and format.

This section of the summary begins with an overview of the characteristics of these new approaches to assessment, and then considers their potential role in advancing the three basic functions of testing. It is important to remember that:

- new assessment methods alone cannot ensure consensus on what children should learn or the levels of skills children should acquire,
- curriculum goals and standards of student achievement need to be determined before appropriate assessment methods can be designed, and
- new assessment methods alone do not necessarily equip teachers with the skills necessary to change instruction and achieve new curricular goals.

Performance Assessment

The move toward new methods of student testing has been motivated by new understandings of how children learn as well as by changing views of curriculum. These views of learning, which challenge traditional concepts of curricula and teaching, also challenge existing methods of evaluating student competence. For example, it is argued that if instruction ought to be individualized, adaptive, and interactive, then assessment should share these characteristics. In general, educators who advocate

Photo credit: Educational Testing Service

Performance assessment covers a broad range of testing methods that require students to create answers or products to demonstrate what they are learning. In this art assessment, students record their observations as they sculpt with clay; the finished product and their notes will become part of their portfolio for the year.

performance assessment believe testing can be made an integral and effective part of learning.

One type of performance assessment uses paper-and-pencil methods such as ''constructed-response'' items, for which students produce their own answers rather than select from a set of choices. Other approaches take performance assessment further along the continuum—from short-answers at one extreme to live demonstrations of student work at the other (see box 1-D). Under ideal circumstances, these methods share the following characteristics:

- they require students to construct responses, rather than select from a set of answers;
- they assess behaviors of interest as directly as possible;
- they are in some cases aimed at assessing group performance rather than individual performance;
- they are criterion-referenced, meaning they provide a basis for evaluating a student's work with reference to criteria for excellence rather than with reference to other students' work;
- in general, they focus on the process of problem solving rather than just on the end result;
- carefully trained teachers or other qualified judges are involved in most of the evaluation and scoring; and

---

[27]Rudman, op. cit., footnote 8, p. 6.

Box 1-D—The Many Faces of Performance Assessment

Performance assessment is a broad term. It covers many different types of testing methods that require students to demonstrate their competencies or knowledge by creating an answer or product. It is best understood as a continuum of formats that range from the simplest student-constructed responses to comprehensive demonstrations or collections of large bodies of work over time. This box describes some common forms of performance assessment.

Constructed-response questions require students to produce an answer to a question rather than to select from an array of possible answers (as multiple-choice items do). In constructed-response items, questions may have just one correct answer or may be more open ended, allowing a range of responses. The form can also vary: examples include answers supplied by filling in a blank; solving a mathematics problem; writing short answers; completing figural responses (drawing on a figure like a graph, illustration, or diagram); or writing out all the steps in a geometry proof.

Essays have long been used to assess a student's understanding of a subject by having the student write a description, analysis, explanation, or summary in one or more paragraphs. Essays are used to demonstrate how well a student can use facts in context and structure a coherent discussion. Answering essay questions effectively requires analysis, synthesis, and critical thinking. Grading can be systematized by having subject matter specialists develop guidelines for responses and set quality standards. Scorers can then compare each student's essays against models that represent various levels of quality.

Writing is the most common subject tested by performance assessment methods. Although multiple-choice tests can assess some of the components necessary for good writing (spelling, grammar, and word usage), having students write is considered a more comprehensive method of assessing composition skills. Writing enables students to demonstrate composition skills—inventing, revising, and clearly stating one's ideas to fit the purpose and the audience—as well as their knowledge of language, syntax, and grammar. There has been considerable research on the standardized and objective scoring of writing assessments.

Oral discourse was the earliest form of performance assessment. Before paper and pencil, chalk, and slate became affordable, school children rehearsed their lessons, recited their sums, and rendered their poems and prose aloud. At the university level, rhetoric was interdisciplinary: reading, writing, and speaking were the media of public affairs. Today graduate students are tested at the Master's and Ph.D. levels with an oral defense of dissertations. But oral interviews can also be used in assessments of young children, where written testing is inappropriate. An obvious example of oral assessment is in foreign languages: fluency can only be assessed by hearing the student speak. As video and audio make it possible to record performance, the use of oral presentations is likely to expand.

Exhibitions are designed as comprehensive demonstrations of skills or competence. They often require students to produce a demonstration or live performance in class or before other audiences. Teachers or trained judges score performance against standards of excellence known to all participants ahead of time. Exhibitions require a broad range of competencies, are often interdisciplinary in focus, and require student initiative and creativity. They can take the form of competitions between individual students or groups, or may be collaborative projects that students work on over time.

Experiments are used to test how well a student understands scientific concepts and can carry out scientific processes. As educators emphasize increased hands-on laboratory work in the science curriculum, they have advocated the development of assessments to test those skills more directly than conventional paper-and-pencil tests. A few States are developing standardized scientific tasks or experiments that all students must conduct to demonstrate understanding and skills. Developing hypotheses, planning and carrying out experiments, writing up findings, using the skills of measurement and estimation, and applying knowledge of scientific facts and underlying concepts—in a word, ''doing science''—are at the heart of these assessment activities.

Portfolios are usually files or folders that contain collections of a student's work. They furnish a broad portrait of individual performance, assembled over time. As students assemble their portfolios, they must evaluate their own work, a key feature of performance assessment. Portfolios are most common in writing and language arts—showing drafts, revisions, and works in progress. A few States and districts use portfolios for science, mathematics, and the arts; others are planning to use them for demonstrations of workplace readiness.

SOURCE: Office of Technology Assessement, 1992.

- students understand clearly the criteria on which they are judged.

Computer and Video Technologies

Data processing technologies have played a significant role in shaping testing as we know it today, and could be important tools for the development of innovative tests. Computers have most commonly been used for the creation of test items and the scoring and reporting of test results. New computer and video technologies, however, used alone or in conjunction with certain types of performance assessment, offer possibilities for enhancing testing in the classroom. As computers have become more available in schools, their use for testing has become more feasible. Research in this field is showing promise in the following areas:

- questions presented and answered on computers can go beyond the traditional multiple-choice format, allowing test takers to create answers rather than select from alternatives presented to them;
- video, audio, and multimedia can make more realistic and engaging questions and tasks available;
- computer-adaptive testing can establish an individual test taker's level of skill more quickly and, under ideal conditions, more accurately than conventional paper-and-pencil testing; and
- integrated learning systems, already found in some classrooms, often come with testing embedded in the instruction and provide ongoing analysis of student progress.

Continued research combining computing power, principles of artificial intelligence, learning theory, and test design could yield significant advances in the form and content of assessment. But a set of impressive technological and economic barriers need to be surmounted: for example, the limited availability (and relatively higher cost) of hardware, compared to paper-and-pencil tests, has prevented more rapid innovation and adoption. And even with more hardware, there is no guarantee that the capacity of that hardware will be adequate to meet constantly increasing software requirements. An even greater barrier is the lack of communication between educators, test developers, and technologists in achieving a consensus on the goals of testing and in shaping a vision for technology in the service of those goals.

Using New Testing Technologies Inside Classrooms

Performance assessment is not new to teachers or students; many techniques have long been used by teachers as a basis for making judgments about student achievement within the classroom. The form and complexity can vary:

- Imagine yourself a rebel at the Boston Tea Party and write a letter describing what occurred and why.
- Complete the following five geometry proofs.
- Describe both the dramatic and situational irony in Dickens' *Hard Times*, specifically using the characters of the Teacher, Mr. McChoakumchild, and the boss businessman in Coketown, Thomas Gradgrind.

As illustrated in box 1-E, what students produce in response to these testing tasks can reveal to the teacher more than just what facts they have learned; they reveal how well the student can put knowledge in context. *Well-crafted classroom performance tasks are useful diagnostic tools that can reveal where a student may be having problems with the material.* They can also help the teacher gauge the pacing and level of instruction to student responses. At their best, these tasks can be exciting learning experiences in themselves, as when a student, required to create a product or answer that puts knowledge into context, is blessed with that flash of inspiration, "Aha! I see how it all comes together now!" In addition, these tests can signal to the students what skills and content they should learn, help teachers adjust instruction, and give students clear feedback.

Much of the research about learning and cognitive processes suggest important new possibilities for tests than can diagnose a student's strengths and weaknesses. Although traditional achievement tests have focused largely on subject matter, researchers are now recognizing that "... an understanding of the learner's cognitive processes—the ways in which knowledge is represented, reorganized, and used to process new information—is also needed."[28]

---

[28]Robert L. Linn, "Barriers to New Test Design," *The Redesign of Testing for the 21st Century*, proceedings of the 1985 ETS Invitational Conference, Eileen E. Freeman (ed.) (Princeton, NJ: Educational Testing Service, 1986), p. 73

Box 1-E—Mr. Griffith's Class and New Technologies of Testing: Before and After

To understand how teaching and testing are traditionally used in the classroom, consider this fictional account of a fourth grade teacher's efforts to understand his students' progress, and the role standardized tests play in that understanding. We start with mathematics, or, as it is known in most fourth grade classrooms, arithmetic.

Mr. Griffith is working on fractions. Among the 28 children in his class, 3 raise their hand to every one of the teacher's prompts, and usually have the answer right. Some of the other children seem to be on safe ground when it comes to adding and subtracting fractions, but appear puzzled over the rules of multiplying. The majority appear lost when it comes to division. Griffith has a sense of these differences based on his constant interaction with his class, but he needs more systematic information to know how to adjust his lessons.

Before

For starters, Griffith turns to his own tests, which are tightly linked to his instructional objectives and to the material he has covered in class. He also assesses the children in other ways: he checks their workbooks, calls on them to do problems at the blackboard, poses questions and invites answers, and eavesdrops while his students work in small groups. As an experienced teacher, Griffith can synthesize his observations of children at work into fluid judgments of their strengths and weaknesses and go that next vital step of adjusting his pedagogy accordingly.

An additional source of information is the summary of statistics from last spring's administration of a nationally normed standardized mathematics test. From these data, Griffith could get a sense of how well the students in his class stack up against others in the school and even in the Nation as a whole, as measured by their performance on that test several months earlier. For example, he might find that Sarah and Jonathan, two of the three students who seem to know all the answers, scored high on the test. But he might also find that Richard, the third one, did less well than his current classroom performance would indicate. (Did he have a bad day in the spring, or did he work on his fractions over the summer?) He might also find that Noreen, another bright child in the class, did very well on the test but still gets stuck when she has to perform at the blackboard.

On the whole, this test data provides information, but probably not enough for Griffith to get a complete picture of his students' learning needs or to structure his lesson plans. One problem is that a handful of his students were not even present for the spring testing, and he has no test data for them. Another problem is that the standardized test scores do not distinguish between fractions and other applications of addition and subtraction. When Griffith moves beyond fractions, there is no guarantee that the next topic on the curriculum will have been covered on the standardized test.

It is not much better with reading and writing. The children read a lot of books on their own, but the reading tests supplied by the district still give passages out of context that have no meaning for many of the students. And, even though Griffith feels it is important to have his students do as much writing as possible, the tests are mainly questions on spelling and vocabulary. If he wants to make the children's scores look good, and the principal happy, he has to drill his students a lot on the mechanics. Important as they are, they do not inspire much enthusiasm in either the students or, truth be known, in Griffith. But scores are important for merit pay in his district, so Griffith knows where his priorities should be.

After

Consider again the situation of Mr. Griffith, our fourth grade teacher. In the last few years, his school has gradually invested in technology. Each class now has several computers linked together in an integrated learning system (ILS) that corresponds to the mathematics and language arts curriculum taught in his school. Money from the PTA made it possible for Griffith to purchase two additional stand alone computers and a VCR, which connect to a television that had been locked in the storage room until a few years back. Occasionally he borrows the school's video camera from the library. While he is far from considering himself a "tekkie," Griffith took a few courses on teaching with computers and has grown pretty comfortable with their use, especially since he knows that his colleague, Mrs. Juster, a computer whiz, is just across the hall and willing to help him when he gets stuck.

Mr. Griffith finds that, as he uses these technologies for teaching, common sense requires that he use them for testing as well. Like the teaching, the testing varies. Some of the testing he does is the same as before, but made simpler by the technology. With the help of a testmaker software package, he can design his own short-answer, essay, or multiple-choice quizzes geared to the material he has been teaching. He appreciates the fact that the

Continued on next page

Box 1-E—Mr. Griffith's Class and New Technologies of Testing: Before and After—Continued

software can automatically translate questions into Spanish, so Maria and Esteban, who recently arrived from El Salvador, can take tests with the rest of the class. The children say these tests are much easier to read than the handwritten ones he had to crank out on the school's ancient mimeograph machine. He keeps better track of their records with ''gradebook'' software that automatically computes and updates student averages and lets him know who is slipping in time for him to set up his little ''fireside chats'' with students.

But the real change has been in being able to link his testing closer to the point for instruction. Griffith has been having his students do a lot of writing on the word processor. Now he has the students pass their writing around on the computer, make comments on each other's works, and save their first drafts. They seem more comfortable making revisions, and he can grade final products that are indeed more finished. He has each student collecting their written work in electronic portfolios on disk; at the end of each semester they chose their best works and print them out for inclusion in the portfolio they take with them to the fifth grade. Some, like Regine, have a hard time deciding what is best and why. She'd like to print it all!

The mathematics they have been working on is included in the software in the ILS: same old fractions and long division—the material that Griffith has watched, over the years, turn some students off mathematics forever while others just breeze through it. But at least now he can get a better handle on where the potholes are for which children. Dana is no problem—he has already moved on to two- and three-digit long division. At the end of his work, the system prints out a report that shows he got all 10 problems in the mini-test right, and completed it in 20 minutes. Griffith makes a note to himself—''Move Dana ahead to the next unit on the program and see how he does. It's far better than having him staring out the window while I'm going over the basics with the other kids.'' Michelle, who did fine with multiplication, continues to have difficulty in division problems. A quick printout of the problems she missed—with the step-by-step procedure she followed—reveals that her problem lies in subtraction—she keeps forgetting principles of carrying. ''Maybe I can get Brad to work with her on some of those problems,'' he thinks. ''Oops, Brad is too much of a tease. Better ask Kevin instead.''

Before it is time for the first grading period, Griffith prints a summary report on all the children's work. There is still a huge range in their skills, especially in mathematics. Even with the bells and whistles added in the computer programs, the curriculum can still be pretty deadly, Griffith knows. He decides to try using some of the new videos Mrs. Juster told him about as ways to get his students more interested in using mathematics to solve problems. ''The one about the abandoned bell tower at the edge of town, in which the bell starts mysteriously ringing, might get their interest,'' he thinks. They like working in groups and digging out the clues in the video; looking for patterns and doing the mathematics to solve the problem might put some of these dry mathematics facts into context. Maybe.

While they are watching the video, Griffith plans to get Elise, a student who just came into his class yesterday from a neighboring school district, started on the computer-adaptive test she will need for placement. It looks like she is quite far behind the other students; this will give a quick picture of her abilities and can be used in determining whether she might benefit from the Chapter 1 program in the school. ''Shoot, I hate to have her miss that video, though. I suppose I can see if she can stay after school and take the test. She'll miss her bus home, though, and I'll be late picking up the baby at the day care center. And then there's the video report I promised to help Lindsey, Scott, and Sherri with. They are working on a report on 'Why we need new playground equipment' and interviewing students playing in the schoolyard after school. I can see they'll need a lot of help with that! Whoever said technology makes teaching easier?''

SOURCE: Fictional scenario prepared by Office of Technology Assessment, 1992.

New diagnostic tests, informed by cognitive science research, may help teachers recognize more quickly the individual learner's difficulties and intervene to get the learner back on track. Similarly, computer-administered tests open up new possibilities for keeping records of a student's errors or ineffective problem-solving strategies, and for providing immediate feedback so that children can recognize their errors while still involved in thinking about the questions.[29]

---

[29]See, for example, Isaac Bejar, ''Educational Diagnostic Assessment,'' *Journal of Educational Measurement*, vol. 21, No. 2, summer 1984, pp. 175-189.

Using New Testing Technologies Beyond Classrooms

Teaching has always been an art more than a science, and what works in one classroom with one teacher does not easily transfer to other classrooms with other teachers.[30] Consequently, many of the methods used by teachers to gauge the progress of their students and adjust their lessons are not standardized. As long as teachers can correct their judgments on a continuing and fluid basis, day by day and hour by hour, teacher experimentation with a wide range of inferential assessment methods presents no particular harm and can offer many benefits.

When judgments about student performance are moved outside the classroom, however, they must be comparable: "... whatever contextual understanding of their fallibility may have existed in the classroom is gone."[31] Using tests fairly and appropriately for management decisions about schools or students, therefore, imposes special constraints. As explained in detail in chapter 6, standardization in test administration and scoring is the first necessary condition to make test results comparable. It is precisely the recognition that individual teachers' judgments may be insufficient as the basis for crucial decisions affecting children's futures that historically has fueled public interest in standardized tests originating from outside the classroom or school.[32]

It is important to recall that the basic concept of direct assessments of student performance is not new. American schools traditionally used oral and written examinations to monitor performance. It was the pressure to standardize those efforts, coupled with the perceived need to test large numbers of children, that led eventually to the invention of the multiple-choice format as a proxy for genuine performance. Evidence that these proxies were more efficient in informing administrative decisions rapidly boosted their popularity, despite their less

obvious relevance to classroom learning. *The modern performance assessment movement is based on the proposition that new testing technologies can be more direct, open ended, and educationally relevant than conventional tests, and also reliable, valid, and efficient.*

How can performance assessments and computer-based tests contribute to system monitoring and selection, placement, and credentialing decisions? A growing number of States are experimenting with answers to this question. Thirty-six States currently use writing assessments and nine others are planning to introduce writing assessment in the near future. Twenty-one States currently use other performance assessment methods including portfolios, constructed response, and hands-on demonstrations; 19 States plan to adopt some or all of these methods. Figure 1-3 shows the current geographic distribution of States using writing and other performance assessments. Some States are using sampling technologies to reduce the direct costs of performance assessments and are seeking to resolve various technical problems. Most States are using these tests in combination with the more familiar multiple-choice test.

To the extent that decisions about school resources could be based on these statewide assessments, they are potentially high stakes. Advocates maintain that performance assessments have a clear advantage over standardized multiple-choice tests, because they assess a wider range of tasks. **Although these assessments do not necessarily provide different estimates of individual student progress than some conventional tests, many educators believe their advantage lies in their more obvious relevance to learning goals.** The involvement of teachers in developing and scoring performance assessments is crucial to keeping them closely linked to curricula and instruction.

Using performance assessments beyond the confines of classrooms raises a set of important research and policy issues:

---

[30]See Richard Murnane and Richard Nelson, "Production and Innovation When Techniques are Tacit: The Case of Education," *Journal of Economic Behavior and Organization*, vol. 5, 1984, pp. 353-373; also Pauly, op. cit., footnote 12.

[31]Stephen Dunbar, Daniel Koretz, and H.D. Hoover, "Quality Control in the Development and Use of Performance Assessments," paper presented at the annual meeting of the National Council on Measurement in Education, Chicago, IL, April 1991, p. 1.

[32]If decisions about children's future opportunities are at stake, then the tests must also demonstrate sufficient "predictive validity," i.e., they must provide reasonably accurate information about individual potential for future behavior in school, work, or elsewhere. For discussion of issues pertaining to the use of test scores in predicting future performance, see, e.g., Henry Levin, "Ability Tests for Job Selection: Are the Economic Claims Justified?" *Testing and the Allocation of Opportunity*, B. Gifford (ed.) (Boston, MA: Kluwer, 1990); and James Crouse and Dale Trusheim, *The Case Against the SAT* (Chicago, IL: University of Chicago Press, 1988).

Figure 1-3—Statewide Performance Assessments, 1991

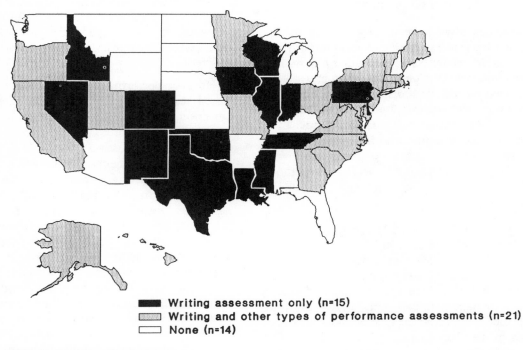

■ Writing assessment only (n=15)
▦ Writing and other types of performance assessments (n=21)
□ None (n=14)

NOTE: Chart includes optional programs.
SOURCE: Office of Technology Assessment, 1992.

- The most common form of performance assessment is the evaluation of written work: essays, compositions, and creative writing have been widely used in large-scale testing programs. Other forms of performance assessment are still in earlier stages of development and, though promising, require considerable experimentation before they can be used for high-stakes decisions.

- If performance assessment is to be successfully adopted, continuing professional development for teachers will be critical. Most teachers receive little formal education in assessment. Performance assessment may provide a great opportunity for teacher development that links instruction with assessment.

- Some parents and educators are worried that a move to greater use of performance assessment could have a negative impact on minority groups. It is critical that the issues of cultural influence and bias be scrutinized in all aspects

of performance assessment: selection of tasks, administration, and scoring.

- Administration and scoring of performance assessment are both time consuming and labor intensive. If the time spent on testing is viewed as integral to instruction, however, new methods could be cost-effective.

Computer technologies, too, may play a powerful role in system monitoring and high-stakes testing of individual students. In particular:

- Adaptive testing, in which the computer selects questions based on individual students' responses to prior questions, can provide more accurate data than conventional tests, and in less time.[33]

- Advances in software could make possible automated scoring that closely resembles human scoring.

- Large item banks made possible by advanced storage technologies could lower the costs of test development by allowing State or district

---

[33]For discussion of the state-of-the-art in computer-adaptive testing, see Bert F. Green, The Johns Hopkins University, "Computer-Based Adaptive Testing in 1991," monograph, May 9, 1991.

testing authorities to tap into common pools of questions or tasks.

- With the combination of large item banks, computer-adaptive software, and computerized test administration, tests would no longer need to be composed in advance and printed on paper; rather, each student sitting at a terminal could theoretically face a completely individualized test. This could reduce the need for tight test security, given that most students cannot memorize the many thousands of items stored in item banks.

An important policy question regarding computers in testing is whether to invest in new technologies for scanning hand-written responses to open-ended test items. Since more tests may one day be administered by computer, investing in new scanning technologies could be wasteful.

Special Considerations for System Monitoring

Performance assessments and computer-based tests could be designed to provide information on the effectiveness of schools and school systems. As with all tests, though, the outcomes of these new tests need to be interpreted judiciously: the relative performance of schools or school systems must be viewed in the context of many factors that can influence achievement.

Because individual student scores are not necessary for system monitoring, innovative sampling methods can be used that offer many important advantages for implementing performance assessments. When sampling is used, inferences can be made about a school system based on testing either a representative subsample of students or by giving each student only a sample of all the testing tasks. These methods can lessen considerably the direct costs of using long and labor-intensive performance tasks, allow broader coverage of the content areas that appear on the test, and still keep testing time limited. Furthermore, sampling methods provide important protection against misuse of a test for other functions (such as selection, placement, or certification), since students do not receive individual scores.

However, the use of sampling methods raises specific concerns: one issue is whether students' less obvious incentives to do well on such tests—given that no individual consequences are attached to performance—could lead to erroneously low esti-

Computers can change testing just as they change learning. Recent advances in computers, video, and related technologies could one day revolutionize testing.

mates of aggregate achievement. A related issue is whether tests administered to samples of students will effectively signal to *all* students what they are expected to learn. A third question is whether it would be fair to administer new testing methods, intended as tools for enriched instruction, to samples of students rather than to all students.

These issues warrant further research as a prerequisite to using new testing methods for system monitoring functions.

Special Considerations for Selection, Placement, and Credentialing

New testing technologies have considerable potential to enrich selection and certification decisions. For example, portfolios of student work can provide richly detailed information about progress and achievement over time that seems particularly relevant and useful for certification decisions. One example is the Advanced Placement (AP) studio art examination, administered by the Educational Testing Service (ETS), which is based on a portfolio of student artwork. This examination is used to award college credit, and, as such, certifies that a student has mastered the skills expected of a first-year college student in studio art.

Tests based on complex computer simulations of "on-the-job" settings are being developed for architecture, medicine, and other professions, as a basis for professional licensing and certification; the integration of graphics, video, and simulation techniques can create tests more closely resembling the actual tasks demanded by those professions. Although promising, these initial efforts have uncovered some technical issues that will require considerably more research before the tests can accurately and fairly assess the skills of interest, and be used to make high-stakes decisions about individuals.[34]

OTA has identified the following central policy issues concerning the design of new tests for selection, placement, and certification.

Technical requirements—These tests must meet very high technical standards. Inferences drawn from them must be based on rigorous standards of empirical evidence not necessarily required of tests used for other functions. Because tests used to select, place, or certify individuals can have potentially long term and significant consequences, their uses need to be limited to the specific functions for which they are designed and validated. Similarly, because test scores are only estimates, very high levels of reliability, or consistency, must be demonstrated for the test as a whole. Finally, because of the amount of day-to-day variability in individuals, no one test score should be used alone to make important decisions about individuals.[35]

Generalizability—Another issue pertains to the content coverage of new assessment formats, such as exhibitions, portfolios, science experiments, or computer simulations. The advantage of these formats is in their coverage of relevant factors of performance and achievement; however, this usually means that only a few such long and complex tasks can be completed by a single child in the allotted time.[36] Are inferences about achievement made on the basis of just a few tasks generalizable across the whole domain of achievement? When each child can complete only a few tasks, there is a much higher risk that a child's score will be specific to that particular task. Selection and certification decisions cannot be made on the basis of these tasks unless results are stable and generalizable.

Security—Currently most high-stakes selection, placement, or certification tests are multiple-choice, and precautions are taken to keep items secret. Scores would be suspect if some (or all) test takers knew the items in advance.[37] Given the relatively low number of performance-based tasks that might appear on some new tests, sharing of information from one cohort of test takers to another could become a problem undermining the test's validity. Computers with enough memory to accommodate very large item banks may provide some technological relief, although the question remains open as to whether a sufficient number of different items could be written at reasonable cost.

Fairness—Most previous legal challenges have targeted tests used to make significant decisions about individuals. Any test designed for selection, placement, or certification will be carefully scrutinized by those concerned with equity and bias. Designing a performance-based selection or certification test will require considerable research to ensure elimination of bias.

---

[34]See, for example, David B. Swanson, John J. Norcini, and Louis J. Grosso, "Assessment of Clinical Competence: Written and Computer-Based Simulations," *Assessment and Evaluation in Higher Education*, vol. 12, No. 3, 1987, pp. 220-246.

[35]An additional reason for insisting on high standards is that high-stakes tests can lead inadvertently to the labeling of individuals—by themselves or by others—with uncertain and potentially harmful consequences. For discussion of these issues see, e.g., U.S. Congress, Office of Technology Assessment, "The Use of Integrity Tests for Pre-Employment Screening," background paper of the Science, Education, and Transportation Program, September 1990.

[36]Increasing the time allotted to assessment does not necessarily imply reduced time for instruction, as long as the two activities are well integrated. But completely "seamless" integration of testing and instruction could raise problems of its own, such as potential infringement of students' rights to know whether they are being tested and for what purposes.

[37]The concept of "test openness" is controversial. Most traditional measurement experts argue that allowing students access to test items in advance would irreparably compromise the test's validity. For opposing viewpoints, however, see, e.g., Judah Schwartz and Katherine A. Viator (eds.), *The Price of Secrecy: The Social, Intellectual, and Psychological Costs of Current Assessment Practice*, A Report to the Ford Foundation (Cambridge, MA: Harvard Graduate School of Education, September 1990); and John Frederickson and Alan Collins, "A Systems Approach to Educational Testing," *Educational Researcher*, vol. 18, No. 9, December 1989, pp. 27-32.

Cost Considerations: A Framework for Analysis

A common challenge posed to advocates of alternative assessment methods is an economic one: can they be administered and scored as efficiently as conventional standardized tests?[38] Indeed, one of the attractive features of commercially published standardized tests is their apparently low cost. As shown in box 1-F, OTA estimated outlays for standardized testing in a large urban school district were approximately $1.6 million for 1990-91 ($0.8 million per test administration), or only about $6 per student per test administration.

But these outlays on contracted materials and services and district testing personnel do not tell the whole story. First, they neglect the dollar value of teacher time devoted to test administration. Because a teacher's many activities are not typically itemized on a school district budget, the costs associated with teacher time spent administering tests are less obvious than other testing expenses. But they can be significant: in the district studied by OTA, the portion of total teacher salaries attributable to time spent administering tests was roughly $1.8 million per test, or $13 per pupil.

Another important component of cost is the time spent by teachers in test preparation. This factor is more variable than administration time and is more difficult to estimate. It depends largely on the degree to which teachers can distinguish their regular instruction from classroom work that is driven by the need to prepare students for specific tests. The question is whether the test preparation activities would take place even in the absence of testing: this issue hinges partly on test content—how closely does the test reflect curricular and instructional objectives?—and partly on how individual teachers allocate their classroom time across various activities, including test-related instruction. (Tests that are intended to be linked to instruction might not be perceived as such by some teachers, and tests that are apparently separate from regular instruction could be useful tools in the hands of other teachers.) In the district OTA studied, teachers reported spending anywhere from 0 to 3 weeks in preparing their students for each test administration—at a cost as high as $13.5 million per test, or close to $100 per pupil.[39]

Just as counting material and testing personnel outlays alone can lead to deceptively low estimates of the total resources devoted to testing, accounting fully for teacher administration and preparation time can lead to deceptively high cost estimates. To correctly account for teacher time requires attention to the indirect or *opportunity costs* of that time. An opportunity cost is defined generally as "... the value of foregone alternative action."[40] With respect to testing, analysis of opportunity costs focuses attention on the following question: to what extent does the time spent by teachers on preparation and administration of tests contribute to the core classroom activities of teaching and learning?

If testing is considered integral to instruction, then teacher time spent on preparing students and on administering the tests has lower opportunity costs than if the testing has little or no instructional value. *To estimate the opportunity costs, then, requires information or assumptions about the degree to which any particular test is intended as an instructional tool, and information or assumptions about the extent to which individual teachers use testing as part of their instructional program.*

As shown in box 1-F, some teachers in the district OTA studied spent as much as 3 weeks preparing students for each of the two standardized tests, plus 4 days administering each test. The worst case would be one in which this time was completely irrelevant to coursework: the district would have incurred steep opportunity costs—about $15 million per test, or close to $110 per pupil. The best case, in which all preparation time was relevant to coursework, would have cost under $2 million per test, or $13 per pupil.

Thus, the total costs of a testing program consist of both direct and opportunity components: direct expenditures on materials, services, and salaries, and

---

[38]The efficiency advantages of standardized multiple-choice tests are discussed in several places in this report. See especially ch. 4 for a historical synopsis, ch. 6 for general discussion of item formats, and ch. 8 for review of technological change in test scoring and administration.

[39]A full accounting of direct costs would also include overhead on the school building and grounds, i.e., depreciation attributable to time spent on test preparation and administration. To simplify the analysis, OTA omitted this element.

[40]David W. Pearce (ed.), *The MIT Dictionary of Modern Economics*, 3rd ed. (Cambridge, MA: MIT Press, 1986), p. 310.

Box 1-F—Costs of Standardized Testing in a Large Urban School District

Because testing policy decisions are still primarily made at the local and State levels, OTA has analyzed the kind of data on standardized testing costs that school authorities would likely include in their deliberations over testing reform. Data for this illustrative example were provided by the director of Testing and Evaluation in a large urban school district with 191,000 enrolled students, among whom 32 percent are in Chapter 1 programs. The district employs 12,000 teachers, including regular classroom and special teachers. The total 1990-91 district budget was $1.2 billion.

Approximately 140,000 students in grades kindergarten through 12 take tests, once a year in kindergarten and twice a year (fall and spring) in all other grades (absenteeism and student mobility account for the large number of untested students). During each test administration, students take separate tests in English, mathematics, social studies, and science. The tests typically consist of norm-referenced questions supplemented with locally developed criterion-referenced items. (In kindergarten, first, second, and third grades, criterion-referenced checklists filled out by teachers supplement the paper-and-pencil tests.) The tests are machine scored by the test publisher, who provides computer-generated score reports to district personnel. Tests are administered by 4,500 regular classroom teachers; there are no other special personnel involved, except for a small group of district staff who design the criterion-referenced items, manage the overall testing program, and conduct research based on test results.

Although the district purchases tests from a large commercial publishing company that has many school districts as customers, the cost figures discussed below are not necessarily representative of other school districts in the United States.

Materials and Services

In most years, the district purchases only a limited supply of test booklets, replacing the complete set only once every few years when they become damaged or when test items are revised. OTA computed average annual expenditures on test booklets based on test publishers' estimates that booklets are recycled typically once every 7 years. As shown in table 1-F1, total annual outlays for the standardized testing program in 1990-91—including materials, contracted scoring and reporting services, and nonteaching personnel—were approximately $1.6 million, or $5.70 per student per test administration.[1]

Teacher Time

Based on the specified time allotments for the various tests in the various grades, and on conversations with district staff, OTA found that full-time teachers in the district spend roughly 2 percent of their annual work time in the *administration* of tests to students. The total salary cost to the district for teacher time spent administering tests was roughly $3.6 million for two testing administrations ($1.8 million per testing cycle).

Table 1-F1—Outlays on Materials, Services, and Personnel

Materials	Cost
Contracted:	
Test booklets: new purchases plus annualized costs based on assumed 7-year cycle	$369,000
Practice books	49,400
Examiner manuals	26,200
Checklists and worksheets	100,600
Kindergarten program	33,300
Other :	
Kindergarten Chapter 1 tests	$3,000
Labels	1,200
Pencils	17,900
Answer sheets	23,000
Headers	2,700
Language battery	1,300
Special tests	14,100
Materials subtotal	$641,700
Services	
Contracted:	
Scoring	$175,600
Report generation	141,800
Collection	14,800
Scanning	146,500
Distribution	9,000
Services subtotal	$487,700
Nonteaching personnel:	
Assistant director	$58,200
Research manager	56,500
Research associates (2)	108,700
Research assistants (3)	127,800
Secretaries	56,500
Clerks	45,600
Nonteaching personnel subtotal	$453,300
Total	**$1,582,700**

SOURCE: Office of Technology Assessment, based on data supplied by a large urban school district, 1990-91 academic year.

---

[1]To understand how this district's cost of standardized testing compares with others, OTA looked at cost data from the November 1988, "Survey of Testing Practices and Issues," conducted by the National Association of Test Directors (NATD). The survey was sent to testing directors in approximately 125 school districts. For 38 districts providing their cost information, the average direct cost per student was $4.80 per year, slightly lower than the $5.70 per student in this example. Most of the districts responding to the NATD survey administer achievement tests only once a year, compared to OTA's example district, which tests twice a year in grades 1 to 12.

In conversations with district teachers, OTA found that the time they spend in classroom *preparation* of students for the standardized tests varies from 0 to 3 weeks per testing administration. Some teachers claim they spend no time doing test preparation that is distinguishable from their regular classroom instruction; others use the standardized test as a final examination and offer students the benefit of lengthy in-class review time. OTA therefore estimated the salary costs for preparation time under three scenarios: 0, 1.5, and 3 weeks (per test). These estimates are summarized in table 1-F2.

Table 1-F2—Salary Costs of Teacher Time Spent on Testing, per Test Administration[a]

Test administration[b]	Test preparation		Total[c]
$1.8 million	0 weeks:	0	$1.8 million
	1.5 weeks:[d]	$7.2 million	9.0 million
	3 weeks:	$13.5 million	15.3 million

[a]Based on average salary of $40,500 per year.
[b]Based on an estimated 2 percent of total time spent on test administration for two testing periods.
[c]Based on 4,500 teachers.
[d]8 days.

SOURCE: Office of Technology Assessment, based on data supplied by a large urban school district, 1990-91 academic year.

Total Direct Costs

The total direct costs of testing can be computed by adding the expenditures on materials and services to the costs of teacher time for test preparation and administration. It is important to note, however, that this analysis does not account for the degree to which teacher time spent on testing is considered to be a necessary and well-integrated part of regular instruction. The importance of indirect or opportunity costs as it pertains to the analysis of testing costs is illustrated in box 1-G.

indirect costs of time spent on testing activities.[41] For a graphical exposition of this concept, see box 1-G.

Federal Policy Concerns

Several proposals now pending before Congress could fundamentally alter testing in the United States. Three issues already on Congress' agenda are proposals for national testing, changes to the National Assessment of Educational Progress (NAEP), and revisions to the program that assists educationally disadvantaged children (Chapter 1). Federal action could also focus on ensuring the appropriate use of tests, and speeding research and development on testing.

These policy opportunities combined with the current national desire to improve schooling provide Congress with an opportunity to form comprehensive, coordinated, and far-reaching test policy. Rather than allowing test activity to occur haphazardly in response to other objectives, decision-makers can bring these several concerns together in support of better learning.

National Testing

As discussed in chapter 3, the past year has witnessed a flurry of proposals to establish a system of national tests in elementary and secondary schools. Momentum for these efforts has built rapidly, fueled by numerous governmental and commission reports on the state of the economy and the educational system; by the National Goals initiative of the President and Governors; by casual references to the superiority of examination systems in other countries (see box 1-H); and most recently by the President's ''America 2000'' plan.

The use of tests as a tool of education policy is fraught with uncertainties. *The first responsibility of Congress is to clarify exactly what objectives are attached to the various proposals for national testing, and how instruments will be designed, piloted, and implemented to meet these objectives.* The following questions warrant careful attention:

- If tests are to be somehow associated with national standards of achievement, who will participate in setting these standards? Will the content and grading standards be visible or invisible? Will the examination questions be

---

[41]In addition to teacher time, there are opportunity costs associated with student time: assuming that instructional time is an investment with economic returns, student time spent on testing can be valued in terms of foregone future income. This follows a ''human capital'' investment model of education. See, e.g., Gary Becker, *Human Capital*, 2nd ed. (New York, NY: National Bureau of Economic Research, 1975). For application of the concept of indirect costs to educational testing see also Walter Haney, George Madaus, and Robert Lyons, Boston College, ''The Fractured Marketplace for Standardized Testing,'' unpublished manuscript, September 1989.

Box 1-G—Direct and Opportunity Costs of Testing

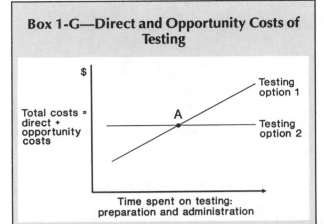

This figure illustrates the relationship between time spent on testing activity and the total costs of testing. Hypothetical test 1 is assumed to contribute little to classroom learning. It costs little in direct dollar outlays, but is dear in opportunity costs. Total costs begin relatively low but rise rapidly with time devoted by teachers and students to activities that take them away from instruction.

Hypothetical test 2, which is a useful instruction and learning tool, requires relatively high direct expenditures. But the opportunity costs of time devoted to testing are relatively low.

At point A, a school district would be indifferent between the two testing programs, if cost was the main consideration.

SOURCE: Office of Technology Assessment, 1992.

kept secret or will they be disclosed after the test?

- If the objective of the test is motivational, i.e., to induce students and teachers to work harder, then the test is likely to be high stakes. What will happen to students who score low? What resources will be provided for students who do not test well? What inferences will be made about students, teachers, and schools on the basis of test results? What additional factors will be considered in explaining test score differences? Finally, will the tests focus the attention of students and teachers on broad domains of knowledge, as desired, or on narrower subsets of knowledge covered by the tests, as often happens?
- If the Nation is interested in using tests to improve the qualifications of the American work force, how will valuable nonacademic skills be assessed? What should be the balance of emphasis between basic skill mastery and higher order thinking skills?
- If there is impatience to produce a test quickly, it is likely to result in a paper-and-pencil machine-scorable test. What signal will this give to schools concerning the need to teach all students broader communication and problem-solving skills?
- What effects will national tests have on current State and local efforts to develop alternative assessment methods and to align their tests more closely with local educational goals?
- Would the national examinations be administered at a single setting or whenever students feel they are ready?
- Would students have a chance to retake an examination to do better?
- Would the tests be administered to samples of students or all students?
- At what ages would students be tested?
- What legal challenges might be raised?

If a test or examination system is placed into service at the national level before these important questions are answered, it could easily become a barrier to many of the educational reforms that have been set into motion, and could become the next object of concern and frustration within the American school system.

Given that a national testing program could be undertaken through State and/or private sector initiatives, the role of Congress is not yet entirely clear. However, to the extent that congressional action regarding NAEP, Chapter 1, and appropriate test use will affect the need for and impact of any national examinations, Congress has a strong interest in clarifying the purposes and anticipated consequences of such examinations. Also, Congress must carefully analyze the pressures the national test movement is exerting on these programs, such as the idea of converting NAEP into a national test for all students.

Future of the National Assessment of Educational Progress

NAEP has proven to be a valuable tool to track and understand educational progress in the United States. It was created in 1969 and is the only regularly conducted national survey of educational achievement at the elementary, middle, and high

---

Box 1-H—National Testing: Lessons From Overseas[1]

The American educational system has a traditional commitment to pluralism in the definition and control of curricula as well as the fair provision of educational opportunities to all children. Lessons from European and Asian examination systems, which have historically been geared principally toward selection, placement, and credentialing, need to be considered judiciously. OTA finds that the following factors should be considered when comparing examination systems overseas with those in the United States:

- Examination systems in almost every industrialized country are in flux. Changes over the past three decades have been quite radical in several countries. Nevertheless, there is still a relatively greater emphasis on tests used for selection, placement, and certification than in the United States.
- None of the countries studied by OTA has a single, centrally prescribed examination that is used for all purposes—classroom diagnosis, selection, and school accountability. Most examinations overseas are used today for certifying and sorting individual students, not for school or system accountability. Accountability in European countries is typically handled by a system of inspectors charged with overseeing school and examination quality. Some countries occasionally test samples of students to gauge nationwide achievement.
- External examinations before age 16 have all but disappeared from the countries in the European community. Primary certificates used to select students for secondary schools have been dropped as comprehensive education past the primary level has become available to all students.
- The United States is unique in the extensive use of standardized tests for young children. Current proposals for testing all American elementary school children with a commonly administered and graded examination would make the United States the only industrialized country to adopt this practice.
- There is great variation in the degree of central control over curriculum and testing in foreign countries. In some countries centrally prescribed curricula are used as a basis for required examinations (e.g., France, Italy, the Netherlands, Portugal, Sweden, Israel, Japan, China and, most recently, the United Kingdom). Other countries are more like the United States in the autonomy of States, provinces, or districts in setting curriculum and testing requirements (Australia, Canada, Germany, India, and Switzerland).
- Whether centrally developed or not, the examinations taken during and at the end of secondary school in other countries are not the same for all students. Syllabi in European countries determine subject-matter

---

[1]This draws on information from George Madaus, Boston College, and Thomas Kellaghan, St. Patricks College, Dublin, ''Student Examination Systems in the European Community: Lessons for the United States,'' OTA contractor report, June 1991.

Continued on next page

---

school levels. It was designed to be an educational indicator, a barometer of the Nation's elementary and secondary educational condition. NAEP reports group data only, not individual scores.

NAEP has also been an exemplary model of careful and innovative test design. As discussed in chapter 3, NAEP has made pioneering contributions to test development and practice: ''matrix'' sampling methods, broad-based processes for building consensus about educational goals, an emphasis on content-referenced testing, and the use of various types of open-ended items in large-scale testing.

If Congress wishes to develop a new national test—to be administered to each child and used as a basis for important decisions about children and schools—OTA concludes that NAEP is not appropriate. This objective would require fundamental redesign and validation of NAEP, and would alter the character and value of NAEP as the Nation's independent gauge of educational progress. It would also greatly increase both the cost and time devoted to NAEP at every level.

A better course for Congress is to retain and strengthen NAEP's role as a national indicator of educational progress. To do this, Congress could:

- require NAEP to include more innovative items and tasks that go beyond multiple choice;
- fund the development of a clearinghouse for the sharing of NAEP data, results of field trials, statistical results, and testing techniques, giving States and local districts involved in the design of new tests better access to the lessons from NAEP;
- restore funding for NAEP testing in more subject areas, such as the fine arts;

Box 1-H—National Testing: Lessons From Overseas—Continued

content and examinations are based on them, organized in terms of traditional subject areas (language, mathematics, sciences, history, and geography) and, in some cases, levels at which the subject is studied (general or specialized). Even in European Community (EC) countries with a national system, the examinations are differentiated: all students do not take the same examination at the same time. The examinations may also be differentiated by locale (depending on the part of the country) or by track (there are high-level, low-level, and various curricular options).

- With differentiated examinations, multiple options give students on lower tracks the chance to choose lower level examinations. It appears, though, that these school-leaving examinations can discourage students who do not expect to do well from staying in school.

- In no other system do commercial test publishers play as central a role as they do in the United States. In EC and other industrialized nations, tests are typically established, tested, and scored by ministries of education, with some local delegation of authority. In Europe, Japan, and the U.S.S.R. the examinations have traditionally been dominated by and oriented toward the universities. In Europe, most examination systems are organized around a system of school inspectors, with quasi-governmental control through the establishment of local boards, or multiple boards in larger countries.

- Psychometrics does not play a significant role in the design or validation of tests in most European and Asian countries. Although issues of fairness and comparability are important, they are treated differently than in the United States.

- Teachers in other countries have considerable responsibility for administering and scoring examinations. In some countries (Germany, the U.S.S.R., and Sweden) they even grade their own students. Teacher contracts often include the expectation that they will develop or score examinations; they are sometimes offered extra summer pay to read examinations.

- Syllabi, topics, and even sample questions are widely publicized in advance of examinations, and it is not considered wrong to prepare explicitly for examinations. Annual publication of past examinations strongly influences instruction and learning.

- In European countries, the dominant form of examination is "essay on demand." These examinations require students to write essays of varying lengths in responses to short-answer or open-ended questions. Use of multiple-choice examinations is limited, except in Japan, where they are as prevalent as in the United States. Oral examinations are still common in some of the German *lander* and in foreign language testing in many countries. Performance assessments of other kinds (demonstrations and portfolios) are used for internal classroom assessment.

- support the continued development of methods to communicate NAEP results to school officials and the general public in accurate and innovative ways (particular emphasis could be placed on informing the public about appropriate ways to interpret and understand such test data and on minimizing misinterpretation by the press and general public);

- add testing of nonacademic skills and knowledge relevant to the world of work;

- restore funding for the assessment of out-of-school youth at ages 13 and 17, to provide a better picture of the knowledge and skills of an entire age cohort;

- request data on the issues surrounding test-takers' motivation to do well on NAEP in various grades;[42]

- expand NAEP to assess knowledge in the adult nonschool population; and

- ensure that matrix sampling is retained, to minimize both costs and time requirements of NAEP.

An experiment in extending the uses of NAEP to provide data on educational progress at the State level and to measure this progress against national standards is now under way.

OTA has identified three potential problems of using NAEP for State-by-State comparisons that

---

[42]In particular, questions have been raised about the accuracy of information derived from tests of 12th graders who are about to graduate. Further trial efforts and research could shed light on this issue. Ed Roeber, Michigan Educational Assessment Program, personal communication, October 1991.

Photo credit: *National Assessment of Educational Progress*

The National Assessment of Educational Progress (NAEP) has pioneered the use of performance assessments in large-scale testing programs. In this science task, 7th and 11th grade students figure out which of the three materials would make the box weigh the most.

Congress should review before making a final decision on a permanent use of NAEP for this purpose. First, States could be pressured to introduce curriculum changes to improve their NAEP performance on certain subjects, regardless of whether such changes have educational merit. For example, following the release in 1991 of the State-by-State results from the first such trial, some States (e.g., the District of Columbia) announced plans to revamp their mathematics curricula. It could be argued that the use of NAEP as a prod to State education authorities to rethink their curricula is a good thing; however, *it is clear that the pressure to perform on the test can outweigh the stimulus for careful*

deliberation about academic policy, and that many States could make changes for the sake of higher scores rather than improved learning opportunities for children. This signifies putting the cart of testing before the horse of curriculum, exactly the kind of outcome feared by the original designers of NAEP who insisted that scores not be reported below broad regional levels of aggregation.

Second, the presentation of comparative scores could lead to intensified school-bashing—even when differences in average State performance are statistically insignificant or when those differences reflect variables far beyond the control of school authorities. Critics of comparative NAEP reporting point out that low-scoring States need real help—financial, organizational, and educational—not just more testing and public humiliation.

Finally, extending NAEP to State-level analysis and reporting is a costly undertaking. NAEP funding jumped from $9 million in 1989 to $19 million in 1991. It is not clear that this extra money provides a proportional amount of useful information: one researcher interested in this question showed that roughly 90 percent of the variance in average State performance on NAEP could be explained by socioeconomic and demographic variables already available from other data.[43] In a time of scarce educational resources, NAEP extensions need to be weighed carefully on the scale of anticipated benefits per dollar. State-by-State comparisons of NAEP performance may not pass this cost-benefit test.[44]

These issues notwithstanding, many education policymakers at the State and national levels have insisted that State-level NAEP could provide new and useful information to support curricular and instructional reform. Their arguments should be taken as potentially fruitful research hypotheses and treated as such: just as new medical treatments undergo careful experimentation and evaluation before gaining approval for general public use, extensions and revisions to NAEP should be postponed pending analysis of research data.

In education, the line between research and implementation is often blurred; few newspapers noted that the 1990 State mathematics results were the first in a "trial" program—the results were

[43]See Richard Wolf, Teachers College, Columbia University, "What Can We Learn From State NAEP?" unpublished document, n.d.

[44]See also Daniel Koretz, "State Comparison Using NAEP: Large Costs, Disappointing Benefits," *Educational Researcher*, vol. 20, No. 3, April 1991, pp. 19-21.

treated as factual evidence of relative effectiveness of State education systems.

The NAEP standard-setting process also raises questions of feasibility and desirability. As discussed in chapter 6, the translation of broad educational goals—such as emphasizing problem-solving skills in the mathematics curriculum—into specific test scores is a complex and time-consuming task. The particular performance standards selected must be validated empirically: how closely educators in different parts of the country will concur on standards of proficiency for children at different stages of schooling is not known. Standard setting has always been a slippery process—in employment, psychological, or educational testing—in large part because of difficulties surrounding the designation of acceptable "cutoff scores." Not surprisingly, controversy surrounded the initial attempts to reach consensus on standards for NAEP, with experts disagreeing among themselves on key definitions and interpretations of items.

Educators and policymakers continue to debate whether nationwide standards are desirable, especially if children who do not reach the defined standards are somehow penalized. In addition to the potential effects on children, turning NAEP into a higher stakes test—with implicit and explicit rewards pegged to achievement of the given proficiency standards—could irreparably undermine NAEP's capacity as a neutral barometer of educational progress.

While continued research on State-by-State NAEP and on standard setting will be useful, Congress needs to find ways to ensure that data from this research are reported as such and that the results are not prematurely construed as conclusive.

Chapter 1 Accountability

Because of its scope and influence, Chapter 1 represents a powerful lever by which the Federal Government affects testing practices in the United States. OTA's analysis of Chapter 1 testing and evaluation requirements (see ch. 3) suggests several congressional policy options that could improve Chapter 1 accountability while reducing the overall testing burden in the United States.

Chapter 1, the largest Federal program of aid to elementary and secondary education, provides sup-

plementary education services for disadvantaged children. Over its 25-year history, Chapter 1 evaluation and assessment requirements have been revised many times. The result is an elaborate web of legal and regulatory requirements with standardized norm-referenced achievement tests as the basic thread. The tests fulfill several functions: Federal policymakers and program administrators use nationally aggregated scores to judge the program's overall effectiveness; and local school districts and States use scores to determine which schools are not making sufficient progress in their Chapter 1 programs, to place children in the program, to assess children's educational needs, and for other purposes.

As a result of the 1988 amendments to Chapter 1, which introduced the "program improvement" concept, Chapter 1 testing became even more critical. At the national level, there has been growing concern that the aggregated test data—collected by school districts with widely divergent expertise in evaluation—do not provide an accurate and well-rounded portrait of the program's overall effectiveness. At the school district level, educators argue that the test data often target the wrong schools for program improvement or miss the schools with the weakest programs in the district or the subject areas and grade levels most in need of help. At the classroom level, teachers tend to feel that their own tests and assessments, as well as some externally designed criterion-referenced tests, afford a much better picture of individual students' progress than do the norm-referenced tests.

Congress' principal challenge vis-à-vis Chapter 1 is to find ways to separate Federal evaluation needs from State and local needs. It is a tough dilemma: to balance the national desire for meaningful and comparable program accountability data against State and local needs for useful information on which to base instructional and programmatic decisions. Congress will consider reauthorization of Chapter 1 in 1993. Hearings and analysis on these complex questions in 1992 would provide an excellent basis for a major revision of the evaluation and testing requirements.

One way to improve Chapter 1 accountability is to create a system that separates national evaluation needs from State and local information needs. It is the perceived need for nationally aggregated data that drives the use of norm-referenced tests. If Congress separated national evaluation purposes from State and local purposes and articulated different requirements for each, State Education Agencies (SEAs) and local education authorities would be free to use a variety of assessment methods that better reflect their own localized Chapter 1 goals. The national data would be used to give Federal policymakers, taxpayers, and other interested groups a national picture of Chapter 1 effectiveness, while the State and local information would be used in modifying programs, placing students, targeting schools for program improvement, deciding on continuation of schoolwide projects, and other purposes.

Congress could obtain national data on Chapter 1 through a well-constructed, periodic testing of Chapter 1 children, similar to the way NAEP is used to assess the progress of all students. This assessment would rely on sampling (rather than testing of every student) and could be administered less frequently than the current tests. In addition to relieving the testing burden on individual students and reducing the time devoted to testing by teachers, principals, and other school personnel, this procedure could also result in higher quality data. As the principal client of the data, the Federal Government could identify the areas to be assessed, instill greater standardization and rigor in test administration and data analysis, and avoid the aggregation problems that arise from thousands of school districts administering different instruments under divergent conditions. This type of Federal assessment could be designed and administered by either an independent body or the Department of Education, with the help of the Chapter 1 Technical Assistance Centers.

The system might be designed to provide a menu of assessment options—criterion-referenced tests, reading inventories, directed writing, portfolios, and other performance assessments—from which States could establish statewide evaluation criteria for Chapter 1 programs. If Congress preferred maximum local flexibility, the discretion to choose among the assessment options could be left to school districts, as long as they administered the instruments uniformly and consistently across schools. The Chapter 1 Technical Assistance Centers could help the States and school districts select and implement appropriate measures.

Either a State or local option would increase the latitude for linking assessments to specific program goals. However, if States or districts were to select instruments that put their Chapter 1 programs in the best light, the information could be misleading. Congress should take steps to see that this does not happen. For example, a strict approach would require programs to show growth in student achievement using multiple indicators, perhaps including one indicator based on a standardized test. A looser version of this option would allow States or districts to develop their own evaluation methods, and set their own standards of acceptable progress, subject to Department of Education approval.

An advantage of separating evaluation requirements would likely be local development of new testing methods, which have not been widely used in Chapter 1 because of the need for national aggregation and comparability. Congress could encourage this choice by reserving some of the Federal Chapter 1 evaluation and research funding to advance the state of the art.

For example, competitive grants could be authorized for local education agencies, SEAs, institutions of higher education, Technical Assistance Centers, and other public and private nonprofit agencies to work on issues such as calibrating alternative assessments, training people to use them, bringing down the cost, and making them more objective. Congress could also consider allowing funds from the 5-percent local innovation set-aside to be used for local development and experimentation.

Since Chapter 1 is a major national influence on the amount, frequency, and types of standardized testing, a broad research and development effort for Chapter 1 alternative assessment would have an impact far beyond Chapter 1. The instruments, procedures, and standards developed by this type of effort would spill over into other areas of education, such as early childhood assessment, and would increase local districts' experimentation in other components of their educational programs.

An important issue for congressional consideration is the appropriate grade levels for Chapter 1 evaluations. There is considerable agreement that testing of children in the early grades is inappropriate, especially if standardized norm-referenced paper-and-pencil tests are used; the 1988 reauthorization eliminated testing requirements for children in kindergarten and first grade. On the other hand, there are compelling arguments that from a program evaluation point of view it is important to have ''pre'' and ''post'' data, which means collecting some baseline information. Lack of a reliable method to demonstrate progress during the early years could discourage principals from channeling Chapter 1 funds to very young children, despite evidence that early intervention is very effective. If testing is required to show progress, these tests should be developmentally appropriate.[45]

A related congressional issue concerns the assessment of school children who have only been in a given school's Chapter 1 program for a short period of time; school districts throughout the country cite the high mobility of Chapter 1 children as a logistical obstacle to meaningful evaluation. Despite regulatory guidance, confusion continues to reign in State and local Chapter 1 offices about how to deal with a mobile student population. Clear and consistent policies regarding testing of these children would alleviate some of that confusion.

Appropriate Test Use

The ways tests should be used and the types of inferences that can appropriately be drawn from them are often not well understood by policymakers, school administrators, teachers, or other consumers of test information. Perhaps most important, many parents and test takers themselves are often at a loss to understand the reasons for testing, the importance of the consequences, or the meaning of the results. School policies about how test scores will be used are important not only to students and parents but also to teachers and other school personnel whose own careers may be influenced by the test performance of their pupils. Many of these problems result from using tests for purposes for which they are not designed or adequately validated. Fairness, due process, privacy, and disclosure issues will continue to fuel public passions around testing.

As reviewed in chapter 2, attempts to develop ethical and technical standards for tests and testing practices have a long history. The most recent attempt to codify standards for fair testing practice (in the *Code of Fair Testing Practices in Education*)[46] led to a set of principles with which most professional testing groups concur.

Educational testing practices in some areas have been defined by Federal legislation. In the mid-1970s, Congress passed laws with significant provisions regarding testing, one affecting all students and parents and the others affecting individuals with disabilities and their parents. In both cases this Federal legislation has had far-reaching implications for school policy, because Federal financial assistance to schools has been tied to mandated testing practices. The Family Education Rights and Privacy Act of 1974—commonly called the "Buckley Amendment" after former New York Senator James Buckley—was enacted in part to attempt to safeguard parents' rights and to correct some of the improprieties in the collection and maintenance of pupil records. The basic provisions of this legislation established the right of parents to inspect school records and protected the confidentiality of information by limiting access to school records (including test scores) to those who have legitimate educational needs for the information and by requiring parental written consent for the release of identifiable data.

Given the growing importance of testing and the precedent for Federal action, several avenues are open if Congress wishes to foster better educational testing practices and appropriate test use throughout the Nation.

One option for congressional action would aim at improved disclosure of information. Individual rights could be better safeguarded by encouraging test users (policymakers and schools) to do a careful job of informing test takers. Many critical decisions about test use, such as the selection and interpretation of tests, are made in a professional arena that is well-protected from open, public scrutiny. This occurs in part because of the highly technical nature of testing design. Although the professional testing community is not unanimous about what constitutes good testing practice, there is considerable consensus on the importance of carefully informing individual test takers (and their parents or guardians in the case of minors) about the purpose of the test, the uses to which it will be put, the persons who will

[45]See, e.g., Robert E. Slavin and Nancy A. Madden, Center for Research on Effective Schooling for Disadvantaged Students, The Johns Hopkins University, "Chapter 1 Program Improvement Guidelines: Do They Reward Appropriate Practices?" paper prepared for the Office of Educational Research and Improvement, U.S. Department of Education, December 1990. See also Nancy Kober, "The Role and Impact of Chapter 1 ESEA, Evaluation and Assessment Practices," OTA contractor report, June 1991.

[46]Joint Committee on Testing Practices, *Code of Fair Testing Practices in Education* (Washington, DC: National Council on Measurement in Education, 1988).

have access to the scores, and the rights of the test taker to retake or challenge test results.[47]

Congress could require, or encourage, school districts to:

- develop and publish a testing policy that spells out the types of tests given, how they are chosen, and how the tests and test scores will be used; and
- notify parents of test requirements and consequences, with special emphasis on tests used for selection, placement, or credentialing decisions.

A second approach for Congress is to encourage good testing practice by modeling and demonstrating such practice at the Federal level. The Federal Government writes much legislation that incorporates standardized testing as one component of a larger program. For example, the Individuals With Disabilities Education Act (Public Law 101-476), formerly the Education for all Handicapped Children Act of 1975 (Public Law 94-142), was designed to assure the rights of individuals with disabilities to the best possible education; this legislation included a number of explicit provisions regarding how tests should be used to implement this program.

Among the provisions were: 1) decisions about students are to be based on more than performance on a single test, 2) tests must be validated for the purpose for which they are used, 3) children must be assessed in all areas related to a specific or suspected disability, and 4) evaluations should be made by a multidisciplinary team.

Through these assessment provisions, Public Laws 101-476 and 94-142 have provided a number of significant safeguards against the simplistic or capricious use of test scores in making educational decisions. Congress could adopt similar provisions in other legislation that has implications for testing. A recent example of Federal legislation that could lead to questionable uses of tests is a provision in the 1990 Omnibus Budget Reconciliation Act. The objective of this provision is to reduce the high loan default rate of students attending postsecondary training programs (largely but not exclusively in

proprietary technical schools). The policy lever is testing: the act requires students without a high school diploma to pass an ''ability-to-benefit'' test, on the assumption that students who are able to benefit from postsecondary training will be more likely to get jobs and pay back their loans than students who are not able to benefit. Basic questions arise about the appropriateness of using existing tests to sort individuals on this broad ''ability'' criterion. Even the most prevalent college admissions tests do not make claims of being able to predict which students will ''benefit'' in the long run, but rather which students will do well in their freshman year.

A third course of action would focus on various proposals to certify, regulate, oversee, or audit tests. If Congress wants to play a more forceful role in preventing misuse of tests—in particular, preventing tests designed for classroom use or system monitoring from being applied to individual selection or certification decisions—this option is the clear choice. If testing continues to increase and takes on even more consequences, pressure for congressional intervention will grow. Proposals include Federal guidelines for educational test use, labeling of all mandated tests and test requirements, labeling of all commercially available tests, and creating a governmental or quasi-governmental entity to regulate, certify, and disseminate information about tests. This last option, which echoes a concept endorsed by the National Commission on Testing and Public Policy, has been discussed in testing policy circles for some years now.[48]

Finally, Congress could pursue more indirect ways to inform and educate consumers and users of tests. This might include supporting continuing professional education for teachers and administrators, or funding the development of better ways to analyze test data and convey the results more effectively to the public.

Federal Research and Development Options

Test development is a costly process. Even for a test or test battery that has already been in use for many years, it can take from 6 to 8 years to write new

---

[47]See, for example, American Psychological Association, *Standards for Educational and Psychological Testing* (Washington, DC: 1985); Joint Committee on Testing Practices, op. cit., footnote 46; and Russell Sage Foundation, *Guidelines for the Collection, Maintenance, and Dissemination of Pupil Records* (New York, NY: 1969), especially Guideline 1.3.

[48]See, e.g., D. Goslin, ''The Present and Future of Assessment: Towards an Agenda for Research and Public Policy,'' draft report of a planning meeting sponsored by the U.S. Department of Education, Mar. 23-25, 1990, draft dated July 19, 1990.

items, pilot test, and validate a major revision.[49] Most investigators working on new testing designs are wading into uncharted statistical and methodological waters. For a new test, consisting of open-ended performance tasks or other innovative items, development and validation are substantially more expensive, even if test content and objectives are clearly defined. For example, the development of a set of new performance measures assessing specific job-related skills for the armed services cost $30 million over 10 years. The results of this sustained research effort, coordinated by the Department of Defense and carried out by the individual service organizations, were a set of hands-on measures, new supervisory ratings, job-knowledge tests, and computer-based simulations representing the skills required in some 30 well-defined jobs. The main purpose of the research was to improve the outcome or criterion measures used to validate the Armed Services Vocational Aptitude Battery, the standardized test used to qualify new recruits for various job assignments.[50]

In elementary and secondary school testing, however, the first step—defining the content that tests should cover—is much more complex than defining specific job performance outcomes for a number of jobs. The omnipresent issue of achieving consensus on content poses formidable barriers to test design. Even in a subject like mathematics, for which there is some agreement on outcomes and standards (as exemplified by the National Council on Teachers of Mathematics' recent work on standards for mathematics education), the definition of those standards took 6 years to develop. In most other subjects consensus on goals and curricula is more difficult to reach, adding substantially to research and development (R&D) costs. Moreover, separate standards, content, and tests would need to be developed for each grade level and subject to be tested.

Another factor making testing R&D expensive is the question of how new assessment methods will affect students and teachers. Much of the interest in developing new assessments (see ch. 6) stems from

the desire to see those assessments eventually become the basis for system monitoring and other high-stakes decisions. Validation studies are therefore critical. Random assignment experiments, which are costly, could encounter legal barriers because students' lives and educational experiences could be affected. Validation studies, therefore, may need to be conducted with quasi-experimental designs, which suffer from various statistical and methodological problems.[51]

Congress has an important role to play in supporting R&D in educational testing, because adequate funding cannot be expected from other sources. Commercial vendors are not likely to make the requisite investments without some assurance of a reasonable return; they face strong market incentives to sell generic products that match the curricula of many school systems. But if these products are so general in their coverage that they reflect only a limited subset of skills common to virtually all curricula, schools may not see the advantage of adding them to an already strapped instructional materials budget. States might be willing to foot the R&D bill, although their education budgets are generally quite constrained. Moreover, in addition to costs associated with consensus-building on test content and evaluation of the anticipated effects of testing, new performance assessment and/or computer-based methods require basic research on learning and cognition. Basic education research has traditionally been a Federal responsibility.

The question becomes how much: how much should the Federal Government spend on educational testing R&D? The answer depends on the choice Congress makes regarding the value of dramatically enlarging the currently available range of testing methods. For example, Federal spending on educational assessment research is roughly $7 million for fiscal year 1992, out of a total education research budget of close to $100 million.[52] This money is divided almost evenly among NAEP (for validation studies, evaluation of trial State assessment, and secondary data analysis); development of new mathematics and science assessments ($6

[49]Rudman, op. cit., footnote 8, p. 8.

[50]See Alexandra Wigdor and Bert Green (eds.), *Performance Assessment for the Workplace*, vol. 1 (Washington, DC: National Academy Press, 1991).

[51]See, e.g., Anand Desai, "Technical Issues in Measuring Scholastic Improvement Due to Compensatory Education Programs," *Socio-Economic Planning Sciences*, vol. 24, No. 2, 1990, pp. 143-153.

[52]Education research and statistics spending in fiscal year 1990 was $94 million. See U.S. Department of Education, *Digest of Educational Statistics, 1990*, op. cit., footnote 1, p. 344.

million over 3 years, administered through the National Science Foundation); and general assessment research (through the Center for Research on Evaluation, Standards, and Student Testing).

Substantially more funding would be needed if Congress chooses to support:

- cognitive science research on learning and testing,
- development of new approaches to consensus building for test content and objectives,
- research on the generalizability of new testing methods across subjects and grades, and
- validation studies of new testing methods.

An intermediate funding approach would be to target Federal dollars toward:

- the creation of a clearinghouse to facilitate continuing and more widespread dissemination of testing research results and innovations,
- continuing professional education for teachers in the applications of new testing and assessment methods and in the appropriate interpretations and uses of test results, and
- the creation of a nationwide computer-based clearinghouse of test items from which States and local districts could draw to develop their own customized tests.

CHAPTER 2

Testing in Transition

Contents

Testing in Transition

Highlights

- Since the 1960s testing in elementary and secondary schools has been caught in a tug between two powerful forces: increased public attention to test scores because of demands for evidence that the schools are educating children, and increased demands from educators and students for tests that more accurately reflect changing educational goals, new curricula, and reforms in teaching.
- State-level concerns about the quality of education were the dominant force behind the rise of high-stakes testing beginning in the mid-1970s. Minimum competency testing, for example, was embraced by many State policymakers who believed that the imposition of external standards would boost educational quality. Since then, however, studies of the effects of this testing have led most educators to question the utility of tests as an instrument of reform.
- Two decades of research about learning and cognition have produced important findings about how children learn and acquire knowledge. These findings challenge most traditional models of classroom organization, curricula, and teaching methods. Among the most important findings are that teaching thinking skills need not await mastery of so-called "basic" skills, and that all students are capable of learning thinking skills. Many educators now charge that significant changes in classrooms cannot go forward if traditional tests are to remain the primary indicator of achievement and program success. The tests must change, they argue, if schools are to change.
- Many of the recent challenges to traditional tests have been directed at the norm-referenced multiple-choice tests most often used to assess educational achievement. It is not just the tests themselves that create controversy, however. Testing practices—the ways tests are used and the types of inferences drawn from them—also create many of the problems associated with testing. Appropriate testing practices are difficult to enforce and few safeguards exist to prevent misuse and misinterpretation of scores, especially once they reach the public.
- Test-use policy is important not only to students and parents but also to teachers and other school personnel whose own careers may be influenced by the test performance of their pupils. Concern for the increasing consequences being attached to test scores has helped fuel a backlash against standardized testing that had been brewing since the expansion of high-stakes testing in the 1970s, when issues of fairness, test bias, due process, individual privacy, and disclosure were debated in Congress and the courts.
- Although demands for accountability have not abated amid this environment of testing reform, most educators now urge the development and implementation of new testing and assessment technologies, and all caution against the use of tests as the sole or principal indicator of achievement.

Overview

Two decades of discussion about school quality have convinced many Americans that their educational system needs substantial reform to meet the demands of the next century. Although the country is far from consensus about exactly what types of reform are needed, nearly all the initiatives call for changes in educational testing.

Some school reformers, primarily at the State level, have called for changes in testing to monitor student progress in mastering fundamentally new curricula. Others have pinned their hopes on more high-stakes testing—including yet-to-be-developed national tests—to spur greater student and teacher diligence. This group includes educators and policymakers who believe that new and better tests can lead to improved learning, as well as those who believe in conventional tests as a catalyst of change. Still others fear that more testing of any type will only exacerbate the problems of test misuse and unfairness, and will be counterproductive to school reform. These debates should not surprise anyone familiar with the U.S. education system: standardized tests have always been prominent, and discussion of educational reform inevitably involves an examination of testing.

Since the 1960s Americans have turned increasingly to testing as a tool for measuring student learning, holding schools accountable for results, and reforming curriculum and instruction. Testing in elementary and secondary schools has, therefore, increased in both frequency and significance. As shown in figure 2-1, revenues from sales of commercially published standardized tests for K-12 more than doubled between 1960 and 1989; i.e., from about $40 million in 1960 to about $100 million in 1989 (in constant 1982 dollars). A recent report of the National Commission for Testing and Public Policy estimates that the 44 million American elementary and secondary students take 127 million separate tests annually, as part of standardized test batteries mandated by States and districts.[1]

Much of this growth in testing occurred during a period of economic, social, and demographic turbulence, and is attributable to Federal, State, and local demands for increased accountability.[2] These strategies for change, such as performance reporting, establishing and enforcing procedural standards, and changing school structure or the professional roles of school personnel, rely on test information about schools and students.[3]

At the Federal level, demands for test-based accountability emerged as a consequence of substantial new financial commitments to education on the part of the Federal Government. State-mandated tests, often designed and administered by State authorities (rather than by commercial vendors) have also grown dramatically; State-level concern with the quality of education, and State-level demands for improvement in the outcomes of schooling, have perhaps been the dominant forces behind

Figure 2-1—Revenues From Sales of Commercially Produced Standardized Tests in the United States, 1960-90

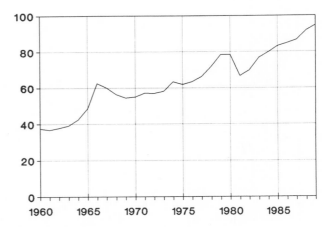

a Sales in 1982 dollars.
NOTE: Sales include K-12 educational tests.
SOURCE: Office of Technology Assessment, based on data from Filomena Simora (ed.), *The Bowker Annual* (New York, NY: Reed Publishing, 1970-90).

the rise of standardized testing in the past two decades.

The pattern of increased testing followed by increased controversy dates to the initial uses of tests to stimulate school reform in the 19th century.[4] In different periods the specific causes of controversy over testing have varied. Today the debate stems from three main factors.

First, many of the people and school systems attempting to redesign curricula and reform teaching and learning feel stymied in their efforts by tests that do not reflect new education goals. Moreover, because tests have increasingly high stakes, reformers find that bold new ideas of curricula and instruction cannot surmount the power of tests to reinforce traditional learning. For example, the basic ''building-block'' approach to student learning—

---

[1] National Commission on Testing and Public Policy, *From Gatekeeper to Gateway: Transforming Testing in America* (Boston, MA: 1990), p. 15. Test publishers claim that the National Commission exaggerates in its estimate of testing. For example, the Vice President for Publishing at one of the largest educational test publishing companies argues that: ''Our data sources indicate that roughly 30 to 40 million standardized tests are administered annually across the country. . . [at an annual] total cost of . . . $100 million to $150 million. . . .'' See Douglas MacRae, ''Topic: Too Much Testing?'' *From CTB Publisher's Desk*, No. 3, Nov. 15, 1990.

[2] The work of Leon Lessinger, ''Accountability for Results,'' *American Education* (Washington, DC: U.S. Office of Education, June-July 1969), is often credited with igniting the most recent wave of accountability in education. For a synthesis and discussion of approaches to accountability in education see Michael Kirst, *Accountability: Implications for State and Local Policymakers* (Washington, DC: U.S. Department of Education, July 1990).

[3] ''An aroused parent group, for example, will follow up on the results of a negative school report card by lobbying the school board for a new principal.'' Kirst, op. cit., footnote 2, p. 7.

[4] See ch. 4.

the idea that children needed to be solidly grounded in the basics before acquiring advanced thinking and problem-solving skills—has been gradually supplanted by new research findings. Curriculum specialists as well as teachers have begun arguing for new approaches to the definition and instruction of ''higher order skills,'' and for changes that could make tests better indicators of learning.

Second, the demand for test-based accountability continues to grow. Advocates of test-based accountability argue it is an efficient and effective way to make students, teachers, and schools work harder. Some go so far as to suggest that raising the stakes of these tests can put America back on the road to global economic hegemony: since teachers will teach and children will study what is tested, the thinking goes, then the tests themselves can drive educational reform.[5] Opponents of this view charge that high-stakes testing sends the wrong signals to students and teachers, and encourages emphasis on test taking and test preparation rather than genuine learning. They also argue that attaching high stakes to tests threatens the validity of the information provided by the tests and leads to erroneous policy inferences.

Third, as the tension surrounding tests increases, so do concerns about the appropriate use of tests and the effects of tests on individual rights. The history of testing is littered with examples of tests being used in ways not intended by their developers, tempting policymakers and the public to draw inferences not supportable by test data.

The three camps—those who support new approaches to assessment and testing, those who think more high-stakes testing will improve education, and those who are worried about ethical and legal aspects of testing—share a common concern for raising the quality of American schooling. But their strategies are crafted from visions of the educational system and the nature of human learning glimpsed through very different prisms.

Changing Views of Teaching and Learning

A quiet but dramatic transformation is occurring in education as researchers and practitioners rethink basic beliefs about teaching and learning. Two decades of research from developmental and cognitive psychology have produced important findings about how children learn and acquire knowledge.[6] The basic concept in this research is that children are active builders of their own knowledge, not merely passive receptacles for information. These research findings and the instructional theories they have spawned raise serious challenges to traditional classroom organizational models, to conventional curricula, and, in turn, to existing forms of testing. Moreover, they have rekindled an awareness of the close links between instructional goals and assessment.

Evolving Views of Learning

In their teaching methods, curricular materials, and testing methods, many schools today embody a behaviorist model of learning first popularized in the 1920s. In this model:

. . . learning is seen to be linear and sequential. Complex understanding can only occur by the accretion of elemental, prerequisite learnings. . . . The whole idea was to break desired learnings into constituent elements and teach these one by one. . . . The implications of this model for instruction are conveyed best by . . . [the] metaphor of a brick wall, i.e., it is not possible to lay the bricks in the fifth layer until the first, second, third, and fourth layers are complete.[7]

This model assumes that more complex skills can be broken down into simple skills, each of which can be mastered independently and out of context. When all requisite components are mastered, then more complex thinking skills can accrue. According to this view, the highest levels of knowledge are achieved only at the later grades and, even then, only by some students. In this conventional model, moreover, the teacher is the active partner in the educational

[5]See e.g., Robert Samuelson, ''The School Reform Fraud,'' *The Washington Post*, June 19, 1991, p. A19.

[6]The following discussion about constructivist and behaviorist models of learning draws on Lauren B. Resnick and Daniel P. Resnick, ''Assessing the Thinking Curriculum: New Tools for Educational Reform,'' paper prepared for the National Commission on Testing and Public Policy, August 1989; Lorrie A. Shepard, University of Colorado at Boulder, ''Psychometricians' Beliefs About Learning,'' paper presented at the annual meeting of the American Educational Research Association, Boston, MA, Apr. 17, 1990.

[7]Shepard, op. cit., footnote 6, p. 15.

process, imparting knowledge to a passive student as though filling an empty jug.

This hierarchical view of complex thinking is challenged by recent research from the cognitive sciences.

One of the most important findings of recent research on thinking is that the kinds of mental processes associated with thinking are not restricted to an advanced or 'higher order' stage of mental development. Instead, thinking and reasoning are intimately involved in successfully learning even elementary levels of reading, mathematics, and other school subjects. Cognitive research on children's learning of basic skills reveals that reading, writing, and arithmetic—the three Rs—involve important components of inference, judgment and active mental construction [see box 2-A]. The traditional view that the basics can be taught as routine skills, with thinking and reasoning to follow later, can no longer guide our educational practice.[8]

In fact, the term ''higher order'' thinking skills seems something of a misnomer in that it implies that there is another set of ''lower order'' skills that need to come first.

Another implication of the hierarchical ''brick wall'' model of learning is the notion that slower learners need to master low-level skills before they can move on to more complex skills. This sort of thinking underlies many compensatory education programs, in which educationally disadvantaged children or children who learn more slowly than their peers spend much of their time confined to remedial classes consisting of drill and practice. By a process of remediation through repetition students are expected to master the low-level skills; many, however, spend a good portion (if not all) of their educational careers confined to the mastery of basic skills through remedial methods. The constructivist model of learning indicates that these students are capable of much more than this; this research suggests that all are naturally engaged everyday in problem solving, making inferences and judgments, and forming theories about how the world works.

Several programs designed specifically to focus on increasing the achievement of disadvantaged

Photo credit: Siemens Corp.

Recent research has emphasized that learning is an active process that can best be supported in the classroom by hands-on activities and experimentation. As curricula and teaching practices change, new tests will also be needed.

learners provide evidence to support the notion that these students are capable of learning far more than basic skills. The Accelerated Schools Program is a reform experiment designed to accelerate the learning of at-risk students and close the ''achievement gap'' while the students are still in elementary school. The program sets high expectations for student learning and focuses on the teaching of critical thinking and problem solving to all students. Although these programs do not yet have a long track record, teachers report delight and surprise at the gains achieved by participating students.[9] Another program, the Higher Order Thinking Skills (HOTS) project, provides Chapter 1 students in grades four through seven with enhanced thinking skills instead of remediation. The HOTS project has yielded compelling anecdotal evidence of substan-

---

[8]Resnick and Resnick, op. cit., footnote 6, p. 2.

[9]Gail Meister, Research for Better Schools, ''Assessment in Programs for Disadvantaged Students: Lessons From Accelerated Schools,'' OTA contractor report, April 1991.

Box 2-A—Fourth Grade Scientists Test a Theory[1]

For nine winters, experience had been their teacher. Every hat they had worn, every sweater they had donned, contained heat. "Put on your warm clothes," parents and teachers had told them. So when the children in Ms. O'Brien's fourth grade science class began to study heat one spring day, who could blame them for thinking as they did?

"Sweaters are hot," said Katie.

"If you put a thermometer inside a hat, would it ever get hot! Ninety degrees, maybe," said Neil.

. . . [With O'Brien's help, the students set out to test these theories.] Christian, Neil, Katie, and the others placed thermometers inside sweaters, hats, and a rolled-up rug. When the temperature inside refused to rise after 15 minutes, Christian suggested that they leave the thermometers overnight. After all, he said, when the doctor takes your temperature, you have to leave the thermometer in your mouth for a long time. Folding the sweaters and hats securely, the children predicted three digit temperatures the next day.

When they ran to their experiments first thing the next morning, the children were baffled. They had been wrong. Now they'll change their minds, and we can move on, O'Brien thought.

But . . . the children refused to give up. "We just didn't leave them in there long enough," Christian said. "Cold air got in there somehow," said Katie.

. . . [O'Brien suggested they adjust their experiments and try again.] If, as they insisted, cold air had seeped inside the clothes overnight, what could they do to keep it out? . . . Neil decided to seal the hat, with the thermometer inside, in a plastic bag. Katie chose to plug the ends of the rug with hats. Others placed sweaters in closets or in desks, far away from the great gusts of cold air they seemed to think swept their classroom at night.

. . . On Wednesday morning the children rushed to examine their experiments. They checked their deeply buried thermometers. From across the room, they shared their bewilderment. All the thermometers were at 68 degrees Fahrenheit. Confused, they wrote in their journals. "Hot and cold are sometimes strange," Katie wrote. "Maybe [the thermometer] didn't work because it was used to room temperature."

Meanwhile, O'Brien wondered in her own journal . . . how long she should let these naive conceptions linger. [She decided to have the students proceed with] . . . one more round of testing. And so the sweaters, hats, and even a down sleeping bag brought from home were sealed, plugged, and left to endure the cold.

. . . For the third day in a row in O'Brien's classroom, the children rushed to their experiments as soon as they arrived. The sweater, the sleeping bag, and the hat were unwrapped. Once again the thermometers uniformly read room temperature. O'Brien led the disappointed children to their journals. But after a few moments of discussion, she realized that her students had reached an impasse. Their old theory was clearly on the ropes, but they had no new theory with which to replace it. She decided to offer them a choice of two possible statements.

"Choose statement A or B," she told them. The first stated that heat could come from almost anything, hats and sweaters included. In measuring such heat, statement A proclaimed, we are sometimes fooled because we're really measuring cold air that gets inside. This, of course, was what most children had believed at the outset. Statement B, of O'Brien's own devising, posed the alternative that heat comes mostly from the sun and our bodies and is trapped inside winter clothes that keep our body heat in and keep the cold air out.

"Write down what you believe," O'Brien told the class. [Although some students clung to the "hot hat" theory and some did not know what to think, most choose theory B.]

"How can we test this new theory?" O'Brien asked. Immediately Neil said, "Put the thermometers in our hats when we're wearing them." And so the children went out to recess that day with an experiment under their hats.

As Deb O'Brien relaxed during recess, she asked herself about the past three days. Had the children really changed their minds? Or had they simply been following the leader? Could they really change their ideas in the course of a few class periods? Would any of their activities help them pass the standardized science test coming up in May? O'Brien wasn't sure she could answer any of these questions affirmatively. But she had seen the faces of young scientists as they ran to their experiments, wrote about their findings, spoke out, thought, asked questions—and that was enough for now.

---

[1]Excerpted from Bruce Watson and Richard Konicek, "Teaching for Conceptual Change: Confronting Children's Experience," *Phi Delta Kappan*, vol. 71, No. 9, May 1990, pp. 680-685.

tial gains in self esteem and enthusiasm for learning—as well as achievement test scores—when children participate in the program for 35 minutes a day over 2 school years.[10]

Additional evidence suggests that thinking and reasoning skills can be taught.[11] A number of programs have been designed to teach thinking and problem-solving skills; some focus on developing these skills within particular disciplines (e.g., mathematics and reading) while others are aimed at enhancing general thinking skills that would, presumably, be applicable in many different settings. The effectiveness of these programs is difficult to evaluate in the absence of appropriate outcome measures. Evaluations show students improving on measures tied to the material taught: students appear to learn to do the things the program teaches. The question of whether that learning generalizes is more difficult to assess, in part because there are few good outcome measures for these skills.[12]

The results of these studies suggest some hopeful beginnings for the design of curricula and teaching methods focused on thinking and reasoning skills. Much of this work is new and experimental. Experimentation is needed to discern how much emphasis to place on general thinking skills and how much to emphasize thinking skills for specific knowledge and information. Moreover, knowledge of how to teach those reasoning skills—at what ages, using what methods—is still very rudimentary.

In sum, although educators have always attempted to foster reasoning skills, research about learning and the structure of knowledge suggests two major changes in how those skills should be taught. **First, thinking skills need not be learned only after other, more basic skills are mastered. Second, all students are capable of learning thinking skills.**

Evolving Views of the Classroom

Recent developments in education have converged to make more and more classrooms into vital laboratories for new teaching and learning methods. First, the growing presence of educational technology in the classroom, especially computers and integrated learning systems, is changing the definitions of what children need to know and how to teach it.

Second, educators are radically rethinking the structure and content of their disciplines. For example, the National Council of Teachers of Mathematics (NCTM) has proposed fundamental changes in the content and delivery of elementary and secondary school mathematics instruction, changes that emphasize the use of manipulative objects and the teaching of analytical reasoning and problem-solving skills. Mathematics educators have recognized that: ''. . . the world is changing so rapidly that, unless those involved in mathematics education adopt a proactive view and develop a new assessment model for the twenty-first century, the mathematical understanding of children will continue to be inadequate into the future;''[13] and they have worked to build consensus on a set of curriculum standards for K-12 education. Initiatives to revisit science curricula and teaching methods have also taken hold, with particular efforts to stress ''hands-on'' science experiments. In addition, many schools are experimenting with the idea of the ''integrated curriculum,'' in which central themes or ideas are taught across disciplines and the school day is no longer divided into discrete periods labeled by subject.

Third, attention is being directed toward the development of materials and methods for cultivating higher order thinking skills (see box 2-B). The emphasis on fostering reasoning skills has been bolstered by the widespread recognition that changing economic and technological conditions will

---

[10]S. Pogrow, ''Challenging At-Risk Students: Findings From the HOTS Program,'' *Phi Delta Kappan*, vol. 71, No. 5, January 1990, pp. 389-397.

[11]For descriptions of some of these efforts see R. Glaser, ''Education and Thinking: The Role of Knowledge,'' *American Psychologist*, vol. 39, No. 2, February 1984, pp. 93-104; Lauren B. Resnick, *Education and Learning to Think* (Washington, DC: National Academy Press, 1987); Lauren B. Resnick and Leopold E. Klopfer (eds.), *Toward the Thinking Curriculum: Current Cognitive Research*, 1989 Yearbook of the Association for Supervision and Curriculum Development (Alexandria, VA: Association for Supervision and Curriculum Development, 1989); and Norman Frederiksen, ''Implications of Cognitive Theory for Instruction in Problem Solving,'' *Review of Educational Research*, vol. 54, No. 3, fall 1984, pp. 363-407.

[12]Resnick, op. cit., footnote 11.

[13]Thomas A. Romberg, E. Anne Zarrinnia, and Kevin F. Collis, ''A New Worldview of Assessment in Mathematics,'' *Assessing Higher Order Thinking in Mathematics*, G. Kulm (ed.) (Washington, DC: American Association for the Advancement of Science, 1990), p. 21.

Box 2-B—Thinking About Thinking Skills

What are "higher order thinking skills"? What do they look like and how do we know when students have them? The first truism seems to be that they are difficult to define; the second is that they are even harder to measure.

Social scientists from many disciplines have studied mental processes such as thinking, problem solving, reasoning, and critical thinking; although they have produced many carefully wrought definitions, consensus about the nature of these processes has eluded them. Educational practitioners, on the other hand, have less interest in understanding the precise nature of all possible thinking processes; instead, practitioners are most concerned about the "... complex thought processes required to solve problems and make decisions in everyday life, and those that have a direct relevance to instruction."[1] One recent attempt to synthesize the perspectives of philosophers, psychologists, and educators has produced the outline of thinking skills shown in table 2-B1. As this table suggests, at least some consensus exists about the kinds of skills educators would like to include in a thinking curriculum.

[1]J.A. Arter and J.R. Salmon, Northwest Regional Educational Laboratory, "Assessing Higher Order Thinking Skills: A Consumer's Guide," unpublished report, April 1987, pp. 1-2.

Table 2-B1—List of Thinking and Reasoning Skills

I. Problem solving
  A. Identifying general problem
  B. Clarifying problem
  C. Formulating hypothesis
  D. Formulating appropriate questions
  E. Generating related ideas
  F. Formulating alternative solutions
  G. Choosing best solution
  H. Applying the solution
  I. Monitoring acceptance of the solution
  J. Drawing conclusions

II. Decisionmaking
  A. Stating desired goal/condition
  B. Stating obstacles to goal/condition
  C. Identifying alternatives
  D. Examining alternatives
  E. Ranking alternatives
  F. Choosing best alternative
  G. Evaluating actions

III. Inferences
  A. Inductive thinking skills
    1. Determining cause and effect
    2. Analyzing open-ended problems
    3. Reasoning by analogy
    4. Making inferences
    5. Determining relevant information
    6. Recognizing relationships
    7. Solving insight problems
  B. Deductive thinking skills
    1. Using logic
    2. Spotting contradictory statements
    3. Analyzing syllogisms
    4. Solving spatial problems

IV. Divergent thinking skills
  A. Listing attributes of objects/situations
  B. Generating multiple ideas (fluency)
  C. Generating different ideas (flexibility)
  D. Generating unique ideas (originality)
  E. Generating detailed ideas (elaboration)
  F. Synthesizing information

V. Evaluative thinking skills
  A. Distinguishing between facts and opinions
  B. Judging credibility of a source
  C. Observing and judging observation reports
  D. Identifying central issues and problems
  E. Recognizing underlying assumptions
  F. Detecting bias, stereotypes, cliches
  G. Recognizing loaded language
  H. Evaluating hypotheses
  I. Classifying data
  J. Predicting consequences
  K. Demonstrating sequential synthesis of information
  L. Planning alternative strategies
  M. Recognizing inconsistencies in information
  N. Identifying stated and unstated reasons
  O. Comparing similarities and differences
  P. Evaluating arguments

VI. Philosophy and reasoning
  A. Using dialogical/dialectical approaches

NOTE: This list is based on a compilation and distillation of ideas from many educators and psychologists. See original source.

SOURCE: J.A. Arter and J.R. Salmon, Northwest Regional Education Laboratory, "Assessing Higher-Order Thinking Skills: A Consumer's Guide," unpublished report, April 1987, p. 3.

require upgrading the cognitive skills of the work force.[14] The combined effects of research on learning and public concern for the state of the education system have led some educators to suggest that reasoning should be considered as "the fourth R."[15] In classrooms across the country, teachers are experimenting with ways to teach critical thinking and comprehension along with basic skills and information.

Implications for Standardized Testing

Educators trying to implement these new ideas and classroom practices have found themselves face to face with the dominance of standardized norm-referenced tests as the sine qua non of educational effectiveness. Many have found their new programs being judged by tests that do not cover the skills and goals central to their innovations. Those working on integrated curricula, a new vision of mathematics, or hands-on learning environments have found their new programs measured by tests designed for very different goals. Thus, a new and energetic movement has emerged focused on developing assessments more closely aligned with new curricula, learning methods, and valued skills.

The press for reform of tests to better match instruction and curricula comes from many sources. Educators are recognizing the potential of computers to change testing just as they are changing learning. Curriculum reform groups, such as the NCTM standards committee, are seeking assessments better matched to their curricular and evaluation standards. Educators working to increase the achievement of disadvantaged learners express frustration that many of their critical program goals are not measured by existing standardized tests.[16] A common theme is that transformation of education cannot occur as long as tests embrace obsolete concepts about learning. Without new assessment instruments, it is difficult to ascertain whether reforms in instruction and curriculum are working.

What implications does a focus on thinking skills and active learning have for test design? Reformers trying to implement a thinking curriculum agree on the need for changes that will better focus on reasoning skills and deep understandings. Test designers have always advanced the idea that an achievement test should be designed to reflect the goals of the curriculum. Most current achievement tests were constructed by careful delineation of the subject matter (e.g., reading, language arts, and mathematics); experts in the subject matter areas were largely responsible for specifying the domains of information and the skills to be mastered. However, ". . . a clear definition of the subject-matter content is essential, but insufficient by itself. An understanding of the learner's cognitive processes—the ways in which knowledge is represented, reorganized, and used to process new information—is also needed."[17]

Until recently most attempts to incorporate cognitive skills into test design were modeled on Bloom's taxonomy of cognitive behaviors,[18] which attempts to organize and classify the cognitive skills children are supposed to acquire. The taxonomy reflects a behavioral approach to learning; educational objectives are written as clearly delineated, mutually exclusive categories of behavior that can be observed, counted, and classified. Tests based on this taxonomy are organized according to a content-by-

---

[14]Although most analysts agree that some improvement in thinking skills will be beneficial, there is disagreement over how high to raise the threshold. The disagreement stems from conflicting interpretations of data on the productivity of the work force currently and on the effects of technological change on future skill requirements. For an eloquent discussion, see Richard Murnane, "Education and the Productivity of the Work Force: Looking Ahead," *American Living Standards*, R. Litan, R. Lawrence, and C. Schultze (eds.) (Washington, DC: Brookings Institution, 1988), pp. 215-246.

[15]R. Glaser, "The Fourth R: The Ability to Reason," paper presented to the Federation of Behavioral, Psychological and Cognitive Sciences Science and Public Policy Seminar, June 1989; and Larry Cuban, "Policy and Research Dilemmas in the Teaching of Reasoning: Unplanned Designs," *Review of Educational Research*, vol. 54, 1984, pp. 655-681.

[16]See Meister, op. cit., footnote 9.

[17]Robert L. Linn, "Barriers to New Test Design," *The Redesign of Testing for the 21st Century*, proceedings of the 1985 ETS Invitational Conference, Eileen E. Freeman (ed.) (Princeton, NJ: Educational Testing Service, 1986), p. 73.

[18]B.S. Bloom (ed.), *Taxonomy of Educational Objectives: The Classification of Educational Goals. Handbook 1—Cognitive Domain* (New York, NY: Academic Press, 1956). This discussion of the applications of Bloom's taxonomy to achievement testing is drawn from Romberg et al., op. cit., footnote 13. See also Edward Haertel and Robert Calfee, "School Achievement: Thinking About What to Test," *Journal of Educational Measurement*, vol. 20, No. 2, summer 1983, pp. 119-132.

behavior matrix. As the example in figure 2-2 demonstrates, one axis of the matrix lists the content areas and the other axis describes the skills test takers are expected to demonstrate within each content area (in this example, computation, comprehension, application, and analysis). Items are designed for each cell in the matrix. Despite changes over time in the specifics of each axis, the matrix approach to test design has persisted because ''. . . it permits a rapid overview of the entire structure [of a test] and relative emphasis on one part or another.''[19]

Some critics of the taxonomic approach feel that the matrix oversimplifies the complexity of knowledge and how students acquire it. Subject matter experts from various content disciplines have criticized the way that such matrices artificially divide both content and skills into mutually exclusive categories, ignoring complex interrelationships. In fact, the matrix form, by its very nature, suggests ''. . . relationships which are simple, numerically restricted and linear . . .''[20]—an outmoded concept that views thinking skills as hierarchically nested atop one another, with the learner moving from simple thinking skills to more complex ones as achievement advances.

Cognitive Research: Implications for New Test Design

Since the publication of Bloom's taxonomy, considerable research has been conducted about the nature of the cognitive processes involved in learning. The findings from cognitive sciences research provide a basis for different kinds of instruction, curriculum materials, and tests that more closely resemble the processes involved in learning and thinking (see box 2-C). Findings from research on learning and cognition imply at least three broad changes for educational tests:

1. Knowledge is a complex network of information and skills, not a series of isolated skills and facts. Tests designed to assess knowledge must reflect this complexity both in the tasks they require children to complete and the criteria they use to evaluate a child's knowledge.

Figure 2-2—Example of Content-by-Behavior Matrix for a 60-Item Mathematics Test

| Behavior | Content areas | | | |
	Number systems	Geometry	Algebra	Total
Computation	15	8	7	30
Comprehension	5	5	5	15
Application	5	3	2	10
Analysis	0	4	1	5
Total	25	20	15	60 items

NOTE: The values in the cells represent the number of items on the test. Matrices like this are used in planning and designing tests.

SOURCE: Office of Technology Assessment, 1992. Based on a concept discussed in Thomas A. Romberg, E. Anne Zarinnia, and Kevin J. Collis, "A New Worldview of Assessment in Mathematics," *Assessing Higher Order Thinking in Mathematics*, G. Kulm (ed.) (Washington, DC: American Association for the Advancement of Science, 1990).

2. The research suggests important new possibilities for tests that can diagnose a student's strengths and weaknesses. Diagnostic tests, informed by cognitive science research, may help teachers recognize more quickly the individual learner's difficulties and intervene to get the learner back on track. The shift toward educationally diagnostic tests is an important one; it represents a move away from seeing tests as predictive indicators of a fixed ''ability to learn'' to tests that can help shape instruction so ''all can learn.''[21]

3. Because research indicates that much learning and thinking is active and occurs within a specific context, assessment of some skills may require testing methods more closely tied to the active learning process. Tasks may need to resemble what students should be able to do, and thus what they spend their time doing in the classroom. It is likely that tests that allow children to manipulate materials, explore naive theories, and demonstrate everyday cognition will more accurately reflect their competence levels across a range of skills. Instruction and assessment can be designed to focus on learning in context; as this happens more, especially in the new forms of assessment commonly referred to as ''performance assess-

---

[19]Romberg et al., op. cit., footnote 13, p. 9.

[20]Ibid., p. 15.

[21]See, e.g., J.W. Pellegrino, ''Anatomy of Analogy,'' *Psychology Today*, vol. 19, No. 10, October 1985, pp. 48-54.

Box 2-C—Tests as Avenues to Individualized Learning

Cognitive and developmental psychologists tend to look for patterns and similarities in the way people think and learn. While research has documented some general patterns, it has also found tremendous individual variation in the rates at which children learn and develop. Other research has drawn attention to the importance of individual differences in social, emotional, and motivational characteristics that affect children's learning. Still others have focused on the modality or "style" by which different children learn. Many have reasoned that if tests can diagnose learning styles, then they can aid in the development of improved instructional techniques matched to individual learning styles. There have been many theories, but no consensus on what those different learning styles look like. Attempts to match learning styles to styles of instruction were initially popular in special education, but the research has not held up in part because the measures for diagnosing learning styles are not reliable enough and do not show expected relationships with achievement.[1]

Nevertheless, the research suggests that the "ability to learn" (a commonly used definition of "intelligence") is not a fixed unitary trait: individuals do not have a certain amount of it that predetermines how well and how much they can learn. The model of learning disabilities provides a well-accepted example of how one or two areas of weakness, such as recognition of written words, can interfere with a child's skills across a broad range of academic areas. While in the past these children were often seen as unable to learn, or worse yet as "dumb," their capabilities are now recognized. Many such children need alternative learning methods in order to acquire necessary skills. Every child brings to any learning situation a complex profile of strengths and weaknesses as well as past learning and experience. Diagnostic tests can describe in detail the actual skills of a child in areas related to instruction. Strengths can then be used by the teacher to support and guide learning in more difficult areas.

One attempt to describe children's skills more broadly is a recent effort to outline "multiple intelligences." Although theories of the multiple components of intelligence have been around for a long time, Howard Gardner's work suggests that most of our current approach to education, as well as assessment, has relied heavily on developing two types of intelligence, which he calls "logical-mathematical" and "linguistic."[2] Drawing on evidence from multiple sources, including neuropsychology and child development, Gardner has proposed an additional five types of intelligences: musical, spatial, bodily-kinesthetic, interpersonal, and intrapersonal. A student can be represented by a profile of "intelligences," each of which is relatively independent of the others.[3]

Several educational pilot programs have grown out of this theory. One, the Key School in Indianapolis, attempts to maximize instruction across all seven areas and uses report cards that evaluate children in each. Another, Project Spectrum, has attempted to develop assessment activities that capture the seven competencies in preschool children. The goal of these efforts is to provide a profile of strengths and weaknesses across the seven areas that can be used to direct educational resources to the child; such a profile could help parents and teachers build on strengths or bolster areas of weakness during the early years.[4]

The theory of multiple intelligences provides one model for broadening traditional views about which skills and competencies are important and require nurturing in the school years. As one policy maker has noted:

> Gardner's work has been important in attacking the monolithic notion of intelligence that has undergirded much of our thinking. We are beginning to see that education is not meant merely to sort out a few children and make them leaders, but to develop the latent talents of the entire population in diverse ways.[5]

---

[1]D. Carnine, "New Research on the Brain: Implications for Instruction," *Phi Delta Kappan*, vol. 71, No. 5, January 1990, pp. 372-377; and Kenneth A. Kavele and Steven R. Forness, "Substance Over Style: Assessing the Efficacy of Modality Testing and Teaching," *Exceptional Children*, vol. 54, No. 3, 1987, pp. 228-239.

[2]Howard Gardner, *Frames of Mind* (New York, NY: Basic Books, 1985). For a fuller discussion of the contributions of Spearman, Guilford, Thurstone, and other researchers whose work was based on different theories of the structure of intelligence, see, e.g., Raymond Fancher, *The Intelligence Men: Makers of the IQ Controversy* (New York, NY: W.W. Norton, 1985).

[3]The work of Robert Sternberg, another modern pioneer of multiple intelligence, while focused largely on adults rather than school children, also has important implications for instruction and assessment. See, for example, his book, *Beyond IQ: A Triarchic Theory of Human Intelligence* (London, England: Cambridge University Press, 1985).

[4]For further description of these programs see Marie Winn, "New Views of Human Intelligence," *New York Times Magazine*, part 2, The Good Health Magazine, Apr. 29, 1990; and Howard Gardner and Thomas Hatch, "Multiple Intelligences Go to School," *Educational Researcher*, vol. 18, No. 8, November 1989, pp. 4-9.

[5]Rexford Brown, Director of Communications for the Education Commission of the States, quoted in Winn, op. cit., footnote 4, p. 30.

ment'' (see ch. 7), the lines between assessment and instruction blur. Assessment becomes feedback to the learner, which in turn promotes further learning and growth.

There are many more specific ways in which the findings from cognitive psychology could find their way into test design, but few areas of cognitive research are ready for immediate translation into new achievement tests. Thus, any test designed using new cognitive findings is likely to require considerable research and development before the thinking skills that underlie the test can be measured with confidence.

The emergence of new theories of cognition and new instructional strategies raises a fundamental question about the nature of the relationship between curriculum and assessment. Those who advocate reforming tests to more closely parallel new theories of learning tend to believe that tests should *follow* curriculum and instruction. In this regard, they echo principles of educational test design well established in the literature of educational measurement.[22] The first step to improving education, according to this view, is to establish what it is students are supposed to learn and how they are most likely to learn it; the next step is to develop instructional approaches; and the last step is to develop assessment instruments that appropriately measure this content and track the learning process.

Tests as Tools of Educational Reform

Everyone would agree that there is bound to be some back-and-forth motion in this process: deciding how children are most likely to learn something can be informed by assessments of their learning in progress. However, another camp of test reformers models the relationship explicitly as one in which tests drive instruction. Since teachers will teach and students will study what is tested, they argue for the development of tests covering content children should learn; curriculum and instruction will then fall into place. This section demonstrates how this view helped spur the rise of high-stakes tests as instruments of policy reform.

Photo credit: American Guidance Service, Inc.

Many educators urge that tasks on tests resemble the skills students should acquire in school. In mathematics, for example, tests like the one pictured above allow children to manipulate materials or use tools such as calculators.

Educational testing has long been viewed as a means to enforce accountability, inform education policy, evaluate educational progress, and reform the structure and content of teaching and learning.[23] Beginning in the mid-1960s and continuing through the 1970s and 1980s, the reliance on tests toward all these ends began to increase at all levels of government, but especially for accountability purposes and most frequently at the State level.

As accountability became a major force in education policy, the response most often took the form of rising demand for standardized achievement testing. Although many States and the Federal Government continued to collect other school performance data (such as dropout rates and various economic indicators), testing was the vehicle of choice. At the Federal level, policymakers wrote requirements for objective evaluations (usually interpreted as standardized tests) into programs of aid to elementary and secondary schools. At the State level, legislatures in 25 States enacted statewide minimum competency tests that affected critical decisions, such as grade

---

[22]See, e.g., William A. Mehrens and Irvin J. Lehmann, *Measurement and Evaluation in Education and Psychology*, 3rd ed. (New York, NY: CBS College Publishing, 1984); and George Madaus and Daniel Stufflebeam, *Educational Evaluation: Classic Works of Ralph W. Tyler* (Boston, MA: Kluwer Academic Publishers, 1989).

[23]See ch. 4 for a fuller discussion of the history of educational testing in the United States.

promotion or high school graduation. And at the local level, school boards and school administrators began to look at tests as a tool for satisfying public demands for accountability, providing information about how their students compared to others, and gauging their schools' progress toward local goals.

To the chagrin of many school people, Federal, State, and local district demands for test-based accountability data often addressed different issues, with each level of government acting as if data collected for the other levels was off the mark or untrustworthy and making little effort to coordinate the multiple testing requirements. It was hardly an accident that policymakers embraced standardized tests as a means to enforce accountability; this was a tradition with roots in the earliest days of the public school movement (as described in greater detail in ch. 4).

One of the appealing aspects of tests is that they enable outsiders—parents, legislators, and the general public—to leverage the internal workings of schools. One commentator has likened tests to ''remote control'' devices, affording policymakers a sense of control over classrooms from a safe distance.[24] Another appealing feature is that testing conforms to a logic that sounds right: if the stakes are high enough, then teachers and students will change their behaviors in ways that improve test scores, leading to increased learning. The facts that tests may not be designed to serve this purpose, and that higher test scores do not necessarily mean increased achievement, are often overlooked. Finally, test scores serve a powerful symbolic function. A steep trend line on a graph can be strong ammunition in political struggles over the quality of schools. Whether the data are reliable and meaningful, though, are issues that are often relegated to the fine print once the headlines have left their marks.

A Climate Ripe for Growth

The reliance on tests as policy tools and the rapid adoption of high-stakes testing programs were not the result of a carefully coordinated national strategy to improve schooling. Rather, they reflected the convergence of several demographic, social, and economic trends that began in the 1960s.

Demographic Trends

The Baby Boomer cohort was a bulge in the demographic python. And as it moved through the K-12 system in the mid-1960s and early 1970s, it created unprecedented demands on school management, particularly in urban and suburban school systems, the centers of growth. As in earlier periods of demographic change, expansion of the school population led to heightened demand for additional sources of information about student achievement, over and above the judgments of teachers and administrators. Moreover, as access to education expanded for minority, immigrant, and low-income children, and in the late-1970s for children with disabilities, schools came under increased pressure to meet the needs of a more diversified student population. Fairness in the allocation of educational opportunities, always a cornerstone of the American public school ethos, rose once again to the top of the education policy agenda.

To confront these demographic changes in an efficient way, schools acted in the 1960s and 1970s in ways that mirrored their reactions to change in decades past: they looked to the world of business, and attempted to adapt techniques such as consolidation, standardization, classification, and, some might argue, bureaucratization. Small districts and rural districts that had lost population to urban and suburban areas consolidated; between school years 1963-64 and 1973-74, the number of public school districts in the United States decreased almost by one-half—from over 31,000 to less than 16,000. Moreover, school systems of all types began relying more on tests to obtain information on larger student bodies in an efficient and objective manner, as well as to make decisions about sorting and tracking students within these bigger organizational structures.

Social Trends

The civil rights movement had a significant effect on American education in general and on testing policy in particular. In addition to raising issues

---

[24]See Larry Cuban, ''The Misuse of Tests in Education,'' OTA contractor report, Sept. 9, 1991. As described briefly in ch. 4, the use of standardized tests in schools began around the same time that expansion in the size of business led to the need for standardized data on the performance of business units. See, e.g., George Madaus, ''Testing as a Social Technology,'' Inaugural Annual Boisi Lecture in Education and Public Policy, Boston College, Dec. 6, 1990; and Alfred Chandler, *The Visible Hand: The Managerial Revolution in American Business* (Cambridge, MA: Harvard University Press, 1977).

about student classification and disaggregation of achievement data, the civil rights movement called attention to the vast disparities that existed in the quantity and quality of education available to children from different racial and ethnic backgrounds. It also helped fuel a broader discussion of the educational inequities experienced by poor and disadvantaged children of all backgrounds, including rural white children, migrant children, and limited-English-proficient children.

Passage of the 1964 Civil Rights Act decisively settled the congressional battles over desegregation that had hampered past school aid bills, and paved the way for a significant Federal role in education. On the heels of the Civil Rights Act, Congress passed a host of social legislation—programs for education, welfare, health, labor, housing, and nutrition—all aimed at improving the lot of the economically disadvantaged. With those programs came a renewed interest in survey research and in the development of outcome-based measures to justify the money being spent.[25]

Economic Trends: Concerns About Competitiveness

The Nation's reaction to the Sputnik launch in 1957 foreshadowed the way that school systems would respond in subsequent decades to perceived threats to America's international competitiveness. Looking for ways to explain second-rate technological performance, leaders and the public seized on the apparently uninspired performance of American students in mathematics and science as a key reason why the United States was losing the space race. Consensus began to emerge that schools needed to place more emphasis on these two subjects. Congress passed the National Defense Education Act, the first substantial influx of Federal aid to elementary and secondary education, targeted at mathematics and science, and also containing a notable provision authorizing funds for guidance counseling and testing to identify high-ability students.

Variations on this pattern of concerns about student achievement igniting public debate and propelling a nationwide response were to be repeated in later decades. For example, when *A Nation at Risk* linked falling Scholastic Aptitude Test (SAT) scores with eroding economic competitiveness, it was the States that responded aggressively by adopting more rigorous graduation requirements, initiating a range of other reforms, and, in some cases, providing significant additional funding for schools (developments that led to more standardized testing, as will be noted later.)[26]

Another trend related to economics merits mention. In the 1970s, educational researchers began applying some of the principles and vocabulary of economics to education, assessing the efficiency and cost-effectiveness of education in terms of inputs and outputs. Most of these studies measured outputs in terms of standardized achievement test scores, some in conjunction with other quantitative measures.[27] This trend in the academic research mirrored the shift occurring in the broader policy community. It was during this period that Congress amended several Federal programs—including the Job Training Partnership Act and the Vocational Education Act—to emphasize outcome measures or performance standards in program evaluation.[28]

Changes in School Finance: Growth in Federal and State Support

The debut of the Federal Government as a significant partner in education during the 1960s, and the surge in State reform initiatives during the 1970s and 1980s, transformed the dynamics of school finance. In school year 1959-60, the lion's share of revenues supporting public elementary and

---

[25]"Some proponents of social legislation resisted any accountability, believing that such could not be measured when including the social goals of the programs." Donald Senese, former assistant secretary for Educational Research and Improvement, personal communication, August 1991.

[26]*A Nation at Risk* is among the most cited government reports on education in the past 50 years, and arguably one of the most influential in spurring a range of school improvement efforts. It is important to note, however, that the findings in that report did not go entirely unchallenged. See, e.g., L. Stedman and Marshall Smith, "Recent Reform Proposals for American Education," *Contemporary Education Review*, vol. 2, fall 1983, pp. 85-104.

[27]For a recent review of this literature see Eric A. Hanushek, "The Economics of Schooling: Production and Efficiency in Public Schools," *Journal of Economic Literature*, vol. 24, 1986, pp. 1141-1177; Richard Murnane, "Interpreting the Evidence on 'Does Money Matter?'" *Harvard Journal on Legislation*, vol. 28, No. 2, summer 1991, pp. 457-464; and Henry M. Levin, "Mapping the Economies of Education: An Introductory Essay," *Educational Researcher*, vol. 18, No. 4, May 1989, pp. 13-16. It is important to note that many of the economists working in this field recognized the limitations of achievement test scores as outcome measures, but the scores did offer a relatively neat quantitative approach to estimating the input-output models of interest.

[28]See, e.g., U.S. Congress, Office of Technology Assessment, "Performance Standards for Secondary School Vocational Education," background paper of the Science, Education, and Transportation Program, March 1989, for discussion of the shift to outcome-based measures of public programs.

secondary education—almost 57 percent—came from local sources; States provided 39 percent and the Federal Government a mere 4 percent. As shown in table 2-1, by 1969-70, a few years after the Federal Elementary and Secondary Education Act had begun channeling over $1 billion annually to schools, the Federal share had risen to 8 percent, with States holding their own, and local support declining. A decade later, States had become the primary source of educational revenues, with a share approaching 47 percent. In recent years, the State share has continued to move up as the Federal share has declined, so that States now provide about one-half the funding for education.

The increase in Federal and State support brought about some important changes in school finance: it helped reduce revenue disparities between school districts, which formerly had depended on local property tax receipts for over one-half their income; and it targeted additional resources to students, subject areas, or urgent problems deemed to warrant Federal or State attention. But with new money came new overseers and greater demands for measurable results. A principal source of Federal accountability requirements was "compensatory education," a program created in 1965 by Title I of the Elementary and Secondary Education Act. Renamed Chapter 1 in 1981, this program has been the cornerstone of Federal aid to elementary and secondary schools. From the beginning, legal requirements to evaluate the effectiveness of this program in meeting the educational needs of educationally disadvantaged children have resulted in increased reliance on standardized norm-referenced tests. As discussed in depth in chapter 3, the Federal Government has had a powerful impact on U.S. testing practice because of the evaluation and reporting requirements of Chapter 1 legislation.

Developments in the Testing Industry

Economic trends influenced assessment in yet another significant way. Advances in testing technology and psychometric research, accompanied by expansion of the testing industry, made wide-scale testing more affordable for school districts and more profitable for testing companies than ever before. While technological, research, and corporate devel-

Table 2-1—Sources of Revenues for Public Elementary and Secondary Schools (In percent)

	1959-60	1969-70	1979-80	1987-88
Federal	4.4%	8.0%	9.8%	6.3%
State	39.1	39.9	46.8	49.5
Local	56.5	52.1	43.4	44.1

SOURCE: U.S. Department of Education, National Center for Education Statistics, *Digest of Educational Statistics, 1990* (Washington, DC: 1991), p. 147.

opments alone did not create the demand for testing—that demand existed well before the advent of specific scoring or testing technologies—they provided powerful efficiency arguments in favor of standardized, machine-scorable tests.

But at the same time as machine-scorable testing was gaining ground as the vehicle of choice to manage the assessment demands of the period, curriculum experts and educational psychologists were busy crafting revised theories of human cognition and learning (as discussed above). Indeed, they, too, were strongly influenced by the apparent decline in American students' performance—compared to students in other nations—and by the fear of America's irreversible loss of international competitiveness. Their response, though, was to rethink thinking, and among the results emerging from this evolving line of research are prescriptions for radical changes in the technologies and uses of educational assessment.

The Net Result

Taken together, these demographic, economic, and social factors created a climate in which the use of tests as policy tools could take root and thrive. As summarized in a seminal National Academy of Sciences report:

> The most significant development in management (and testing) in recent years has been the increasing demand for central oversight of educational results. This comes partly because of the increased reliance of local schools on State funds since the late 1960s, partly because education has come to be viewed explicitly as a weapon with which to combat poverty and increased equality, and partly because of a suspicion that teachers and local administrators are falling down on the job.[29]

[29]Alexander K. Wigdor and Wendell R. Garner (eds.), *Ability Testing: Uses, Consequences, and Controversies*, part 1, report of the committee (Washington, DC: National Academy Press, 1982), p. 170.

States, Tests, and Minimum Competency

Although the Federal Government has wrought changes in education of indisputable importance, the main arena for the events commonly thought of as the school reform movement has been the States. Education reform can mean many things and can be conducted in quite different ways. In general, the term connotes efforts to improve the quality of educational outcomes through changes in one or more aspects of the school system. Some reforms, such as the decentralization of decisionmaking that took place in the New York City schools in the late 1960s,[30] address the actual organization of schooling. Others focus on curriculum, teacher or administrator salary structures, or student tracking and grouping policies.[31]

Spurred by public demands for more accountability in education, States have taken on new and increasingly activist roles in education—and in education reform—over the past 15 years. In general, State-initiated reforms of the 1970s were ''top down'' in nature: States identified their priorities, often in the forums of the legislature and State Board of Education, and set standards for all local school systems.

Tests have been essential components of most State-mandated reforms and have been asked to fulfill many new functions, such as determining the allocation of resources or persuading individuals and organizations to change behavior. In fact, States have been the main practitioners of high-stakes educational testing. For these reasons, the State experience with mandated reforms is a good illustration of some of the effects of externally developed standards on educational practices.

Minimum Competency Testing: Definition

Perhaps the most significant manifestation of the vigor with which States approached reform was the growth of minimum competency testing (MCT) that occurred during the late 1970s and continued into the 1980s. MCT refers to programs mandated by State or local agencies that have the following characteristics:

- All or almost all students in designated grades take paper-and-pencil tests designed to measure a set of skills deemed essential for future life and work.
- The State or locality has established a passing score or acceptable standard of performance on these tests.
- The State or locality may use test results to: a) make decisions about grade-level promotion, high school graduation, or the awarding of diplomas; b) classify students for remedial or other special services; c) allocate certain funds to school districts; or d) evaluate or certify school districts, schools, or teachers.[32]

Within this general framework, minimum competency tests can vary greatly in their design, format, uses, and applications to high-stakes decisions.

Impetus for MCT

MCT is a genuine example of a grassroots phenomenon, with the impetus coming mostly from outside the educational system.[33] Fueled first by popular writers, employers, and the media, and later by a proliferation of education reform panels, a movement began to catch fire among parents and other citizens who were already somewhat disillusioned with the schools. In the minds of this group, the symptoms of educational distress were all around, apparent to anyone who dared open his eyes: standards had been relaxed to the point that a high school diploma no longer meant anything; students were leaving school without the basic reading and mathematics skills they needed to succeed in work or higher education; pupils were being promoted to higher grades automatically, regardless of achievement; too little time was being spent on instruction and too much on ''frills''; and too many teachers

[30]See, e.g., Diane Ravitch, *The Great School Wars: New York City, 1805-1973* (New York, NY: Basic Books, 1974), especially pp. 251-404.

[31]For a review of recent school reform efforts, see, e.g., Educational Testing Service, *The Education Reform Decade*, policy information report (Princeton, NJ: 1990). For analysis of the role of testing in the reform movements of the 1970s and 1980s, see Douglas A. Archbald, University of Delaware, and Andrew C. Porter, University of Wisconsin, Madison, ''A Retrospective and an Analysis of the Roles of Mandated Testing in Education Reform,'' OTA contractor report, January 1990.

[32]Ronald A. Berk, ''Minimum Competency Testing: Status and Potential,'' *The Future of Testing*, Barbara S. Plake and Joseph C. Witt (eds.) (Hillsdale, NJ: L. Erlbaum Associates, 1986), pp. 88-144.

[33]Archbald and Porter, op. cit., footnote 31. See also Barbara Lerner, ''Good News About American Education,'' *Commentary*, vol. 91, No. 3, March 1991, pp. 19-25.

were incompetent.[34] A symbol that became inextricably linked with deteriorating educational quality and perhaps more responsible than any other for erosion in public confidence was the steady drop in SAT scores that began in 1963 and persisted through the 1970s.[35]

This movement, which led to the adoption of MCT by many States, was an outgrowth of the "back to basics" movement of the 1970s—itself a backlash against the educational experimentation and general social permissiveness that had characterized the previous decade. A public grown suspicious of such innovations as schools without walls and student-centered learning, or the elimination of dress codes and the expansion of electives, came to believe that major changes—more rigorous standards, a curriculum rooted in the "three Rs"—were needed. But many people believed that since local teachers and administrators were part of the problem, they could not be relied on to make the needed reforms without outside pressure. Seeking support from the Federal Government was an unappealing alternative to those who feared an infringement on State and local control of education or the enactment of Federal mandates.

Eventually public pressure focused on the States as the level of government best positioned to direct education reform. State Government was close enough to grassroots to understand community standards and needs, but possessed enough authority to put pressure on recalcitrant school districts. It was largely elected State officials—State legislators and State Board of Education members—who found themselves at the center of the debate over education reform. It is significant that elected officials, more than professional educators, took the lead on MCT. Many State legislators were already sympathetic with the back to basics movement and were willing, even anxious, to show their support through sponsoring legislation. In addition, the fact that State

legislators were not part of the educational establishment may explain their faith in the power of tests to bring about major change in education. Finally, as some researchers have observed: "As non-educators, enthusiasts of competency testing [were] free to focus on the results and to pay little heed to the processes by which they might be achieved."[36] State legislators may have viewed this freedom as a plus; by enacting MCT they could appear to be doing something significant about education reform without seeming to encroach too much on local control or venture into instructional areas they knew little about.

The basic idea behind MCT was an appealing one to many State policymakers. In developing the tests, States could create some uniform, external standards that emphasized those skills deemed especially important to literacy and life success. By further tying these standards to promotion, graduation, or other educational way stations, it would focus instruction and learning on critical areas.[37]

The Rise of MCT

By the mid-1970s, the climate was ripe for action in many States. States had already begun to pick up a greater share of the costs of education, and the principle that he who pays the piper calls the tune is a time-honored one in the educational arena. And in many States, the use of tests as accountability tools was a well-established principle (witness the existence of State licensing examinations in a range of professional fields, or the State Regents' examinations in New York). In addition, early MCT programs in Denver, Florida, and Georgia had set a precedent and piqued the interest of policymakers from other States.

The major expansion in MCT that occurred during the 1970s and 1980s was a watershed event in testing policy. Prior to 1975, only a few States mandated MCT. The peak growth period for statewide compe-

[34]Berk, op. cit., footnote 32.

[35]George Madaus, ''Testing and Policy—True Love, Shot Gun Wedding or Marriage of Convenience?'' paper presented at the annual meeting of the National Council on Measurement in Education, New Orleans, LA, April 1984. The sudden (and short-lived) upturn in Scholastic Aptitude Test scores beginning in 1979 is evidence for some analysts of the effectiveness of the minimum competency testing movement. See Lerner, op. cit., footnote 33, for the most ardent formulation of this causal argument.

[36]Walt Haney and George Madaus, ''Making Sense of the Competency Testing Movement,'' *Harvard Educational Review*, vol. 48, No. 4, November 1978.

[37]Critics took a much dimmer view of what they saw as the real function of minimum competency testing: ''When penalties associated with failing a certification test are severe enough, instruction and study will adjust to prepare pupils to pass it. The test becomes a coercive device to influence both the curriculum and instruction. Unleashing the fear of diploma denial or retention in grade bullies the instructional delivery system into line.'' P. Airasian and G. Madaus, ''Linking Testing and Instruction: Policy Issues,'' *Journal of Educational Measurement*, vol. 20, No. 2, summer 1983.

tency testing was between 1975 and 1979 (see figure 2-3). In fact, MCT accounted for most of the overall growth in educational testing in the post-1975 era. By 1980, 29 States had implemented legislation that required students to pass criterion-referenced examinations and 8 more had such legislation pending.[38] Some States used the examinations to determine eligibility for remedial programs and promotions and some required it for graduation. By 1985, growth in such programs had leveled off, although 33 States were still mandating statewide minimum competency testing; 11 of these States required the test as a prerequisite for graduation.[39]

Minimum competency tests were altogether different creatures from the ''off-the-shelf'' norm-referenced achievement tests that had dominated standardized testing up to that point. Most MCT instruments were custom-made in State education offices or by vendors working from State specifications, and unlike commercial tests, were designed from the start as high-stakes instruments. Most States required students to achieve a predetermined passing score for grade promotion or diploma receipt; usually students were allowed to take the test over if they did not obtain a passing score the first time. Some States mandated remediation for students who did not pass, while in other States it was optional.

Minimum competency tests are criterion-referenced; they measure performance in relation to specified skills objectives in such areas as vocabulary, reading comprehension, mathematical computation, and, in some cases, functional skills (filling out a job application, for instance, or conducting simple financial transactions). The multiple-choice format is by far the most common, although some competency tests use other approaches, such as essay writing, oral examinations, and problem solving.

Two other features distinguish MCTs from other types of tests. First, because they use specific passing scores, they require some type of standard-setting process to determine and justify the ''cutoff

Figure 2-3—Number of States Conducting Minimum Competency Tests

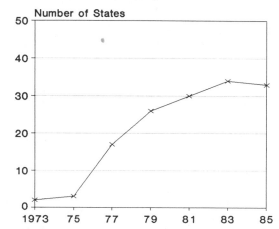

SOURCE: U.S. Congress, Office of Technology Assessment, "State Educational Testing Practices," background paper of the Science, Education, and Transportation Program, December 1987; supplemented by data from Ronald A. Berk, "Minimum Competency Testing: Status and Potential," *The Future of Testing,* Barbara S. Plake and Joseph C. Witt (eds.) (Hillsdale, NJ: L. Erlbaum Associates, 1986), p. 96.

score.''[40] Since there is no fixed, scientific approach to determining what knowledge a person needs to ''function'' in society, this can be a murky process. Second, MCT instruments are always administered on a census basis: each student takes the test. This does not mean, however, that the tests are not also used as instruments of *school-level* accountability. Many States and districts aggregate individual student scores to derive passing rates or average scores for entire schools. The demand for this type of comparative information has actually increased, with business leaders and policymakers often linking support for expensive reform packages to the willingness of State Education Agencies (SEAs) and school districts to accept public disclosure of test results. (Nineteen States now produce public reports comparing districts or schools on State test results.[41])

The Second Wave of State-Mandated Reform

A Nation at Risk and other reform reports of the 1980s set in motion a second wave of State-

[38]Berk, op. cit., footnote 32.

[39]U.S. Congress, Office of Technology Assessment, "State Educational Testing Practices," background paper of the Science, Education, and Transportation Program, December 1987.

[40]See ch. 6; Robert Linn, George Madaus, and Joseph Pedulla, ''Minimum Competency Testing: Cautions on the State of the Art,'' *American Journal of Education,* November 1982, pp. 1-35; and Richard Jaeger, ''An Iterative Structured Judgment Process for Establishing Standards on Competency Tests: Theory and Application,'' *Educational Evaluation and Policy Analysis,* vol. 4, No. 4, winter 1982, pp. 461-475.

[41]Archbald and Porter, op. cit., footnote 31.

Photo credit: Arana Sonnier

The 1970s witnessed increased public demands for accountability in education. States initiated reforms that included mandated tests, as well as course and graduation requirements. Students in this ninth grade algebra class are required to take the course by Louisiana State law.

mandated reform. Reacting to criticisms that not enough students were taking advanced courses in science, mathematics, foreign languages, and other areas deemed critical to American international competitiveness, States assumed greater control of graduation requirements, making them more rigorous.[42] In addition, States pushed for and obtained

more authority over curriculum, usually making them more prescriptive and enforcing a greater degree of consistency across the State.[43] Many States with statewide (rather than locally determined) textbook adoption policies also began scrutinizing more closely the match between their textbooks and their curriculum guidelines.[44]

Under public pressure to demonstrate gains in test scores, some States also undertook major "curriculum alignment" efforts, which linked curricular objectives, textbooks, lessons, instructional methods, and assessment. Curriculum alignment is a common strategy at the classroom and school level, but it is only recently that entire districts and States have experimented with it. The idea behind curriculum alignment is straightforward: if the goal is to improve test scores, then instruction should focus on what is tested. At the State level, however, alignment is not always easy to achieve. SEAs must contend with traditions of local curriculum autonomy and wide differences among school districts according to a whole range of characteristics. Moreover, the local variables that affect course content and classroom instructional practice are not easily influenced by State policies.

Nonetheless, many States have gradually tightened control over those curriculum variables that they *can* influence. Districts under pressure to raise test scores on State tests have done the same.[45] In practice, curriculum alignment can range from State officials selecting a norm-referenced test based on how well it matches with loosely defined State education goals, to States conducting exhaustive content analyses to ensure detailed matches among tests, curriculum, and textbook objectives. Off-the-shelf standardized tests—the staple of State testing for decades—increasingly were augmented or re-

---

[42]William Clune, Paula White, and Janice Patterson, *The Implementation and Effects of High School Graduation Requirements: First Steps Toward Curricular Reform* (New Brunswick, NJ: Rutgers, The State University of New Jersey, Center for Policy Research in Education, 1989).

[43]In a survey of 27 State social studies specialists, 26 said course requirements and guidelines had become more specific in the last 4 to 5 years. The investigators concluded: "Despite great differences among the states, a very strong generalization emerges from the study, namely, that the current 'flavor' of social studies throughout most of the country is highly prescriptive. Many prescripts have been applied in recent years to students, teachers, and curricula." Council of State Social Studies Specialists, *Social Studies Education, Kindergarten-Grade 12* (Washington, DC: National Council for the Social Studies, 1986).

[44]Harriet Tyson-Bernstein, *A Conspiracy of Good Intentions* (Washington, DC: Council for Basic Education, 1988); and Harriet Tyson-Bernstein, "Three Portraits: Textbook Adoption Policy Changes in North Carolina, Texas and California," occasional paper for the Institute for Educational Leadership, 1989.

[45]Ken Komoski, director of the Educational Products Information Exchange, as cited by Lynn Olson, "Districts Turn to Nonprofit Group for Help in 'Realigning' Curricula to Parallel Tests," *Education Week*, vol. 7, No. 8, Oct. 28, 1987, pp. 17, 19. Textbook manufacturers market their books in "big-market" States and districts by demonstrating (in documentation and in sections of the books themselves) the alignment of their textbook content with State curriculum frameworks through "correlational analyses."

**Table 2-2—Improvements in Student Achievement Associated
With Curriculum Alignment**

Locale	Subject	Grade	Period	Gain[a] (in percent)
Alabama	3Rs	3, 6, 9	1981-86	1-13%
	3Rs	11	1983-85	4-8
Connecticut	3Rs	9	1980-84	6-16
Detroit	3Rs	12	1981-86	19
Maryland	3Rs	9	1980-86	13-25
	Social studies	9	1983-86	23
New Jersey	Reading/mathematics	9	1977-85	16-19
	Reading/mathematics	10	1982-85	8-11
South Carolina	Readiness	1	1979-85	14
	Reading/mathematics	1-3, 6, 8	1981-86	12-20

[a]Figures represent the increased percentage of students who have mastered standards of quality during the period in question.

SOURCE: W. James Popham, "The Merits of Measurement-Driven Instruction," *Phi Delta Kappan*, vol. 68, No. 9, May 1987, pp. 679-682. Note, numbers in right-most column denote the range of percentage increases across the different grade levels and tests in columns on left.

placed by custom-developed tests designed to assess State curriculum guidelines and goals.

MCT: Lessons for High-Stakes Testing

One problem with drawing conclusions about the effects or influences of State-mandated tests on school improvement is that testing is but one of many forces that shape the learning experiences of young people. Indeed, mandated testing is as much a *result* of widely held beliefs about curriculum, teaching, and learning as it is a *cause* of educational outcomes.

Even so, researchers have made some thorough analyses of State experiences with MCT and other State-mandated reforms and drawn some conclusions about their effects. In general, these researchers have concluded that the movement, which began amid such optimism, has produced results that are on the whole disappointing. A summary and analysis of key findings from studies of MCT are summarized below.

Test Score Gains

A number of States and districts can point to gains over time on minimum competency and other State tests. Gains tend to be more apparent in districts and States that have systematically pursued test and curriculum alignment. For example, on the Texas Assessment of Basic Skills in mathematics, 70 percent of ninth graders achieved mastery in 1980; by 1985, the figure had risen to 84 percent. On the reading portion of the same assessment, passing rates increased from 70 percent to 78 percent during the same period.[46] Similarly, in South Carolina, the percentage of first graders passing the basic skills reading test rose from 70 percent in 1981 to 80 percent in 1984, and for mathematics the passing rate went from 68 to 81 percent during the same period[47] (see table 2-2).

Impressive as these gains might be, their credibility was severely undermined by analysts who looked more closely at the timing and generality of the trends in test scores.[48] Among the findings in this body of research, the most damning to the MCT movement were: 1) that scores on some tests in some places rose more rapidly and more significantly than in other places, 2) scores rose on tests even in States without MCT,[49] 3) scores began to rise before MCT could have had much impact, and 4) all States were reporting performance of their students on nationally normed achievement tests above the national average, a statistical impossibility (see box 2-D).

---

[46]Office of Technology Assessment, op. cit., footnote 39, p. 272.

[47]See W. James Popham, Keith L. Cruse, Stuart Rankin, Paul Sandifer, and Paul L. Williams, "Measurement Driven Instruction: It's on the Road," *Phi Delta Kappan*, vol. 66, 1985, pp. 628-634; cited in Lorrie Shepard and Katharine Dougherty, "Effects of High-Stakes Testing on Instruction," paper presented at the annual meeting of the American Educational Research Association, Chicago, IL, April 1991.

[48]See especially Daniel Koretz, *Trends in Educational Achievement* (Washington, DC: Congressional Budget Office, April 1986); and Congressional Budget Office, *Educational Achievement: Explanations and Implications of Recent Trends* (Washington, DC: August 1987).

[49]See also Gerald Bracey, rejoinder to Barbara Lerner, *Commentary*, vol. 92, No. 2, August 1991, p. 10.

Box 2-D—The Lake Wobegon Effect: All the Children Above Average?

In radio personality Garrison Keillor's fictional town of Lake Wobegon, "all the women are strong, all the men are good-looking, and all the children are above average." To statisticians, of course, average is simply a representation of central tendency, and is a point drawn from an array of numbers. In many norm-referenced tests (NRTs), average represents the "median" and shows that one-half the test takers scored above this point and one-half below. It is statistically impossible for everyone to be above average—but "above average" is in some sense an American ideal.

The word average connotes a certain hum-drum, undistinguished level of achievement, especially when applied to people. Just as the citizens of mythical Lake Wobegon want all their children to be above average, teachers, principals, and parents want to show that their children are doing well.

Thus, the desire for higher test scores may overwhelm the desire to improve actual learning. Similarly, in reporting scores, calculations and methods may be used that do not give a full or accurate picture. Such excessive emphasis on test scores can compromise the value of information, as well as give misleading views of how children and schools "rank" with regard to one another. For example, students and teachers may focus their efforts on improving performance on samples of what is to be learned, rather than on the body of knowledge from which the samples are drawn, and rising test scores may then be erroneously interpreted as reflecting genuine gains in achievement. Schools or districts seeing the scores of their students rise may be lulled into a false sense of complacency.

Or consider another possible example of how test scores used alone can lead to inaccurate inferences about achievement gains. A school system adds a number of academic high school course requirements in order to increase achievement levels. After several years, test scores go up considerably and administrators conclude that increased course requirements have raised achievement levels throughout the district. However, this gain has been attained at the expense of a number of low-achieving students dropping out. True achievement has not risen; but the lowest scoring students are no longer represented in the data. In this case, achievement test scores examined in combination with another achievement indicator (drop-out statistics) might have demonstrated that the gains were artificial.

The so-called Lake Wobegon phenomenon is by now a familiar example of how excessive focus on test scores can provide misleading information. Issued in 1987 by a group called the Friends for Education, the Lake Wobegon report asserted that all States reporting statewide test scores ranked above the national average; however, many of these same States were doing very poorly on other indicators such as graduation and literacy rates.[1]

The Lake Wobegon report sparked controversy and debate; critics charged that the report contained many inaccuracies and misunderstandings of the technical nature of test scores. Although subsequent analyses by testing experts have acknowledged that such errors do exist in the report, they have largely confirmed the basic conclusions of the Lake Wobegon report—achievement test scores can give a highly exaggerated picture of achievement.[2] Although the causes of the problem are complex and are difficult to collect data about, some of the most well-understood contributions to the Lake Wobegon phenomenon are shown below.

Dated norms. Before a standardized NRT is released, it is administered to a national sample of students to obtain "norms"—that is, the distribution of scores for children across the Nation. That set of norms, which acts as a national standard, will then be used for about 7 years before a new form of the test is developed and "re-normed" on a new sample of children. When there are upward trends in genuine achievement, old norms become easier to master because children know more than those in prior years.[3] When old norms are used, the average performance of students today is being compared with students who took the test up to 7 years ago. Thus, today's children will appear above average.

---

[1]J. Cannell, *Nationally Normed Elementary Achievement Testing in America's Public Schools: How All 50 States Are Above the National Average* (Daniels, WV: Friends for Education, 1987).

[2]See Daniel Koretz, "Arriving in Lake Wobegon: Are Standardized Tests Exaggerating Achievement and Distorting Instruction?" *American Educator*, vol. 12, No. 2, summer 1988, pp. 8-15, 46-52; Robert L. Linn, Elizabeth Graue, and Nancy M. Sanders, "Comparing State and District Test Results to National Norms: Interpretations of Scoring 'Above the National Average,'" paper presented at the annual meeting of the American Educational Research Association, San Francisco, CA, March 1989.

[3]See, e.g., Linn et al., op. cit., footnote 2.

Repeated use of nonsecure tests. Because the same tests are present in the district and given over a period of years, teachers and students become increasingly familiar with the test questions. This is one of the factors that can contribute to a very focused "teaching to the test" and leads to the difficulty in defining the gray area between legitimate test preparation activities and outright cheating (e.g., by having students practice actual test questions). The demarcation between legitimate test preparation activities (e.g., giving practice, coaching, and explanation of instructions to students) and dubious or even unethical practices may vary from school system to school system.[4] Even if all test preparation activities are legitimate and teaching to the test is minimized, however, some gains can probably be attributed to the increased familiarity with a particular form of a test that comes with use of a single test over a number of years.

Selection of closely aligned tests. Standardized achievement tests vary in content, emphasis, and form. Administrators typically select tests that most closely match the curricular objectives of their State or district. Students will tend to score higher on a test that is closely aligned with their own curricula than will students who have been taught a different, less closely aligned curricula. Because the norming group of any test is composed of schools which vary in their degree of alignment, a district with a highly aligned curriculum will score higher than the norming group. Thus, administrators who select a highly aligned test, or have a customized test made for them, will often find their students scoring better than the national norming group ". . . even if their level of achievement is in some broader sense equivalent, simply because their curricula match the test more closely and thus prepare them better for it."[5]

Selection of students to be tested. Testing manuals usually explain that certain students, such as non-English speakers or special education students have been excluded from the norming sample. However, when the tests are being administered in schools, specific decisions about which children to exclude—who has mastered English well enough to take the test, for example—have to be made at the district and school level. Because many of the students who will be excluded (including truant or chronically absent children) will score well below average, these decisions can have a major impact on a school or district's average score. Schools that decide to exclude all such students are likely to have a higher average than schools with policies that attempt to include all students for whom the test can be considered valid. If the exclusionary policies for a district are more liberal than those used to obtain the norming sample, that district is likely to appear "above average."

Although embarrassing to some State policymakers, the Lake Wobegon report illustrated the potential mischief caused by high-stakes testing: higher test scores without more learning. And since the publication of the original study, other researchers have replicated the basic result. For example, one recent longitudinal study of a large urban district that uses a high-stakes commercial achievement test found that the improved performance seen over a 4-year period on that test was not confirmed when a different test was also administered in the fourth year. Preliminary data indicate that the ". . . results of this district's high-stakes test overstate achievement [in mathematics] by as much as 8 academic months by the spring of grade 3."[6] Policymakers (and the public) are interested in mathematics achievement broadly defined, not just as defined by one particular test. These results suggest that ". . . information provided to the public by accountability-oriented tests can be seriously misleading."[7]

The Lake Wobegon episode taught policymakers and the testing community a number of important lessons about norms, test selection, teaching to the test, and the distorting effects of high-stakes testing. Perhaps the greatest significance of the phenomenon was to demonstrate the validity of a warning that has been provided by educational testing experts for many years: no single test should ever be the basis for important policy decisions about schools or individuals.[8]

---

[4]For views on the difference between ethical and unethical test preparation activities see William A. Mehrens and John Kaminski, "Methods for Improving Standardized Test Scores: Fruitful, Fruitless, or Fraudulent?" *Educational Measurement: Issues and Practice*, vol. 8, spring 1989, pp. 14-22; and Thomas M. Haladyna, Susan B. Nolen, and Nancy S. Haas, "Raising Standardized Achievement Test Scores and the Origins of Test Score Pollution," *Educational Researcher*, vol. 20, No. 5, June-July 1991, pp. 2-7.

[5]Koretz, op. cit., footnote 2, p. 14

[6]Daniel Koretz, Robert Linn, Stephen Dunbar, and Lorrie Shepard, "The Effects of High Stakes Testing On Achievement: Preliminary Findings About Generalizations Across Tests," paper presented at the annual meeting of the American Educational Research Association, Chicago, IL, April 1991.

[7]Ibid.

[8]See, e.g., Anne Anastasi, *Psychological Testing* (New York, NY: Macmillan Publishing Co., 1988).

Proponents of high-stakes testing, however, counter these arguments with data from the National Assessment of Educational Progress (NAEP). Unlike the high-stakes tests, for which score increases can be attributed to test-taking skills rather than genuine achievement, NAEP trends are considered by most experts as a better gauge of trends in achievement.[50] Thus, the fact that NAEP scores have gone up in the 1970s and 1980s has become a linchpin in the pro-MCT argument.[51]

But, once again, closer inspection of the timing and significance of NAEP trends suggests a more complex picture, one that defies simple attribution to MCT or any other single policy. First, NAEP scores did rise in the 1970s and 1980s, but the rise actually began to be noticed as early as the 1974 assessment, well before MCT was in operation in all but one or two States.

Second, the magnitude of the rise was considerably less impressive than the magnitude recorded on other standardized tests. Although some might argue that NAEP underestimates true achievement because NAEP test takers perceive no particular incentive to do their best, even correcting for this possibility would not erase the large gap between increases on other tests and the increases on NAEP.

Third, the most impressive aspect of longitudinal analysis of NAEP scores is the narrowing of the achievement gap between minority and white students: "... the average achievement of Blacks and of Hispanic students is substantially higher now than a decade ago."[52] This is hailed by some as the most convincing proof of the value of MCT,[53] while others note that: 1) the narrowing of the gap is explained largely by improvements at the low end of the range of achievement, 2) the overall gap between achievement of minority and white students remains quite large, and 3) gains among minority students in basic literacy and numeracy skills may have come at the expense of gains in higher order skills, which, according to NAEP data have been stagnant at best.

Undue Emphasis on Basic Skills

Prompted by these trends in NAEP, a number of researchers have investigated the hypothesis that basic skills improvements may have been made possible by a shift of instructional resources away from higher order academic skills. NAEP reports, for example, have emphasized the lack of progress in so-called higher order skills during the period of progress in basic skills. But other studies have been more optimistic. Researchers working with the Iowa Tests of Basic Skills, for example, produced evidence contradicting NAEP's: performance of comparable samples of 9-, 13-, and 17-year-olds increased between 1979 and 1985 on higher order questions even more than on basic skills items, continuing a trend observed from 1971 on.[54]

Contradictory evidence about test score trends notwithstanding, there is widespread agreement that State-mandated testing, and MCT in particular, had damaging effects on classroom behavior of teachers and students. One study combined analysis of survey data and intensive interviews with teachers and school administrators, and concluded that the testing reinforced the already excessive emphasis on basic skills and stymied local efforts to upgrade the content of education being delivered to all students. The authors of this study write:

Although [the] ability of a Statewide testing program to control local activity may be praiseworthy in the minds of some educational critics, the activity the program stimulated was not reform. Responding to testing did not encourage educators to reconsider the purposes of schooling; their purpose quickly became to raise scores and lower the pressure directed toward them. Responding to testing did not encourage educators to restructure their districts; they redirected time, money, and effort so that some parts of their systems could more expeditiously address the test score crisis while leaving the parts unaffected by testing or producing 'good' scores unscathed. Responding to testing did not encourage educators to rethink how they should teach or how they should administer schools; once

[50]For a fuller discussion of the origins and technical characteristics of the National Assessment of Educational Progress, see ch. 3.

[51]See Lerner, op. cit., footnote 33.

[52]Robert Linn and Stephen Dunbar, "The Nation's Report Card Goes Home: Good News and Bad About Trends in Achievement," *Phi Delta Kappan*, vol. 72, No. 2, October 1990, pp. 127-133.

[53]See Lerner, op. cit., footnote 33.

[54]See Elizabeth Witt, Myunghee Han, and H.D. Hoover, "Recent Trends in Achievement Test Scores: Which Students are Improving and on What Levels of Skill Complexity?" paper presented at the annual meeting of the National Council on Measurement in Education, Boston, MA, 1990.

again they addressed process only in the parts of their system that felt the direct impacts of testing.[55]

Narrowing Effect

While there is agreement among many studies of MCT that local districts have changed curriculum, instructional methods, and textbooks to align them more with the content of MCT instruments, there are differences of opinion about whether this is a good or bad trend. Some studies have bemoaned the narrowing effect that MCT seems to have had on instructional strategies, content coverage, and course offerings. The values embodied by MCT— that there is a fixed body of knowledge that students must absorb by a certain age, that mastery of this content is reflected in student responses to paper-and-pencil tests, and that student failure on the test is the school's responsibility to correct—tend to reinforce educational practices that are mechanical, superficial, and fragmented, such as passive learning, drill and practice, and adherence to age-grade distinctions and subject-matter boundaries.[56] Moreover, alignment to a State standard does not reflect the meaningful differences between localities.

Effects on Achievement and on Teacher Behavior

Recent research suggests that improvements on high-stakes tests do not generalize well to other measures of achievement in the same domain. For example, in one study mathematics performance on a conventional high-stakes test was found to not generalize to other tests for which students have not been specifically prepared. The authors of this study caution, therefore, that: "... information provided to the public by accountability oriented tests can be seriously misleading."[57] The evidence is somewhat contradictory about the extent to which teachers

modify their instructional practices in ways that are likely to produce higher test scores. One-half of the respondents to one nationally representative survey of eighth grade mathematics teachers (n=552) said they did not prepare students at all for mandated tests; of those who said they did, almost one-half reported spending no more than several periods a year on these efforts (and mathematics is one of the most tested areas).[58] It is also important to note, however, that of the group who said that testing influenced their instruction, 30 percent said they increased basic skills emphasis; 24 percent said they added emphasis on topics covered on the test; and 19 percent said they decreased their emphasis on project work, since it was not directly assessed by the test.[59]

Research studies that focus in particular on teachers in districts with high-stakes testing conditions—such as MCT, school evaluation tests, or externally developed course-end tests—demonstrate a greater influence of testing on curriculum and instruction. A study of four elementary classrooms with both mandated State and district objectives-based testing found that students spent up to 18 hours annually taking tests and about 54 hours receiving instruction that appeared to be directly oriented toward the tests.[60] Teachers of New York Regents courses, which have high-stakes testing at the end of the course, report spending anywhere from a few class periods to about 10 class periods (out of 175) reviewing and preparing for the examinations. Even the upper number reflects a rather modest direct effect of testing.[61]

One recent study, which sought to disentangle the effects of high-stakes testing on teaching and learning, showed fairly convincing evidence of

---

[55]H.D. Corbett and B. Wilson, "Unintended and Unwelcome: The Local Impact of State Testing," paper presented at the annual meeting of the American Educational Research Association, Boston, MA, April 1990, pp. 10-11.

[56]Archbald and Porter, op. cit., footnote 31. Also see ibid.

[57]Daniel Koretz, Robert Linn, Stephen Dunbar, and Lorrie Shepard, "The Effects of High Stakes Testing on Achievement: Preliminary Findings About Generalizations Across Tests," paper presented at the annual meeting of the American Educational Research Association, Chicago, IL, April 1991, p. 20.

[58]Thomas Romberg, Anne Zarrinia, and Steven Williams, *The Influence of Mandated Testing on Mathematics Instruction: Grade 8 Teachers' Perceptions* (Madison, WI: National Center for Research in Mathematical Science Education, University of Wisconsin-Madison, 1989), pp. 33-39. Nevertheless, the authors concluded that changes in instruction brought about by the tests were incompatible with the kinds of changes sought by the mathematics community. See discussion below.

[59]See also Shepard, op. cit., footnote 6.

[60]Claire Rottenberg and Mary Lee Smith, "Unintended Effects of External Testing in Elementary Schools," paper presented at the annual meeting of the American Educational Research Association, Boston, MA, April, 1990.

[61]Douglas Archbald, "Curriculum Control and Teacher Autonomy," paper presented at the annual meeting of the American Educational Research Association, Boston, MA, April 1990.

testing influencing teacher practices. This study found that:

- teachers felt pressured to improve test scores; 79 percent reported "great" or "substantial" pressure by district administration and the media;
- teachers reported giving greater emphasis to basic skills instruction than they would have in the absence of the mandatory tests;
- one-half the teachers reported giving less emphasis to subjects not on the tests;
- one-half the teachers reported spending 4 or more weeks per year giving students worksheets and practice exercises to review content they expected to be on the test and to prepare students for the tests: 68 percent of the teachers reported conducting these preparation activities "regularly," i.e., throughout the school year and not just in the days or weeks prior to testing; and
- the majority of teachers could identify numerous beneficial uses of the tests, such as ". . . setting instructional goals, providing feedback about student strengths and weaknesses, and identifying gaps in instruction . . . [but] these benefits . . . were offset or greatly outweighed by negative effects such as the amount of instructional time given to test preparation, the amount of stress experienced, unfair or invalid comparisons, and the demoralizing effects on teachers and students."[62]

These findings on the effects of high-stakes testing on teacher behavior, which the authors of the study described above caution are not necessarily generalizable, raise fundamental questions about the use of tests for instructional reform.

Misuse of MCT Data for School Comparisons

Another lesson from the MCT experience is that if test data are available they will be used to make comparisons and judgments about districts, schools, and students regardless of the data's original purpose, the ways in which it was collected, or how many caveats are issued as warnings about potential misuse. These types of comparisons, furthermore, ignore differences between school districts with large variations in student populations, resources,

and other factors affecting instruction; not only are the comparisons damaging to the self esteem of students and schools, they are also potentially misleading to policymakers seeking information on how to improve the schools.

Conclusions

Viewing the MCT glass as at least half-full, proponents have argued for more high-stakes testing and, in particular, for more high-stakes testing that covers advanced skills. Their argument is simply that if it worked for the basic skills it can work for the higher order skills.[63] These supporters of high-stakes testing argue that MCT worked because it:

- defined a single performance standard tied to powerful incentives (promotion or graduation);
- allowed teachers latitude in choosing whatever instructional methods they thought would be most appropriate to bring their students closer to the defined standards of performance;
- signaled to students the importance of acquiring basic skills in order to become productive citizens in a democracy; and
- conveyed to all students that they could acquire the necessary skills.

Critics contend that MCT is not a genuine tool of reform because it:

- does not provide school systems with information on to how to improve instruction, but rather serves to reinforce the instructional methods already in place;
- ignores differences between school districts with large variations in student populations, resources, and other factors affecting instruction; and
- creates conditions under which true reform is not possible, by emphasizing test scores rather than improved learning.

In the current debate over testing, it is common to hear both sides invoke the lessons of the minimum competency movement. Proponents focus on the powerful effects of high-stakes testing on clarifying and reinforcing curricula, and argue that once the right curricula are established tests will make them work. Critics fear that more high-stakes testing will reinforce outmoded curricula, provide misleading

---

[62]For a detailed discussion of methods, sample, and results, see Lorrie Shepard and Katherine Dougherty, "Effects of High Stakes Testing on Instruction," paper presented at the annual meeting of the American Educational Research Association, Chicago, IL, April 1991.

[63]Lerner, op. cit., footnote 33.

information to policymakers, and create artificial obstacles to educational and economic opportunity.

The positive and negative lessons of MCT, and of 100 years of prior experience with standardized tests, should inform policy for the future of testing in America. Although some of the evidence is contradictory, even confusing, one thing is clear: test-based accountability is fraught with uncertainties—it is no panacea. Specific proposals for tests intended to catalyze school improvement must be scrutinized on their individual merits, with certain cautions in mind. First, the evidence seems clear that as the stakes attached to test results heat up, so do teacher and student efforts to do better on the tests, which can lead to instructional activities that do not necessarily promote real learning. Second, there is a compelling rationale to design high-stakes tests that: a) sharpen incentives for students and teachers to practice for them, but b) contain material worth practicing for. Experience to date suggests that designing such tests is harder than originally imagined and that none has yet been implemented successfully.[64] Third, it is dubious that mandated testing alone has the potential to effect the sorts of restructuring needed to substantially reform education.

Increased Concern About the Appropriate Use of Tests

Testing policy in the United States has been influenced by the tugs of two countervailing tides: pressure for more testing with higher stakes on one hand, and cries for a slower pace and more careful examination of consequences on the other. As the influence of educational tests expanded in the 1970s and 1980s, a counterbalancing trend emerged. Individuals with different interests—parents, students, scholars, lawyers, writers, civil libertarians—began questioning the role of tests in their own and others' lives and sounding alarms about the effects of tests on individual privacy, equal opportunity, and fairness in the allocation of future opportunities. This

antitesting movement encompassed a variety of sentiments, from skepticism about the validity of tests to apprehension about the damaging effects of their misuse. In addition, the trend gained momentum from the growth of consumerism and some key victories in Congress and the courts. The themes of this backlash against standardized testing, in the past and today, have tended to cluster around certain passion-inspiring issues: fairness, bias, due process, individual privacy, and disclosure.

In the late 1960s, for example, the idea of a ''self-fulfilling prophecy'' gained a foothold in the American consciousness, supported in part by a controversial study of teacher expectations. In this study, teachers were told that a test had identified a subset of children as ''bloomers'' whose achievement could be expected to flourish during the school year.[65] Despite the fact that these bloomers were actually chosen at random, many showed impressive gains, outpacing their ''nonbloomer'' classmates. This study, which has since been found to contain many weaknesses, caught the public fancy and helped to support the arguments of many that disadvantaged children were failing in school due to teachers' low expectations about their abilities. It also alerted the public to the potential dangers of labeling children on the basis of test scores, and thus limiting their educational futures.[66]

As this example illustrates, it is not only the tests themselves that create controversy. Testing practices and policies—the ways tests are used and the types of inferences drawn from them—also create many of the problems associated with testing. There is widespread agreement among educators, analysts, measurement experts, and test publishers that tests are often used for functions for which they were not designed or validated, and that test results are often misinterpreted.

What Constitutes Fair Testing Practice?

Attempts to develop ethical and technical standards for tests and testing practices have a long

---

[64]The possibility that certain types of performance assessments might solve the dilemma has generated enthusiastic research and experimentation. See ch. 6.

[65]Robert Rosenthal and Lenore Jacobson, *Pygmalion in the Classroom: Teacher Expectation and Pupils' Intellectual Development* (New York, NY: Holt, Rinehart and Winston, 1968).

[66]For other sources on the self-fulfilling prophecy and rejoinders to the original study see Ray C. Rist, ''Student Social Class and Teacher Expectations: The Self-Fulfilling Prophecy in Ghetto Education,'' *Harvard Educational Review*, vol. 40, No. 3, August 1970, pp. 411-451; J.D. Elashoff and Richard E. Snow (eds.), *Pygmalion Reconsidered* (Worthington, OH: Jones, 1971); and Samuel S. Wineburg, ''The Self-Fulfillment of the Self-Fulfilling Prophecy: A Critical Appraisal,'' and replys by Robert Rosenthal and Ray C. Rist, *Educational Researcher*, vol. 16, No. 9, December 1987, pp. 28-44.

history. These efforts have been made primarily by professional groups involved in the design and administration of tests, such as psychologists and educational measurement specialists. Although discussions of such standards began at the turn of the century, the first organized efforts, at mid-century, resulted in the adoption of a formal code of ethics for psychologists in 1952 and a set of technical recommendations regarding test use developed by three professional groups in 1954.[67] This latter document, known in its most recent version as the *Standards for Educational and Psychological Testing* (hereafter referred to as the *Standards*), has been revised three times in the intervening years.[68]

Some of these technical standards pertain to tests themselves: the methods by which they should be developed, the data required to support their use, and evidence of their fairness. Although aimed primarily at the developers and publishers of tests, the standards have relevance for test users, who must evaluate the adequacy of the tests they buy or commission.

Many of the technical standards contain guidelines for test use: appropriate procedures for the selection, administration, and interpretation of tests, and guidelines affecting the rights of test takers. The two incidents quoted below, for example, represent violations of principles of appropriate testing practice.

A high school newspaper carried a page one headline: "Meet the geniuses of the incoming class" and listed all pupils of IQ 120 and up with numerical scores. Then under a heading: "These are not geniuses, but good enough" were listed all the rest, with IQ scores down to the 60's.

****

A new battery of tests for reading readiness was introduced in a school. Instead of the customary two or three, 12 beginners were this year described by the test as not ready for reading. They were placed in a special group and given no reading instruction. The principal insisted that if the parents or anyone else tried to teach them to read "Their little minds would crack under the strain." In at least two cases parents did teach them to read with normal progress in the first semester, and later mental tests showed IQ's above 120.[69]

As these examples suggest, one of the major problems with the professional *Standards* is that most of the principal interpreters of educational test results (such as policymakers, school administrators, teachers, and journalists) are unaware of them and are untrained in appropriate test use and interpretation.

A set of testing standards should consider the needs of three main participants in the testing process: 1) the test developer who constructs and markets tests, 2) the test user (usually the institution that selects tests and uses them to make some decision), and 3) the test taker who takes the test ". . . by choice, direction, or necessity."[70] Some form of consumer protection or assurance is needed for both the test user and the test taker, but particularly for the latter: ". . . who is still the least powerful of the three."[71] As depicted in figure 2-4, the test-taker's fate rests on the assumption that good testing practice has been upheld by both the test developer when it constructed the test and the test user (such as the school) when it selected, interpreted, and made a decision on the basis of the test. With few exceptions, the test taker has no direct contact with or access to the test developer; the test user serves as the primary filter through which testing information reaches the test taker.[72] Just as the patient undergoing an electrocardiogram must assume that the machine is soundly built and correctly calibrated, that the technician is admini-

---

[67]The American Psychological Association, the American Educational Research Association, and the National Council on Measurement in Education; and Walter Haney and George Madaus, "The Evolution of Ethical and Technical Standards for Testing," *Handbook of Testing*, R. Hambleton (ed.) (Amsterdam, The Netherlands: North-Holland Publishing Co., in press).

[68]In 1966, 1974, and 1985.

[69]American Psychological Association, quoted in Haney and Madaus, op. cit., footnote 67.

[70]Melvin R. Novick, "Federal Guidelines and Professional Standards," *American Psychologist*, vol. 36, No. 10, October 1981, p. 1035.

[71]James V. Mitchell, Jr., "Testing and the Oscar Buros Lament: From Knowledge to Implementation to Use," *Social and Technical Issues in Testing: Implications for Test Construction and Usage*, Barbara S. Plake (ed.) (Hillsdale, NJ: L. Erlbaum Associates, 1984).

[72]For college and graduate admissions tests such as the SAT, ACT, and GRE, test takers do have direct contact with test developers. On these tests, students register directly with the test developers and receive explanations of the test, scoring methods, test-taking strategies, as well as score reports from them. Records of test scores, in these cases, remain in the hands of test developers, so privacy protection must also be assured by the developer. In contrast, the reponsibility for and control of the test-takers' scores remains with the school system for most educational achievement tests administered during elementary and secondary years.

Figure 2-4—Appropriate Testing Practice in Education: Four Major Obligations of Test Developers and Test Users to Test Takers[a]

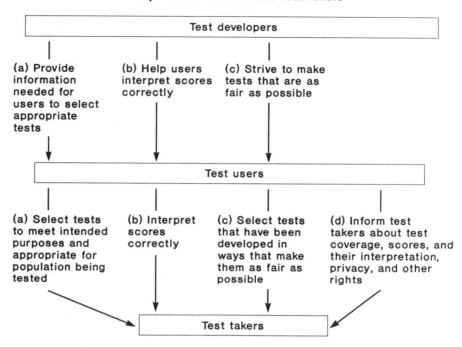

[a]This chart is based on *The Code of Fair Testing Practices in Education* which outlines four areas of major obligation to test takers: 1) developing/selecting tests, 2) interpreting scores, 3) striving for fairness, and 4) informing test takers. See the *Code* for the specific principles in each area.
NOTE: For some kinds of tests, such as college admissions tests, test developers have direct contact with test takers; in these cases, they are also obligated to the set of principles (d) regarding appropriately informing test takers.
SOURCE: Joint Committee on Testing Practices, *Code of Fair Testing Practices in Education* (Washington, DC: National Council on Measurement in Education, 1988).

stering the test properly, and that the physician is interpreting the information appropriately, so must the test taker assume that the choice of test, its method of administration, and its interpretation are correct. Currently, few mechanisms exist to assure such protection for educational tests.

The assurance of good testing practice for the test taker is further complicated by the absence of information about tests. Testing manuals, which document development and validation processes, are highly technical, and considerable training is required to evaluate the statistical properties of much of this test data. In addition, most tests are closely supervised by developers and users, in order to maintain the secrecy of test items, which is important to assuring that the test remains fair for all current and future test takers.[73] The compulsory nature of most schoolwide testing programs presents

yet another complication: students and their parents can exercise little choice about whether a child should be tested. In sum, a social and ethical tension exists between the need for close professional supervision of tests and the need for open public discussion and knowledge about tests by test takers—especially those whose educational opportunities may be affected by their use.

Since the 1977 version of the *Standards*, more attention has been given to the rights of the persons being tested. This attention to consumers' rights, however, appears to conflict somewhat with the need for test security. For example,

Concerning testing, the 1977 *Standards* states that "Persons examined have the right to know results, the interpretations made, and where appropriate the original data on which final judgements were made." In light of the very next sentence, the

[73]In fact the ethical principles of psychologists prohibit them from releasing tests to unqualified persons; dissemination of any standardized test risks invalidating the test and giving some test takers an unfair advantage over others.

modifier "where appropriate" looms large and uncertain: "Test users avoid imparting unnecessary information which would comprise test security. . . ." An obvious question remains: When do the rights of test takers leave off and the need for test security begin?[74]

Agreement about what constitutes good testing practice is far from unanimous even among professionals; as the above example suggests, considerable latitude of interpretation is allowed for any one of the standards. For the most part each standard is a general principle, a goal to strive for and uphold; the specific criteria by which it is met are not explicitly stated. The principles governing the appropriate administration of standardized achievement tests in schools are a good example. What one school district may call legitimate test preparation activities (practice, coaching, and explanation of instructions to students), another may deem dubious or even unethical. These different interpretations are one of the principal causes of test score "inflation."[75]

Recently some professional groups have been working to translate the more technical *Standards* into principles for untrained users of tests, such as administrators, policymakers, and teachers. The *Code of Fair Testing Practices in Education*[76] (for basic provisions, see figure 2-4) attempts to outline the major obligations that professionals who use or develop educational tests have to individual test takers. These principles are widely agreed on and endorsed by professional groups as central to the fair and effective use of tests.[77]

What agreement is there about the rights of test takers? Is there a consistent set of ethical principles that should be followed? Most professional groups seem to agree that test takers should be provided with certain basic information about:

- content covered by the test and type of question formats;
- the kind of preparation the test taker should have and appropriate test-taking strategies to use (e.g., should they guess or not?);
- the uses to which test data will be put;
- the persons who will have access to test scores and the circumstances under which test scores will be released to anyone beyond those who have such access;
- the length of time test scores will be kept on record;
- available options for retesting, rescoring or cancelling scores; and
- the procedures test takers and their parents or guardians may use to register complaints and have problems resolved.[78]

An important question arises regarding the principle of "informed consent," defined by the *Standards* as:

> The granting of consent by the test taker to be tested on the basis of full information concerning the purpose of the testing, the persons who may receive the test scores, the use to which the test score may be put, and such other information as may be material to the consent process.[79]

Since most children cannot give truly informed consent, an adult serving as a proxy must give consent. Although in most cases such a proxy will be the parent, there appears to be certain circumstances under which school officials are allowed to grant permission for collecting and using pupil information. Currently, the *Standards* suggest that test data collected on a schoolwide basis or by a legislated requirement are exempt from parental informed

[74]Haney and Madaus, op. cit., footnote 67, p. 6.

[75]See, e.g., Thomas M. Haladyna, Susan Bobbit Nolen, and Nancy S. Haas, "Raising Standardized Achievement Test Scores and the Origins of Test Score Pollution," *Educational Researcher*, vol. 20, No. 5, June-July 1991, pp. 2-7.

[76]Authored by the Joint Committee on Testing Practices initiated by the American Educational Research Association, the American Psychological Association, and the National Council on Measurement in Education in 1988. Joint Committee on Testing Practices, *Code of Fair Testing Practices in Education* (Washington, DC: National Council on Measurement in Education, 1988).

[77]Similar efforts are under way in other countries. For example, a number of professional groups in Canada, drawing on the experience of the Joint Committee who developed the *Code*, have begun working on a set of principles for Canadian testing programs.

[78]See, e.g., American Educational Research Association, American Psychological Association, and National Council on Measurement in Education, *Standards for Educational and Psychological Testing* (Washington, DC: 1985); Joint Committee on Testing Practices, op. cit., footnote 76; Russell Sage Foundation, *Guidelines for the Collection, Maintenance, and Dissemination of Pupil Records* (New York, NY: 1969); U.S. Department of Education, Office of Educational Research and Improvement, *Your Child and Testing* (Washington, DC: 1980).

[79]American Educational Research Association et al., op. cit., footnote 78, pp. 91-92.

consent—consent is given in this case by school officials.[80]

Informed consent also implies that the test takers are aware that they are being tested. As high-stakes tests are now conducted, children are certainly well aware that they are being tested: instructions, setting, and testing booklets all serve to clearly mark the testing session as something different from the everyday business of the classroom. Parents and children are usually notified in advance when tests will be given, in part so that parents can assure that their children are well rested and fed on testing day. Conditions and circumstances of testing are made clear so that all children have the chance to do their best.

How can parents be assured that tests are being used appropriately by schools to make decisions, particularly about individual students? One of the persistent problems with tests is that they are used for purposes not originally intended. Those being tested are not always directly informed about the uses and purposes of testing. Although it has long been considered to be the ethical responsibility of test administrators and developers to assure that tests are used only for purposes intended, there are few, if any, safeguards to assure this. Furthermore there are even fewer protections for the test score information once it is obtained—scores that sit in a child's record can be used by anyone who has access to that record whether or not that person knows anything about the particular test that was administered. It is difficult to prevent the misuse of test-based information once that information has been collected.

How is Fair Testing Practice Encouraged or Enforced?

It follows from this analysis that the first step toward fair testing practice is agreement on a set of principles or guidelines about appropriate and inappropriate test practices. Achieving such a consensus is not always a simple or clear-cut process. But given that some agreement already exists about what

constitutes appropriate and inappropriate test use, how can these practices be encouraged or enforced and unfair practices be discouraged?

Right now there are four mechanisms for encouraging fair and appropriate testing practices: professional self-regulation, education, litigation, and legislation.

Professional Self-Regulation

Professional self-regulation is the primary mechanism for promoting good testing practices in education. Standards and codes for testing developed by professional associations, critical reviews of tests by experts, and individual professional codes of ethics all contribute to better testing practices among testing professionals; nevertheless, many professionals agree that these codes lack sufficiently strong enforcement mechanisms.[81] The Buros Institute of Mental Measurement has long been concerned with the education of test users and the assurance of quality tests. As part of these efforts the Institute publishes the *Mental Measurement Yearbook* (MMY), first published in 1938, which contains critical reviews by experts of nearly all commercially available psychological and educational tests. Recently, Institute personnel concluded that 41 percent of the tests reviewed in *The Eighth Mental Measurements Yearbook* were lacking in reliability and/or validity data.[82] In the years before his death, Oscar Buros often lamented the lack of effect that either the *Standards* or the Buros Institute had on test quality or use. In a speech in 1968, for example, Buros reported the following:

> At present, no matter how poor a test may be, if it is nicely packaged and if it promises to do all sorts of things which no test can do, the test will find many gullible buyers. When we initiated critical test reviewing in *The 1938 Yearbook*, we had no idea how difficult it would be to discourage the use of poorly constructed tests of unknown validity. Even the better informed test users who finally become convinced that a widely used test had no validity after all are likely to rush to use a new instrument

---

[80]The *Standards* read: "... informed consent should be obtained from test takers or their legal representatives before testing is done except (a) when testing without consent is mandated by law or governmental regulation (e.g., statewide testing programs); (b) when testing is conducted as a regular part of school activities (e.g., schoolwide testing programs and participation by schools in norming and research studies); or (c) when consent is clearly implied (e.g., application for employment or educational admissions)." Ibid., p. 85.

[81]See, e.g., George Madaus, "Public Policy and the Testing Profession—You've Never Had it so Good?" and reactions by former National Council on Measurement in Education presidents William E. Coffman, Thomas J. Fitzgibbon, Jason Millman, and Lorrie A. Shepard, in *Educational Measurement: Issues and Practice*, winter 1985, pp. 5-16.

[82]Mitchell, op. cit., footnote 71.

which promises far more than any good test can possibly deliver.[83]

In addition, the efforts by professionals to self-regulate are often aimed at developing technically sound tests and thus at the transactions between test developers and test users. Less attention has been directed toward the even more intractable problem of how to assure that tests are used appropriately *once developed and chosen by a school*. How can good testing policies be assured once a testing program, over which test takers have no choice about participation, is put in place?

Education and Public Discussion

Education and public discussion about tests, their limitations (as well as their value), and the principles of appropriate test use is the second way better testing practices could be encouraged. If the general public, parents, and test takers understood what questions to ask about tests and what protections to expect, then those who administer and choose tests would be more accountable for their testing practices. A number of testing experts believe that more open examination of test use and its social consequences could help encourage better practices on the part of those responsible for administering and interpreting tests.[84]

Teachers, principals, school boards, superintendents, and others who set testing policies for schools are another audience for educational efforts. Some proposals have recommended mandatory training for teachers to help them better understand tests and good testing practices.[85] Recently several professional associations jointly drew up a set of "Standards for Teacher Competence in Educational Assessment of Students," which established guidelines for what teachers should know in order to use various assessment techniques appropriately.[86] Others have called for better training of administrators and have encouraged rewarding of administrators for good assessment practices in their schools.[87]

Litigation

Litigation is the third route toward better testing practice. "Before the 1960's, the courts were rarely concerned with testing or evaluation of students. Most likely, their concern was limited because, under the standard of 'reasonableness,' standardized testing was a subject left principally to the professional discretion of school teachers and administrators."[88] And since the courts showed little interest in test-related issues, as characterized in this quotation, lawyers had no incentive to bring legal actions about testing practices.

As the use of tests increased, so did their potential for causing legally significant harm to test takers.[89] The court's "hands off" approach changed in the 1970s and 1980s, with the filing of several lawsuits challenging the uses of standardized tests in education. The activism of parents, civil rights advocates, and civil liberties groups was an important spur to the development of case law in this area. Overall, however, educational tests have received far fewer legal challenges than have employment-related tests.[90]

Most litigation involving standardized educational tests involves individuals who, alone or as a class, claim violations of fundamental rights. These include the constitutional rights of due process and equal protection, and the rights guaranteed by Federal laws, such as civil rights, equal opportunity, and education of individuals with disabilities. The issues tend to center on the use of tests for classification, exclusion, and tracking, or the privacy of individual test takers. In these cases, the defendants are usually State and local school administra-

---

[83]Oscar K. Buros, "The Story Behind the Mental Measurements Yearbooks," *Measurement and Evaluation in Guidance*, vol. 1, 1968, p. 94.

[84]Mitchell op. cit., footnote 71; and Walter Haney, "Testing Reasoning and Reasoning About Testing," *Review of Educational Research*, vol. 54, No. 4, winter 1984, pp. 597-654.

[85]John R. Hills, "Apathy Concerning Grading and Testing," *Kappan*, vol. 72, No. 7, March 1991, pp. 540-545; and Richard J. Stiggins, "Assessment Literacy," *Phi Delta Kappan*, vol. 72, No. 7, March 1991, pp. 534-539; and Robert Lynn Canady and Phyllis Riley Hotchkiss, "It's a Good Score! Just a Bad Grade," *Phi Delta Kappan*, vol. 71, No. 1, September 1989, pp. 68-73.

[86]American Federation of Teachers, National Council on Measurement in Education, and National Education Association, "Standards for Teacher Competence in Educational Assessment of Students," unpublished document, 1990.

[87]Hills, op. cit., footnote 85.

[88]James E. Bruno and John C. Hogan, "What Public Interest Lawyers and Educational Policymakers Need to Know About Testing: A Review of Recent Cases, Laws and Areas of Future Litigation," *Whittier Law Review*, vol. 7, No. 4, 1985, p. 917.

[89]Donald N. Bersoff, "Social and Legal Influences on Test Development and Usage," in Plake (ed.), op. cit., footnote 71.

[90]See Wigdor and Garner (eds.), op. cit., footnote 29, for an overview of legal issues in employment and educational testing.

tors. Some of the earliest challenges to testing practices focused on racial discrimination. Under attack were certain classification and tracking policies—not uncommon in Southern schools resisting desegregation—that used I.Q. and other tests in ways that resulted in resegregation. Federal courts quickly barred these types of programs.[91]

Often it is the testing policy or the way a test is being used, rather than the test itself, that is challenged in court. In addition, most legal challenges have dealt with tests used for the so-called "gatekeeping" functions: college admissions, minimum competency, or special education placement. *Thus, tests are most likely to receive legal scrutiny and challenge when they are used to make significant decisions about individual students.* In general, the courts have most often sought guidance from and upheld the *Standards.*

Some of the most significant cases involving due process and testing were spawned by the minimum competency movement. The first such case, the landmark *Debra P.* v. *Turlington,* claimed that the Florida law requiring students to pass a functional literacy test before obtaining a high school diploma violated the student plaintiffs' rights to due process and equal protection, as well as the Equal Educational Opportunities Act. After examining such issues as whether the test assessed skills that were actually taught, whether there was adequate notice of the requirement, whether students had access to adequate remediation, and whether they had opportunities to take the test over, the court enjoined Florida from implementing the law until 1982-83, after the vestiges of the State's formerly segregated school system were presumed to have dissipated.

As in other cases, the court referred to the *Standards* in reaching its decision. However, this case also demonstrated quite clearly the considerable latitude for interpretation and professional judgment required to translate the *Standards* into specific recommendations for practice. During the trial, two testing experts, both of whom were members of the committee who drew up the *Standards* in 1974, offered divergent and conflicting expert views about the kind of validity evidence the State of Florida should have provided.[92]

Photo credit: Daniel Broun, OTA staff

Resorting to the courts to settle issues of good testing practice is often a last recourse. Most legal challenges to educational tests have occurred when these tests have been used for selection, certification, or placement of students.

The body of case law reveals some broad themes about how courts view tests, and some general principles about acceptable and unacceptable uses of tests. In general, courts have a great respect for well-constructed, standardized tests that are clearly tied to the curriculum. They do not find them arbitrary or irrelevant to the legitimate State interest in improving education. A minimum competency test, for example, is a reasonable method of assessing students' basic skills. In addition, Federal courts have hesitated to interfere in the education process or second guess local school district personnel.

Courts tend to look at how the results of the tests are used. If there are allegations that tests were used to deny graduation diplomas, place students in lower education tracks, or misclassify students as mentally disabled—any situations in which a test taker can claim serious injury—then the cases will be given more careful scrutiny. Cases involving historically vulnerable groups of students, such as minorities and children with disabilities, also raise flags.

[91]Norman J. Chachkin, "Testing in Elementary and Secondary Schools: Can Misuse Be Avoided?" *Test Policy and the Politics of Opportunity Allocation: The Workplace and the Law,* Bernard R. Gifford (ed.) (Boston, MA: Kluwer, 1989).

[92]See Haney, op. cit., footnote 84.

Usually Federal lawsuits involving the use of tests have been successful only where there was a claim that the test violated some other, independently established Federal right, such as the right of due process or protection from racial discrimination.[93] State courts have shown similar deference to local judgment.

Court decisions have established some other basic guidelines about tests and their applications. Tests should accurately reflect their intended content. Students should have opportunities to learn the material on the tests in school. Students should receive adequate notice to prepare for the tests. The examinations should not be used as the sole factor in determining placement or status. The scoring procedures should accurately assess mastery of the content.[94]

Courts have protected the privacy of the parent-child relationship when testing of a very personal nature, such as certain psychological and diagnostic tests, has interfered with family relationships or the parents' rights to rear their children. On the flip side, courts have also tended to protect the security of tests by reaffirming the applicability of copyright laws to test materials.

Resorting to the courts to settle issues of good testing practice is often a last recourse. However, many testing experts as well as educators feel that courts are not the optimal arena in which to set policies regarding tests and their use. "If educators have a difficult time matching students with appropriate educational placements, judges have no experience at all."[95]

One clear alternative to courts as watchdogs is to encourage school systems and policymakers to be more careful about the testing policies they implement. Many school testing policies are not set clearly and explicitly nor are they publicly available. As one litigator, involved for many years in testing and tracking litigation in schools, has written: ". . . the most difficult part of such litigation is the process of factual investigation to determine *exactly*

what use is being made of what tests in a particular district."[96]

A recent case in New York State suggests that educational administrators may have an important role to play in providing guidance and supervision regarding the fairness of school testing policies. The mother of an eighth grade student who had been excluded from enrichment programs because of her test scores on the Iowa Tests of Basic Skills (ITBS) appealed that decision. The district superintendent denied her appeal, supporting the school board's policy of using this test as the screening criteria for the enrichment program. This mother then appealed her case to the New York State Commissioner of Education who, after reviewing the evidence about the ITBS, issued an order prohibiting the district's use of test scores as the sole determinant for eligibility for educational enrichment programs. In part the order reads:

> Given the proviso in the ITBS testing manual, respondents' use of its test scores as a screening device that automatically excludes a student from further consideration for placement in an enrichment program is inconsistent with the specific guidelines provided by the developers of the ITBS test. Furthermore, because the results of a single test may be adversely affected by factors such as anxiety, illness, test-taking ability, ability to process directions or general distractibility (which have little to do with ability or achievement), use of standardized test scores as a screening device may serve to exclude pupils prematurely who are otherwise eligible. Based on the foregoing, I conclude that respondents'(the district) policy which denies a student the possibility of further consideration for placement in an enrichment program solely on the student's failure to achieve above a certain score on a subpart of the ITBS is not a legitimate measure for screening a student's capacity for success in an enriched program and is, therefore, *arbitrary, capricious and contrary to sound educational policy.*[97]

As the attorney cited above notes:

> As we (litigators) accumulate more knowledge about both test construction and test misuse in

---

[93]Chachkin, op. cit., footnote 91.

[94]Bruno and Hogan, op. cit., footnote 88.

[95]William H. Clune, "Courts as Cautious Watchdogs: Constitutional and Policy Issues of Standardized Testing in Education," report prepared for the National Commission on Testing and Public Policy, 1988, p. 1.

[96]Chachkin, op. cit., footnote 91, p. 186, emphasis added.

[97]Order #12433 of the State Education Department of New York, issued Dec. 7, 1990 by Thomas Sobol, Commissioner of Education, p. 3, emphasis added.

educational settings, it will become easier for attorneys to gather these facts and litigation will continue and expand. For this reason, policymakers, legislators, and educational administrators are well advised to conduct their own reviews for the purpose of restricting test use to appropriate functions within their institutions and systems.[98]

Federal Legislation

Federal legislation is the fourth avenue to improved test practice. Some of the practices commonplace today in educational testing are the result of legislative efforts. In the mid-1970s, Congress passed a series of laws with significant provisions regarding testing and assessment, one affecting all students and parents and the others affecting individuals with disabilities and their parents. In both cases, this Federal legislation has had far-reaching implications for school policy because Federal financial assistance to schools has been tied to compliance with these legislated mandates regarding appropriate testing practices.

The Family Education Rights and Privacy Act of 1974 (FERPA)—FERPA, commonly called the "Buckley Amendment" after former New York Senator James Buckley, was enacted in part to attempt to safeguard parents' rights and to correct some of the improprieties in the collection and maintenance of pupil records. This legislation drew heavily on a set of voluntary guidelines regarding pupil records, called the Russell Sage Foundation Conference Guidelines, drawn up in 1969 by a panel of education professors, school administrators, sociologists, psychologists, professors of law, and a juvenile court judge.[99] The basic provisions of this legislation are twofold. First it establishes the right of parents to inspect school records. Second, it protects the confidentiality of information by limiting access to school records (including test scores) to those who have legitimate educational needs for the information and by requiring written parental consent for the release of identifiable data (see table 2-3).

Table 2-3—Federally Legislated Rights Regarding Testing and School Records

I. The Family Education Rights and Privacy Act of 1974
A. Right to inspect records:
1. Right to see all of a child's test results that are part of the child's official school record.
2. Right to have test results explained.
3. Written requests to see test results must be honored in 45 days.
4. If child is over 18, only the child has the right to the record.
B. Right to privacy: Rights here limit access to the official school records (including test scores) to those who have legitimate educational needs.

II. The Education of All Handicapped Children Act of 1975 and The Handicapped Rehabilitation Act of 1973
A. Right to parent involvement:
1. The first time a child is considered for special education placement, the parents must be given written notice in their native language, and their permission must be obtained to test the child.
2. Right to challenge the accuracy of test scores used to plan the child's program.
3. Right to file a written request to have the child tested by other than the school staff.
4. Right to request a hearing if not satisfied with the school's decision as to what are the best services for the child.
B. Right to fairness in testing:
1. Right of the child to be tested in the language spoken at home.
2. Tests given for placement cannot discriminate on the basis of race, sex, or socioeconomic status. The tests cannot be culturally biased.
3. Right of child to be tested with a test that meets special needs (e.g., Braille or orally).
4. No single test score can be used to make special education placement decisions. Right to be tested in several different ways.

SOURCE: E.B. Herndon, *Your Child and Testing* (Washington, DC: U.S. Department of Education, National Institute of Education, October 1980), pp. 26-27.

FERPA was an early victory for the proponents of public disclosure of test results and to date their only significant success in the Federal arena. During the 1980s, several "truth in testing" bills were introduced in Congress, intended to make tests more accessible to individuals who took them. Amid press reports about serious scoring mistakes and the publication of books accusing major testing companies of greed and arrogance, these bills gained momentum for a while, but none were enacted. The

---

[98]Chachkin, op. cit., footnote 91, p. 186.

[99]With respect to "informed consent," the Russell Sage Foundation Conference *Guidelines*, op. cit., footnote 78, state that: ". . . no information should be collected from students without the prior informed consent of the child and his parents," p. 16. However, these guidelines also specify the types of data for which the notion of *representational* consent can be accepted. Representational consent means that permission to collect data is given by appropriately elected officials, such as the State Legislature or local school board. The *Guidelines* go on to clarify that: "no statement of consent, whether individual or representational, should be binding unless it is freely given after: The parents (and students where appropriate. . .) have been fully informed, preferably in writing, as to the methods by which the information will be collected; the uses to which it would be put; the methods by which it will be recorded and maintained; the time period for which it will be retained; and the persons to whom it will be available, and underwhat conditions," p. 17.

drive for Federal action to ensure better testing practices has since stalled.

These bills were patterned, to some extent, on legislation passed by New York and California requiring testing companies to disclose to State commissions information about tests and testing procedures, as well as the answers to test questions. In general these laws have contained three main provisions: 1) that test developers file information about the reliability and validity of the test with a government agency, 2) that they inform students what their scores mean, how scores will be used and how access to the scores will be controlled, and 3) that individual test takers have access to corrected questions (after the test), not just the score they receive. It is largely this third provision that has made this type of legislation so controversial; the first two provisions (assuring access to information about the test's development and assuring that the test taker is appropriately informed and privacy protected) are basic tenets of good testing practice.[100] The premise behind these laws is that by increasing public scrutiny of tests, their development and their uses, potential harm to individuals can be headed off in the early stages—as when a testing company makes a scoring error—and the tests themselves will become more accurate and fair.

Legislation Affecting Individuals With Disabilities—The Rehabilitation Act of 1973 bars recipients of Federal funds from discriminating against individuals with disabilities. In the educational arena, the act has been interpreted to protect against misclassification of people as retarded, learning disabled, or mentally disabled in other ways.

One of the most consistent recommendations of testing experts is that a test score should never be used as the single criterion on which to base decisions about individuals. Significant legal challenges to the overreliance on I.Q. test scores in special education placements led to an exemplary Federal policy on test use in special education decisions. The Education for All Handicapped Children Act of 1975 (Public Law 94-142) was designed to assure the rights of individuals with disabilities to the best possible education. Congress included eight provisions designed to protect students and ensure fair, equitable, and nondiscriminatory use of tests in implementing this program. Among the provisions were: 1) decisions about students are to be based on more than performance on a single test, 2) tests must be validated for the purpose for which they are used, 3) children must be assessed in all areas related to a specific or suspected disability, and 4) evaluations should be made by a multidisciplinary team.[101] This legislation provides, then, a number of significant safeguards against the simplistic or capricious use of test scores in making educational decisions.

Conclusion: Toward Fair Testing Practice

Legal challenges have affected testing practices in some important ways. First, they have "... made the [psychological and testing] profession, as well as society in general, more sensitive to racial and cultural differences and to how apparently innocent and benign practices may perpetuate discrimination. [Second, they have] ... alerted psychologists to the fact that they will be held responsible for their conduct."[102] Third, by drawing some attention to the rights of test takers and responsibilities of test administrators, they have accelerated the search for better means of assessing human competencies in all spheres.[103]

Even after the enactment of FERPA and 25 years of court challenges, the current level of protection against test misuse remains rather low when compared with some other areas of consumer interest. Protections consist primarily of warnings in test publishers' manuals and a handful of State laws. Few public school districts, except for the very largest, have staffs with adequate backgrounds in psychometrics, fully trained in professional ethics and responsibilities governing test use and misuse. For most school systems, there is an abundance of public and government pressure to test students extensively, but a minimum of support to help them

---

[100]The truth in testing legislation has focused primarily on college and graduate admissions tests, "... probably in part because such tests seem to have more visible consequences for the fate of individual test-takers than did testing of students below the college age, but surely also because college age test-takers had considerably more political clout than test-takers too young to vote." Mehrens and Lehmann, op. cit., footnote 22, p. 629; and Haney, op. cit., footnote 84.

[101]John Salvia and James E. Ysseldyke, *Assessment in Special and Remedial Education*, 3rd ed. (Boston, MA: Houghton Mifflin Co., 1985).

[102]Donald N. Bersoff, "Testing and the Law," *American Psychologist*, vol. 36, No. 10, October 1981, p. 1055.

[103]Ibid.

make ''. . . proper, cautious interpretations of the data which are produced.''[104]

As educational test use expands, examination of the social consequences of test use on children and schools must also be a priority. More social dialog and openness about what constitutes acceptable and unacceptable testing practices should be encouraged. Furthermore, tests used for the gatekeeping functions of selection, placement, and certification should be very carefully examined and their social consequences considered. If high-stakes testing spreads into new realms, such as a national test, we can expect to see the number of court challenges and the demand for legislative and regulatory safeguards multiply. Options for Congress to consider to foster better testing practice are discussed in chapter 1.

[104]Chachkin, op. cit., footnote 91.

Educational Testing Policy: The Changing Federal Role

Contents

Table

Educational Testing Policy: The Changing Federal Role

Highlights

- As the Federal financial commitment to education expanded during the 1960s and 1970s, new demands for test-based accountability emerged. Federal policymakers now rely on standardized tests to assess the effectiveness of several Federal programs.
- Evaluation requirements in the Federal Chapter 1 program for disadvantaged children, which result in more than 1.5 million children being tested every year, have helped escalate the amount of testing in American schools. Questions arise about whether results of Chapter 1 testing produce an accurate picture of the program's effectiveness, about the burden that the testing creates for schools, teachers, and children, and about the usefulness of the information provided by the test results.
- The National Assessment of Educational Progress (NAEP) is a unique Federal effort begun in the 1960s to provide long-term and continuous data on the achievement of American school children in many different subjects. NAEP has become a well-respected instrument to help gauge the Nation's educational health. Recent proposals to change NAEP to allow for comparisons in performance between States, to establish proficiency standards, or to use NAEP items as a basis for a system of national examinations raise questions about how much NAEP can be changed without compromising its original purposes.
- National testing is a critical issue before Congress today. Many questions remain about the objectives, content, format, cost, and administration of any national test. *thesis*

The role of the Federal Government in educational testing policy has been limited but influential. Given the decentralized structure of American schooling, few decisions supported with test information are made at the Federal level. States and local school districts make most of the decisions about which tests to give, when to give them, and how to use the information. The Federal Government weighs in primarily by requiring test-based measures of effectiveness for some of the education programs it funds, operating its own testing program through the National Assessment of Educational Progress (NAEP), and affording some limited protections and rights to test takers and their parents (see ch. 2).

This circumscribed Federal role has nevertheless influenced the quantity and character of testing in American schools. As Federal funding has expanded over the past 25 years, so has the Federal appetite for test-based evidence aimed at ensuring accountability for those funds. This growth in Federal influence has evolved with no specific and deliberate Federal policy on testing. Most Federal decisions about testing have been made in the context of larger program reauthorization bills, with evaluation questions treated as program issues rather than testing policy issues. As discussed in the preceding chapter, Congress did consider several bills in the 1970s and 1980s related to test disclosure and the rights of test takers; only the Family Education Rights and Privacy Act of 1974 became law.

This picture is changing. Congress now faces several critical choices that could redefine the Federal role in educational testing. In three policy areas, Congress has already played an important role, and its decisions in the near term could have significant consequences for the quantity and quality of educational testing. Accountability for federally funded programs is the first area. The tradition of achievement testing as a way to hold State- or district-level education authorities accountable is as old as public schooling itself. Continued spending on compensatory education has become increasingly dependent on evidence that these programs are working. Thus, for several decades now the single largest Federal education program—Chapter 1 (Compensatory Education)—has struggled with the need for evaluation data from States and districts that receive Federal monies. Increasing reliance on standardized norm-referenced achievement tests to monitor Chapter 1 programs indicates an increasing Federal influence on the nature and quantity of testing. Congress has revised its accountability requirements on several occasions, and in today's atmosphere of test reform, the $6 billion Federal Chapter 1 program can hardly be ignored. The basic policy question is whether the Federal Government is well served by the information derived from the tests used today and whether modifications could provide improved information.

Second, Federal support for collection of educational data, traditionally intended to keep the Nation informed about overall educational progress, is now viewed by some as a lever to influence teaching and learning. Thus, the 20-year-old NAEP, widely acclaimed as an invaluable instrument to gauge the Nation's educational health, has, in the past few years, attracted the attention of some policymakers interested in using its tests to change the structure and content of schooling.

A third and related issue is national testing. In addition to various suggested changes to NAEP, a number of proposals have emerged recently—from the White House, various agencies of the executive branch, and blue ribbon commissions—to implement nationwide tests. Although the purposes of these tests vary, it is clear they are intended to bring about improved achievement, not simply to estimate current levels of learning. The idea of national testing seems to have gained greater public acceptability. Proponents argue that "national" does not equal "Federal," and that national education standards do not require Federal determination of curricula and design of tests. Others fear that national testing will lead inevitably to Federal control of education.

OTA analyzed the development and effects of the current Federal role in testing and examined pending proposals to change that role. This chapter discusses OTA's findings vis-á-vis Chapter 1, NAEP, and national testing.

Chapter 1, Elementary and Secondary Education Act: A Lever on Testing

The passage of the 1965 Federal Elementary and Secondary Education Act (ESEA) heralded a new era of broad-scale Federal involvement in education and established the principle that with Federal education funding comes Federal strings. The cornerstone of ESEA was Title I (renamed Chapter 1 in 1981), which is still the largest program of Federal aid to elementary and secondary schools.[1] The purpose of Title I/Chapter 1, both then and now, is to provide supplementary educational services, primarily in reading and mathematics, to low-achieving children living in poor neighborhoods. With an appropriation of $6.2 billion for fiscal year 1991,[2] Chapter 1 channels funds to almost every school district in the country. Some 51,000 schools, including over 75 percent of the Nation's elementary schools, receive Chapter 1 dollars, which are used to fund services to about 5 million children in preschool through grade 12. Given its 25-year history and broad reach, the effect of Chapter 1 on Federal testing policy is profound.

History of Chapter 1 Evaluation

From the beginning, the Title I/Chapter 1 law required participating school districts to periodically evaluate the effectiveness of the program in meeting the special educational needs of educationally disadvantaged children, using ". . . appropriate objective measures of educational achievement"[3]—interpreted to mean norm-referenced standardized tests. Congress has revised the evaluation requirements many times to reflect changing Federal priorities and address new State and local concerns.

During the 1960s and 1970s, the Title I evaluation provisions generally became more prescriptive and detailed. In 1981, a dramatic loosening of Federal requirements occurred: while evaluations were still required, Federal standards governing the format, frequency, and content of evaluations were deleted. In the absence of Federal guidance, confusion about just what was required ensued at the State and local

[1]The remainder of this section is from Nancy Kober, "The Role and Impact of Chapter 1 Evaluation and Assessment Requirements," OTA contractor report, May 1991.

[2]Of this $6.2 billion, approximately $5.5 billion is distributed by formula to local school districts. The remainder is used for three State-administered programs for migrant students, students with disabilities, neglected and delinquent children, and for other specialized programs and activities, such as State administration and technical assistance.

[3]Public Law 89-10.

Photo credit: UPI, Bettmann

President Johnson signing the Elementary and Secondary Education Act of 1965 at a school in Johnson City, Texas. The enactment of this law was a milestone in Federal education policy.

levels. Congress responded by gradually retightening the evaluation requirements. The most recent set of amendments, the 1988 reauthorization, made Chapter 1 assessment more consequential and controversial than ever before by requiring Chapter 1 schools to modify their programs if they could not demonstrate achievement gains among participating children—the so-called ''program improvement provisions.''

Through all these revisions, the purposes of Title I/Chapter 1 evaluation have remained much the same: to determine the effectiveness of the program in improving the education of disadvantaged children; to instill local accountability for Federal funds; and to provide information that State and local decisionmakers can use to assess and alter programs.

Specific Requirements for Evaluating Programs

Title I/Chapter 1 is a partnership between Federal, State, and local governments, and the evaluation provisions reflect this division of responsibility. Evaluation of the effects of Chapter 1 on student achievement begins at the project level—usually the school. Test scores of participating children are collected from schools, analyzed, and summarized by the local education agency (LEA). Each LEA reports its findings to the State education agency (SEA), which aggregates the results in a report to the U.S. Department of Education. (States can, if they wish, institute additional requirements regarding the format, content, and frequency of Chapter 1 evaluations.) Congress, by statute, and the Department of Education, through regulations and other written guidance (particularly the guidance in the Department's Chapter 1 Policy Manual[4]), set standards for SEAs and LEAs to follow in evaluating and measuring progress of Chapter 1 students. The Department also compiles the State data and sends Congress a report summarizing the national achievement results, along with demographic data for Chapter 1 participants.

---

[4]U.S. Department of Education, *Chapter 1 Policy Manual* (Washington, DC: April 1990).

Standardized Tests and Mandated Evaluations

Since the creation of the Title I/Chapter 1 Evaluation and Reporting System (TIERS) in the mid-1970s, the Department has relied on norm-referenced standardized test scores as an available, straightforward, and economical way of depicting Chapter 1 effectiveness. The law, for its part, gives an imprimatur to standardized tests, through numerous references to "testing," "scores," "objective measures," "measuring instruments," and "aggregate performance." Chapter 1 evaluation has become nearly synonymous with norm-referenced standardized testing.

The purpose of TIERS has changed little since it became operative in 1979: to establish standards that will result in nationally aggregated data showing changes in Chapter 1 students' achievement in reading, mathematics, and language arts. To conform with TIERS, States and local districts must report gains and losses in student achievement in terms of Normal Curve Equivalents (NCEs), a statistic developed specifically for Title I. NCEs resemble percentile scores, but can be used to compute group statistics, combine data from different norm-referenced tests (NRTs), and evaluate gains over time. (Gains in scores, which can range from 1 to 99, with a mean of 50, reflect an improvement in position relative to other students.[5]) To produce NCE scores, local districts must use an NRT or another test whose scores can be equated with national norms and aggregated. Thus, although the Chapter 1 statute does not explicitly state that LEAs must use NRTs to measure Chapter 1 effectiveness, the law and regulations together have the effect of requiring NRTs because of their insistence on aggregatable data and their reliance on the NCE standard.

The 1988 law, as interpreted by the Department of Education, changed the basic evaluation provisions in ways that increased the frequency and significance of standardized testing in Chapter 1. Specifically, the law:

- through the new "program improvement" provisions, put teeth into the longstanding Title I/Chapter 1 requirement that LEAs use evaluation results to determine whether and how local programs should be modified. Schools with stagnant or declining aggregate Chapter 1 test scores must develop improvement plans, first in conjunction with the district and then with the State, until test scores go up.
- gave the Department the authority to reinstate national guidelines for Chapter 1 evaluation (which had been eliminated in 1981) and required SEAs and LEAs to conform to these standards.
- focused greater attention on (and, through regulation, required measurement of) student achievement in higher order analytical, reasoning, and problem-solving skills.
- directed LEAs to develop "desired outcomes," or measurable goals, for their local Chapter 1 programs, which could include achievement outcomes to be assessed with standardized tests.
- expanded the option for high-poverty schools to operate schoolwide projects,[6] as long as they can demonstrate achievement gains (i.e., higher test scores) among Chapter 1-eligible children.
- as interpreted by the Department, required LEAs to conduct a formal evaluation that met TIERS standards every year, rather than every 3 years. (In actual practice, most States required annual evaluations.)

Other Uses of Tests in Chapter 1

Producing data for national evaluations is only one of several uses of standardized tests in Chapter 1. Under the current law and regulations, LEAs are required, encouraged, or permitted to use tests for all the following decisions:

- identifying which children are eligible for Chapter 1 services and establishing a "cutoff score" to determine which children will actually be served;
- assessing the broad educational needs of Chapter 1 children in the school;

---

[5]Mary Kennedy, Beatrice F. Birman, and Randy E. Demaline, *The Effectiveness of Chapter 1 Services* (Washington, DC: U.S. Department of Education, 1986), p. E-2.

[6]Under the schoolwide project option, schools with 75 percent or more poor children may use their Chapter 1 funds for programs to upgrade the educational program for all children, without regard to Chapter 1 eligibility; in exchange for this greater flexibility, these schools must agree to increased accountability.

- determining the base level of achievement of individual Chapter 1 children before receiving services (the "pretest");
- assessing the level of achievement of Chapter 1 children after receiving services (the "post-test"), in order to calculate the change data required for national evaluations;
- deciding whether schools with high proportions of low-achieving children should be selected for projects over schools with high poverty;[7]
- allocating funds to individual schools;
- establishing goals for schoolwide projects;
- determining whether schoolwide projects can be continued beyond their initial 3-year project period;
- annually reviewing the effectiveness of Chapter 1 programs at the school level for purposes of program improvement;
- deciding which schools must modify their programs under the "program improvement" requirements;
- determining when a school no longer needs program improvement;
- identifying which individual students have been in the program for more than 2 years without making sufficient progress; and
- assessing the individual program needs of students that have participated for more than 2 years.

In addition, Congress and the Department of Education use standardized test data accumulated from State and local evaluations for a variety of purposes:

- justifying continued appropriations and authorizations;
- weighing major policy changes in the program;
- targeting States and districts for Federal monitoring and audits; and
- contributing to congressionally mandated studies of the program.

Competing Tensions

Chapter 1 is a good example of how Congress must weigh competing tensions when making decisions about Federal accountability and testing. For example, in Chapter 1, as in other education programs, the need for Federal accountability must be weighed against the need for State and local flexibility in program decisions. The Federal appetite for statistics must be viewed in light of the undesirable consequences of too much Federal burden and paperwork—lost instructional time and declining political support for Federal programs, to name a few. The Federal desire for succinct, "objective," and aggregatable data must be judged against the reality that test scores alone cannot provide a full and accurate picture of Chapter 1's other goals and accomplishments (e.g., redistributing resources to poor areas, mitigating the social effects of child poverty, building children's self esteem, and keeping students in school). Finally, the Federal need for summary evaluations on which to formulate national funding and policy decisions must be weighed against the local need for meaningful, child-centered information on which to base day-to-day decisions about instructional methods and student selection.

The number of times Congress has amended the Chapter 1 evaluation requirements suggests how difficult it is to balance these competing tensions.

Effects of Chapter 1 on Local Testing

Chapter 1 has helped create an enormous system of local testing. Almost every Chapter 1 child is tested every year, and in some cases twice a year, to meet national evaluation requirements. In school year 1987-88, over 1.6 million Chapter 1 participants were tested in reading and just under 1 million in mathematics. Sometimes this testing is combined with testing that fulfills State and local needs; other times Chapter 1 has caused districts to administer tests more frequently, or with different instruments, than they would in the absence of a Federal requirement.

Because SEAs and LEAs often use the same test instruments to fulfill both their own needs and Chapter 1 requirements, and because States and districts expanded their testing programs during roughly the period when Chapter 1 appropriations were growing, it is difficult, perhaps impossible, to sort out which entity is responsible for what degree of the total testing burden. Although States and districts often coordinate their Chapter 1 testing with other testing needs, many LEAs report that without

---

[7] A proposal to amend Title 1 so that all funding would be distributed on the basis of achievement test scores was put forth in the late 1970s by then-Congressman Albert Quie (R-MN). The proposal was not accepted, but a compromise provision was adopted, which remains in the law today, permitting school districts to allocate funds to schools based on test scores in certain limited situations.

Photo credit: Julie Miller, Education Week

Classrooms like this in Jefferson Parish, Louisiana, benefit from the extra assistance for disadvantaged students provided by Chapter 1 of the Elementary and Secondary Education Act. Testing has always been a big part of Chapter 1 activity.

Chapter 1, they would do less testing. A district administrator from Detroit, for example, estimated that her school system conducts twice as much testing because of Chapter 1.[8] The research and evaluation staff of the Portland (Oregon) Public Schools noted that in the absence of a Chapter 1 requirement to test second graders, their district would begin standardized testing later, perhaps in the third or fourth grade.[9] (In school year 1987-88, about 22 percent of Chapter 1 public and private school participants were in grades pre-K through one and were already exempted from testing. Another 26 percent of the national Chapter 1 population were in grades two and three; these children must be tested under current requirements.) One State Chapter 1 coordinator said that without Chapter 1, his State would require only its State criterion-referenced instrument, and not NRTs. At the school level,

principals and teachers express frustration with the amount of time spent on testing and tracking test data in Chapter 1 and the degree of disruption it causes in the academic schedule.

National studies of Chapter 1 and case studies of its impact in particular districts have uncovered some significant concerns about the appropriateness of using standardized tests to assess the program's overall effectiveness, make program improvement decisions, and determine the success of schoolwide projects. Over the years, Chapter 1 researchers and practitioners have raised a number of technical questions about the quality of Chapter 1 evaluation data and have expressed caveats about its limitations in assessing the full impact and long-term consequences of Chapter 1 participation. With the new requirements that raised the stakes of evaluation, debate over the data's validity and limitations has

[8]Sharon Johnson-Lewis, director, Office of Planning, Research and Evaluation, Detroit Public Schools, remarks at OTA Advisory Panel meeting, June 28, 1991.

[9]This and the other observations about the impact of Chapter 1 on testing practices are taken from Kober, op. cit., footnote 1. Case studies of the Philadelphia, PA, and Portland, OR, public schools helped inform OTA's analysis and are cited throughout this chapter.

become more heated. For example, there is evidence from Philadelphia, Portland, and other districts that because of measurement phenomena, test results do not always target for program improvement the schools with the lowest achievement or the weakest programs. Similarly, schools with schoolwide projects have argued that a 3-year snapshot based on test scores does not always provide adequate time or an accurate picture of the project's success compared with more traditional Chapter 1 programs.

State and local administrators have also expressed concerns about the effect of Chapter 1 testing on instruction. While administrators and teachers are loathe to admit to any practices that could be interpreted as ''teaching to the test,'' there is some evidence from case studies and national evaluations that teachers make a point to emphasize skills that are likely to be tested. In districts such as Philadelphia and Portland, where a citywide test tied to local curriculum is also the instrument for Chapter 1 evaluation, teachers can readily justify this practice. Discomfort arises, however, when local administrators and teachers feel they are being pressed by Federal requirements to spend too much time drilling students in the type of ''lower order'' skills frequently included on commercially published NRTs, or when teachers hesitate to try newer instructional approaches, such as cooperative learning and active learning, for fear their efforts will not translate into measurable gains.

Of more general concern is the broad feeling that for the amount of burden it entails, Chapter 1 test data is not very useful for informing local program decisions. According to case studies and other analyses, teachers and administrators use federally mandated evaluation results far less often than other more immediate and more student-centered evaluation methods—e.g., criterion-referenced tests (CRTs), book tests, teacher observations, and various forms of assessment—to determine students' real progress and make decisions about instructional practices. Frequently the mandated evaluations are viewed as a compliance exercise—a ''hoop'' that States and local districts must jump through to obtain Federal funding.

Although Chapter 1 teachers, regular classroom teachers, and administrators do occasionally employ

other types of assessment to make decisions about Chapter 1 students and projects, these alternative forms are not entrenched in the program in the same way that NRTs are, and are seldom considered part of the formal Chapter 1 evaluation process. While the Chapter 1 law contains some nods in the direction of alternative assessment—particularly for measuring progress toward desired outcomes and evaluating the effects of participation on children in preschool, kindergarten, and first grade—the general requirements for evaluation cause local practitioners to feel that NCE scores are the only results that really matter. They believe that alternative assessment will not become a meaningful component of Chapter 1 evaluation without explicit encouragement from Congress and the Department.

One bottom line question remains: what does the large volume of testing data generated by Chapter 1 evaluation tell Congress and other data users about the achievement of Chapter 1 children? To answer this question, it is useful to consider the data from a 10-year summary of Chapter 1 information, as shown in table 3-1.[10] The first thing that is apparent from the summary data is how the millions of individual test scores required for Chapter 1 evaluation are aggregated into a single number for each grade for each year. Average annual percentile gains in achievement—comparing average student pretest scores and average post-test scores—have hovered in the range of 2 to 6 percentiles in reading, and 2 to 11 percentiles in mathematics. For some grade levels, in some years, there have been greater improvements, but in general the gains have been modest and the post-test scores have remained low. For example, in 1987-88 the average post-test score for Chapter 1 fourth graders was the 27th percentile in reading and the 33rd percentile in mathematics. In analyzing these data it is important to understand that Chapter 1 children, by definition, are the lowest achieving students in their schools, and that once a child's test scores exceed the cutoff score for the district that child is no longer eligible for Chapter 1 services. There has been some upward trend, more pronounced in mathematics than in reading, but overall closing of the gap has been slow. In addition, because there is no control group for Chapter 1 evaluation, it is difficult to assess what these post-test scores really mean, i.e., how well Chapter

---

[10]For the complete tables of data referred to in this discussion, see U.S. Department of Education, *A Summary of State Chapter 1 Participation and Achievement Information for 1987-88* (Washington, DC: 1990).

Table 3-1—Achievement Percentiles for Chapter 1 Students Tested on an Annual Cycle, 1979-80 to 1987-88

| Grade | \multicolumn{9}{c}{Changes in percentile ranks for reading} |

Grade	1979-80	1980-81	1981-82	1982-83	1983-84	1984-85	1985-86	1986-87	1987-88
\multicolumn{10}{l}{Changes in percentile ranks for reading}
2	2	2	2	2	2	3	2	4	4
3	4	5	3	4	4	4	4	5	5
4	3	4	4	4	4	5	5	6	5
5	3	5	5	5	5	6	5	4	4
6	4	6	5	6	5	5	5	5	5
7	2	3	4	3	4	6	4	3	4
8	3	4	5	4	4	4	4	3	4
9	2	4	4	4	3	2	3	2	3
10	−1	2	1	2	1	2	2	2	2
11	−3	3	1	−1	0	2	3	3	2
12	2	0	2	0	1	0	0	2	0
\multicolumn{10}{l}{Changes in percentile ranks for mathematics}
2	2	5	5	3	6	6	9	10	11
3	1	3	5	5	6	4	6	7	7
4	3	6	5	4	5	6	6	8	8
5	4	4	6	8	7	7	9	7	7
6	6	8	6	8	7	6	7	7	7
7	4	3	5	7	5	6	6	5	4
8	4	5	5	6	5	5	4	4	5
9	1	1	2	3	1	2	2	5	4
10	−2	1	0	2	1	2	4	3	4
11	1	2	1	1	2	3	4	3	3
12	2	0	1	0	3	2	2	4	−1

SOURCE: Beth Sinclair and Babette Gutmann, *A Summary of State Chapter 1 Participation and Achievement Information for 1987-88* (Washington, DC: U.S. Department of Education, 1990), pp. 49-50.

1 children would achieve in the absence of any intervention.[11]

For purposes of this analysis, *the real question is whether the information from these test scores is necessary or sufficient to answer the accountability questions of interest to Congress.* For the disadvantaged population targeted by the program, the achievement score gains are evidence of improvement. Thus, when taken together with other evaluative evidence about the program's impact, the test scores support continued funding. But whether the test scores reveal anything significant about what and how Chapter 1 children are learning remains ambiguous. And in the light of unanticipated effects of the extensive testing, it is not clear that the information gleaned from the tests warrants the continuation of an enormous and quite costly evaluation system in its present form.

Ripple Effects of Chapter 1 Requirements

Title I/Chapter 1 established a precedent for achievement-based accountability requirements adopted in many subsequent Federal education programs. In the migrant education program added in 1966, the bilingual education program added in 1967, the Head Start program enacted in the Economic Opportunity Amendments of 1967, and programs that followed, Congress required recipients of Federal funds to evaluate the effectiveness of the programs funded.[12] As a result of Federal requirements, State and local agencies administer a whole range of tests—to place students, assess the level of participants' needs, and determine progress. Even when NRTs are not explicitly required, they are often the preferred mode of measurement for Federal accountability because they can be applied consistently, are relatively inexpensive, and leave a clearly under-

---

[11]One of the more vexing evaluation problems has been to infer ''treatment effects'' from studies with no control group. For discussion and analysis of methods designed to correct for ''regression to the mean'' and other statistical constraints, see Anand Desai, ''Technical Issues in Measuring Scholastic Improvement Due to Compensatory Education Programs,'' *Socio-Economic Planning Sciences*, vol. 24, No. 2, 1990, pp. 143-153.

[12]For discussion of outcome-based performance measures in vocational education and job training programs see, e.g., U.S. Congress, Office of Technology Assessment, ''Performance Standards for Secondary School Vocational Education,'' background paper of the Science, Education and Transportation Program, April 1989.

stood and justifiable trail for Federal monitors and auditors.

The 1965 ESEA had another, less widely recognized impact on State testing practices. Title V of the original legislation provided Federal money to strengthen State departments of education, so that they could assume all the administrative functions bestowed on them by the new Federal education programs. This program helped usher in an era of increased State involvement in education and would have a significant impact down the road as States assumed functions and responsibilities far beyond those required by Federal programs or envisioned by Congress in 1965.

Chapter 1 Testing in Transition

OTA finds that because of its size, breadth, and influence on State and local testing practices, Chapter 1 of ESEA provides a powerful lever by which the Federal Government can affect testing policies, innovative test development, and test use throughout the Nation.

OTA's analysis brings to light several reasons why Congress ought to reexamine and consider significant changes to the Federal requirements for Chapter 1 evaluation and assessment.

- National policymakers and State and local program administrators have different data needs, not all of which are well served by NRTs.
- The implementation of the 1988 program improvement and schoolwide project requirements has underscored some of the inadequacies and limitations of using NRTs for local program decisions, while simultaneously increasing the consequences attached to these tests.
- While the uses and importance of evaluation data have changed substantially as a result of the 1988 amendments, the methods and instruments for collecting this data have remained essentially the same since the late 1970s. A better match is needed between the new goals of the law, particularly the goal to improve the quality of local projects, and the tools used to measure progress toward those goals.

As Congress approaches Chapter 1 reauthorization, it should examine how all the pieces that affect testing under the umbrella of Chapter 1 fit

Photo credit: The Jenks Studio of Photography

Research has shown that early intervention is important, and many schools like this one in Danville, Vermont, use Chapter 1 funds for preschool and kindergarten programs.

together. Many pieces are interrelated, but they do not always work harmoniously. For example, the timing and evaluation cycles for Federal, State, and local testing in existing law are not well coordinated. As part of this review, Congress should pay particular attention to the need to revise language that inadvertently endorses norm-referenced testing in situations where that type of testing may be inappropriate. Options such as data sampling may meet congressional needs. Clearer legislative language could help maintain and improve accountability, because States and local districts would know better what was expected.

The following questions can guide congressional deliberations regarding changes in Chapter 1:

- What information does Congress need to make policy and funding decisions about Chapter 1? Is Congress getting that information, and is it timely and useful?
- What information does the Department of Education need to administer the program?
- How do the data needs of State and local agencies differ from those of the Federal Government and each other?
- Is it realistic to serve national, State, and local needs with the same information system based on the same measurement tool?
- How well do NRTs measure what Chapter 1 children know and can do?
- Is the nationally aggregated evaluation data that is currently generated accomplishing what

Congress intended? Specifically, do aggregates of aggregates of averages of NCE gains and negative gains present a meaningful and valid national picture of how well Chapter 1 children are achieving?

- To what extent is the value of cumulative data symbolic rather than substantive? For example, is being able to point to a rising line on a chart as important as having accurate, meaningful data about what Chapter 1 children know and can do? Can symbolic or oversight needs be fulfilled with less burdensome types of testing?
- What other types of data, beyond test scores, might meet Federal policymakers' criteria for objectivity?

In summary, OTA finds that Congress should revisit the Chapter 1 assessment and evaluation requirements in the attempt to lessen reliance on NRTs, reduce the testing burden, and stimulate the development of new methods of assessment more suited to the students and the program goals of Chapter 1. A careful reworking of the requirements could have widespread salutary effects on the use of educational tests nationwide. Congressional options for achieving these ends are identified in chapter 1 of this report.

National Assessment of Educational Progress

By the late 1960s, Title I/Chapter 1 and other Federal programs had produced a substantial amount of data concerning the achievement of disadvantaged children and other special groups of students. State and local testing told SEAs and LEAs how their students stacked up against national norms on specific test instruments. What was missing, however, was a context—a nationally representative database about the educational achievement of elementary and secondary school children as a group, against which to confirm or challenge inferences drawn from State, local, or other nationwide testing programs.

Although policymakers and the public could draw from a wide variety of statistics to make informed decisions on such issues as health and labor, they were operating in a vacuum when it came to education. The Department of Education produced a range of quantitative statistics on school facilities, teachers, students, and resources, but had never collected sound and adequate data on what American students knew and could do in key subject areas.

Francis Keppel, U.S. Commissioner of Education from 1962 to 1965, became troubled by this dearth of information and initiated a series of conferences to explore the issue.[13] In 1964, as a result of these discussions, the Carnegie Corp. of New York, a private foundation, appointed an exploratory committee and charged it with examining the feasibility of conducting a national assessment of educational attainments. By 1966, the committee had concluded that a new battery of tests—carefully constructed according to the highest psychometric standards and with the consensus of those who would use it—would have to be developed.[14]

The vision became a reality in 1969, when the U.S. Office of Education began to conduct periodic national surveys of the educational attainments of young Americans. The resulting effort, NAEP, sometimes called ''the Nation's report card,'' has the primary goal of obtaining reliable data on the status of student achievement and on changes in achievement in order to help educators, legislators, and others improve education in the United States.

Purpose

Today, NAEP remains the only regularly conducted national survey of educational achievement at the elementary, middle, and high school levels.[15] To date it has assessed the achievement of some 1.7 million young Americans. Although not every subject is tested during every administration of the program, the core subjects of reading, writing, mathematics, science, civics, geography, and U.S.

---

[13]In 1963, Keppel is reported to have lamented the fact that: ''Congress is continually asking me about how bad or how good the schools are and we have no dependable information. They give different tests at schools for different purposes, but we have no idea generally about the subjects that educators value. . . .'' OTA interview with Ralph W. Tyler, Apr. 5, 1991.

[14]This early history of the National Assessment of Educational Progress (NAEP) is taken from the National Assessment of Educational Progress, *General Information Yearbook* (Washington, DC: National Center for Education Statistics, 1974); and George Madaus and Dan Stufflebeam (eds.), *Educational Evaluation: Classic Works of Ralph W. Tyler* (Boston, MA: Kluwer Academic Publishers, 1989). Conversations with Frank Womer, Edward Roeber, and Ralph Tyler, all involved in different capacities in the original design and implementation of NAEP, enriched the material found in published sources.

[15]National Assessment of Educational Progress, *The Writing Report Card* (Princeton, NJ: Educational Testing Service, 1986).

Photo credit: Office of Technology Assessment, 1992

Known as the Nation's Report Card, the National Assessment of Educational Progress issues summary reports for assessments conducted in a number of academic subject areas. These reports also analyze trends in achievement levels over the past 20 years.

history have been assessed more than once to determine trends over time. Occasional assessments have also examined student achievement in citizenship, literature, art, music, computer competence, and career development.

Safeguards and Strengths

The designers of the NAEP project took extreme care and built in many safeguards to ensure that a national assessment would not, in the worst fears of its critics, become any of the following: a stepping stone to a national individual testing program, a tool for Federal control of curriculum, a weapon to "blast" the schools, a deterrent to curricular change,

or a vehicle for student selection or funds allocation decisions.[16] An understanding of NAEP's design safeguards is crucial in order to comprehend what NAEP was and was not intended to do and why it is unique in the American ecology of student assessment. NAEP has seven distinguishing characteristics.

NAEP reports **group data** only, not individual scores. NAEP results cannot be used to infer how particular students, teachers, schools, or districts are achieving or to diagnose individual strengths and weaknesses. Prevention of these levels of score reporting was a prerequisite to gaining approval for

---

[16]Tyler, op. cit., footnote 13.

the original development and implementation of NAEP.[17]

NAEP is essentially a battery of **criterion-referenced** tests in various subject areas (although its developers prefer the term "objective-referenced," since NAEP tests are not tied to any specific curriculum but measure the educational attainment of young Americans relative to broadly defined bodies of knowledge). Unlike many commercially published NRTs, NAEP scores cannot be used to rank an individual's performance relative to other students. This emphasis on criterion-referenced testing represents an important shift toward outlining how children are doing on broad educational goals rather than how they are doing relative to other students. NAEP is the only test to provide this kind of information on a national scale.

NAEP has pioneered a survey methodology known as **"matrix sampling."** This approach grew out of item-response theory, and has been hailed as an important contribution to the philosophy and practice of student testing.[18] Under this method, a sample of students across the country is tested, rather than testing all students (which would be considered a "census" design). Furthermore, the students in the matrix sample do not take a "whole" test, or even the same subject area tests, nor are they all given the same test items. Rather, each student takes a 1-hour test that includes a mix of easy, medium, and difficult questions. Thus, NAEP uses a method of sampling, not only of the students, but also of the content that appears on the test. Any student taking a NAEP test only takes one-seventh of the test in a 1-hour testing session. *Because of matrix sampling, a much wider range of content and goals can be covered by the test than most other tests can allow.* This broad coverage of content is the essential foundation of a nationally relevant test, as well as a test that is relatively well protected against the negative side effects that can occur with teaching to a narrow test. It is probable that these important strengths of NAEP, which make it a robust and nationally credible test, would be difficult to incor-

porate into a test designed to be administered to individuals (unless it were a prohibitively long test). In addition, because no individual students can be assigned scores, the matrix sampling approach imposes an important technological barrier against the use of NAEP results for making student, school, district, or State comparisons, or for sorting or selecting students.

NAEP provides **comparisons over time**, by testing nationally representative samples of 4th, 8th, and 12th graders on a biennial cycle. (Prior to 1980, NAEP tested on an annual cycle.) This form of sampling deters the kinds of interpretation problems that can arise when different populations of test takers are compared.[19] Due to cost constraints, the out-of-school population of students that had been sampled in early NAEP administrations was eliminated.

NAEP strives for **consensus about educational goals.** NAEP's governing board employs a consensus-building process for establishing content frameworks and educational objectives that are broadly accepted, relevant, and forward looking. Panels of teachers, professors, parents, community leaders, and experts in the various disciplines meet in different locales and work toward agreement on a common set of objectives for each subject area. These objectives are then given to item writers, who come up with the test questions. Before the items are administered to students, they undergo careful scrutiny by specialists in measurement and the subject matter being tested and are closely reviewed in the effort to eliminate racial, ethnic, gender, and other biases or insensitivities.[20]

Recognizing that changing educational objectives over time can complicate its mandate to plot trends in achievement, NAEP has developed a valuable process for **updating test instruments.** Using this process, NAEP revises test instruments to reflect new developments in curricular objectives, at the same time maintaining links between current and past levels of achievement of certain fixed objec-

[17]See, e.g., James Hazlett, University of Kansas, "A History of the National Assessment of Educational Progress, 1963-1973," unpublished doctoral dissertation, December 1973.

[18]The principles of matrix sampling are now used in many State assessment programs, as well as in other countries. See chs. 6 and 7 for additional discussion.

[19]For example, this was a major problem in using the decline in Scholastic Aptitude Test scores as a basis for the inference that overall achievement had fallen. See Robert Linn and Stephen Dunbar, "The Nation's Report Card Goes Home: Good News and Bad About Trends in Achievement," *Phi Delta Kappan*, vol. 72, No. 2, October 1990, pp. 127-133.

[20]National Assessment of Educational Progress, op. cit., footnote 15.

Photo credit: National Assessment of Educational Progress

In addition to information about the Nation as a whole, the National Assessment of Educational Progress (NAEP) reports for four regions of the country as well as by sex, race/ethnicity, and size and type of community. NAEP does not report results for individual students, but generates information by sampling techniques.

tives. In mathematics and reading, for example, representative samples of students are assessed using methods that have remained stable over the past 20 years, while additional samples of students are tested using instruments that reflect newer methods or changed definitions of learning objectives. Thus, the 1990 mathematics assessment allowed some students to use calculators, a decision generally praised by the mathematics teaching community. The NAEP authors took care to note, however, that the results of these samples were not commensurate with the mathematics achievement results from prior years.

Although NAEP is predominantly a paper-and-pencil test relying heavily on multiple-choice items, certain assessments include **open-ended questions or nontraditional formats.** For example: the writing assessment requires students to produce writing samples of many different kinds, such as a persuasive piece or an imaginative piece; the 1990 assessment also included a national "writing portfolio" of works produced in classrooms; the science assessment combines multiple-choice questions with essays and graphs on which students fill in a response; and the 1990 mathematics assessment included several questions assessing complex problem-

solving and estimation skills, as recommended by the mathematics teaching profession.

During its early years, NAEP experimented with even more varied test formats and technologies, conducting performance assessments in music and art that were administered by trained school personnel and scored by trained teachers and graduate students. Although many of its more innovative approaches were suspended due to Federal funding constraints,[21] many State testing programs continue to use the performance assessment technologies pioneered by NAEP. Moreover, NAEP continues to be a pioneer in developing open-ended test items that can be used for large scale testing; this is possible largely due to matrix sampling.

Accomplishments

All of these strengths have lent NAEP a degree of respect that is exceptional among federally sponsored evaluation and data collection efforts. NAEP has produced 20 years of unparalleled data and is considered an exemplar of careful and innovative test design. NAEP reports are eagerly awaited before publication and widely quoted afterward. In addition, NAEP collects background data about students' family attributes, school characteristics, and student attitudes and preferences that can be analyzed to help understand achievement trends, such as the relationship between television and reading achievement.

Because of NAEP, the Nation now knows, among other trends, that Black students have been narrowing the achievement gap during the past decade, 9-year-olds in general read better now than they did 10 years ago, able 13-year-olds do less well on higher order mathematics skills than they did 5 years ago, and children who do homework read better than those who do not.

Caveats

A relatively recent issue has emerged with potential consequences for NAEP administration and for interpretation of NAEP results. Researchers have begun to question whether NAEP scores tend to *underestimate* knowledge and skills of American students, precisely because NAEP is perceived as a low-stakes test. The question is whether students perform at less than their full ability in the absence

---

[21]For discussion of the 1974 funding crisis, see Hazlett, op. cit., footnote 17, pp. 297-299.

of extrinsic motivation to do well. It is not purely an academic question: much of today's debate over the future of American education and educational testing turns on public perceptions of the state of American schooling, perceptions based at least in part on NAEP.

Some empirical research on the general question of motivation and test performance has already demonstrated that the issue may be more important than originally believed. For example, one study found that students who received "... special instructions to do as well as possible for the sake of themselves, their parents, and their teachers ..." did significantly better on the Iowa Tests of Basic Skills than students in the control group who received ordinary instructions.[22] This result supports the general findings in research discussed in the preceding chapter;[23] and another analyst's observation that "... when a serious incentive is present (high school graduation), scores are usually higher."[24]

Prompted by these and other findings, several researchers are conducting empirical studies to determine the specific motivational explanations of performance on NAEP. One study involves experimental manipulation of instructions to NAEP test takers; the other involves embedding NAEP items in an otherwise high-stakes State accountability test.[25] Data are to be collected in spring 1992. The results of these studies will shed light on an important aspect of how NAEP scores should be interpreted.[26]

The 1988 Amendments

The original vision of NAEP has been diminished by years of budget cuts and financial constraints. Some of what NAEP once had to offer the Nation has been lost as a result. Concomitantly, over the past few years, new pressures have arisen in the attempt to adapt NAEP to serve purposes for which it was never intended. Some of this pressure has come from policymakers frustrated with the lack of effect of

NAEP results in shaping educational policy and the relatively "low profile" of the test and the results. Responding in part to this pressure, Congress took some cautious steps in 1988 to amend NAEP to provide new types of information.

One dilemma that surfaced during NAEP's first two decades was that its results did not appear to have much impact on education policy decisions, especially at the State and local levels. While theoretically NAEP could provide benchmarks against which State and local education authorities could measure their own progress, many educators argued that the information was too general to be of much help when they made decisions about resource allocations. Others observed that since NAEP carried no explicit or implicit system for rewards or sanctions, there was simply no incentive for States and localities to pay much attention to its results.

Had NAEP not been so highly respected, criticisms about its negligible influence on policy might have been considered minor, but given NAEP's reputation, its lack of clout was viewed as a major lost opportunity. Pressure mounted to change NAEP to make State and local education authorities take greater heed of its message. These voices for change were quickly met by experts who reissued warnings from the past: that any attempts to use NAEP for purposes other than analyzing aggregate national trends would compromise the value of its information and ultimately the integrity of the entire NAEP program.[27] The principal concerns were:

1. that turning NAEP into a high-stakes test would lead to the kinds of score "inflation" or "pollution" that have undermined the credibility of other standardized tests as indicators of achievement (see ch. 2); and

2. that using NAEP to compare student attainment across States would induce States to change their curricula or instruction for the

[22]Steven M. Brown and Herbert J. Walberg, University of Illinois at Chicago, "Motivational Effects on Test Scores of Elementary School Students: An Experimental Study," monograph, 1991.

[23]See Daniel Koretz, Robert Linn, Stephen Dunbar, and Lorrie Shepard, "The Effects of High Stakes Testing on Achievement: Preliminary Findings About Generalization Across Tests," paper presented at the annual meeting of the American Educational Research Association, Chicago, IL, April 1991.

[24]See Paul Burke, "You Can Lead Adolescents to a Test But You Can't Make Them Try," OTA contractor report, Aug. 14, 1991, p. 4.

[25]Robert Linn, University of Colorado at Boulder, personal communication, November 1991.

[26]For discussion of general issues regarding the public's understanding of National Assessment of Educational Progress scores, see Robert Forsyth, "Do NAEP Scales Yield Valid Criterion-Referenced Interpretations?" *Educational Measurement: Issues and Practice*, vol. 10, No. 3, fall 1991, pp. 3-9; and Burke, op. cit., footnote 24.

[27]The strongest early warnings about NAEP were found in Harold Hand, "National Assessment Viewed as the Camel's Nose," *Phi Delta Kappan*, vol. 47, No. 1, 1965, pp. 8-12; and Harold Hand, "Recipe for Control by the Few," *Educational Forum*, vol. 30, No. 3, 1966, pp. 263-272.

sake of showing up better on the next test, rather than as a result of careful deliberations over what should be taught to which students and under what teaching methods.

When NAEP came up for congressional reauthorization in 1988, it was amid a climate of growing public demands for accountability at all levels of education (fueled in part, ironically, by NAEP's own reports of mediocre student achievement in critical subjects). Almost a decade of serious education reform efforts had made little visible impact on American students' test scores, especially relative to those of international competitors.

Trial State Assessment

Congress responded by authorizing, for the first time, State-level assessments, to be conducted on a voluntary, trial basis. Beginning with the 1990 eighth grade mathematics assessment and the 1992 fourth grade mathematics and reading assessments, NAEP results were to be published on a State-by-State basis for those States that chose to participate. Congress considered this amendment a trial, to be followed up with careful evaluation, before the establishment of a full-scale, State-level NAEP program could be considered.

While proponents believed that the experiment would yield useful information for SEAs, critics worried that a State-by-State assessment would invite fruitless comparisons among States that did not take into account other factors influencing achievement; would put pressure on States to teach to the test or find other ways to artificially inflate scores; or would lead to general "education bashing." Most importantly, critics cautioned that with the State assessment Congress would eventually succumb to pressure to allow assessments and comparative reporting by district, by school, or even by student—a travesty of NAEP's original purpose and design.

Thirty-seven States, the District of Columbia, Guam, and the Virgin Islands participated in the first trial State assessment of mathematics, conducted in 1990. Results were released in June 1991.[28] As expected, some media reports focused on the inevitable question of: "Where does *your* State rank?" In

general, however, the consequences of the trial will not be apparent for some time. In addition to analyzing the effects of the trial on the quality and validity of NAEP data and on State and local policy decisions, observers are likely to focus on whether the information will be worth the high cost of administering the State assessments, and whether the cost of the State programs will crowd out other necessary expenditures or improvements in the basic NAEP program.

Standard Setting

The 1988 reauthorization made another fundamental revision in the original concept of NAEP. From its inception, NAEP had reported results in terms of proficiency scales, pegged to everyday descriptions of what children at that performance level could do. For example, a 200 score in reading meant that students ". . . have learned basic comprehension skills and strategies and can locate and identify facts from simple informational paragraphs, stories, and news articles."[29] NAEP has been commended for its accuracy in describing how things are. In the late 1980s, however, it came under criticism because it was silent on how things *ought to be*. Those who saw NAEP as a potential tool for reforming schools or measuring progress toward the President's and the Governors' National Goals for the year 2000 thought that NAEP should set proficiency standards—benchmarks of what students should be able to do. As with the statewide assessment proposal, the recommendation for proficiency standards raised the hackles of many educators, researchers, and policymakers. Opponents of the proposal said it would undermine local control of education; increase student labeling, tracking, and sorting; and compromise NAEP's original purpose and validity.

The 1988 amendments created a new governing body, the National Assessment Governing Board (NAGB), and charged it with identifying ". . . appropriate achievement goals for each age and grade in each subject area." NAGB has completed the standard-setting process for mathematics in 4th, 8th, and 12th grades, and in doing so, generated considerable controversy. Many observers felt that the

[28]See Ina V.S. Mullis, John A. Dossey, Eugene H. Owen, and Gary W. Phillips, Educational Testing Service, *The State of Mathematics Achievement*, prepared for the National Center for Education Statistics (Washington, DC: U.S. Department of Education, Education Information Branch, June 1991).

[29]For analysis of National Assessment of Educational Progress' definitions of literacy see John B. Carroll, "The National Assessments in Reading: Are We Misreading the Findings?" *Phi Delta Kappan*, vol. 68, No. 6, February 1987, pp. 424-430.

mathematics standards were hammered out too quickly, before true consensus was achieved.

Adding the trial State assessment and standard-setting activity increased NAEP funding from about $9.3 million in fiscal year 1989 to over $17 million in fiscal year 1990 (nominal dollars).

NAEP in Transition

When authorization for the trial State assessments and standard-setting processes expires, Congress will face the issue of whether to continue and expand these efforts. As of now, Congress has authorized planning for the 1994 trial, but has not appropriated funds for the implementation of the trial itself. The Administration's ''America 2000 Excellence in Education Act'' recommends authorization of State-by-State comparisons in five core subject areas (mathematics, science, English, history, and geography) beginning in 1994 as a means of monitoring (and stimulating) progress toward the National Goals. The Administration's bill also suggests that tests used in NAEP be made available to States that wish to use them for testing at school or district levels at their own expense.

In conclusion, the basic question facing Congress is whether to make NAEP even more effective at what it was originally intended to do, or to explore ways that NAEP could serve new purposes. OTA finds that any major changes in NAEP should be carefully evaluated with respect to potential effects on NAEP's capacity to serve its original purpose.

National Testing

Overview

Perhaps the proposals with the most far-reaching implications for the Federal role in testing are those calling for the creation and implementation of a national testing program. Although the objectives of the various national testing proposals are somewhat unclear, they appear to rest on two basic assumptions: first, that the skills and knowledge of most American schoolchildren do not meet the needs of a changing global economy; and second, that new tests can create incentives for the teaching and learning of the appropriate knowledge and skills. Momentum for these efforts has built rapidly, fueled by numerous governmental and commission reports on the state of the economy and of the educational system; by the National Goals initiative of the

Photo credit: National Assessment of Educational Progress

The National Assessment of Educational Progress has developed and pilot tested a variety of hands-on science and mathematics tasks. In this example, students watch an administrator's demonstration of centrifugal force and then respond to written questions about what occurred in the demonstration.

President and Governors; by casual references to the superiority of examination systems in other countries; and most recently by the President's ''America 2000'' plan.

Taken together, the questions of purpose and balance between local control and national interest frame the debate regarding the desirability of national testing. This debate must reflect both the needs of the Nation and the well being of individual students.

Congress provides the best forum for review of this question. Commitment to such a test represents a major change in education policy and should not be undertaken lightly. A number of issues must be considered in weighing the concept.

Will testing create incentives that motivate students to work harder? What are the effects of tests on the motivation of students? Tests should reward classroom effort, rather than undermine it. Tests built on comparing students to one another, for example, may reinforce the notion that effort does not matter, since the bell curve design of norm referencing always places some students at the top, some at the bottom, and most in the middle.

Furthermore, if the test is of no consequence to the students, they may not be motivated to try hard or to study to prepare for it. The motivation of those who do poorly on tests must be carefully considered. Those students who repeatedly experience failure on tests (starting in the earliest years of schooling), without any assistance or guidance to help them master test content, are unlikely to be motivated by a high-stakes test. Positive motivational effects are likely only if students perceive they have a good chance of achieving the rewards attached to strong test performance.

How broad will the content and skills covered be? Can just one test be offered to all students at a particular grade level, or will there need to be a range of tests at various levels and disciplines? This affects the testing burden on any one student and the range of levels at which testing can be focused. In some European countries, for example, students take subject-specific examinations at a choice of levels. Some examinations take many hours or are administered over several days, with combinations of testing items and formats that call on a range of performance by the student.

Would the test be voluntary or mandatory? Voluntary tests sound appealing. However, if a test becomes very widely used or needed for access to important resources, it will no longer be truly voluntary. Choosing not to take a test may not be a neutral option; negative consequences may result for those who choose not to be tested. This is especially true if a test is used for selection or credentialing; without a test result in hand, what chance does the student have? Furthermore, voluntary tests do not provide an accurate picture if the goal is school accountability. If only those students, schools, districts, or States that feel they can do well on a test participate in it, the results give an inaccurate picture of achievement. The claim that an important test can be voluntary should be taken with a grain of salt.

What happens to those who fail? Are there resources provided to help them? If consequences for failure are high and a student has no recourse once the examination has been taken, the wisest choice for a student who is having difficulty in school is to skip the examination altogether. The negative effects of examinations on students who do not do well have been a matter of serious concern in many European countries. Some countries have been dismayed to find that some students leave

school before required high-stakes examinations are offered, rather than face the indignity and stigma that accompanies failure. This has also occurred with high school graduation examinations in some parts of this country. Rather than punishing those who do not succeed at standards that seem unattainable, tests can be designed to make standards more explicit and the path to their acquisition more clear. However, if it is certain that low scores do not mean failure but that additional or refocused resources will be provided to the student, testing can have positive outcomes.

Who will design the tests and set performance standards? In the decentralized U.S. educational system, national testing proposals raise questions of State and local responsibility for determining what is taught and how it is taught. Can any test content be valid for the entire Nation? Who shall be charged with determining test content? It is important to recall that achievement tests by definition must assess material taught in the classroom. As the content of a test edges away from the specifics of what is delivered in classrooms, based on State-defined curricular goals, and searches instead for common elements, it can become either a test of ''basic skills'' or of more general skills and understandings. In the latter case, however, the test risks becoming more a measure of aptitude than one of achievement. (See also, ch. 6, box 6-A.) Similarly, setting performance standards on a national basis assumes the feasibility of consensus not only on what is taught and measured, but also on what constitutes acceptable performance, and on procedures to distinguish among levels of performance.

Will the content and grading standards be visible or invisible? Will the examinations be secret or disclosed? Experience from the classroom and other countries suggests that students are more motivated and will learn better when they understand what is expected of them and when they know what competent performance looks like. It is important to note that in Europe the impact of examinations on teaching and learning—what is taught and learned and how it is taught and learned—is mediated through the availability of past examination papers. The tradition in this country is just the opposite. Most high-stakes examinations are kept secret, in part because of high development costs. For a national examination to have salutary effects on learning, the additional costs of item disclosure should be weighed against the larger impact of the examination on teaching and learning.

Would the examination be administered at a single setting or several times, perhaps when students feel ready? This question affects students' control over the opportunity to study and prepare for an examination. If students can schedule a test when they feel they have mastered the material, they are more likely to be motivated by a realistic expectation of success. Conversely, accountability examinations are more likely to require single-sitting administration if they measure achievement within a common timeframe.

Do students have a chance to retake an examination to do better? Allowing retakes suggests a mastery model in which effort is rewarded and students can try again if they do not master the material the first time. It reinforces the idea that students can learn what they need to know.

Would the tests be administered to samples of students or individuals? If a test is intended to increase student motivation, then it will have to be an individual test. However, tests administered to individuals need safeguards to meet high technical standards if they will affect the future opportunities of individuals.

At what age are students to be tested? American elementary schoolchildren are tested far more often than their European counterparts, especially with standardized examinations. Much of the rationale for this testing is related to the selection of children for Chapter 1 services and for identification of progress within those programs. This testing has had a spill-over effect greatly influencing overall elementary school testing practice. However, the use of multiple-choice, standardized norm-referenced testing of elementary school children in general, and young (prior to grade three) children in particular, is under attack by those who see the negative consequences of early labeling. Thus, the suggestion of a new national examination at this age stands in contrast with efforts in many States to reduce early childhood standardized testing and to use instead teacher assessments, checklists, portfolios, and other forms of performance-based assessments.

What legal challenges might be raised? Legal challenges based on fairness have become a part of the American landscape. Public policy in this country is based on assurances of equal protection under the law; furthermore, cultural and racial diversity make equity issues far more significant in this country than in most others. Tests must meet these challenges by careful design that assures that the administration and scoring procedures are fair, the content measures what all participants have been taught, and the scores are used for the purposes understood and agreed to by the participants.

What test formats will be used? Tests send important signals to students about the kinds of skills and knowledge they need to learn. Tests that rely on a single format, such as multiple choice, are likely to send a limited message about necessary skills. As noted earlier, the United States and Japan are the only countries to rely almost exclusively on multiple-choice paper-and-pencil examinations for testing. Current proposals for national tests range from the use of multiple-choice norm-referenced standardized tests to the use of "state-of-the-art" assessment practices. Test format and procedures for scoring go hand in hand. Because performance assessments generally involve scoring by teachers or other experts, they are more expensive than machine-scorable tests. A diversity of formats in tasks and items may be the best means of balancing tradeoffs between the kinds of skills and understandings that any one test can measure and the costs of testing.

Conclusions

The answers to these questions will shed light on the larger questions of whether or not national testing is desirable. Goals must be clearly set to determine the kind of tests, content, costs, and potential linkages to curriculum. For example, if Congress sets as its goal increasing student effort for higher achievement by testing in specific subjects, one would expect mandatory tests, administered to all individuals, with the content made explicit through a common syllabus covering a broad scope of material, with past test items made public so students can study and practice for them. If other countries are to be a guide, this kind of examination is not used for testing children under the age of 16 or even 18. Some States are already using tests of this sort (e.g., New York Regents, California Golden State Examinations) for students as high school-leaving examinations. Congress should consider how the participation of these States would be affected, or how these tests could serve as models for use, or be calibrated to match some national standard.

Furthermore, if the goal is to encourage performance that includes direct measures of complex tasks, then written essays, portfolios of work over time, or oral presentations may be called for. These tests would be considerably more costly to develop, administer, and score than machine-scored norm-referenced examinations. Tests of this type are not as carefully researched and may be challenged if used prematurely for high-stakes outcomes like selection or certification.

At present, there is controversy over the use of many test results. The development and use of tests is complicated, both in terms of science and politics. **If a test is placed into service at the national level before these important questions are answered,** **OTA finds that the test could easily become a barrier to many of the educational reforms that have been set into motion and become the next object of concern and frustration within the American educational system.**

Congress should consider the questions of test desirability and use first, and then consider policy directions that emerge from these conclusions. This deliberation cannot be separated from a comprehensive look at the other issues discussed in this section, specifically, the role of NAEP in the national testing mosaic, the ways testing is used for Chapter 1 purposes, and how students' interests are to be protected. The policy implications of these choices are considered collectively in chapter 1.

Lessons From the Past: A History of Educational Testing in the United States

Contents

Lessons From the Past: A History of Educational Testing in the United States

Highlights

- Since their earliest administration in the mid-19th century, standardized tests have been used to assess student learning, hold schools accountable for results, and allocate educational opportunities to students.
- Throughout the history of educational testing, advances in test design and innovations in scanning and scoring technologies helped make group-administered testing of masses of students more efficient and reliable.
- High-stakes testing is not a new phenomenon. From the outset, standardized tests were used as an instrument of school reform and as a prod for student learning.
- Formal written testing began to replace oral examinations at about the same time that American schools changed their mission from servicing the elites to educating the masses. Since then tests have remained a symbol of the American commitment to mass education, both for their perceived objectivity and for their undeniable efficiency.
- Although standardized tests were seen by some as instruments of fairness and scientific rigor applied to education, they were soon put to uses that exceeded the technical limits of their design. A review of the history of achievement testing reveals that the rationales for standardized tests and the controversies surrounding test use are as old as testing itself.

The burgeoning use of tests during the past two decades—to measure student progress, hold students and their schools accountable, and more generally solidify various efforts to improve schooling—has signified to some observers a "... profound change in the nature and use of testing. ...."[1] But the use of tests for the dual purposes of measuring and influencing student achievement is not a historical anomaly. The three principal rationales for student testing—classroom feedback; system monitoring; and selection, placement, and certification—have their roots in practices that began in the United States more than 150 years ago. And many of the points that frame the testing debate today, such as the potential for test misuse, echo arguments that have been sounded since the beginning of standardized student testing.

This chapter surveys the evolution of student testing in American schools, and develops four themes:

1. Tests in the United States have always been used to ascertain the effects of schooling on children, as well as to manage school systems and influence curriculum and pedagogy. Tests designed and administered from beyond classrooms have always been more useful to administrators, legislators, and other school authorities than to classroom teachers or students, and have often been most eagerly applied by those seeking school reform.

2. The historical use of standardized tests in the United States reflects two fundamentally American beliefs about the organization and allocation of educational opportunities: fairness and efficiency. The fairness principle involves, for example, assurances to parents that their children are offered opportunities similar to those given children in other schools or neighborhoods. Efficiency refers to the orderly provision of educational services to all children. These have been the foundation blocks for the

---

[1] George Madaus, quoted in Edward B. Fiske, "America's Test Mania," *The New York Times*, Apr. 10, 1988, section 12, p. 18. See ch. 3 of this report for a detailed account of the rise of testing in the 1970s and 1980s.

297-933 0 – 92 – 8 QL 3

American system of mass public schooling; testing has been a key ingredient of the mortar.

3. Increased testing has engendered tension and controversy over its effects. These tensions reflect the centrality of schooling in American life, and competing visions of the purposes and methods of education within American pluralism. *Demand* for tests stems in large part from demand for fair treatment of all students; the *use* of tests, however, especially for sorting and credentialing of young persons, has always raised its own questions of fairness.

4. As long as schooling continues to play a central role in American life, and as long as tests are used to assess the quality of education, testing will occupy a prominent place on the public policy agenda. The search for better assessment technologies will continue to be fraught with controversies that have as much to do with testing per se as with conflicting visions of American ideals and values.

This chapter focuses on testing through four chronological periods. The first section begins with the initial educational uses of standardized written examinations in the mid-19th century and continues through the development of mental (intelligence) measurement near the end of that century. The next section covers the onset of intelligence and achievement testing in the schools, a movement spurred largely by managerial and administrative concerns and supplied, in large part, with the newly developing tools of "scientific" testing. The third section focuses on trends in educational testing from the end of World War I through the end of World War II, a period marked by important technological advances as well as refinements in the art and science of testing. The last section of this chapter is a discussion of the pivotal role of testing in the struggle for racial equality, increased educational access, and international technological competitiveness in the years after World War II.

Achievement Tests Come to American Schools: 1840 to 1875

Overview

The period from 1840 to 1875 established several main currents in the history of American educational testing. First, formal written testing began to replace oral examinations administered by teachers and schools at roughly the same time as schools changed their mission from servicing the elite to educating the masses. Second, although the early standardized examinations were not designed to make valid comparisons among children and their schools, they were quickly used for that purpose. Motivated in part by a deep commitment to fairness in educational opportunities, the use of tests soon became controversial precisely over challenges to their fairness as a basis for certain types of comparisons—challenges leveled by some teachers and school leaders, although not by the most active crusaders on behalf of free and universal education. Third, the early written examinations focused on the basics—the major school subjects—even though the objectives of schooling were understood to be considerably broader than these topics. Finally, from their inception standardized tests were perceived as instruments of reform:[2] it was taken as an article of faith that test-based information could inject the needed adrenalin into a rapidly bureaucratizing school system.

Demography, Geography, and Bureaucracy

Tests of achievement have always been part of the experience of American school children. In the colonial period, school supervisors administered oral examinations to verify that children were learning the prescribed material. Later, as school systems grew in size and complexity, the design, purposes, and administration of achievement testing evolved in an effort to meet new demands. Well before the Civil War, schools used externally mandated written examinations to assess student progress in specific curricular areas and to aid in a

---

[2]"Reform" means different things to different people, especially with respect to education. In this report, the word is intended neutrally, i.e., as "change," although it clearly connotes the intention to improve, upgrade, or widen children's educational experiences. The possibility that good intentions can lead to unintended consequences is the central theme in such works as Michael B. Katz, *The Irony of Early School Reform* (Cambridge, MA: Harvard University Press, 1968). See also Lawrence Cremin, *The Transformation of the School: Progressivism in American Education, 1876-1957* (New York, NY· Vintage Books, 1964) for an even broader exploration of change, i.e., as "transformation" of the school.

variety of administrative and policy decisions.[3] As early as 1838 American educators began articulating ideas that would soon be translated into the formal assessment of student achievement.

What were the main factors that led to this interest in testing? What were the main purposes for testing? Some of the answers lie in the demography and political philosophy that shaped the 19th century American experience.

Between 1820 and 1860 American cities grew at a faster rate than in any other period in U.S. history, as the number of cities with a population of over 5,000 increased from 23 to 145.[4] That same period saw an average annual immigration of roughly 125,000 newcomers, mostly Europeans (see figure 4-1).[5] Coincident with this immigration and urbanization, the idea of universal schooling took hold. By 1860 "... a majority of the States had established public [primary] school systems, and a good half of the nation's children were already getting some formal education."[6] Some States, like Massachusetts, New York, and Pennsylvania, were moving toward free secondary school as well.

Although it is difficult to establish a causal link between these demographic and educational changes, surely one thing that attracted European immigrants was the ideal of opportunity embodied in the American approach to universal schooling. Following his visit to the United States in 1831 to 1832, the Frenchman Alexis de Tocqueville shared with his countrymen his conviction that there was no other country in the world where "... in proportion to the population there are so few ignorant and at the same time so few learned individuals. Primary instruction is within the reach of everybody; superior instruction is scarcely obtained by any."[7]

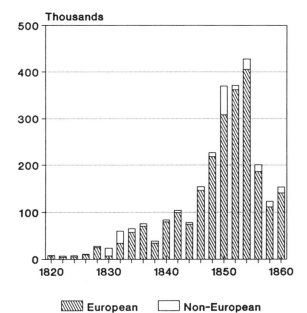

Figure 4-1—Annual Immigration to the United States: 1820-60

SOURCE: Office of Technology Assessment, based on data from U.S. Department of Commerce, Bureau of the Census, *Historical Statistics of the United States, Colonial Times to 1970* (Washington, DC: 1975), pp. 105-111.

At the same time, it could be argued that population growth and increased heterogeneity necessitated the crafting of institutions—such as universal schooling—to "Americanize" the masses. The 20th century social philosopher Hanah Arendt wrote, for example, that education has played a "... different, and politically incomparably more important, role [in America] than in other countries," in large part because of the need to Americanize the immigrants.[8]

The concept of Americanization extended well beyond the influx of immigrants who arrived in the latter half of the 19th century, however. The

[3]Many historians of American educational testing focus on the influence of the intelligence testing movement, which began at the end of the 19th century. See, e.g., Daniel Resnick, "The History of Educational Testing," *Ability Testing: Uses, Consequences, and Controversies*, part 2, Alexandra Wigdor and W. Garner (eds.) (Washington, DC: National Academy Press, 1982), pp. 173-194; or Walter Haney, "Testing Reasoning and Reasoning About Testing," *Review of Educational Research*, vol. 54, No. 4, winter 1984, pp. 597-654.

[4]David Tyack, *The One Best System: A History of American Urban Education* (Cambridge, MA: Harvard University Press, 1974), p. 30.

[5]U.S. Department of Commerce, Bureau of the Census, *Historical Statistics of the United States: Colonial Times to 1970*, part 1 (Washington, DC: U.S. Government Printing Office, 1975), p. 106.

[6]Cremin, op. cit., footnote 2, p. 13. This chapter relies heavily on Cremin's work, but also on important educational historiography of David Tyack, Michael Katz, Ira Katznelson, Margaret Weir, and Carl Kaestle.

[7]See Alexis de Tocqueville, *Democracy in America*, vol. 1 (New York, NY: Vintage Books, July 1990), p. 52.

[8]Hannah Arendt, "The Crisis in Education," *Partisan Review*, vol. 25, No. 4, fall 1958, pp. 494-495. See also Diane Ravitch, *The Great School Wars: New York City, 1805-1973* (New York, NY: Basic Books, 1974), p. 171, for her treatment of some of the early American educators (like William Henry Maxwell in New York) who saw schooling as the "... antidote to problems that were social, economic, and political in nature."

foundation for a political role for education had already been laid in the colonial and post-Revolutionary periods, as religious, educational, and civic leaders began considering the possible relationships between lack of schooling, ignorance, and moral delinquency. These leaders, especially in the burgeoning cities, advocated public schooling for poor children who lacked access to church-run charity schools or to common pay schools (schools available to all children in an area but for which parents paid part of the instructional costs).

Up until the mid-19th century, the pattern of education consisted of private schools run by paid tutors, State-chartered academies and colleges with more formal programs of instruction, benevolent societies, and church-run charity schools—in sum, a "hodge-podge" reflecting the many:

> . . . motives that impelled Americans to found schools: the desire to spread the faith, to retain the faithful, to maintain ethnic boundaries, to protect a privileged class position, to succor the helpless, to boost the community or sell town lots, to train workers or craftsmen, to enhance the virtue or marriageability of daughters, to make money, even to share the joys of learning.[9]

Population growth and density created new strains on schools' capacity to provide mass education.[10] According to census statistics, public school enrollments grew from 6.8 million in 1870 to 15.5 million by 1900. By the turn of the century, almost 80 percent of children aged 5 to 17 were enrolled in some kind of school.[11] Mass public education could no longer be viable without fundamental institutional adaptations. Expanding enrollments also placed new strains on the public till as public school began overshadowing private and charity schools. In direct expenditures, the percentage of total education spending attributable to the public schools grew from less than one-half in 1850 to more than 80 percent in 1900.[12] In terms of foregone income as well, the costs were impressive: the income that students aged 10 to 15 would have earned were they not in school increased from an estimated nearly $25 million in 1860 to almost $215 million in 1900.[13] Not surprisingly, this spending inevitably led to calls for evidence that the money was being used wisely.

The size and concentration of the growing student population increased the taxpayers' burden and created new institutional demands for efficiency similar to those that governed the evolving nature of many American institutions. One way schools could demonstrate sound fiscal practice was by organizing themselves according to principles of bureaucratic management. "Crucial to educational bureaucracy was the *objective and efficient classification*, or grading, of pupils."[14] According to Henry Barnard, a prominent figure in the common school movement, it was not only inefficient, but also inhumane, to fill a classroom with children of widely varying ages and *attainment*.[15] On this assumption, the mid-19th century reformers sought additional information that would make the classification more rational and efficient than the prevailing system of classification, based primarily on age. They turned their attention toward achievement tests.

The result was one of many ironies in the history of educational testing: the classification and grouping of students, essentially a Prussian idea, became a pillar in the public school movement that was an American creation. No less an American educational statesman than Horace Mann, who saw universal

---

[9]David Tyack and Elisabeth Hansot, *Managers of Virtue: Public School Leadership in America, 1820-1980* (New York, NY: Basic Books, 1982), p. 30. See also Katz, op. cit., footnote 2, p. 131. Katz writes that: ". . . the duty of the school was to supply that inner set of restraints upon passion, that bloodless adherence to a personal sense of rights, which would counteract and so reform the dominant tone of society."

[10]For a more detailed analysis of the shifts from rural to urban education, see, e.g., Tyack, op. cit., footnote 4. Also, see Michael B. Katz, *Class, Bureaucracy, and Schools* (New York, NY: Praeger, 1972).

[11]Bureau of the Census, op. cit., footnote 5, p. 369. See also Tyack, op. cit., footnote 4, p. 66, who cites a report by W.T. Harris with similar data.

[12]Tyack and Hansot, op. cit., footnote 9, p. 30.

[13]Ibid., p. 44, emphasis added.

[14]Ibid., p. 44, emphasis added. It is worth recalling that the early exponents of bureaucracy spoke of its formalism—manifest in classification systems of the type discussed here—in positive terms, i.e., as an improvement over earlier forms of organization that were at once less fair and less efficient. See, e.g., Max Weber, *The Theory of Social Economic Organization*, edited and translated by A.M. Henderson and T. Parsons (New York, NY: MacMillian Publishing Co., 1947). The appeal of tests as both fair and efficient tools of management is a main theme in this chapter.

[15]Tyack, op. cit., footnote 4, p. 44, emphasis added. Barnard's lifelong commitment to school improvement for the masses, coupled with his belief in the importance of conserving the social and economic status of the privileged classes, personifies an important aspect of the American experiment with democratic education. See also Merle Curti, *The Social Ideas of American Educators* (Paterson, NJ: Pageant Books, Inc., 1959), pp. 139-168.

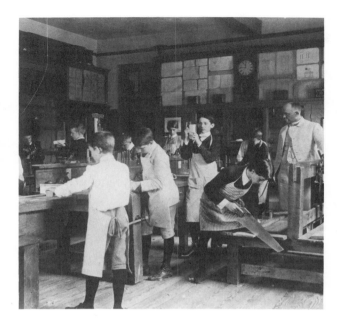

Teachers have always assessed student performance directly. These photos were taken circa 1899 for a survey of Washington, DC schools.

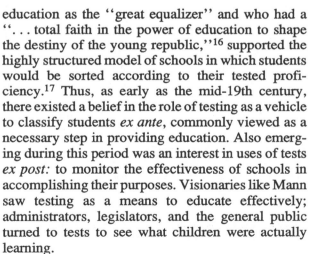

education as the "great equalizer" and who had a "... total faith in the power of education to shape the destiny of the young republic,"[16] supported the highly structured model of schools in which students would be sorted according to their tested proficiency.[17] Thus, as early as the mid-19th century, there existed a belief in the role of testing as a vehicle to classify students *ex ante*, commonly viewed as a necessary step in providing education. Also emerging during this period was an interest in uses of tests *ex post:* to monitor the effectiveness of schools in accomplishing their purposes. Visionaries like Mann saw testing as a means to educate effectively; administrators, legislators, and the general public turned to tests to see what children were actually learning.

In fact, it was during Horace Mann's tenure as Secretary of the (State) Board of Education that Massachusetts became the site of "... the first reported use of a written examination ... *after some harassment by the State Superintendent of Instruction about the shortcomings of the schools....*"[18] From its inception, this formal written testing had two purposes: to classify children (in pursuit of more efficient learning)[19] and to monitor school systems by external authorities. Under Mann's guidance, the State of Massachusetts moved from subjective oral examinations to more standardized and objective written ones, largely for reasons of efficiency. Written tests were easier to administer and offered a streamlined means of classifying growing numbers of students.

[16]Cremin, op. cit., footnote 2, pp. 8-9.

[17]Katz, op. cit., footnote 2, pp. 139-140.

[18]Resnick, op. cit., footnote 3, p. 179, emphasis added.

[19]Tyack, op. cit., footnote 4, p. 45. Tyack notes that classification preceded standard examinations: "... the proper classification was only the beginning. In order to make the one best system work, the schoolmen also had to design a uniform course of study and standard examinations." But he does not describe the criteria for classification used prior to the standard examinations, which would be important to analyze the comparative fairness of formal and informal classification systems. It appears, though, always to have involved some type of proficiency testing, the difference being between the looser and more subjective classroom-based tests and the more formal externally administered tests.

It is important to point out what "standardization" meant in those days. It did not mean "norm-referenced" but rather that ". . . the tests were published, that directions were given for administration, that the exam could be answered in consistent and easily graded ways, and that there would be instructions on the interpretation of results."[20] The model was quite consistent with the assumed virtues of bureaucratic management. The efficient flow of information was not unique to education or educational testing; it was becoming a ubiquitous feature of American society.[21]

Perhaps more important, though, was the evolving role of testing as a vehicle to ensure fairness and evenhandedness in the distribution of educational resources: *one way to ascertain whether children in the one-room rural schoolhouse were receiving the same quality of education as their counterparts in the big cities was to evaluate their learning through the same examinations.* Thus, standardized testing came to serve an important symbolic function in American schools, a sort of technological embodiment of principles of fairness and universal access that have always distinguished American schools from their European and Asian counterparts. As the methods of testing later became increasingly quantitative and "scientific" in appearance, the tests gained from the growing public faith in the ability of science and rational decisionmaking to better mankind.

But Mann had other reasons for introducing standardized testing. He had been engaged in an ideological battle with the Boston headmasters, who perceived him as a "radical." This disagreement reflected a wider schism in the Nation between reformers like Mann who believed in stimulating student interest in learning through greater emphasis on the "real world," and hard-liners who believed in discipline, rote recitation, and adherence to texts.[22] Although Mann and his compatriots eventually won, setting American public education on a unique historical course, one of their more potent weapons in the battle was one that might today be associated with a hard-line, top-down approach to school reform: when two of Mann's allies were appointed to examine the status of the grammar schools, ". . . they gave written examinations with questions previously unknown to the teachers [and] . . . published a scathing indictment of the Boston grammar schools in their annual report. . . ."[23]

The Logic of Testing

The fact that the first formal written examinations in the United States were intended as devices for sorting and classifying but were used also to monitor school effectiveness suggests how far back in American history one can go for evidence of test misuse. The ways in which these tests were used for monitoring was logical: to find out how students and their schools are performing, it made sense to conduct some sort of external measurement process. But the motivation for the standardized examinations in Massachusetts was, in fact, more complicated and reveals a pattern that would become increasingly familiar. *The idea underlying the implementation of written examinations, that they could provide information about student learning, was born in the minds of individuals already convinced that education was substandard in quality.* This sequence—perception of failure followed by the collection of data designed to document failure (or success)—offers early evidence of what has become a tradition of school reform and a truism of student testing: tests are often administered not just to discover how well schools or kids are doing, but rather to obtain external *confirmation*—validation—of the hypothesis that they are not doing well at all.[24]

---

[20]Resnick, op. cit., footnote 3, p. 179.

[21]George Madaus, for example, writes that the movement toward standardization and conformity began in 1815 with efforts in the Army Ordnance Department to develop ". . . administrative, communication, inspection, accounting, bureaucratic and mechanical techniques that fostered conformity and resulted in the technology of interchangeable parts . . . [and that] these techniques . . . were well known throughout the textile mills and machines shops of New England when Horace Mann introduced the standardized written test. . . ." George Madaus, "Testing as a Social Technology," unpublished monograph, Inaugural Annual Boisi Lecture on Education and Public Policy, Boston College, Dec. 6, 1990, pp. 26-27. See also Katz, op. cit., footnote 2, pp. 5-11, for an account of the dramatic changes in the structure and management of American business during Mann's lifetime.

[22]See Katz, op. cit., footnote 10, pp. 115-153, for a fuller discussion of the origins and ramifications of this ideological struggle.

[23]Ibid., p. 152. See also Madaus, op. cit., footnote 21.

[24]Although testing was not yet considered a scientific enterprise (that would come later in the century, with the emergence of psychology and the concepts of mental measurement—see below), the logic of its application had traces of the inductive model: from empirical observations of the schools, to hypotheses explaining those observations, to the more systematic and less anecdotal collection of data in order to test the hypotheses. For a physicist's views on the basic fallacies in mental "measurement," however, see David Layzer, "Science or Superstition? A Physical Scientist Looks at the IQ Controversy," *The IQ Controversy: Critical Readings*, N.J. Block and Gerald Dworkin (eds.) (New York, NY: Pantheon Books, 1976), pp. 194-241.

The use of formal, written achievement tests in Massachusetts (and soon afterwards in many other places), as already emphasized, was motivated largely by administrative concerns.[25] The tests themselves often focused on a rather narrow set of outcomes, selected principally to put the headmasters in the worst possible light. There was a profound mismatch between the content covered in those early achievement tests and the objectives of common schooling those tests were intended to gauge. Given the schools' broad democratic agenda, and given the environment of demographic and geographic shift in which the agenda was to be carried out, the estimation of educational quality by a "... test of thirty questions on the subjects scheduled for study during the year ... given to about half the eighth grade, one thousand students,"[26] is a telling early example of the limitations of tests in measuring the range of knowledge students acquire during a school year.

From their inception, written achievement tests were among the more potent weapons of reform of teaching and school administration. For example, Samuel Gridley Howe, an ally of Mann, looked to tests to provide "... a single standard by which to *judge and compare the output of each school,* 'positive information in black and white,' [in place of] the intuitive and often superficial written evaluation of oral examinations."[27]

The tests Mann and Howe encouraged covered a narrow range of school material; there was no attempt to link students' test performance with specific features of school organization or pedagogy; and the schoolmasters usually selected which students took the tests.[28] But these technical issues did not interfere with the use of test results as a basis for reform. Mann, for one, successfully convinced

his fellow Bostonians that the tests were able to "... determine, beyond appeal or gainsaying, whether the pupils have been faithfully and competently taught."[29] Teachers, for their part, went along with the testing as long as they saw it as a way to wield power over their students.[30]

Effects of Test Use

Not surprisingly, soon after the first application of tests came criticisms that have also become a steady presence in school life. First, there was public amazement at the poor showing of the test-takers: "Out of 57,873 possible answers, students answered only 17,216 correctly and accumulated 35,947 errors in punctuation in the process. Bloopers abounded: one child said that rivers in North Carolina and Tennessee run in opposite directions because of 'the will of God.'" Second, it was feared that the tests were driving students to learn by rote: ... [according to Howe] they could give the date of the embargo but not explain what it did."[31]

Nevertheless, test use continued, and from the earliest applications, test use raised key questions. Consider, for example, that the main beneficiaries of test information were not the teachers and principals, who might have used it to change aspects of their specific institutions, but rather State-level policymakers and administrators. Thus, while there might have been a casual acceptance of the principle that tests could provide information necessary to effect change, there was apparently much less agreement—or perhaps just simple naivete—as to how and where the changes would be initiated. "The most important reported result, *an unintended one from the standpoint of the [Boston] school committee,* was to make city teachers and principals accountable to supervisory authority at the State level."[32] Tests became

[25]Schools were not alone in their growing admiration for quantification. Prison reformers, abolitionists, and others were also fond of statistics. For a lucid discussion of the reverence for science and quantitative methods, which would peak at the turn of the century, see Paula S. Fass, "The IQ: A Cultural and Historical Framework," *American Journal of Education,* vol. 88, No. 4, August 1980, pp. 431-458.

[26]Resnick, op. cit., footnote 3, p. 179.

[27]Tyack, op. cit., footnote 4, p. 35, emphasis added.

[28]"Even within the grade, [the Boston test] was not a fair sample of students, since the schoolmasters were free to choose who would take the test." Resnick, op. cit., footnote 3, p. 179.

[29]Quoted in Paul Chapman, *Schools as Sorters: Lewis M. Terman, Applied Psychology, and the Intelligence Testing Movement, 1890-1939* (New York, NY: New York University Press, 1988), p. 33.

[30]Robert Hampel, University of Delaware, personal communication, May 1991.

[31]Tyack, op. cit., footnote 4, p. 35. According to Tyack, Howe knew how "abstruse and tricky" the test items were, but thought it was a fair basis for comparison of students nonetheless. Given the reference to punctuation errors, it seems that the tests included at least some written work; in any event, we know that multiple choice was not invented until several decades later, which suggests that test format is not the sole determinant of content validity, fairness, or the tendency to learn.

[32]Resnick, op. cit., footnote 3, p. 180, emphasis added.

important tools for education policymakers, despite their apparently limited value to teachers, students, and principals.

A related development offers yet another illustration that current problems in educational testing are not all new. Although the written examinations were intended to provide information about schools and students, that information was not necessarily meant to become a basis for *comparisons*. Yet that is quickly what happened, as illustrated in the case of examinations used for high school admission: "Although only a minority of students took the [standard short-answer] exam, performance [on the exam] . . . could function, within the larger communities, to compare the performance of classes from different feeder schools."[33]

The case cited in this example points to a pervasive dilemma in the intended and actual uses of tests. On the one hand, information about student performance was understood to be essential as a basis for organizing classroom learning and judging its output; on the other hand, once the information was created, it was quickly appropriated to uses for which it had not been designed—specifically, to comparisons among schools and districts. The fact that the jurisdictions were different in so many fundamental ways as to render the comparisons virtually meaningless did not seem to matter. Nevertheless, by the 1870s many school leaders were beginning to question the comparisons: ". . . a careful observation of this practice for years has convinced me that such comparisons are usually unjust and mischievous."[34] At the same time, there was widespread agreement that ". . . the classroom was part of the production line of the school factory [and that] examinations were the means of judging the value added to the *raw material . . .* during the course of the year."[35]

In the latter part of the 19th and early 20th centuries, changing demography would continue to influence school and test policy. Other factors would also begin to play a role: the development of psychology and "mental measurement" as a science, and the increasing influence of university and business interests on performance standards for the

secondary schools. These are the main topics in the next section of the chapter.

Science in the Service of Management: 1875 to 1918

During the period from 1875 to the end of World War I, the development and administration of a range of new testing instruments—from those that sought to measure mental ability to those that attempted to assess how well students were prepared for college—brought to the forefront several critical issues related not only to testing but to the broader goals of American education. First, as instruments that were designed to discern differences in individual intelligence became available, the concept of classifying and placing students by ability gained greater acceptance, even among those who espoused the democratic ideals of fairness and individuality.

Second, as research on mental measurement continued, it gave rise to new debates about the role of heredity in determining intellectual ability and the effects of education. Some theorists used the results of intelligence and aptitude tests to support claims of natural hierarchy and of racial and ethnic superiority.

Third, mirroring the structural changes occurring in businesses and other American institutions, school systems reorganized around the prevailing principles of efficient management: consolidation of small schools and districts, classification of students, bureaucratization of administrative responsibilities. Within these new arrangements, tests were viewed as an important efficiency tool.

Fourth, by the end of World War I, standardized achievement tests were available in a variety of basic subjects, and the possibilities for large-scale group testing had been demonstrated. The results of these tests gave reformers (including college presidents) ammunition in their push for improvements in educational quality.

Fifth, the implementation of mass testing in World War I ushered in a new era of educational testing as well.

---

[33]Ibid. For an indepth study of the role of tests and other criteria in admissions decisions at Philadelphia's Central High School, see David F. Labaree, *The Making of an American High School: The Credentials Market and the Central High School of Philadelphia, 1838-1939* (New Haven, CT: Yale University Press, 1988), especially chs. 3 and 4.

[34]Emerson White (an early leader in the National Education Association), quoted in Tyack, op. cit., footnote 4, p. 49.

[35]John Philbrick, quoted in ibid., p. 49, emphasis added.

Issues of Equity and Efficiency

The analysis in the preceding section of this chapter raises a perplexing question about the role of testing in American education: how could the emerging American and democratic theory of education be reconciled with standardized tests that covered, at best, a small portion of what schooling was supposed to accomplish, and, at worst, were used in ways that violated basic democratic principles of fairness? Part of the answer in the early years of testing lay in the role of curriculum in the public school philosophy. Horace Mann, for example, was "... inclined to accept the usual list of reading, writing, spelling, arithmetic, English grammar, and geography, with the addition of health education, vocal music (singing would strengthen the lungs and thereby prevent consumption), and some Bible reading."[36] Thus, it might be argued that one reason Mann favored the formal examinations was that they signaled the importance of learning the major subjects, which, in his view, was the first step toward achieving the broader goals of morality, citizenship, and leadership. Learning the major subjects was a necessary—if insufficient—condition for education writ large.[37]

Another factor was that because standardized tests were new, there was no established methodology for designing them or judging whether test scores accurately reflected learning. Furthermore, school reformers seemed relatively unconcerned that emphasizing the basics might compromise the broader objectives of schooling. Generally they viewed the basics as just that: the necessary building blocks on which the broader objectives of education could be erected.

If that explanation helps resolve the curious acceptability of short tests as proxies for complex educational goals, it does not offer any obvious clues to the paradox that the use of tests to track students had its roots in the movement to universalize and democratize education. Again, Mann's thinking on the subject can shed some light. Although "Mann was one of the first after Rousseau to argue that education in groups is not merely a practical necessity but a social desideratum,"[38] he had an equally powerful belief in individuality. Mann's answer was to tailor lessons in the classroom to meet the needs of individual children: "... children differ in temperament, *ability*, and interest ..." and need to be treated accordingly.[39] From here, then, it was not a far leap to embracing methods that, because they were purported to measure those differences, could be used to classify children and get on with the educational mission.

Mann was not alone. The American pursuit of efficiency would become the hallmark of a generation of educationists, and would create the world's most fertile ground for the cultivation of educational tests.

An Intellectual Bridge

Some social scientists have characterized mental measurement—a branch of psychology that blossomed during the late 19th and early 20th centuries and prefigured modern psychological testing—as "... the most important single contribution of psychology to the practical guidance of human affairs."[40] Psychological testing was able to flourish because of its appeal to individuals of nearly every ideological stripe. It was not just the hereditarians and eugenicists who were attracted to such concepts as "intelligence" and the "measurement" of mental ability; many of the early believers in the measurement of mental and psychophysical processes were progressives, egalitarians, and communitarians committed to the betterment of all mankind.

Mann, for one, embraced phrenology—an approach to the assessment of various cognitive capacities based on physical measurement of the size of areas of the brain—without reservation, joining the ranks of such advocates as Ralph Waldo Emerson, Walt Whitman, William Ellery Channing, Charles Sumner, and Henry Ward Beecher, as well

---

[36]Cremin, op. cit., footnote 2, p. 10.

[37]The belief that learned persons were better, in the moral sense, has been pervasive throughout the history of American education. See, e.g., Curti, op. cit., footnote 15. A major figure in the measurement of ability and achievement, Edward Thorndike, produced empirical results showing the high correlation between intellectual attainment and morality. See, e.g., Tyack and Hansot, op. cit., footnote 9, p. 156.

[38]Cremin, op. cit., footnote 2, p. 11.

[39]Ibid.

[40]Lee Cronbach, "Five Decades of Public Controversy Over Mental Testing," *American Psychologist*, January 1975.

as a host of respected physicians.[41] Phrenology attributed good or base character traits to differences in physical endowments; Mann and others saw in this doctrine a persuasive rationale for education as a means of cultivating every individual's admirable *propensities* and checking his coarser ones. One might say, then, that phrenology symbolized to Mann a unique chance to mobilize support for social intervention.[42]

Phrenology was a methodological bridge from crude comparisons based on written achievement examinations, to measures that were at once more scientifically rigorous and more sensitive to innate differences in ability.[43] The principal intelligence researchers whose work would ultimately be translated into the American science of mental testing—Galton, Wundt, and Binet—had each dabbled in phrenology before devising their methods for assessing human intelligence.

Mental Testing

In the late 19th century, European and American psychologists began independently seeking ways to corroborate and measure individual differences in mental ability. Sir Francis Galton in England and J. McKeen Cattell in the United States conducted a series of studies—mostly dealing with sense perception but some focusing on intellectual aptitude—that may be said to mark the beginning of modern intelligence testing.[44] It was Cattell, in fact, who coined the term "mental test" in a paper published in 1890.

In an effort to trace the hereditary origins of mental differences, Galton conducted the first em-

pirical studies of the heritability of mental aptitude and developed the first mental test, although he did not call it that.[45] Although the more extreme views of some of these early researchers have long since been repudiated, and although some veered off into distasteful and unsupportable conclusions about hereditary differences (see box 4-A), their work nevertheless stimulated interest in intelligence testing that persists today.

The French psychologist and neurologist Alfred Binet also had a very strong influence on the development of intelligence tests in America and on their uses in schools, although not necessarily in the ways Binet himself would have liked. Empirically based definitions of intelligence and accounting explicitly for age were two of Binet's most important contributions to the science of mental testing. For Binet "intelligence" was not a measurable trait in and of itself, like height or weight; rather, it was only meaningful when tied to specific observable behaviors. But what behaviors to observe? Answering this question led Binet to his second major insight: ability to perform various mental behaviors varied with the age of the individual being observed. His research, therefore, consisted of giving children of different ages sets of tasks to perform; from their performances he computed average abilities—for those tasks—and how individual children compared on those tasks.[46] Neither the concept that intelligence existed as a unitary trait, nor the concept that individuals have it in fixed amounts from birth, are attributable to Binet. Moreover, to Binet and coworker Theodore Simon, intelligence meant ". . . judgment, otherwise called good sense, practical

[41]About Mann's attraction to phrenology, historian Lawrence Cremin wrote: "It reached for naturalistic explanation of human behavior; it stimulated much needed interest in the problem of child health; and it promised that education could build the good society by improving the character of individual children. What a wonderful psychology for an educational reformer!" Op. cit., footnote 2, p. 12.

[42]Curti, op. cit., footnote 15, pp. 110-111. Michael Katz points out that ". . . to Mann and others of his time [intelligence] meant . . . a capacity that could be developed, not an innate limit on potential . . . an important point because it shows that 'intelligence' is partly a social/cultural construction that we shouldn't reify. . . ." Personal communication, Aug. 18, 1991.

[43]The history of phrenology contains some amusing ironies. Franz Gall, for example, one of the founders of the discipline, had to suffer the embarrassment of having his own brain weigh in "at a meager 1,198 grams," considerably lighter than the brains of real geniuses like Turgenev. For discussion see Stephen Jay Gould, *The Mismeasure of Man* (New York, NY: Norton, 1981), p. 92. And Francis Galton, whose own phrenologist surmised that his ". . . intellectual capacities are not distinguished by much spontaneous activity in relation to scholastic affairs. . . ." (Raymond E. Fancher, *The Intelligence Men: Makers of the IQ Controversy* (New York, NY: W.W. Norton & Co., 1985), p. 24), was later credited with launching the science of individual differences and of mental testing.

[44]Walter S. Monroe, *Ten Years of Educational Research, 1918-1927* (Urbana, IL: University of Illinois, 1928), p. 89.

[45]Borrowing methods of data collection and analysis from mathematics and astronomy, he also invented a statistical procedure that his student Karl Pearson would later turn into what is still the most powerful tool in the statistician's arsenal, the correlation coefficient.

[46]Had the United States' move to universal public schooling begun in the late 19th century, and not in the middle, it is likely that the first achievement tests (described in the first section of this chapter) would have been more focused on innate ability and aptitude rather than on mastery of subjects taught in school. As will be shown below, however, the strands of ability and achievement ultimately did converge, largely due to the work of Terman and Thorndike.

Box 4-A—Mental Testers: Different Views

Although Charles Darwin himself never extrapolated from his biological and physical theory of evolution to evolution of cognitive abilities, Sir Francis Galton, his second cousin, made the leap. Galton's basic theory was that mental abilities were distributed unevenly in the population, and that while a certain amount of nurturing could have an effect, there was, as with physical ability, an upper bound predetermined by one's natural (genetic) endowments.

At the same time, researchers in the German laboratory of Wilhelm Wundt had also been involved in early studies of mental differences, with a focus on physical differences in sensation, perception, and reaction time. Apparently Wundt himself was not terribly interested in the development of tests for mental processes independent of the physical senses, but some of his students in the United States—such as Cattell—became prominent figures in the debate over hereditary origins of intelligence.

Although the name of Alfred Binet is commonly associated with the notion of IQ, Binet himself had strong reservations about using intelligence test data to classify and categorize children, and was opposed to the reduction of mental capacities to a single number. One reason had to do with his awareness of the difficulty of keeping the data purely objective. Another reason was his fear that "... individual children [would be] placed in different categories by different diagnosticians, using highly impressionistic diagnostic criteria ... [and] ... that the diagnosis was of particular moment in borderline cases."[1]

With his colleague Theodore Simon, Binet undertook an inductive study of children's intelligence: "... they identified groups of children who had been unequivocally diagnosed by teachers or doctors as mentally deficient or as normal, and then gave both groups a wide variety of different tests in their hopes of finding some that would differentiate between them."[2] Eventually they developed the key insight that the age of the child had to be considered in examining differences in test performance. The 1905 Binet/Simon test proved a workable model to make discriminations among the normal and subnormal populations of children. Binet, it should be noted, differed with many of his contemporaries on the role of heredity in intelligence. Binet believed that intelligence was fluid, "... shaped to a large extent by each person's environmental and cultural circumstances, and quantifiable only to a limited and tentative degree."[3]

Binet's followers took a different road than Binet himself would likely have chosen. Unlike those who worked in the tradition of Galton and who focused on measurement of young adults at the upper end of the ability distribution, Binet had devoted much of this part of his career to diagnosing retardation among children at the lower end of the distribution. And in fact, Binet's view of intelligence as a blend of multiple psychological capacities—attention, imagination, and memory among them—is enough to distinguish him from a generation of intelligence testers who followed, especially in the United States.

---

[1]Raymond E. Fancher, *The Intelligence Men: Makers of the IQ Controversy* (New York, NY: W.W. Norton & Co., 1985), p. 70.

[2]Ibid., p. 70.

[3]Ibid., p. 82.

---

sense, initiative, the faculty of adapting one's self to circumstances. ... A person may be a moron or an imbecile if he is lacking in judgment; but with good judgment he can never be either."[47] These characteristics of the Binet-Simon tradition were altered when the concepts of mental testing were imported to the United States.

Several Americans revised the Binet-Simon scale and adapted it for use in the United States. Stanford Professor Lewis Terman was perhaps the most

influential and successful of the American mental testers. His 1912 revisions, called the Stanford Revision, caught on quickly and marked the beginning of large-scale individual intelligence testing in the United States.[48] As discussed in box 4-A, the *technology* of intelligence testing in the United States—in particular the connection between test performance and age in the formation of intelligence scales—was directly influenced by Binet; but the *philosophy underlying the use and interpretation of*

---

[47]A. Binet and T. Simon, *The Development of Intelligence in Children*, translated by E.S. Kite (Baltimore, MD: Williams and Wilkins, 1916), pp. 42-43. For discussion of the Binet-Simon tradition in intelligence testing, see, e.g., Robert Sternberg, *Metaphors of Mind* (Cambridge, England: Cambridge University Press, 1990).

[48]Monroe, op. cit., footnote 44, p. 90.

the tests was inherited from Galton and his followers. Several historians have noted the mixed lineage of American testing; one has summarized it eloquently, noting that:

> . . . it was only as the French concern with personality and abnormality and the English preoccupation with individual and group differences, as measured in aggregates and norms, were superimposed on the older German emphasis on laboratory testing of specific functions that mental testing as an American science was born.[49]

Testing in Context

There is a tendency in the psychological literature to overstate the influence of Galton, Binet, and the other pioneers of mental testing on the demand for educational tests among American school authorities. That demand grew from a range of social and economic forces that produced similar calls for efficiency and compartmentalization in the workplace. Interest in the application of tests undoubtedly would have arisen even without the hereditarian influences of Galton and others who thought humankind could be bettered through gradual elimination of the subnormally intelligent.[50]

What was happening in the schools in the midst of these intellectual storms? For one thing, immigration was becoming an even more dominant influence on American political and social thinking. By 1890, some 15 percent of the American population was foreign born, and the quest for Americanization was continuing full steam. These ''new'' immigrants came from Southern and Eastern Europe (Austria, Hungary, Bulgaria, Italy, Poland, and Russia among others), and their numbers were beginning to overtake the traditional immigrants arriving from Northern Europe (Anglo-Saxons, French, Swiss, and Scandinavians). The effects on schools were staggering.

These abrupt demographic shifts affected many aspects of American life, but schools had a unique charge to maintain order in a society undergoing massive change and fragmentation and to inculcate American democratic values into massive numbers of immigrants. ''Just as mass immigration was a symbol for—even the embodiment of—cultural

Photo credit: Tamara Cymanski, OTA staff

Schools in America have played a central role in preparing immigrants for life in their new home. Challenged by the goals of educating massive numbers of newcomers fairly and efficiently, schools relied heavily on standardized testing.

disruption, education became its dialectical opposite, an instrument of order, or direction, of social consolidation.''[51] Because American schools were committed to principles of democratic education and universal access, instruments designed to bring order to schools without violating principles of fairness and equal access were extremely attractive.

Indeed, standardized tests offered even more than that. For one thing, they held promise as a tool for assessing the current condition of education, a means to gather the data from which reforms for integrating the masses could be designed. In what was perhaps the first effort to blend objective evaluation with journalistic-style muckraking, Joseph Mayer Rice conceived the idea of giving a uniform spelling test (and later, arithmetic and language tests) to large numbers of pupils in selected

---

[49]Fass, op. cit., footnote 25, p. 433. See also Cremin, op. cit., footnote 2, p. 100.

[50]See, e.g., Gould, op. cit., footnote 43, for a fuller discussion of the role of testing in the eugenics movement and how it influenced public policy in the 1920s and 1930s.

[51]Fass, op. cit., footnote 25, p. 432.

cities. His findings, published in 1892, were based on data he had collected on some 30,000 children, and documented the absence of a relationship between the time schools spent on spelling drills and children's performance on objective tests of spelling.[52] "In one study, [Rice] . . . found that [instructional time] varied from 15 to 30 minutes per day at different grade levels . . . [but that] tests of student performance on a common list of words revealed that the extra 15 minutes a day made no difference in demonstrated spelling ability."[53] When Rice's results were presented to a major meeting of school superintendents in 1897, they were ridiculed; ultimately, however, a few farsighted educators concurred with Rice's analysis.[54]

Managerial Efficiency

Schools were not alone in their attempts to adapt to changing times. The following description of change in the railroad industry could just as well describe emerging trends in school administration:

> . . . it meant the employment of a set of managers to supervise . . . functional activities over an extensive geographical area; and the appointment of an administrative command of middle and top executives to monitor, evaluate, and coordinate the work of managers responsible for the day-to-day operations. It meant, too, the formulation of brand new types of internal administrative procedures and accounting and statistical controls. . . .[55]

In other sectors of American enterprise, engineers, researchers, and managers were applying scientific principles to enhance efficiency. In agriculture, for example, research and technology was transforming the nature and scale of farming. Progressive educators, who were familiar with the commercial precedents, ". . . commonly used the increased productivity of scientific farming as an analogy for the scientifically designed educational system they hoped to build."[56]

The newly evolving business organizations also employed modes of classification and bureaucratic control that bore remarkable similarity to those adopted by school systems as they shifted from largely rural, decentralized organizations to urban, centralized ones. "Scientific management," a relatively late addition to the set of new business organizational principles invented around the turn of the century, was based on the proposition that managers could ascertain the abilities of their workers and assign them accordingly to the jobs where they would be the most productive.

Managerial efficiency was but one way in which business thinking coincided with school policy. The other principal point of convergence had to do with the demand for "skilled" labor. Just as division of labor according to ability was seen as a vehicle to improve productivity on the shop floor, classification and ranking of students was seen as a prerequisite to their efficient instruction. The relationship is perhaps best illustrated by the statements of Harvard President Charles Eliot, in 1908. Society, he said, is:

> . . . divided . . . into layers . . . [with] distinct characteristics and distinct educational needs . . . a thin upper [layer] which consists of the managing, leading, guiding class . . . next, the skilled workers . . . third, the commercial class . . . and finally the thick fundamental layer engaged in household work, agriculture, mining, quarrying, and forest work. . . . [The schools could be] . . . reorganized to serve each class . . . to give each layer its own appropriate form of schooling.[57]

It was an obvious leap, then, for business executives to join with progressives in calling for reform of schools along the corporate model. Hierarchy, bureaucracy, and classification—all served by the science of testing—would become the institutional environment charged with producing educated persons capable of functioning in the hierarchical, bureaucratic, and classified world of business.[58]

---

[52]Haney, op. cit., footnote 3, p. 600.

[53]Resnick, op. cit., footnote 3, p. 180.

[54]Monroe, op. cit., footnote 44, pp. 88-89.

[55]Alfred Chandler, *The Visible Hand: The Managerial Revolution in American Business* (Cambridge, MA: Harvard University Press, 1977), p. 87. Chandler's description of changes in railroad management suggests another analogy with school administration. Daily reports—from conductors, agents, and engineers—detailed every aspect of railroad operations; these reports, along with information from managers and department heads, were used to make day-to-day decisions and, at the executive level, to compare the performance of operating units with each other and with other railroads (p. 103).

[56]Tyack and Hansot, op. cit., footnote 9, p. 157.

[57]Tyack, op. cit., footnote 4, p. 129.

[58]For a critical analysis of testing and social/economic stratification in the United States, see, e.g., Clarence Karier, "Testing for Order and Control in the Corporate Liberal State," in Block and Dworkin (eds.), op. cit., footnote 24, pp. 339-373.

The advocates of the corporate model of school governance, such as Stanford Education Dean Ellwood P. Cubberley, argued that to manage efficiently, the modern school superintendent needed "rich and accurate flows of information" on enrollments, buildings, costs, student promotions, and student achievement.[59] Cubberley advocated the creation of "scientific standards of measurement and units of accomplishment" that could be applied across systems and used to make comparisons. Fulfilling this need for data, Cubberley maintained, would require new types of school employees—efficiency experts ". . . to study methods of procedure and to measure and test the output of its works";[60] a recommendation that indeed came to pass as large, urban systems hired census takers, business managers, and eventually evaluation experts and psychologists.

Achievement and Ability Vie for Acceptability

Despite initial opposition from teachers, the use of achievement tests as instruments of accountability began to gain support. By 1914 the National Education Association was endorsing the kind of standardized testing that Rice had been urging for two decades. The timing was exquisite: on one front, there was the "push" of new technology that promised to be valuable to testing, and on the other, a heightened "pull" for methods to bring order to the chaotic schools.

Two approaches to testing competed for dominance in the schools in the early 20th century. One had its antecedents in the intelligence testing movement, the other in the more curriculum-oriented achievement testing that grew out of Rice's examples.

Between 1908 and 1916, Edward Thorndike and his students at Columbia University developed standardized achievement tests in arithmetic, handwriting, spelling, drawing, reading, and language ability. Composed of exercises to be done by students, the arithmetic test was similar in format to the types of tests traditionally administered by teachers. The handwriting and composition tests, by contrast, consisted of samples of handwriting and essays against which pupil performances were compared.[61] By 1918, there were well over 100 standardized tests, developed by different researchers to measure achievement in the principal elementary and secondary school subjects.[62]

Student achievement was not all that would come under the microscope of standardized assessment. In the first decade of the 20th century, following the advice of Cubberley and other advocates of scientific management, ". . . leaders of the school survey movement examined and quantified virtually every aspect of education, from teaching and salaries to the quality of school buildings."[63] Indeed, Thorndike's proclamation of 1918—"whatever exists at all exists in some amount"—formed the cornerstone of his educational measurement edifice.[64] By 1922, John Dewey would lament the victory of the testers and quantifiers with these words: "Our mechanical, industrialized civilization is concerned with averages, with percents. The mental habit which reflects this social scene subordinates education and social arrangements based on averaged gross inferiorities and superiorities."[65]

Thorndike's approach to achievement tests mirrored in important ways that taken by reformers in Massachusetts some 70 years earlier: just as they had reached a foregone conclusion about the quality of Boston schools before the first tests were given, Thorndike's tests actually came *after* he had already decided that the schools were failing. His 1908 study of dropouts, followed the next year by a remarkable statistical analysis conducted by Leonard Ayres,

---

[59]Tyack and Hansot, op. cit., footnote 9, p. 157.

[60]Ellwood P. Cubberly, *Public School Administration* (Cambridge, MA: The Riverside Press, 1916), p. 338.

[61]Monroe, op. cit., footnote 44, p. 90.

[62]Cremin, op. cit., footnote 2, p. 187. A report by Walter Monroe in 1917 documented over 200 such tests. See Chapman, op. cit., footnote 29, p. 34.

[63]Chapman, op. cit., footnote 29, pp. 34-35.

[64]In later writings, Thorndike was more humble. For example, he wrote: "Existing instruments (for measuring intellect) represent enormous improvements over what was available twenty years ago, but three fundamental defects remain. Just what they measure is not known; how far it is proper to add, subtract, multiply, divide, and compute ratios with the measures obtained is not known; just what the measures obtained signify concerning intellect is not known. . . ." Edward L. Thorndike, E.O. Bregman, M.V. Cobb, and Ella Woodyard, *The Measurement of Intelligence* (New York, NY: Columbia University, Teachers College, Bureau of Publications, 1927).

[65]Tyack, op. cit. footnote 4, p. 198.

KANSAS STATE NORMAL SCHOOL.

Test II.

State Normal School.
EMPORIA, KAN.
Bureau of Educational Measurements and Standards.

Put Pupil's Score Here.

THE KANSAS SILENT READING TEST.

Devised by F. J. Kelly

FOR

Grades 6, 7 and 8.

City............................ State..................... Date...............

Pupil's Name.. Age........... Grade.............

School.................................... Teacher.................

Directions for Giving the Tests.

After telling the children not to open the papers ask those on the front seats to distribute the papers, placing one upon the desk of each pupil in the class. Have each child fill in the blank spaces at the top of this page. Then make clear the following:

Instructions to be Read by Teacher and Pupils Together.

This little five-minute game is given to see how quickly and accurately pupils can read silently. To show what sort of game it is, let us read this:

Below are given the names of four animals. Draw a line around the name of each animal that is useful on the farm:

cow   tiger   rat   wolf

This exercise tells us to draw a line around the word cow. No other answer is right. Even if a line is drawn *under* the word cow, the exercise is wrong, and counts nothing. The game consists of a lot of just such exercises, so it is wise to study each exercise carefully enough to be sure that you know exactly what you are asked to do. The number of exercises which you can finish thus in five minutes will make your score, so do them as fast as you can, being sure to do them right. Stop at once when time is called. Do not open the papers until told, so that all may begin at the same time.

The teacher should then be sure that each pupil has a good pencil or pen. Note the minute and second by the watch, and say, BEGIN.

Allow exactly five minutes.

Answer no questions of the pupils which arise from not understanding what to do with any given exercise.

When time is up say STOP and then collect the papers at once.

Photo credit: Rutgers University Press

The first educational test using the multiple-choice format was developed by Frederick J. Kelly in 1915. Since then, multiple choice has become the dominant format of standardized achievement tests.

called attention to an alarming problem.[66] For reasons that neither Thorndike nor Ayres professed to understand entirely, the schools were full of students who were not progressing. In New York City, for example, Ayres reported that 23 percent of the 20,000 children studied were above the normal age for their grade.

Where could concerned educators of the time turn for explanations? It is useful to review in this context the staggering demographic changes of the time, a phenomenon that so utterly consumed the collective psyche that Thorndike, Ayres, or anyone else thinking about the schools could not have helped but try to explain their findings in terms of the changing national origin of students. Between 1890 and 1917, the total U.S. population grew from 63 million to over 100 million, largely as a result of immigration. During the same period, the population aged 5 to 14 grew from just under 17 million to over 21 million; similarly, the public school enrollment rate climbed from about 50 percent in 1900 to 64 percent in 1920, and average daily attendance went from 8 million to just under 15 million.[67]

The effects of immigration and population growth on the issues Thorndike and Ayres grappled with, however, were somewhat surprising. While Ayres's initial research question—"Is the immigrant a blessing or a curse?"[68]—reveals something about the anti-immigrant zeitgeist, his answers, based on the data analysis he presented, revealed a healthy objectivity. Ayres concluded that:

1. there was no evidence that the problems of students being above normal age for their grade or dropping out were most serious in those cities having the largest foreign populations;

2. "... children of foreign parentage drop out of the highest grades and the high school faster than do American children;

3. ... there are more illiterates among the native whites of native parentage than among the native whites of foreign parentage;"[69] and

4. "... the proportion of children five to fourteen years of age attending school is greater among

---

[66]See Leonard Ayres, *Laggards in Our Schools: A Study of Retardation and Elimination in City School Systems* (New York, NY: Russell Sage Foundation, Charities Publication Committee, 1909), p. 8.

[67]For analysis of the effects of child labor laws on school attendance, see David Goldston, History Department, University of Pennsylvania, "To Discipline and Teach: Compulsory Education Enforcement in New York City, 1874-94," unpublished monograph, n.d.

[68]Ayres, op. cit., footnote 66, p. 103.

[69]Ibid., p. 115. Ayres did not cite the source for his illiteracy statistics, which he presumably collected himself. Census data suggest a somewhat different picture from the one presented by Ayres. In 1900, for example, about 5 percent of the native white population was estimated to be illiterate, as compared to almost 13 percent of the foreign born. Had Ayres included the census category "Negro" (and other races), he might have found—as did the census—a staggering illiteracy rate of 44 percent in 1900. See Bureau of the Census, op. cit., footnote 5, Series H 664-668, p. 382.

those of foreign parentage and foreign birth than among Americans."[70]

Finally, he concluded from his analysis that: ". . . in the country at large [the schools] reach the child of the foreigner more generally than they do the child of the native born American," which was a source of great humiliation to "national pride."[71]

Experimentation and Practice

Although Ayres may not have been aware of it, his work actually vindicated the basic tenets of the achievement-oriented testers, who tended to focus on school curricula and the extent to which children were actually mastering the substantive content of schooling. Their approach to assessment was to develop quantitative and qualitative measures of student "productions;" and the ". . . early versions of standardized tests were developed by public school systems, often in collaboration with university centers, to reflect the curriculum of the schools in a particular city."[72]

This approach to assessment recognized implicitly that institutional factors were largely responsible for the sorry situation in the schools. Moreover, if school practices changed, then children's opportunities for success would improve, and it was believed that the kind of information provided by the standardized achievement tests could light the way to effective reform.

Much to the frustration of the dedicated educators who had mounted them, the effects of school reform efforts were typically disappointing. In New York, for example, in 1922, nearly one-half of all students were above the normal age for their school grade, and there was enormous variability in ages of pupils in any given grade.[73]

This sort of experience did not dissuade educators from the idea of using tests to effect change, but rather persuaded many of them that poor student achievement stemmed from low innate ability. In other words, even the achievement tests of Thorn-

dike were inadequate to measure—and remedy—the problems of schools, because those tests did not adequately measure basic intelligence. The statements of New York Superintendent William Ettinger underscore the intrinsic appeal of the intelligence test model:

> . . . rapid advance in the technique of measuring mental *ability and accomplishments* means that we stand on the threshold of a new era in which we will increasingly group our pupils on the basis of both intelligence and accomplishment quotients and of necessity, provide differentiated curricula, varied modes of instruction, and flexible promotion to meet the crying needs of our children.[74]

Thus, for Ettinger and others, the achievement tests available at the time were still not standardized enough—they did not get at the root causes of difference in student performance.

New York was not alone. Oakland, California, was the site of one of the first attempts at large-scale intelligence testing of students. During the 1917 and 1918 academic years, 6,500 children were given the Stanford-Binet, as well as a new test written by Arthur Otis (one of Lewis Terman's students who would eventually be credited with the invention of the multiple-choice format[75]). The experiment in Oakland was significant because it was one of the first attempts to use intelligence tests to classify students: "Intelligence tests were used at first to diagnose students for special classes; later their adoption led to the creation of a systemwide tracking plan based on ability. . . . The experiment with testing in Oakland . . . would provide a blueprint for the intelligence testing movement after the war."[76]

The Influence of Colleges

Another institutional force exerted pressure on the schools during this period. The university sector sent a clear message of dissatisfaction with the quality of high school graduates, and urged a return to the high standards to which the elite colleges had been accustomed in earlier times. Many academic leaders

---

[70]Ayres, op. cit., footnote 66, p. 115.

[71]Ibid., p. 105.

[72]Edward Haertel and Robert Calfee, "School Achievement: Thinking About What to Test," *Journal of Educational Measurement*, vol. 20, No. 2, summer 1983, p. 120.

[73]Tyack, op. cit., footnote 4, p. 203.

[74]Ibid.

[75]See ch. 8.

[76]Chapman, op. cit., footnote 29, p. 56.

were attracted to the intelligence test as a filter in their admissions process. The President of Colgate, along with leaders of the Carnegie Foundation, the University of Michigan, Princeton, Lehigh, and other higher education institutions, argued that too many children were in college who did not belong there.

As early as 1890, Harvard President Charles William Eliot proposed a cooperative system of common entrance examinations that would be acceptable to colleges and professional schools throughout the country, in lieu of the separate examinations given by each school. The interest of Eliot and like-minded college presidents in a standardized set of national examinations went beyond their immediate admissions needs. Their broader objective was to institute a consistent standard that could be used to gauge not only the quality of high school students' preparation, but also, by inference, the quality of the high schools from which those students came. The ultimate aim was to prod public secondary schools to standardize and raise the level of their instruction, so that students would be better prepared for higher education. Eliot expressed consternation that ''. . . in the present condition of secondary education one-half of the most capable children in the country, at a modest estimate, have no open road to colleges and universities.''[77]

Getting colleges and universities to agree on the subjects to be included and the content knowledge to be assessed in a common college entrance examination was no easy task. Anticipating the minimum competency testing movement by almost a century, the opponents of a standard college entrance examination voiced early concerns about whether these tests could lead to State examinations that would eventually be used for awarding degrees as well as college admission.

Eventually the advocates of common examinations were able to garner enough support to form the College Entrance Examination Board in 1900. In 1901, the first examinations were administered around the country in nine subjects. While in later years college admissions examinations would come to resemble tests of general intelligence, the early examinations of the College Board were closely tied to specific curricular requirements: ''. . . the hallmark [of the examinations] was their relation to a carefully prescribed area of content. . . .''[78]

Within a relatively short period of time, the College Board became a major force on secondary school curricula. The Board adopted the practice of formulating and publicizing, at least a year before a new examination was introduced, a statement describing the preparation expected of candidates. Developed in consultation with scholarly associations, these statements, in the opinion of one observer, ''. . . became a paramount factor in the evolution of secondary school curriculum, with a salutary influence on both subject matter and teaching methods.''[79] This glowing assessment was not shared by all educators. By the end of World War I, many school superintendents shared the concerns of one California teacher who wrote the following to the Board in 1922:

> These examinations now actually dominate, control, and color the entire policy and practice of the classroom; they prescribe and define subject and treatment; they dictate selection and emphasis. Further, they have come, rightly or wrongly, to be at once the despot and headsman professionally of the teacher. Slight chance for continued professional service has that teacher who fails to ''get results'' in the ''College Boards,'' valuable and inspiring as his instruction may otherwise be.[80]

World War I

Army testing during World War I ignited the most rapid expansion of the school testing movement. In 1917, Terman and a group of colleagues were recruited by the American Psychological Association to help the Army develop group intelligence tests and a group intelligence scale. This later became the Alpha scale, used by the Army to quickly and efficiently determine which recruits were capable for service and to assign them to jobs.[81]

---

[77]Much of the discussion of the early history of the College Board comes from John A. Valentine, *The College Board and the School Curriculum: A History of the College Board's Influence on the Substance and Standards of American Education, 1900-1980* (New York, NY: College Entrance Examination Board, 1987). Eliot is quoted on p. 3.

[78]From the autobiography of James B. Conant, quoted in ibid., p. 21.

[79]Claude M. Fuess, quoted in ibid., p. 19.

[80]Ibid., p. 29.

[81]Monroe, op. cit., footnote 44, p. 95.

The administration of group intelligence tests during the war stands out to this day as one of the largest social experiments in American history. Prior to World War I, most intelligence tests had been administered to individuals, not large groups. In a period of less than a month, the Army's psychologists developed and field tested an intelligence test. Almost as quickly, the Army began applying the tests to what today would clearly be called "high-stakes decisions." The Alpha tests, for the normal population, and the Beta tests, for the subnormal, both loosely structured after Binet's tests for children, were given to just under 2 million young Army men, and the results were used as the basis for job assignments. "In short, the tests had *consequences*: in part on the basis of a short group examination created by a few psychologists in about a month, testee number 964,221 might go to the trenches in France while number 1,072,538 might go to offices in Washington."[82]

The results from this testing were mixed. For one thing, validation studies were less than conclusive and Army personnel (and others) criticized the validity of the tests. In one such study (the typical validation study used officers' ratings of soldiers' proficiencies as the outcome or criterion measure), correlations between performance on the Alpha test and officers' ratings were in the low 0.60s, and on the Beta test in the 0.50s.[83] The Army itself had mixed feelings about the testing program, and eventually it discontinued testing its peacetime force.

One of the most important outputs of the program was the mass of data that could be mined by eager intelligence theorists. Some theorists reached particularly controversial and inflammatory conclusions, most notably that 1) a substantial proportion of American soldiers were "morons," which was presented as evidence that the American "stock" was deteriorating; and 2) in terms of test performance, the ranking of intelligence was white Americans first, followed by Northern Europeans in second place, with immigrants from Southern and Eastern Europe a distant third. These findings helped fuel the work of a small but vocal group of eugenicists, such as Carl Brigham, who advocated ". . . selective breeding [to create] a world in which all men will equal the top ten percent of present men. . . ."[84] This reasoning contributed to congressional debate over restrictive immigration legislation.[85]

Testing Through World War II: 1918 to 1945

Overview

Several themes emerged during the period of 1918 to 1945 that continue to be relevant to testing policy. A basic lesson of the period was that in a society constantly struggling with tradeoffs between equity and efficiency, an institution that claims to serve both objectives at once commands attention. If achievement and intelligence tests had been viewed purely in terms of more efficient classification, they would have undoubtedly encountered even more public opposition than they did. But because the tests were promoted as tools to aid in the efficient allocation of resources according to principles of

[82]Tyack, op. cit., footnote 4, p. 204.

[83]A 0.5 validity coefficient does not mean that predictions of soldiers' future performance based on their test scores were right about one-half the time. Rather, it suggests a linear and nonrandom relationship (0 correlation would signify complete randomness) between the score and the criterion variable. It should be noted that today's tests used for selection and placement (e.g., the Scholastic Aptitude Test for college admissions or the General Aptitude Test Battery for employment) have predictive validities (correlation coefficients) in the 0.2 to 0.4 range. See, e.g., Frank Hartigan and Alexandra Wigdor, *Fairness in Employment Testing* (Washington, DC: National Academy Press, 1989). For a critique of the policy to use employment tests with low predictive validity, see, e.g., Henry Levin, "Issues of Agreement and Contention in Employment Testing," *Journal of Vocational Behavior*, vol. 33, No. 3, December 1988, pp. 398-403.
Since the days of the Army Alpha, the psychometric quality of tests used in screening and selection has improved considerably; in fact, there is little evidence that the criterion measures for the Army Alpha were psychometrically sound, or that other test features would pass today's scientific muster. Stephen Jay Gould made this point quite forcefully in his book *The Mismeasure of Man* (op. cit., footnote 43): his experiment that demonstrated how Harvard students, hardly an illiterate lot, performed on the Beta version of the test—designed for recruits who could not read—is often cited as prima facie evidence of the low psychometric quality of the Army intelligence tests.

[84]Karier, op. cit., footnote 58, p. 347. Some of the early faith in eugenics was fueled by the writing of H.H. Goddard, as described in Gould (op. cit., footnote 43), Fancher (op. cit., footnote 43), and other histories. However, it is important to note that Goddard later recanted his findings concerning the allegedly low intelligence levels of immigrants and Black Americans, and publicly apologized for the effects those findings might have had. For discussion, see Carl Degler, *In Search of Human Nature* (Cambridge, England: Oxford University Press, 1991).

[85]See, e.g., Gould, op. cit., footnote 43.

"meritocracy," they appealed to a wide spectrum of the American polity.[86]

Second, the development of mental measurement—part of the broader emergence of psychology as a bona fide science—coincided with profound demographic and geographic shifts in American society. New educational testing models were cultivated in this crossroads of technological push (psychology) and social pull (the need to reform schools and schooling). Windows of opportunity of this sort are rare in history; how society capitalizes on them can have deep and long lasting impacts.

Third, it is important to distinguish technology of testing from ideology of test use. The history of testing in America suggests that political, social, and economic uses for testing can substantially exceed the technical limits imposed by test design.[87]

Fourth, there appears to be a trend from highly specific and curriculum-oriented achievement tests toward tests of increasingly general cognitive ability. This trend has historically been associated with attempts to extend principles of accountability to larger and larger jurisdictions, i.e., from schools to districts to States and ultimately to the Nation as a whole. As shown by the developments in college admissions testing, for example, the move toward consolidation of admissions criteria and the perceived need to influence secondary school education nationwide led eventually to the adoption of a test designed explicitly to assess aptitude, which later was renamed "developed ability," rather than achievement of specific curricular goals. This trend has been reinforced, historically, by several other factors:

- the incentives for efficiency, made particularly important by the commitment to assess massive numbers of students over many different learning objectives;

- the recurring interest in using tests as a way to mitigate the cultural differences in a heterogeneous population; and
- the tendency to shift blame for the quality of education, i.e., to explain low achievement in terms of low innate ability of students rather than in terms of poor management and instruction.

Fifth, growth in the use of standardized tests often coincides with heightened demand for greater unification in curricula. Although the history does not demonstrate a fixed direction of causality, it does suggest the following sequence: initially there is growing recognition that many schools are not doing as well as they should; next there is awareness of a fragmented school system which, if nothing else, makes it difficult to obtain systematic information about what is really happening in classrooms; and finally there is a simultaneous push for standardization in measurement—to facilitate reliable comparisons and standardization of instruction—to remedy the fragmentation.

A Legacy of the Great War

Despite the questionable foundations and effects of the Army's intelligence testing experiments, the terrain had been plowed, and on the conclusion of World War I, schools were only too willing to partake of the harvest. At long last, it seemed to many school leaders, there was a technology that could be deployed in the service of elevating the quality of education provided to the Nation's youth. "Better testing would allow [the schools] to perform their sifting scientifically,"[88] i.e., to classify children according to their innate abilities and in so doing, protect the slow witted from the embarrassments of failure while allowing the gifted to rise to their rightful levels of achievement.

World War I, in effect, set in motion the process that would result—in an incredibly short time—in

---

[86]The word "meritocracy" was coined by the English sociologist Michael Young in a satirical essay. See Michael Young, *The Rise of the Meritocracy, 1870-2033: An Essay on Education and Equality* (London, England: Thames and Hudson, 1958). Paula Fass notes that: "The IQ established a meritocratic standard which seemed to sever ability from the confusions of a changing time and an increasingly diverse population, provided a means for the individual to continue to earn his place in society by his personal qualities, and answered the needs of a sorely strained school system to educate the mass while locating social talent." Fass, op. cit., footnote 25, p. 446.

[87]Historian Michael Katz disagrees:
I can't agree with . . . the point . . . that there's a difference between the purpose of testing (or the technology or science of testing) and the uses to which testing is put. . . . This argument creates a false dichotomy which seems to reflect a naive view of scientific and technological development as self-contained and unaffected by their context. Clearly, this wasn't so; psychology and testing as research enterprises were products of time and place with all that implies.
Katz, op. cit., footnote 42.

[88]Tyack, op. cit., footnote 4, p. 206.

national intelligence testing for American school children. By the end of the first decade after the war, standardized educational testing was becoming a fixture in the schools. A key development of the period was the publication of test *batteries*, which "... relieve[d] the teacher or other user from the task of selecting the particular tests to be used ... [and which provided] a method for combining the several achievement scores into a single measure." Many testmakers included detailed instructions and scoring procedures for using achievement and intelligence tests in conjunction with each other, in order to gauge "... how well a school pupil is capitalizing his mental ability."[89]

The proponents of testing were extraordinarily successful: "... one of the truly remarkable aspects of the early history of IQ testing was the rapidity of its adoption in American schools nationwide."[90] Another aspect was that researchers obtained their data not from a controlled laboratory or limited trial programs, but from real schools in which millions of students were taking the tests. This period of testing, then, involved a complicated two-way interaction between the research community and the public, with the mass testing of children—and the use of test results to support important administrative decisions— occurring even as research on the validity and usefulness of tests continued to develop.

It is not surprising that testing engendered public controversy, given that its most visible manifestation in those days was in *selection*. Had the tests been used to diagnose learning disorders among children and to create appropriate interventions, they would have likely enjoyed more public support. But the tests were mostly used as they had been during the war, namely to classify (i.e., label and rank) individuals, and to assign them to positions accordingly. A U.S. Bureau of Education Survey conducted in 1925 showed that intelligence and achievement tests were increasingly used to classify students.[91] Group-administered intelligence tests were most likely to be used for classification of pupils into homogeneous groups, and educational achievement tests were most likely to be used to supplement

teachers' estimates of pupils' ability. Related survey data showed that 90 percent of elementary schools and 65 percent of high schools in large cities grouped students by ability, and that the use of intelligence tests as the basis for classification was widespread.

By the fall of 1920 the *World Book* had published nearly half a million tests, and by 1930 Terman's intelligence and achievement tests (the latter published as the Stanford Achievement Test) had combined sales of some 2 million copies per year. If test production and sales are any indicator of social preferences, the data suggest a marked preference for achievement measures over tests of innate intelligence. Between 1900 and 1932, there were some 1,300 achievement tests on the market, as compared to about 400 tests of "mental capacities."[92] High school tests, vocational tests, assessments of athletic ability, and a variety of miscellaneous tests had been developed to supplement the intelligence tests, and statewide testing programs were becoming more common.[93]

The Iowa Program

In 1929, the University of Iowa initiated the first major statewide testing program for high school students. Directed by E.F. Lindquist, the Iowa program had several remarkable features: every school in the State could participate on a voluntary basis; every pupil in participating schools was tested in key subjects; new editions of the achievement tests were published annually; and procedures for administering and scoring tests were highly structured. Results were used to evaluate both students and schools, and schools with the highest composite achievement received awards. In addition, Lindquist was among the first to extend the range of student abilities tested. The Iowa Tests of Basic Skills and the Iowa Test of Educational Development became tools for diagnosis and guidance in grades three to eight and in high school, respectively. The Iowa program was also a significant demonstration of the feasibility of wide-scale testing at a reasonable cost.

[89]Monroe, op. cit., footnote 44, p. 99.

[90]Fass, op. cit., footnote 25, p. 445.

[91]W.S. Deffenbaugh, Bureau of Education, U.S. Department of the Interior, "Uses of Intelligence Tests in 215 Cities," City School Leaflet No. 20, 1925.

[92]Chapman, op. cit., footnote 29, (citing data from Hildreth), p. 149.

[93]Monroe, op. cit., footnote 44, pp. 96, 106, and 111.

E.F. Lindquist (1901-1978), at left, one of the fathers of standardized achievement testing, directed the Iowa testing programs. In 1952, E.F. Lindquist developed the basic circuitry design for the first electronic scoring machine, as shown below.

Photo credit: University of Iowa Press

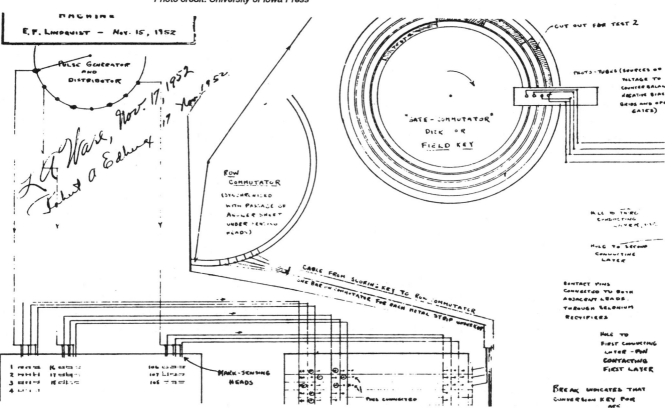

Photo credit: University of Iowa Press

By the late 1930s, Iowa tests were being made available to schools outside the State.[94]

Under Lindquist, the Iowa program had a remarkable influence on swinging the pendulum of educational testing back in the direction of diagnosis and monitoring, and away from classification and selection. Indeed, the distinction between intelligence and standardized achievement tests, in their design and content as well as their scores, was always fuzzy. In any event, the use of intelligence tests encountered substantially heavier criticism than the use of achievement tests—if not on the grounds of their relative design strengths and weaknesses, then on the extent to which they became the basis for classifying and labeling children early in their lives.

Multiple Choice: Dawn of an Era

The achievement tests that gained popularity during the 1920s looked very different from the pre-World War I educational tests. Achievement tests were designed largely with the purpose of sorting and ranking students on various scales. This model of test design has dominated achievement testing ever since.

One of the most significant developments was the invention of the multiple-choice question and its variants. The Army tests marked the first significant use of the multiple-choice format, which was developed by Arthur S. Otis, a member of the Army testing team who later became test editor for *World Book*. In the view of the Army test developers, the multiple-choice format provided:

> . . . a way to transform the testees' answers from highly variable, often idiosyncratic, and always time-consuming oral or written responses into easily marked choices among fixed alternatives, quickly scorable by clerical workers with the aid of superimposed stencils.[95]

The multiple-choice item and its variant, the true-false question, were quickly adapted to student tests and disseminated for classroom use, marking another revolution in testing. Lindquist and coworkers at the Iowa program later invented mechanical and later electromechanical scoring machines that would make possible the streamlined achievement testing of millions of students.[96]

Not surprisingly, the rapid spread of multiple-choice tests kindled debate about their drawbacks. Critics accused them of encouraging memorization and guessing, of representing "reactionary ideals" of instruction, but to no avail. Efficiency and "objectivity" won out; by 1930 multiple-choice tests were firmly entrenched in the schools.

Critical Questions

In the late 19th and early 20th centuries, the potential for science to liberate the schools from their shackles of inefficiency was almost universally accepted. As suggested earlier, this fact helps explain the apparently ironic marriage of testing and progressivism.

But if the spirit of progressivism catapulted scientific-style testing, it was that same progressivism that ultimately reined it in. In a nutshell, the intelligence testers went too far. When Brigham used the Army data to argue that Blacks were naturally inferior; when Robert Yerkes wrote that one-half of the white recruits were morons; when H. H. Goddard suggested that the intellectually slovenly masses were about to take over the affairs of state; or when a popular writer named Albert Wiggam ". . . declared that efforts to improve standards of living and education are folly because they allow weak elements in the genetic pool to survive, [and] that 'men are born equal' is a great 'sentimental nebulosity' . . .";[97] it became clear to progressives like John Dewey that testing had run amok.

Thus, in the days immediately following the first World War, the "heyday of intelligence testing" was confronted by a kind of field day of antitesting muckraking. And the muckrakers were progressives: most notably, Walter Lippman, whose 10 articles in the *New Republic* attempted to remind readers that ". . . the Army Alpha had been designed as an

---

[94]Julia J. Peterson, *The Iowa Testing Programs* (Iowa City, IA: University of Iowa Press, 1983), pp. 1-6.

[95]Franz Samelson, "Was Early Mental Testing (a) Racist Inspired, (b) Objective Science, (c) A Technology for Democracy, (d) The Origin of Multiple Choice Exams, (e) None of the Above? Mark the RIGHT Answer," *Psychological Testing and American Society: 1890-1930*, Michael M. Sokal (ed.) (New Brunswick, NJ: Rutgers University Press, 1987), p. 116.

[96]See discussion in ch. 8.

[97]Cronbach, op. cit., footnote 40, p. 9. For a comprehensive survey of the questionable scientific basis for intelligence testing, see Gould, op. cit., footnote 43.

instrument to aid classification, not to measure intelligence.''[98] It was almost as though Lippman, an early supporter of tests to aid in the efficient management of schools, suddenly recognized that the very same tests could be put to different ends. ''Intelligence testing,'' Lippman warned, ''could . . . lead to an intellectual caste system in which the task of education had given way to the doctrine of predestination and infant damnation.''[99]

College Admissions Standards: Pressure Mounts

The admissions procedures established by the College Board had some clearly beneficial effects on education. They succeeded in enforcing some degree of uniformity in the college admissions process, helped raised the level of secondary school instruction, engendered serious discussion about the appropriate curriculum for college-bound youth, and built solid, cooperative relationships among higher education institutions throughout the country.[100]

Nevertheless, several influential colleges continued to express concern that most secondary schools did not take the mission of college preparation seriously and did not organize their curricula within the College Board's guidelines. Moreover, despite the board's energetic efforts at standardization, a large portion of the Nation's colleges continued to rely to some extent on their own examinations.[101]

In addition, college leaders were coming to a more sophisticated recognition of the limitations of achievement-type tests, including the College Board tests, in helping admissions officers discriminate between students who had stockpiled memorized knowledge and students with more general intellectual ability. Harvard was particularly sensitive to the apparently high number of applicants who, ''. . . as a result of constant and systematic cramming for examinations . . . manage to gain admission without having developed any considerable degree of intellectual

power.''[102] Partly in response to this problem Harvard developed a plan that in a fundamental way presaged the eventual swing from curriculum-centered achievement tests toward more generalized tests of intellectual ability: the plan called for a shift from separate subject examinations to ''comprehensive'' examinations designed to measure the ability to synthesize and creatively interpret factual knowledge.

At Columbia University, as well, the pressure was on to do something about the admissions process. The arrival of increasing numbers of immigrants, many of them Eastern European Jews living in New York City, fueled the xenophobia. Columbia's President, Nicholas Butler, for example, found the quality of the incoming students (in 1917) ''. . . depressing in the extreme . . . largely made up of foreign born and children of those but recently arrived. . . .''[103] To counteract this trend, Butler adopted the Thorndike Tests for Mental Alertness, hoping that ''. . . would limit the number of Jewish students without a formal policy of restriction.''[104]

In 1916, the College Board began developing comprehensive examinations in six subjects. These examinations included performance types of assessment such as essay questions, sight translation of foreign languages, and written compositions. While the comprehensive examinations enabled colleges to widen the range of applicants, university leaders continued to watch with interest the development and growing acceptance of intelligence tests.

Responding to the demand for standardization and for tests that could sort out applicants qualified for college-level work from those less qualified, the College Board developed the Scholastic Aptitude Test (SAT). The test was administered for the first time in 1926; one-third of the candidates who sat for College Board examinations took the new test, and the SAT was off to a promising start.[105]

---

[98]Cremin, op. cit., footnote 2, p. 190.

[99]Walter Lippman, ''The Abuse of the Tests,'' *The New Republic*, Nov. 15, 1922, p. 298.

[100]Valentine, op. cit., footnote 77, p. 17.

[101]Ibid., pp. 32-33.

[102]Claude M. Fuess, *The College Board: Its First Fifty Years* (New York, NY: College Entrance Examination Board, 1967), quoted in ibid., p. 24.

[103]Harold Wechsler, *The Qualified Student* (New York, NY: John Wiley, 1977), p. 155.

[104]James Crouse and Dale Trusheim, *The Case Against the SAT* (Chicago, IL: University of Chicago Press, 1988), p. 20. See also Resnick, op. cit., footnote 3, p. 188.

[105]Valentine, op. cit., footnote 77, p. 35.

In addition to reinforcing the growing popularity of multiple-choice items, the SAT made several other contributions to the testing enterprise. First, the College Board took pains to try to prevent misinterpretation of SAT results. The board's manual for admissions officers cautioned that the new tests could not predict the subsequent performance of students with certainty and further warned of the pitfalls of placing too much emphasis on scores. Second, the board also adopted procedures from the outset to ensure confidentiality of test scores and examination content.[106] Third, the unique scoring scale, from 200 to 800, with 500 representing the average, indicated where students stood relative to others, a concept that helped lay the underpinnings for the eventual dominance of norm-referenced testing.

Given the central role of colleges and universities in American life generally and their specific influence on secondary education standards, it is perhaps not surprising that examinations designed for selection soon became the basis for rather general judgments about individuals' ability and achievement, or that in later years, the SAT would become the basis even for inter-State comparisons of school systems. Clearly the SAT was not designed or validated for either of those purposes,[107] as its designers have attempted to clarify time and again; the fact that it was appropriated to those ends, therefore, stands out as a warning of how tests can be misused.

Testing and Survey Research

Along with the increased use of standardized tests for tracking in the elementary and secondary grades and for college admissions, the period between the wars also saw the first uses of standardized tests in large-scale school surveys. These studies, which paved the way for the kinds of program evaluations that would become so important in education policy analysis in the 1960s, had several aims. Researchers, journalists, and charitable foundations seized on surveys as a way of calling attention to inequities and shortcomings in public education. Understandably, these studies met resistance from school superintendents, who resented being called on the carpet by outsiders. But as the old guard of superintendents were gradually replaced by people more familiar with the role of quantitative analysis in educational reform, and as superintendents came to see the benefits of an outside inventory of school needs, particularly in terms of increased public support for more funding, attitudes softened.[108]

The links between achievement test scores and later college performance were further challenged by Ralph Tyler's analysis of data generated in the "Eight-Year Study" (1932 to 1940).[109] In looking for evidence of a link between formal college-preparatory work in high school and eventual college performance, Tyler reached several important conclusions. First, his research revealed that certain basic tenets of the progressive movement, e.g., deemphasizing rigid college entrance requirements in the high school curriculum, did not produce graduates who were less well prepared for college work than those in traditional classrooms. Second, Tyler's research ". . . confirmed the importance of following student progress on a continuous basis, recording data from standardized tests as well as other kinds of achievement."[110] Third, it set an important precedent for the use of achievement scores as a control variable in large-scale survey-based studies. Finally, the study demonstrated the

---

[106]Ibid., pp. 31-37.

[107]The Scholastic Aptitude Test is intended as a source of additional information, over and above high school grades, to predict freshman grade point average. While its predictive validity has been documented, even that rather modest mission—as compared with overall judgments of individual ability or State education systems—is controversial. See, for example, Crouse and Trusheim, op. cit., footnote 104.

[108]Tyack and Hansot, op. cit., footnote 9, p. 163.

[109]The study involved a group of 30 public and private secondary schools, which had been invited to revise substantially their course offerings and provide a more flexible learning environment for students intending to go to college. Cooperating with these 30 schools were some 300 colleges and universities that had agreed to waive their formal admissions requirements. Tyler examined the effects of high school work on college performance among 1,475 pairs of students—each consisting of a graduate of one of the 30 schools and a graduate of another school not in the study, matched as closely as possible on race, sex, age, aptitude test scores, and background variables.

[110]Resnick, op. cit., footnote 3, page 186.

potential power of educational research as an agent of change.[111]

Another development in the years between the wars was high-speed computing, first applied to testing in 1935. Although there was by then little argument with the idea of standardized testing, the cost-effectiveness of using electronic data processing equipment to process massive numbers of tests was icing on the cake. One report showed that the cost of administering the Strong Inventory of Vocational Interests dropped from $5 per test to $.50 per test as a result of the computer.[112]

Testing and World War II

Once again, new research ground was broken on the eve of world war. But unlike the experience with the Army Alpha program in World War I, the testing that took place during the second World War did not substantially affect educational testing; nor did it engender much public controversy. For one thing, testing was already so well ensconced in the public mind—several million standardized tests were administered annually by the outbreak of the war—that the testing of 10 million Army recruits hardly seemed out of the ordinary. Second, the Army testing program did not focus on innate ability and the hereditarian issue. And third, it did not seem to rest on assumptions of a unitary dimension of intelligence. Rather, it seems that the theoretical and empirical studies initiated by Thurstone, Lindquist, and others had succeeded in persuading the Army psychologists to consider alternative models with which to estimate soldiers' abilities and future performance.

"Multiple assessment," which examined distinct mental abilities, such as verbal comprehension, word fluency, number facility, spatial visualization, associative memory, perceptual speed, and reasoning, was one of two significant technological developments in testing during this period.[113] Another was the transfer of testing technology from the schools to the military. For example, elements of the Iowa Tests of Basic Skills and the Iowa Test of Educational Development were borrowed by the Army for their World War II testing program, establishing the credibility of tests based on notions of multiple dimensions of ability.

Equality, Fairness, and Technological Competitiveness: 1945 to 1969

Overview

Much of the controversy over student testing during the post-World War II period revolved around its uses in classification and selection. Although there had always been some dissent, controversy over student testing had entered a relatively quiet phase in the late 1920s, allowing the psychometric community to refine its craft and the educational community to create "... the most tested generation of youngsters in history."[114] But astute listeners in the early post-war years could detect faint rumblings of conflict; by the end of the 1960s testing would once again be in the eye of storm over educational and social policy.

Three sets of forces came to bear on the schools in general and on testing policy in particular during the 1950s and 1960s: demographic change, due largely to new immigration, which once again challenged the American ideal of progressive education; technological change, brought into sharp relief by the launching of Sputnik, which ignited nation-

---

[111]Commenting on the Eight-Year Study, Lee Cronbach and Patrick Suppes wrote:
   Although the study was carried out as planned, one cannot escape the impression that the central question was of minor interest to the investigators and the educational community. The main contribution of the study was to encourage the experimental schools to explore new teaching and counseling procedures.
Lee Cronbach and Patrick Suppes (eds.), *Research for Tomorrow's Schools: Disciplined Inquiry for Education* (New York, NY: MacMillan Publishing Co., 1969), pp. 66-67. George Madaus (personal communication, 1991) notes that the Eight-Year Study was a turning point in the design of tests: it supported Tyler's argument that direct measures of performance needed to precede the design of indirect measures. See also G. Madaus and D. Stufflebeam (eds.), *Educational Evaluation: Classical Works of Ralph W. Tyler* (Boston, MA: Kluwer, 1989).

[112]Resnick, op. cit., footnote 3, p. 190. For more discussion of the technology of testing see ch. 8.

[113]To this day, the debate between the unitary and multidimensional intelligence theorists rests in stalemate, largely because each camp uses different mathematical models to analyze test scores. As Howard Gardner has neatly pointed out: "Given the same set of data, it is possible, using one set of factor-analytic procedures, to come up with a picture that supports the idea of a 'g' factor; using another equally valid method of statistical analysis it is possible to support the notion of a family of relatively discrete mental abilities." Howard Gardner, *Frames of Mind*, 2nd ed. (New York, NY: Basic Books, 1985), p. 17, and ch. 6 of this report.

[114]Cremin, op. cit., footnote 2, p. 192. Daniel and Lauren Resnick would later embellish this theme, arguing that "American children were the most tested in the world—and the least examined." See Daniel P. Resnick and Lauren Resnick, "Standards, Curriculum and Performance: A Historical Perspective," *Educational Researcher*, vol. 14, No. 4, April 1985, p. 17.

Photo credit: Marjory Collins

Testing of children has often involved oral as well as written work. These first grade pupils at the Lincoln School of Teachers' College, Columbia University, are recording their voices for diction correction, circa 1942.

wide interest in science and mathematics education as well as higher standards of schooling overall; and the awakening of the public conscience to the problems of racial inequality in the Nation's public schools, which led to wholly new approaches to school governance, financing, and participation.

Access Expands

Enrollment in public elementary and secondary schools jumped from 25 million in 1949-50 to 46 million in 1969-70, or from 17 percent of the total

population to over 22 percent. The number of high school graduates went from just over 1 million in 1950 to 2.6 million in 1970. The trend was even more impressive in the postsecondary sector: total enrollments in institutions of higher education went from 2.6 million in 1949-50 to 8 million in 1969-70. While part of the enrollment growth is explained by the size of the "baby boom" cohort, the increase in the proportion of the population enrolled in school signifies progress toward the goal of universal access.

The timing of this upsurge in participation suggests that through decades of increased reliance on standardized tests, the progressive spirit in American education had not only survived, but had actually flourished. Several points need to made in this regard. First, recall that student classification had been viewed by the early progressives as a means to render schooling more efficient: it was when tests became designed and used to classify students on the basis of innate ability—and to allocate educational resources accordingly—that some of the Progressives began to protest. Although the proponents of testing could argue that their approach was intended to ensure continued high standards of school quality, the resulting sorting and tracking of children was anathema to many leaders of the Progressive movement (Dewey, in particular).[115]

Second, both sides claimed to have the welfare of children and the Nation at heart. It was commonly agreed that schooling needed to improve; the dispute arose over the choice of strategy. One side favored increased access to education by all students, and tolerated or supported testing as a way to manage massive public education more efficiently. The implicit assumption was an egalitarian one: all children could learn. The other side also favored testing; but the underlying assumption was that some children were innately more capable of learning than others, and that classification would keep standards high for the more able students while

---

[115]On the acceptability of testing by the Progressive movement, see also Cronbach, op. cit., footnote 40, p. 8. While Cronbach concedes that the testers themselves may have gone too far in their reliance on the new science of measurement, he seems to place more of the blame for controversy on the popular press: "Virtually everyone favored testing in schools; the controversies arose because of incautious interpretations made by the testers and, even more, by popular writers."

sparing the slower ones the embarrassment of failure.[116]

The Test of General Educational Development (GED) played an interesting role in expanding educational access. The GED was formulated by the U.S. Armed Forces Institute, in cooperation with the American Council on Education, to address the problems of returning service personnel who had been inducted before graduating from high school. Patterned after the Iowa Test of Educational Development and constructed with substantial input from Lindquist, the GED was intended to enable out-of-school youth and adults to demonstrate knowledge for which they would receive academic credit and in some cases a high school equivalency diploma.[117]

Thus, the postwar enrollment boom and the development of the GED could be viewed as a victory for universal access. But the analysis would be remiss without repeating the obvious: these developments took place in an education culture fully infused with standardized tests. Indeed, it would be possible to argue—as some did—that tests *opened gates of opportunity*, that access to school was enhanced, not encumbered, by objective tests.[118] In later years this theme would be echoed by some minority leaders, who argued that standardized tests allowed children the opportunity to demonstrate their ability more effectively—and more fairly—than they had been able to in the highly subjective environments of their impoverished classrooms.[119] This curious nature of testing—it could be assigned responsibility for enhancing or for confining opportunities for advancement—sheds light on its powerfully symbolic role in American society generally and in education specifically.

Developments in Technology

American enchantment with technology during the 1950s produced several strides in the field of testing. Most noteworthy was the automatic scoring machine, a form of optical scanner invented by the Iowa Testing Program. The machine enabled tests to be processed in large volume and at a reasonable cost.[120] During the next 12 years, the Iowa program, through its engineering spinoff, the Measurement Research Center, perfected several generations of scanners, each smaller but more powerful than the last.[121]

With this equipment, national testing programs became feasible. Although the optical scanning equipment did not in itself drive up demand for testing, it gave an efficiency edge to tests that could be scored by machine and enabled school systems to implement testing programs on a scale that had previously been unthinkable. An enormous jump in testing ensued. One estimate of the number of commercially published tests administered in 1961

---

[116]The tension between access and standards has been a longstanding motif in education policy debates. Lawrence Cremin illustrates it eloquently in his summary of former Harvard President James Conant's conflicted views on the subject:

For Conant . . . the mixing of youngsters from different social backgrounds with different vocational goals in comprehensive high schools is important to the continued cohesiveness and classlessness of American society, important enough to maintain in the face of the difficulty of providing a worthy education to the academically talented in the context of that mixing. Hence, the central problem for American education is how to preserve the quality of the education of the academically talented in comprehensive high schools.

Cremin, op. cit., footnote 2, p. 23.

[117]Peterson, op. cit., footnote 94, p. 82.

[118]Christopher Jencks and David Reisman argue that the "conservatives" in the debate over college admissions policies were those who disliked tests and who preferred the old-fashioned criteria (e.g., that sons of alumni should be granted preference); and that the "liberals" were those who favored ". . . seeking out the ablest students . . . wherever they might come from." They go on to suggest that while the liberals appear to have been winning, there has been a ". . . rising crescendo of protest, especially from the civil rights movement and others who believe in a more egalitarian society, against the use of tests to select students and allocate academic resources." See their seminal work, *The Academic Revolution* (New York, NY: Doubleday, 1969) pp. 121 ff.

[119]See, e.g., Donald Stewart, "Thinking the Unthinkable: Standardized Testing and the Future of American Education," speech before the Columbus Metropolitan Club, Columbus, OH, Feb. 22, 1989. Stewart, who is president of the College Entrance Examination Board, notes that:

In a country as multicentric and pluralistic as ours, only a standardized test that works like the SAT is going to be valuable . . . in providing some . . . national sense of the levels of educational ability of different individuals and also different groups.

He goes on to note that:

. . . the SAT has made it possible for students from every background and geographic origin to attend even the most prestigious institutions.

[120]Peterson, op. cit., footnote 94, p. 89.

[121]Ibid., p. 163.

was 100 million[122]—just under 3 tests per year, on average, for each student enrolled in grades K-12.[123]

In 1958, Iowa also introduced computerization to the scoring of tests and production of reports to schools. This early and rather primitive application of computers to the field of testing helped propel two decades of research and development that culminated in highly sophisticated programs of computer-based testing.

But technology played an important role not just in the design and implementation of tests, but as a catalyst to renewed interest in the use of testing to improve education. By the mid-1950s, a major expansion in educational opportunities was taking place amid a continued reliance on standardized tests to diagnose and classify students and monitor school quality. The impetus for this expansion came in large part from America's rude awakening to global technological advance: the Soviet launching of Sputnik (Oct. 4, 1957) spurred many Americans to question whether the battlefield victories in World War II were sufficient for America to win the peace that followed. As in prior periods of perceived external challenge, the policy response centered on education, and as in prior periods, the education reforms involved increased testing. The general idea behind the National Defense Education Act of 1958 was to provide Federal funds for upgrading mathematics and science education in particular.

One means for accomplishing this goal was the allocation of Federal dollars to support the development and maintenance of:

> . . . a program for testing aptitudes and abilities of students in public secondary schools, and . . . to identify students with outstanding aptitudes and abilities . . . to provide such information about the aptitudes and abilities of secondary school students as may be needed by secondary school guidance personnel in carrying out their duties; and to provide information to other educational institutions relative to the educational potential of students seeking admissions to such institutions. . . .[124]

Race and Educational Opportunity

The birth of the modern civil rights movement was a watershed in American history and marked a turning point in the history of schooling. It also altered the course of testing policy and raised new debates about the design and use of various tests in school and the workplace.

In 1954, the *Brown* v. *Board of Education* Supreme Court decision ruled out racial segregation in schools, thereby establishing the legal prescription for completing the mission of the public school movement. It had taken about 100 years to address this glaring anomaly in a school system predicated on the ideal of universal access. *Brown* had no immediate and direct consequences for testing, but it set in motion social and ideological forces that would, in years to come, bring student testing into new arenas of controversy and, for the first time, into the courts.

In a second significant court case, *Hobson* v. *Hansen* (1967), filed on behalf of a group of Black students in Washington, DC, the policy of using tests to assign students to tracks was challenged on the grounds that it was racially biased. The judge concurred; although the test was given to all students, the court found that because the test was standardized to a white, middle class group, it was inappropriate to use for tracking decisions.[125]

The explicit rejection of the notion of "separate but equal" in *Brown* set the tone for challenges such as *Hobson*, which found that tests used for classification could result in the kinds of racially segregated classrooms (or schools) explicitly outlawed by *Brown*. A new branch of applied statistics emerged, concerned with the analysis of group differences in test scores in order to determine the potential "adverse impact" of test use in certain kinds of decisions.

---

[122]David Goslin, *The Search for Ability* (New York, NY: Russell Sage, 1963).

[123]Total K-12 enrollments in the 1959-60 school year were just over 36 million. See U.S. Department of Education, *Digest of Education Statistics, 1990* (Washington, DC: U.S. Government Printing Office, 1991), p. 47.

[124]National Defense Education Act, Public Law 85-864.

[125]269 F. Supp. 401 (D.D.C. 1967).

Controversies emerged over the effects of tests in correcting or exacerbating racial inequality.[126] Two other points need to be made about this period. First, the civil rights movement led to the development of a wide range of social programs, which in turn created new demands for accountability measures to ensure that Federal money was being well spent. A century after accountability became a purpose of student testing at the State and local level, the model was being applied on a grand scale to national issues. The 1965 Elementary and Secondary Education Act in particular opened the way for new and increased uses of norm-referenced tests to evaluate programs.

Second, controversy over the quite obvious increased reliance on testing for selection and monitoring decisions did not abate; on the contrary, even the notion of using certain kinds of ability tests to classify children into categories such as ''educably mentally retarded,'' for the purpose of giving them special educational treatment, came under strident criticism by parents and leaders who viewed the classification as potentially harmful to their children's long-term opportunities.

Recapitulation

Testing of students in the United States is now 150 years old. From its earliest incarnation coinciding with the birth of mass popular schooling, testing has played a pivotal role in the American experiment with democratic education. That experiment has been unique in many ways. Not only did it begin well before most other industrialized countries expanded schooling to the masses, but it was carried out in a uniquely American, decentralized system: today 40 million children attend schools scattered across some 15,000 local school districts. If there have been taboos in American education, they have concerned national curriculum, national standards, and national testing.[127]

Yet for all its diversity, the American system also shows some remarkable uniformity and stability.

Beneath the surface of institutional independence lies a strong unifying force, a tacit agreement that a principal objective of schooling is *community*: ''E pluribus unum'' does not stop at the schoolhouse door. But neither does it come with a handy recipe to make it work. Indeed, the apparently endless struggle over the structure, content, and quality of American education—and of educational tests—stems in part from the tension between the judgments of teachers, parents, and students on the one hand, and the quest for community, State, or even national standards, on the other.

Teachers in their classrooms have always used all kinds of tests—everything from spot quizzes to group projects—as part of the continuous process of assessment of individual student learning. At the same time, as this chapter has shown, standardized examinations have been used at least since the mid-19th century to keep district and State education authorities, and the legislatures that fund them, informed about the general quality of schools and schooling. From their inception, these tests have been used to inform institutional decisions about student placement and resource allocation, and they have been seen as a way to influence teaching and learning standards.

Today the United States stands again at the crossroads of major transition in student testing. The issues framing today's public policy debate—perceived decline in academic standards, shifts in the demographic composition of the student population, heightened awareness of global technological competition, and lingering inequality in the allocation of educational and economic opportunities—have been evolving for two centuries. Lessons from the history of educational testing provide important background to the development of testing policies for the future.

---

[126]The most vehement debate was sparked by the 1969 publication of an article by Arthur Jensen questioning whether school intervention programs (such as Head Start) could affect IQ, which was largely determined by heredity. See Arthur Jensen, ''How Much Can We Boost IQ and Achievement?'' *Harvard Educational Review*, vol. 39, winter 1969. For review of this controversy see, e.g., Cronbach, op. cit., footnote 40; Mark Snyderman and Stanley Rothman, *The IQ Controversy: The Media and Public Policy* (New Brunswick, NJ: Transaction Books, 1988); and Fancher, op. cit., footnote 43.

[127]This picture is changing. See discussion in chs. 1 and 2 of this report.

How Other Countries Test

Contents

Tables

How Other Countries Test[1]

Highlights

- There are fundamental differences in the history, purposes, and organization of schooling between the United States and other industrialized nations. Comparisons between testing in the United States and in other countries should be made prudently.
- The primary purpose of testing in Europe and Asia is to control the flow of young people into a limited number of places on the educational pyramid. Although many countries have recently implemented reforms designed to make schooling available to greater proportions of their populations, testing has remained a powerful gateway to future opportunity.
- No country that OTA studied has a single, centrally administered test used for the multiple functions of testing.
- Standardized national examinations before age 16 have all but disappeared from Europe and Asia. The United States is unique in its extensive use of examinations for young children.
- Only Japan uses multiple-choice tests as extensively as the United States. In most European countries, students are required to write essays "on demand."
- Standardized tests in other countries are much more closely tied to school syllabi and curricula than in the United States.
- Commercial test publishers play a much more influential role in the United States than in any other country. In Europe and Asia, tests are usually established, administered, and scored by ministries of education.
- Testing policies in almost every industrialized country are in flux. The form, content, and style of examinations vary widely across nations, and have changed in recent years.
- Teachers have considerably greater responsibility for development, administration, and scoring of tests in Europe and Asia than in the United States.

International comparisons of student test scores have become central to the debate over reform of American education. Reports suggesting that American students rank relatively low compared to their European and Asian peers, especially in mathematics and science, have coincided with growing fears of permanent erosion in America's economic competitiveness, and have become powerful weapons in the hands of school reformers of nearly every ideological stripe.

A recent addition to this arsenal of comparative education politics is the examination system itself: many education policy analysts in the United States who envy the academic performance of students in Europe and Asia also envy the structure, content, and administration of the examinations those children take. In the current debate over U.S. testing reform options, it is common to hear rhetoric about the advantages of national examinations in other industrialized countries; some commentators have gone so far as to suggest that tougher examinations in the United States, modeled after those in other countries, could motivate greater diligence among students and teachers and alter our slipping global competitiveness.[2]

But these arguments are based on an exaggerated sense of the role of schools in explaining broad economic conditions, and on misplaced optimism about the effects of more difficult tests on improving

---

[1]Material in this chapter draws extensively on the OTA contractor report by George F. Madaus, Boston College, and Thomas Kellaghan, St. Patricks College, Dublin, "Examination Systems in the European Community: Implications for a National Examination System in the United States," April 1991.

[2]See, e.g., Robert Samuelson, "The School Reform Fraud," *The Washington Post*, June 19, 1991, p. A19.

education.[3] The rhetoric that advocates national testing using the European model tends to neglect differences in the history and cultures of European and Asian countries, the complexities of their respective testing systems, and the fact that their education and testing policies have changed significantly in recent years.

Explaining international differences in test scores is a delicate business.[4] Similarly, drawing inferences from other countries' testing policies requires attention to the educational and social environments in which those tests operate. As a backdrop to the analysis in this chapter, it is important to keep in mind some basic issues affecting the usefulness of international comparisons of examination practices.

- Testing policies are in transition in most industrialized countries, where the pressures of a changing global economy have a ripple effect on public perceptions of the adequacy of schooling.
- Parents in Europe and Asia, like their counterparts in the United States, tend to praise their own children's schools while decrying the decline in standards and quality overall.[5]
- There is considerable variation in the structures and conduct of school systems *within* Europe and Asia. For example, there is probably as much difference in the degree of centralization of curriculum between Germany and France as there is between France and the United States. These differences are reflected in testing policies that vary from country to country in important ways. In Australia, Germany, Canada, or Switzerland, for example, provincial (or

State) governments have considerably more autonomy in the design and administration of tests than in France, Italy, Sweden, or Israel. Test format differs too: Japan relies heavily on multiple choice and Germany still uses oral examinations, while in most other countries the dominant form is "essay on demand."

- The functions of testing have different historical roots in Europe and Asia than in the United States. Steeped in the traditions of Thomas Jefferson, Horace Mann, and John Dewey, the American school system has been viewed as the public thoroughfare on which all children journey toward productive adulthood. Universal access came relatively later in Europe and Asia, where opportunities for schooling have traditionally been rationed more selectively and where the benefits of schooling have been bestowed on a smaller proportion of the population. Although recent reforms in many European countries have opened doors to greater proportions of children, the role of tests has remained principally one of "gatekeeper"— especially at the transition from high school to postsecondary.[6] In this country higher education is available to a greater proportion of college-age children than in any other industrialized country.
- There is considerable variation among European and Asian countries with respect to both the age at which key decisions are made and the permanence of those decisions. For example, second chances are more likely in the United States and Sweden than in most other countries, which do not provide many options for students

---

[3]See, e.g., Clark Kerr, "Is Education Really All That Guilty?" *Education Week*, vol. 10, No. 3, Feb. 27, 1991, p. 30; Lawrence Cremin, *Popular Education and Its Discontents* (New York, NY: Harper and Row, 1990); and Richard Murnane, "Education and the Productivity of the Work Force: Looking Ahead," *American Living Standards*, Robert E. Litan, Robert Z. Lawrence, and Charles L. Schultze (eds.) (Washington, DC: Brookings Institution, 1988), pp. 215-246.

[4]See Iris Rotberg, "I Never Promised You First Place," *Phi Delta Kappan*, vol. 72, No. 4, December 1990; and the rejoinder by Norman Bradburn, Edward Haertel, John Schwille, and Judith Torney-Purta, *Phi Delta Kappan*, vol. 72, No. 10, June 1991, pp. 774-777. For discussion of how American postsecondary education ought to be factored into international comparisons, see Michael Kirst, "The Need to Broaden Our Perspectives Concerning America's Educational Attainment," *Phi Delta Kappan*, vol. 73, No. 2, October 1991, pp. 118-120.

[5]James Irving, director of Learning and Assessment Policy Division, New Zealand Ministry of Education, personal communication, February 1990. For the United States, the latest Gallup poll shows ratings of public schools have remained basically stable since 1984. The most striking aspects are the higher ratings the public in general give their local schools (42 percent rate them an "A" or "B") compared to the grades they give the Nation's schools overall (only 21 percent rate them an "A" or "B"). Most significant, however, is the enormous confidence parents of children currently in school give to the schools their own children attend (73 percent rate these schools an "A" or "B"). It is suggested that the more firsthand knowledge one has about the public schools, the more favorable one's perception of them. Stanley M. Elam, Lowell C. Rose, and Alic M. Gallup, "The 23rd Annual Gallup Poll of the Public's Attitudes Toward the Public Schools," *Phi Delta Kappan*, vol. 73, No. 1, September 1991, p. 54.

[6]See Max A. Eckstein and Harold J. Noah, "Forms and Functions of Secondary-School Leaving Examinations," *Comparative Education Review*, vol. 33, No. 3, August 1989, p. 303. It is important to note that Japanese children enjoy considerably greater access to schooling than is commonly believed. For a summary of myths and data regarding Japanese education, see William Cummings, "The American Perception of Japanese Education," *Comparative Education*, vol. 25, No. 3, September 1989, pp. 293-302.

who bloom late or have not done well on tests. In Japan, children are put on a track early on: the right junior high school leads to the right high school, which leads to the right university, which is the prerequisite for the best jobs. Japanese employment reflects the rigidity that begins with schooling: job mobility is neglible, ''career-switching'' a totally alien concept. Employment opportunities for French, German, and British students are significantly affected, albeit in varying degrees, by performance on examinations.

The purpose of this chapter is to consider lessons for U.S. testing policy that can be drawn from the experiences of selected European and Asian countries. The first section provides an overview of education and testing systems in the European Community (EC) and other selected countries. The second considers lessons for U.S. testing policy. The last section contains ''snapshots'' of examination systems in selected countries.

Teaching and Testing in the EC and Other Selected Countries[7]

Origins and Purpose of Examinations

The university has always played a central role in examination systems in most European countries.[8] In France, for example, the *Baccalaureat* (or *Bac*) was established by Napoleon in 1808 and has been traced to the 13th century *determinance*, an oral examination required for admission to the Sorbonne. The *Bac* was the passport to university entrance in France until recently, when additional admissions requirements were developed by the more prestigious schools.

Universities also played an important role in the establishment of examinations in Britain. London created a matriculation examination in 1838, which in 1842 became the earliest formal written school examination.[9] The system established at the Society

of Arts, taken as an exemplar by other systems, was modeled on the written and oral examinations used at the University of Dublin. Oxford and Cambridge established systems of ''locals,'' examinations graded by university ''boards'' to assess local school quality. In 1858, they began to use these examinations for individual students and, in 1877, to select them for university entrance. Other universities (Dublin and Durham) followed the same path and established procedures for examining local school pupils. The system of university control of examinations continued throughout the second half of the 19th century.

During the 18th and 19th centuries European countries also began to develop examinations for selection into the professional civil service. The purposes of the examinations were to raise the competency levels of public functionaries, lower the costs of recruitment and turnover, and control patronage and nepotism. Prussia began using examinations for filling all government administrative posts starting as early as 1748, and competition for university entrance as a means to prepare for these examinations followed. The British introduced competitive examinations for all civil service appointments in 1872.

Public examination systems in Europe, therefore, developed primarily for selection, and when mass secondary schooling expanded following World War II, entrance examinations became the principal selection tool setting students on their educational trajectories. In general, testing in Europe controlled the flow of young people into the varying kinds of schools that followed compulsory primary schooling. Students who did well moved on to the academic track, where study of classical subjects led to a university education; others were channeled into vocational or trade schools.

In the last two decades, the duration of compulsory schooling has become longer; the trend has

[7]The 12 members of the European Community (EC) are Belgium, Denmark, France, Germany, Greece, Ireland, Italy, Luxembourg, The Netherlands, Portugal, Spain, and the United Kingdom. Much of the general discussion of EC education and examination systems is taken from Madaus and Kellaghan, op. cit., footnote 1. For comparative data on U.S. and Japanese education, see, e.g., Edward R. Beauchamp, ''Reform Traditions in the United States and Japan,'' *Educational Policies in Crisis*, William K. Cummings, Edward Beauchamp, Shogo Ichikawa, Victor N. Kobayashi, and Morikazu Ushiogi (eds.) (New York, NY: Praeger Publishers, 1986).

[8]In the United States, secondary schooling is more closely linked, in structure and content, with primary than with university education. Other countries' elite secondary schools are closely linked to universities. See Martin Trow, ''The State of Higher Education in the United States,'' in Cummings et al., op. cit., footnote 7, p. 177.

[9]Some professional bodies had already introduced written qualifying examinations (Society of Apothecaries in 1815 and Solicitors in 1835). The London examination initiated in 1842 was the first formal school examination of its kind.

generally been to provide access to comprehensive schooling for more students and to provide a wider variety of academic and vocational choices. Examinations that filter students into different kinds of schools, once given at the end of primary school (around age 11), now take place around age 16 or even 18. The uses and formats of these "school-leaving" examinations are evolving as more options have become available and larger percentages of students seek and can gain access to postsecondary education. In several countries, school-leaving examinations that were once considered a passport to higher education have evolved into first stage or qualifying examinations, which are followed by more diversified examinations for specific prestigious universities or lines of study administered by the university itself. Examples are the French *Baccalaureat*, the German *Abitur*, and the Japanese *Joint First Stage Achievement Test* (JFSAT).[10]

Standardized examinations are not generally used outside the United States for purposes other than certification or selection. However, some exceptions are noteworthy. In Sweden, standardized examinations are used as scoring benchmarks to help teachers grade students uniformly and properly in their regular classes. Examination results in a few countries serve not only to evaluate student performance but also to evaluate the quality of a teacher or school. This was the approach, now abandoned, in England during the second half of the 19th century, when "payment by results" was based on student scores.[11] Today student scores in China have taken on this school accountability function, in that "Key Schools" in China receive extra resources in recognition of their better examination results.[12]

Central Curricula

In most EC countries curriculum is prescribed by a central authority (usually the Ministry of Education). However, the level of prescription varies from system to system. In Germany, curricula are determined by each of the 11 States,[13] in France the curriculum is quite uniform nationwide, and in Denmark individual schools enjoy considerable discretion in the definition of curricula. The trend in several countries has been to allow schools a greater say in the definition of curricula during the compulsory period of schooling; school-based management and local control are not uniquely American concepts.

The United Kingdom[14] seems to be moving in the other direction. In the past, curricula in the United Kingdom were determined by the local education authorities and even individual schools. Independent regional examination boards exerted a strong influence on the curricula of secondary schools. The central government significantly tightened its grip around the regional boards beginning in the mid-1980s, and since the Education Reform Act of 1988 the U.K. has moved toward adoption of a common national curriculum.

Divisions Between School Levels

Most European countries have maintained the conventional division between primary, secondary, and third-level education. The primary sector offers free, compulsory, and common education to all students; the secondary level is usually divided into lower and upper levels. The duration of primary schooling can vary among the States or provinces of a given country.

---

[10]This has changed slightly with the change from the Joint First Stage Achievement Test (JFSAT) to the Test of the National Center for University Entrance Examinations (TNCUEE). The JFSAT was required only for those candidates applying to national and local public universities (approximately 49 percent of total 4-year university applicants), not those applying to private universities. Some applicants for private universities now also take the TNCUEE. Shin'ichiro Horie, Press and Information Section, Embassy of Japan, personal communication, Aug. 2, 1991.

[11]In 1862, the British Government adopted the Revised Code of 1862, which established the criteria for the award of government grants to elementary schools. Each child of 6 and over was to be examined individually by one of Her Majesty's Inspectors toward the end of each school year. Attendance records were also taken into consideration. Thus, each child over 6 could earn the school 4 shillings for regular attendance and a further 8 shillings for successful performance in the annual examination. Clare Burstall, "The British Experience With National Educational Goals and Assessment," paper presented at the Educational Testing Service Invitational Conference, New York, NY, October 1990.

[12]Eckstein and Noah, op. cit., footnote 6, p. 307.

[13]This is also the case in Canada and Australia, where each of the provinces or States sets its own curricula.

[14]The term "United Kingdom" (England, Wales, Scotland, and Northern Ireland) is used throughout this document. Testing practice in Northern Ireland, England, and Wales is similar, but Scotland is unique, with a completely different structure of testing and examinations. Scotland has only one examining board, with close connections to the central Scottish Education Department; the other countries in the United Kingdom each have several examining boards. Desmond Nuttall, director of the Centre for Educational Research, London School of Economics and Political Science, personal communication, June 1991.

Table 5-1—Data on Compulsory School Attendance and Structure of the Educational Systems in the European Community

	Comprehensive attendance (age)	Horizontal structure of system (years)	Compulsory curriculum/schools (lower secondary grades)	Differentiated curriculum/schools (grades)
Belgium[a] [b]	6-16 (16-18 P-T)	6-3-3 or 6-2-2-2	7-10[c]	11-12
Denmark	7-16	7-3-2 or 7-2-3	8-10	11-12
France	6-16	5-4-3	6-9	10-12
Germany[b]	6-15	4-6-3	5-6[c]	5-13
Greece	6-15	6-3-3	7-9	10-12
Ireland[a]	6-15	6-3-2 or 3	7-9[c]	7-12
Italy	6-14	5-3-5	6-8	9-13
Luxembourg	5-15	6-7	—	7-13
Netherlands	6-16	6-3-3	7-10[c]	7-12
Portugal	6-12	4-2-3-2-1	5-9	10-12
Spain	6-15	5-3-3(1)	6-8	9-13
United Kingdom	5-16	6-4-2	7-10	11-12

[a]Belgium and Ireland have an additional 2 years preprimary education integrated into the primary school system. All other countries have provision outside the formal educational system for early childhood education.

[b]Belgium and Germany are federations. There are two States in Belgium with completely independent educational systems. There are 11 States in the former Federal Republic of Germany (16 in the new Germany). Each of the 11 States determines its curriculum under terms agreed by the Council of State Ministers of Education.

[c]A number of countries are less advanced than others in comprehensiveness of their school structures.

SOURCE: George F. Madaus, Boston College, and Thomas Kellaghan, St. Patricks College, Dublin, "Examination Systems in the European Community: Implications for a National Examination System in the United States," OTA contractor report, April 1991, table 3.

Most European countries at one time required a national school examination at the end of primary schooling. These examinations were intended to clarify for teachers the standards that were expected, provide a stimulus to pupils, and certify completion of a phase of formal education. They were used for admission to secondary education and for preemployment screening. But these examinations raised many concerns about their limiting effects on the curriculum and about the tendency among some schools to retain students in grade in order to prevent the low achievers from presenting themselves for examinations.

Perhaps most important, however, were the changes in the philosophy of education that led to raising the school-leaving age and provision of adequate space in secondary schools to accommodate all students. Secondary education was once highly selective, with relatively low participation rates beyond the primary level, and with major divisions between two or three types of schooling. The most exclusive was the "grammar school," "gymnasium," or "lycee," which prepared students for third-level education

and professional occupations. Typically, the school systems of Europe offered a classical academic curriculum in the liberal arts. As numbers of students in this line of study grew, the traditional academic curriculum became diversified, subjects were presented at different levels, and some students took practical or commercial-type subjects.[15]

After the second World War, and particularly during the 1960s, demographic, social, ideological, and economic pressures led to various reviews of education. All the EC countries have made some moves to provide comprehensive lower secondary education (up to age 15 or 16), but these patterns are varied (see table 5-1). Several countries have established comprehensive lower secondary school curricula. Denmark and Britain have gone the furthest, with 10 years of comprehensive education. Greece, Portugal, Spain, Italy, and France also have relatively long periods of comprehensive education. There are some comprehensive schools in Germany but, on the whole, the German States have resisted the development of a thorough-going comprehensive system. Both major components of the tradi-

---

[15]The alternative to the academic secondary school were schools offering technical curricula to prepare students for skilled manual occupations. These schools also expanded their range of offerings as the numbers of students grew, but they typically provided practical, usually short-term, continuing education.

Table 5-2—Upper Secondary Students in General Education and in Technical/ Vocational Education, by Gender, 1985-86 (in percent)

	Girls		Boys	
	General education	Technical/vocational education	General education	Technical/vocational education
Belgium[a]	56%	44%	53%	47%
Denmark	40	60	26	74
France[b]	65[c]	35	58[c]	42
Germany[b]	51	49	57	43
Greece	83	17	62	38
Ireland	79	21	86	14
Italy[d]	26	74[e]	22	78[e]
Luxembourg	38	62	29	71
Netherlands	49	51	43	57
Portugal[f]	99	1	99.8	0.2
Spain	58	42	53	47
United Kingdom	53	47	57	43

[a]Lower and upper secondary education.
[b]1986-87.
[c]Includes upper secondary technological education.
[d]1984-85.
[e]Includes preschool and primary teacher training.
[f]Technical/vocational education was abolished in 1976. New courses were introduced on an experimental basis in 1983/84.

SOURCE: European Communities Commission, *Girls and Boys in Secondary and Higher Educational* (Brussels, Belgium: 1990), table 3b.

tional German school structure (the classical *gymnasium* and the vocational school) have been sufficiently strong and successful to resist possible merging. In particular, vocational education, often seen by students as more enticing than the *gymnasium-Abitur*-university route, has been consolidated and improved and is generally regarded as a success of educational policy.[16]

Today the term "general education" is used to describe the activities of schools that include university-preparation curricula as well as programs designed for students who are not likely to go on to university. Nevertheless, the upper secondary level in all European countries is still quite differentiated, especially in Germany and Italy. (In Italy the system is so complicated that it has been described as a "jungle."[17]) As shown in table 5-2, in 8 of the 12 EC countries a majority of students follow a curriculum of general education, but a sizable number of students are in technical/vocational education courses. Comprehensive high schools in the United King-

dom, France, and, to a somewhat lesser extent, Germany, have begun to resemble the typical comprehensive American high school.

These shifts toward comprehensive schooling have resulted in changed testing policies. Today none of the EC countries administers a national examination at the end of primary schooling.[18]

Variation in the Rigor and Content of Examinations

Specified examinations for leaving secondary school and moving into higher levels of schooling vary across locales, kinds of degrees, subject areas, and competitiveness of the program or of the university. For example, while the French *Bac* retains a large core of general education subjects that all candidates are required to take (albeit with different weights), the 4 options offered in 1950 had grown to 53 in 1988.[19]

[16]Madaus and Kellaghan, op. cit., footnote 1, pp. 53-54.

[17]Ibid., p. 55.

[18]Ibid. Note, however, that Italy uses school-based primary examinations set, administered, and scored by the pupils' own teachers. The United Kingdom has plans to introduce nationwide assessment at ages 7 and 11, but these will be scored by teachers and used for accountability, and are not intended to be used for selection. Some schools in Belgium also administer an examination at the end of primary schooling, but this is a local school option, not a national policy.

[19]Information about the *Bac* was provided to OTA by Sylvie Auvillain of the French Embassy, July 1991. See also the final section in this chapter for a more detailed discussion of the French examination system.

On the basis of examination performance, a candidate is usually awarded a certificate or diploma that contains information on performance on each subject in the examination in letters (A, B, C, D, E) or numbers (1, 2, 3, 4, 5). Usually, grades are computed by summing marks on sections of questions and on clusters of questions or papers. The final allocation of grades may also take into account grade distributions in previous years. These marks or grades are used in making university admissions decisions.

The certificate or diploma may also confer the right to be considered for (if not actually admitted to) some stratum of the social, professional, or educational world. Certificates are credentials, and certification therefore plays a dual role: educationally, in establishing standards of academic achievement, and socially, in justifying the classification of individuals into categories that determine their shares of educational resources and employment opportunities.

Because government manages and finances higher education, and scholarships often cover almost all university costs in some countries, stiff entry competition is seen as a fair and appropriate way to distribute scarce educational resources.

Psychometric Issues

Two major criteria for European examinations are objectivity and comparability. The central concern is whether the examinations reflect what is in the syllabus and whether they are scored fairly. Since, as noted below, most of the examination questions are essay questions that cannot be machine scored, it is not surprising that these issues of fairness are foremost. In the United States, test fairness issues have been analyzed primarily through statistical methods. This statistical apparatus, known as psychometrics, has been honed over seven decades of research and practice. It attempts to identify item or test bias,[20] and determine the reliability and validity of tests. Although European educators attempt to ensure that examinations reflect what is in the syllabus (i.e., content validity) and whether they are scored fairly (i.e., reliability), they do not typically conduct intensive pretesting and item analysis; quantitative models of item-response theory, equating, reliability, and validity receive little or no attention. Unlike the United States, Europe does not have an elite psychometric community with strong disciplinary roots, or an extensive commercial test industry.[21] Only the United Kingdom has made any attempt to apply to their examinations psychometric principles of the type developed in the context of U.S. testing, and they are still not in widespread use.

Essay Format and the Cost Question

Because examinations in European countries require students to construct rather than select answers, the examinations are considerably more expensive to score than the multiple-choice tests common in the United States. (Multiple-choice tests, on the other hand, are relatively expensive to design. See ch. 6 for discussion.) In general, the more open-ended a test is, the more expensive it will be to score, since scoring requires labor-intensive human judgment as opposed to machine scoring. The achievement tests used in other countries typically assess mastery and understanding of a subject by asking students to write. A few require oral presentations (Germany, France, and foreign language examinations in many countries). Some of the German *Abitur* requires students to give practical demonstrations in subjects such as music and the natural sciences.

These tests are expensive—to grade them takes the time of trained professionals (teachers, examiners, university faculty, or some combination). For example, written examinations taken at age 16+ in Great Britain and Ireland cost roughly $110 per student.[22] (In Ireland, candidates pay about 40 percent of the cost.) These costs may be tolerable in countries where a small percentage of the age cohort takes the examination. But in the United States, with nearly five times as many students in this age group, testing the 3 million 16-year-olds in U.S. schools using the British or Irish model would cost about $330 million. Looked at from the perspective of one State, Massachusetts, it would cost almost $7 million to test all 65,000 16-year-old-students using the model of essay on demand; at present, Massachusetts spends just $1.2 million to test reading,

[20]For a recent summary and discussion of the meanings of test bias see, e.g., Walter Haney, Boston College, ''Testing and Minorities,'' draft monograph, January 1991. See ch. 6 for an explanation of reliability, validity, and other psychometric concepts.

[21]Madaus and Kellaghan, op. cit., footnote 1, pp. 57-58.

[22]Ibid., pp. 30-31.

writing, and arithmetic achievements of students in three grades and three subjects.[23]

An additional factor to be included in a cost analysis is the potential effect of tests on retention. In the United Kingdom, for example, many students remain in school an extra year to repeat the General Certificate of Secondary Education (GCSE) if they did not pass the first time, or to repeat the more advanced ''A levels'' if they wish to try for a higher grade.

Tradition of Openness

Individual test takers in the United States can request prior year examinations and sample examination booklets for some tests used for selection, i.e., the Scholastic Aptitude Test (SAT); in addition, third-party vendors offer test preparation classes or software to enable students to practice for these examinations. In general, however, there is a greater emphasis on test security in the United States than in other countries,[24] where both the examinations and correct responses are made public following an examination and become the subject of much discussion. In France, for example, examination questions make front page news, and in Germany, answer scripts are returned to students who may question the way they were graded with their teachers. If a problem cannot be resolved between the student and teacher, the matter is referred to the Ministry of Education.

In the United States, legal challenges since 1980 have made the disclosure of college admissions tests available to test takers who wish to review them, but the examinations are not routinely publicized as in Europe. Some observers contend that releasing examination questions helps focus student and teacher awareness on the facts, concepts, or skills required in order to do well on the test, and that ''teaching to the test'' is therefore a good thing. Multiple-choice examinations, however, which are quite inexpensive to score, are very costly to develop, because of the time and effort spent pretesting items and attempting to eliminate various biases. Releasing such tests in advance, therefore, could jeopardize their validity; this is important because of the high costs of creating new items.

The Changing State of Examinations in Most Industrialized Countries

There have been important changes in European test policies in the past three decades; many of the most dramatic changes have been undertaken in the last few years. France abolished centralized examinations at age 16+ with the aims of postponing selection, making assessment more comprehensive, and giving a greater role to teachers in assessing students. However, the examinations were reinstituted in the 1980s, at least partly because the resources to support a school-based system of assessment had not been made available to the schools.[25] The United Kingdom is overhauling its examination system. Even in Japan, where success in examinations has been the central feature of the educational experience, politicians and educators are debating and reevaluating the form and functions of national examinations.

A major force affecting examination policies has been expansion of the educational franchise. Rising participation rates and rising expectations of individuals with diverse ethnic and socioeconomic backgrounds have changed attitudes toward the assessment of student progress and the uses of tests for important economic and social decisions. Historical criticisms of the narrowing effects of these examinations on students' educational experiences have become politically significant. Many commentators always judged tests unsuitable for low-achieving students, an argument that has gained credence in the light of data suggesting that in order to avoid the examinations these students are likely to leave school early and enter the labor force without

---

[23]It should be noted that the United States has some experience with nationally standardized written examinations. The Advance Placement (AP) program, for instance, includes tests comprised of short answer and essay items. Currently the AP test costs $65 per subject per student, paid for in most cases by the student rather than the school system. This financial burden prevents some poor students from taking the tests required for college credit. Some States (Florida and South Carolina), pay all AP fees and others (Indiana and Utah) subsidize or help students in need, but most States have no official policy, although the Educational Testing Service reduces the fee to $52 for those with need. Jay Mathews, ''Low Income Pupils Find Exam Fees a Real Test: California Questions Who Should Foot the Bill,'' *The Washington Post*, Apr. 25, 1991, p. A3.

[24]Public Law 100-297, which authorizes the U.S. Secretary of Education to approve comprehensive tests of academic excellence, specifies that, besides being conducted in a secure manner, ''. . . the test items remain confidential so that such items may be used in future tests.'' This law has been passed, but funding has not been appropriated.

[25]Madaus and Kellaghan, op. cit., footnote 1, p. 60.

benefit of any formal certification.[26] The apparent correlation between participation rates and school-leaving examination policies is striking: in the United Kingdom, for example, the participation rate drops from almost 100 percent at age 15 to just under 70 percent at age 16—when examinations must be taken. In contrast, some 95 percent of all American 16-year-olds are still in school (see table 5-3).

As noted above, a second area where examination policies have changed is the elimination of standardized examinations at the primary level. Furthermore, at the secondary level there has been a move toward greater reliance on assessments developed and scored by teachers. In four EC countries (Belgium, Greece, Portugal, and Spain), national examinations have been abolished and certification is entirely school based at both primary and secondary levels. In other countries, teachers may mark examinations set by an outside body or contribute their own assessments, which are combined with the results of the standardized examinations. This was the pattern in Britain from the 1960s onward, and virtually every GCSE examination includes an assessment (of things like oral work, projects, and portfolios) by teachers. Although the national program is bringing more centralized curriculum to the United Kingdom, the national curriculum assessment relies extremely heavily on teacher assessments.[27]

A third trend has been the shift in emphasis from selection to certification and guidance about future academic study. This shift has been made possible, especially at lower educational levels, by the expansion of places in secondary schools. Furthermore, as the examinations have become more varied, selection for traditional third-level education is no longer a concern for as many students. Increasing numbers are now turning to apprenticeships or technical training.

Other Considerations

There are other important variables that affect the administration, costs, and outcomes of testing. These include the numbers of students to be tested, preselection of students prior to testing, the homogeneity of the student population and of the teaching

Table 5-3—Enrollment Rates for Ages 15 to 18 in the European Community, Canada, Japan, and the United States: 1987-88

	Age 15	Age 16	Age 17	Age 18
Belgium	95.8	95.5	92.7	72.0
(of whom, part-time) ...	(2.2)	(3.6)	(4.6)	(4.6)
Denmark	97.4	90.4	76.9	68.6
France	95.4	88.2	79.3	63.1
(of whom, part-time) ...	(0.3)	(7.9)	(10.0)	(5.2)
Germany[a]	100.0	94.8	81.7	67.8
(of whom, part-time) ...			(0.1)	
Greece[b]	82.1	76.2	55.2	43.6
Ireland[b]	95.5	83.9	66.4	39.6
Italy	—	—	—	—
Luxembourg[c]	—	—	83.4	71.1
(of whom, part time) ...			(15.8)	(15.8)
Netherlands[d]	98.5	93.4	79.2	59.7
Portugal		32.1	36.9	29.2
Spain	84.2	64.7	55.9	30.4
United Kingdom	99.7	69.3	52.1	33.1
Canada	98.3	92.4	75.7	56.9
Japan[c]	96.6	91.7	89.3	3.2
(of whom, part-time) ...	(2.6)	(1.9)	(1.7)	(1.4)
United States[b]	98.2	94.6	89.0	60.4

[a]Apprenticeship is classified as full-time education.
[b]1986-87.
[c]Excluding third level.
[d]Excludes second level part-time education.

SOURCE: George F. Madaus, Boston College, and Thomas Kellaghan, St. Patricks College, Dublin, "Student Examination Systems in the European Community: Lessons for the United States," OTA contractor report, June 1991, table 5; information for this table from Organisation for Economic Cooperation and Development, *Education in OECD Countries, 1987-88* (Paris, France: 1990), table 4.2, except figures for Portugal which are for secondary education in 1983-84 and come from European Communities Commission, *Girls and Boys in Secondary and Higher Education* (Brussels, Belgium: 1990), table 1c.

profession, centralization and consistency of teacher training to support common standards, and the number of days in the school year. These issues need to be included in efforts to compare testing policies across countries. There is no one model that could be described as the European examination system and, more importantly, no one model that can be transplanted from its European or Asian setting and be expected to thrive on American soil.

Lessons for the United States

What lessons from European and Asian testing policies apply to the American scene? To address that question OTA focused attention on three basic

---

[26]In Britain and Ireland, the number of such students are about 11 and 8 percent, respectively. Ibid., p. 15. (This estimate appears low to other researchers. Max Eckstein, professor of Education, Queens College, City University of New York, personal communication, 1991).

[27]Nuttall, op. cit., footnote 14.

issues: the functions, format, and governance of testing.[28]

Functions of Testing

This report concentrates on three basic functions of educational testing: instructional feedback to teachers and students, system monitoring, and selection, placement, and certification (see ch. 1). European and Asian testing systems, though different from country to country, tend to emphasize the last group of functions, i.e., selection, placement, and certification.[29] There is in other countries almost no reliance on student tests for accountability or system monitoring, activities that are typically handled through various types of ministerial or provincial inspectorates; this fact itself suggests an important lesson for U.S. educators.

Selection, Placement, and Credentialing

If one wished to import testing practices from overseas, an obvious strategy would be to expand and intensify the use of student testing for selection, placement, and certification decisions. Indeed, this appears to be at least one of the ideas behind some proposals for national achievement testing in the United States.[30] OTA finds that the European and Asian experience with testing for these functions leads to three important lessons for U.S. policymakers.

First, in most other industrialized countries, the significance of testing is greatest at the transition from secondary to postsecondary schooling. Standardized examinations before age 16 have all but disappeared from the EC countries. Primary certificates used to select students for secondary schools have been dropped as comprehensive education past the primary level has become available to all students. Current proposals for testing all fourth graders with a common externally administered and graded examination would make the United States

the only industrialized country to adopt this practice.[31]

Second, the continued reliance on student testing as a basis for allocating scarce publicly funded postsecondary opportunities has, in Europe and Asia, come under intense criticism. Having relatively recently attempted to relax stringent elementary and secondary school tracking systems, many countries have been reluctant to hold on to stiff examination-based criteria for admission to third-level schooling. As a result, admissions policies have been in flux. It would be ironic if U.S. policymakers, in an attempt to import the best features of other countries' models, adopted a system of increased selectivity—even at the postsecondary level—just when those countries were evolving in the other direction.

In this context it is important to note the fundamental differences in the relationships between secondary and postsecondary schooling in the United States and elsewhere. In most other industrialized countries, there is a strong link between secondary schools and the universities for which they prepare students; in the United States, on the other hand, high school graduates face a vast array of postsecondary opportunities, diverse in their location, academic orientation, and selectivity. Although periodically in American educational history there have been attempts to influence secondary school curricula and academic rigor through changes in college admissions policies, the postsecondary sector in the United States has remained basically independent of the system of primary and secondary public schools. Restructuring the linkages between these sectors along the lines of the European model, and changing the examination system accordingly, could bring about changes in the quality of American high school education; but the benefits of such a policy need to be weighed against the uncertain effects it would have on the U.S. postsecondary

---

[28]This framework was suggested by Max Eckstein, professor of Education, Queens College, City University of New York, who chaired an OTA workshop on lessons from testing in other countries, January 1991.

[29]Classroom testing, conducted by teachers to assess on a regular basis the progress of their students, is likely to be much the same around the world—teacher-developed quizzes, end-of-year examinations, and graded assignments do not vary much from Stockholm to Sacramento, from Brussels to Buffalo.

[30]See, e.g., Madaus and Kellaghan, op. cit., footnote 1, for an overview of national testing proposals. It should be noted that many advocates of high-stakes selection and certification tests view their principal role as stimulus to improved learning and teaching. Although this might be considered a fourth function of testing, this report treats the potential motivating effects of tests as a crosscutting issue affecting the utility of tests designed to serve any of the three main functions.

[31]As discussed earlier, the United Kingdom has implemented a new system of national assessment at ages 7 and 11, for purposes of accountability (system monitoring).

sector, considered by many to be the best in the world.[32]

The third lesson concerns the equity effects of increased testing for what are commonly called "gatekeeping" functions. Europe has a long history of controlled mobility among nations, and an equally long history of efforts to deal with changing ethnic and national composition of its population. What is relatively new in many countries, however, is the commitment to widening educational and economic opportunities for all citizens. As a result of this shift in social and economic expectations, the use of rigorous academic tests as gatekeepers has come under fire in many countries. In France, for example, the expansion of options under the *Bac* emerged from the struggle of the 1960s to reform not only the schools but much else in French society.

In discussions with many educators and policymakers from European countries, OTA found a fairly common and growing concern with the equity implications of educational testing; European (and to a lesser extent Asian) education policymakers are in fact looking to the United States for lessons about how to design and administer tests fairly. Although the ultimate resolution of complex equity issues escapes predictability, there is no doubt that continued cross-cultural and transnational exchanges among policymakers and educators grappling with these issues will be invaluable.

System Monitoring

European and Asian nations tend not to use student examinations to gauge the performance of their school systems. That function is still handled primarily by inspections carried out at the ministerial or provincial government levels. There has been heightened interest in using the results of international comparative test score data for policymaking, although exactly how to use the data for internal policy analysis is a relatively new question.[33] Nevertheless, three lessons for the United States emerge from the European and Asian experiences.

First, other countries considering the adoption of some kind of test-based accountability system tend to view the American National Assessment of Educational Progress (NAEP) as a model. The fact that NAEP uses a sampling methodology, addresses a relatively wide range of skills, and is a relatively "low-stakes" test make it appealing as a potential complement to other data on schools and school systems. One lesson for American policymakers, therefore, is to approach changes to NAEP cautiously (see also ch. 1 for a thorough discussion of NAEP policy options).

The second lesson is to consider nontest indicators of educational progress that could be valid for monitoring the quality of schools. In this regard, careful study of the ways in which inspectors operate in other countries—how they collect data, what kind of data they collect, how their information is transmitted, how they maintain neutrality and credibility—could be fruitful.[34]

Finally, the European and Asian approach to system monitoring suggests a general caution regardless of whether tests, inspections, or other data are utilized. Public perception of the adequacy of schools in most countries depends on which schools are in question: parents typically like what their own children are doing, but complain about the system as a whole. It is difficult to pinpoint the causes of this dual set of attitudes;[35] in any event, it is fairly clear that there is greater enthusiasm for reform in general than for changes that might affect one's own children. Like the "not-in-my-back yard" ("NIMBY") problem faced by environmental policymakers, education policymakers in many countries face a formidable "NIMSY" problem: education reform may be OK, so long as it is "not-in-my-school yard." American, European, and Asian educators and policymakers who have struggled with the NIMSY problem in their attempt to respond effectively to analyses of various types of system monitoring data could learn much from one another.

---

[32]See Kirst, op. cit., footnote 4, for discussion of the quality of U.S. colleges and universities.

[33]The Organisation for Economic Cooperation and Development (OECD) has been sponsoring, along with the U.S. Department of Education, an ongoing collaborative effort to better understand and utilize comparative data on student achievement.

[34]For discussion of multiple indicators of education, see U.S. Department of Education, National Center for Education Statistics, *Education Counts: An Indicator System to Monitor the Nation's Educational Health* (Washington, DC: 1991).

[35]One explanation that caused a stir in policy circles was the finding that statewide achievement scores in every State were above the national average. See discussion in ch. 2 of this report.

Test Format

In European countries, the dominant form of examination is "essay on demand." These are examinations that require students to write essays of varying lengths. Use of multiple-choice examinations is limited, except in Japan, where multiple-choice tests are common at all levels of elementary and secondary schooling and are used as extensively as in the United States. Performance assessments of other kinds (demonstrations, portfolios) may be used for internal classroom assessment, but not generally for systemwide examinations because of costs.

The lesson from this mixture of test formats overseas is a complicated one. On the one hand, European experience could lead American policymakers to eliminate, or at least reduce significantly, multiple-choice testing; surely some critics of U.S. testing policy would embrace this position. But this inference would be erroneous, given the conflicting evidence from the overseas examples. For example, if one of the purposes of testing is to raise standards of academic rigor, the French and Japanese examples offer conflicting models: both countries typically rank higher than the United States in comparisons of high school students' achievement, but they rely on diametrically different methods of testing.

If there is a lesson, then, it is that testing in and of itself cannot be the principal catalyst for educational reform, and that changes in test format do not automatically lead to better assessments of student achievement, to more appropriate uses of tests, or to improvements in academic performance. The fact that European countries do almost no multiple-choice testing is not, in itself, a reason for the United States to stop doing it; rather it is a reason to consider whether: a) reliance on the multiple-choice format satisfies the numerous objectives of testing; and b) whether alternative formats in use in other countries, such as essays and oral examinations, could better serve some or all objectives of testing in the United States.

In considering alternative test formats and the experience of other countries, it is important to keep two additional issues in mind. First, as discussed in chapters 4 and 8 of this report, the combination of multiple-choice and electromechanical scoring tech-

nologies made the concept of mass testing in the United States economically feasible. To the extent that this type of testing went hand in hand with the American commitment to schooling for all, it will be interesting to observe whether increased efficiency of test format will evolve as an important consideration in European countries committed to expansion of school opportunities for the masses.

Second, one of the important advantages of the multiple-choice format is that tests based on many different questions are usually more reliable and generalizable than tests based on only a few questions or tasks.[36] It allows for statistical analysis of test reliability and validity both before and after tests are administered. In addition, multiple-choice tests allow for statistical analysis of items and student responses, not as easily accomplished with performance assessments. If criteria such as reliability and validity remain a central concern among American educators, the adoption of European testing methods will necessitate substantial investments in research and development to bring those methods up to acceptable reliability and validity standards.

Governance of Testing

None of the countries studied by OTA has a single, centrally prescribed examination that is used for all three functions of testing. Moreover, the countries of Europe and Asia exhibit considerable variation in the degree of centralized control over curriculum and testing. In some countries, there are centrally prescribed curricula that are used as a basis for the standardized examinations students take, while elsewhere decisionmaking is more decentralized. An obvious lesson, then, is that the concept of a single national test is no less alien in other countries than it has been in the United States. Nevertheless, there are important differences in the governance of tests between the United States and other industrialized countries.

Testing and Curriculum

Although most countries allow some local control of schooling, in general there is greater national agreement over detailed aspects of curriculum than there is in the United States. This sense of a shared mission is reflected in tests that probe content mastery at much deeper levels than most of the

---

[36]See discussion of generalizability in ch. 6.

standardized tests in the United States.[37] As explained elsewhere in this report, however, this has more to do with the politics of testing than with the technology of testing: the United States has a long history of decentralized decisionmaking and school governance, and an aversion to the idea of curricula defined for the Nation as a whole. Standardized tests that can be used across the United States have therefore been limited to skills and knowledge common to most school districts—which has meant basic reading, writing, and arithmetic.[38] The pursuit of consensus in the United States for anything beyond the basics has proved difficult, though not impossible; the best example to date is NAEP, considered by most educators who are familiar with it as an important complement to the kinds of information provided on nationally normed standardized tests. Nevertheless, even NAEP items fall short of the complexity, depth, and specificity of content material attained in written examinations overseas.

Three important lessons regarding governance of tests emerge for U.S. policy. First, consensus on the goals and standards of schooling appears easier to establish in Europe and Asia than in the decentralized and diverse U.S. education system. As a consequence, national examinations in Europe and Asia can be very content and syllabus specific. In the United States, on the other hand, achieving national consensus usually means limiting examinations to basic skill areas common to 15,000 school districts. Even NAEP, which consists of items derived from elaborate consensus-seeking processes, does not assess achievement at a level of detail and complexity comparable to typical essay examinations in other countries. The lesson from abroad, then, is that syllabus-specific tests can be national only in countries where curriculum decisions are made centrally or where consensus can be easily attained.

The second lesson, related to the first, concerns the sequencing of curriculum and test design. European and Asian experience does not demonstrate that national testing raises the academic rigor

of curricula, but rather that national consensus on goals and standards of schooling allows for consistent curricula that can be tested by syllabus-based national examinations. Indeed, the importance of keeping the horse of curriculum and instruction before the cart of assessment (one of OTA's central findings in this report) is reinforced by the overseas experience.

The third lesson concerns the effects of heavily content-driven examinations on student behavior. Syllabi, topics, criteria of excellence, and questions from prior examinations are widely publicized in other countries, where preparing for tests is encouraged. This emphasis on curricular content conveys an important signal to students in Europe and Asia: "study hard and you can succeed." In the United States, students are encouraged to work hard, but their success in gaining admission to college or in finding good jobs often depends on many other factors besides their performance on tests closely tied to academic courses they have taken. While there is clearly a need for tests that can assess fairly the differences in knowledge and skills of individuals from vastly diverse and locally controlled school environments,[39] there may also be considerable merit in the use of examinations that reinforce the value of studying material deemed worthy of learning.[40]

The Private Sector

Only in the United States is there a strong commercial test development and publishing market. The importance of this sector, in terms of research, development, and influence on the quality and quantity of testing, cannot be overstated. Even when States and districts create their own tests, they often contract with private companies. In Europe and Asia, testing policies reside in ministries of education.

There is a certain paradox about the preference for public administration of tests in other countries and private markets in this country. Given that European and Asian countries typically have less trouble than

---

[37]See, e.g., National Endowment for the Humanities, *National Tests: What Other Countries Expect Their Students to Know* (Washington, DC: 1991), for examples of test questions faced by students in Europe and Japan.

[38]For discussion of how multiple-choice items can assess certain "higher order thinking skills" see ch. 6.

[39]See Donald Stewart, "Thinking the Unthinkable: Standardized Testing and the Future of American Education," speech before the Columbus Metropolitan Club, Columbus, OH, Feb. 22, 1989.

[40]This issue turns on distinctions between aptitude testing and achievement testing (see ch. 6). For discussion of the historical development of these approaches to testing, see ch. 4. See also James Fallows, *More Like Us* (Boston, MA: Houghton-Mifflin, 1989), pp. 152-173.

the United States in defining national goals and standards of education, the ability to specify testing needs and contract with private vendors for test development and production ought to be relatively easier in other countries than in the United States. On the other hand, given that fragmentation in curricular standards and educational goals in the United States raise formidable barriers to market transactions, one might expect greater reliance on nonprofit or governmental organization of testing.

The Role of Teachers

Considerable responsibility is vested in teachers in other countries for the administration and scoring of standardized examinations. This practice is based on the premise that examinations with heavy emphasis on academic content should be developed and graded by professionals charged with delivering that content and respected for their ability to ascertain whether children are learning it. The important lesson for U.S. testing policy, then, is that faith in the professional caliber of teachers is a necessary condition for a credible system of examinations that requires teachers' judgments in scoring.

It is important to note that many European countries have only one or very few teacher training institutes, guaranteeing more consensus on the principles of pedagogy and assessment than in the United States, where teacher education occurs in thousands of colleges and universities. The centralized model of teacher training in other countries reinforces the professional quality of teaching, and makes it relatively easier to implement national curricula. The American tradition emphasizes standardized testing as a source of information to check teachers' judgments and to assure that children in diverse schools and regions are being treated equitably. The lesson from the European model, then, is that a centralized system of teacher preparation can increase the homogeneity of teaching and curriculum and reduce the need for assessments designed to assure that all children are receiving similar educational experiences. This suggests a familiar theme: changing testing will not necessarily improve teaching, but changes in teaching can lead to different approaches to testing.

U.S. policymakers wishing to adopt examinations on European or Asian models will need to balance the need for increased reliance on teacher judgments with public demand for a system that provides an independent ''second opinion,'' especially when test results have high stakes.

Snapshots of Testing in Selected Countries[41]

The People's Republic of China

The first examinations were attributed to the Sui emperors (589-618 A.D.) in China. With its flexible writing system and extensive body of recorded knowledge, China was in a position much earlier than the West to develop written examinations. The examinations were built around candidates' ability to memorize, comprehend, and interpret classical texts.[42] Aspirants prepared for the examinations on their own in private schools run by scholars or through private tutorials. Some took examinations as early as age 15, while others continued their studies into their thirties. After passing a regional examination, successful applicants traveled to the capital city to take a 3-day examination, with answers evaluated by a special examining board appointed by the Emperor. Each time the examination was offered, a fixed number of

---

[41]In the following country profiles all data on area and total population come from Mark S. Hoffman (ed.), *The World Almanac and Book of Facts, 1991* (New York, NY: Pharos Books, 1990); age of compulsory schooling and total school enrollment figures come from the United Nations Educational, Scientific and Cultural Organization (Unesco), *Statistical Yearbook* (Louvain, Belgium: 1985 and 1989). School enrollment figures include ''pre-first level,'' ''first level,'' and ''second level'' students. Data on number of school days comes from Kenneth Redd and Wayne Riddle, Congressional Research Service, ''Comparative Education: Statistics on Education in the United States and Selected Foreign Nations,'' 88-764 EPW, Nov. 14, 1988.

For comparison purposes, current U.S. data are: size, 3.6 million square miles; population, 247.5 million. Mark S. Hoffman (ed.), *The World Almanac and Book of Facts, 1990* (New York, NY: Pharos Books, 1989). School enrollment: 46.0 million. U.S. Department of Education, National Center for Education Statistics, *The Condition of Education, 1991, vol. 1, Elementary and Secondary Education* (Washington, DC: U.S. Government Printing Office, 1991).

[42]Stephen P. Heyneman and Ingemar Fagerlind, ''Introduction,'' in The World Bank, *University Examinations and Standardized Testing* (Washington, DC: 1988), p. 3.

Size	3,705,390 square miles, slightly larger than the United States
Population	1,130,065,000 (1990)
School enrollment	177.8 million (1988)
Age of compulsory schooling	6 to 16
Number of school days	September 1 to mid-July—exact number of days not available
Selection points and major examinations	1. Provincial examinations at end of 9th year of compulsory schooling 2. Central examinations set by the State for university and college entrance
Curriculum control	National, central control

aspirants were accepted into the imperial bureaucracy.[43]

Education in China today is largely centrally controlled. Curricula and the examinations that accompany them are used as a reflection of political philosophy and as a means of maintaining cultural cohesion, as well as to reinforce common loyalties in a population of over 1 billion people, speaking several major languages, distributed over a huge land mass (larger than the United States). There remains a sharp separation between academic schooling and vocational schooling, and examinations are the basis for making these selections at the end of the 9 years of compulsory schooling. Students may then enter general academic schools, vocational or technical schools, or "key schools," which accept the top cadre of students and receive superior resources in part based on the test results of their students. The examinations at this level are prepared by provincial education bureaus and are administered on a city-wide basis.

At the end of upper secondary school, students seeking university entrance take a centralized examination that provides no choice of subjects, specializations, or options. This examination is developed by the National State Education Commission and administered by provincial higher education bureaus who assign candidates to schools based on scores, specialties, and places available. The same is true for

technical schools. The Central Ministry of Labor and Personnel develops and administers a nationwide entrance examination for skilled worker schools. Strict quotas are assigned for overall opportunities for further study and to particular programs at specific institutions, based on a master plan of national and regional development goals. The size, wealth, and general power of certain municipalities (Beijing, Shanghai, and Tientsin) have enabled them to assume control over the examination mechanism, which in other locations may be directed by the central or provincial authority.

The number of candidates for university entrance is huge—in 1988, 2.7 million students prepared for the national college admission test. Less than one-quarter were accepted for study. Overall, about 2 percent of Chinese first graders eventually go on to higher education.[44] The format of the examinations, once extended answer/essay format, is beginning to change to short-answer and multiple-choice questions. Nevertheless, examinations are still scored by hand rather than machines. Some analysts suggest that, given the huge numbers of examinees, it is only a matter of time before machine-scorable formats are introduced, reinforcing the already strong emphasis in Chinese schools on rote learning and recall of facts.[45]

The pendulum of Chinese higher education admission policy has swung with political pressures. After 1,000 years and a well-established tradition of using examinations to control admission to higher education and further training, the Chinese abolished examinations during the cultural revolution, with the goal of eliminating status distinctions. Selection was to be based instead on political activism and "correctness" of social origin. The pendulum swung back again with the new regime in 1976, when examinations were reestablished as a means of allocating university places on basis of merit. Student scores rather than political orthodoxy have again become the major criterion to advancement. Examinations confer status in China. It is not uncommon to inquire about a persons' status in

[43]William K. Cummings, "Evaluation and Examination," *International Comparative Education Practices: Issues and Prospects*, Thomas Murray (ed.) (Oxford, England: Pergamon Press, 1990), p. 90.

[44]Harold J. Noah and Max A. Eckstein, "Tradeoffs in Examination Policies: An International Comparative Perspective," *Oxford Review of Education*, vol. 15, No. 1, 1989, p. 22.

[45]Ibid.

society by asking: ''How many examinations has he (or she) passed?''[46]

The Union of Soviet Socialist Republics (U.S.S.R.)[47]

Soviet society has been characterized by central control and planning, and this centralization extends to the educational system.[48] The 15 republics and subrepublics that made up the U.S.S.R. had shared a central curriculum and common school organization. Considerable local discretion had been provided, however, in education policy as it pertained to the secondary school-leaving certificate, the *attestat zrelosti* (maturity certificate). This certificate was based on accumulated course grades and an examination that was predominantly oral in nature. Each of the 15 republics was responsible for setting the content and standards of the examination, and the teachers who prepared the students dominated the process of setting the questions and evaluating the responses.[49]

Because there was so little comparability in grading, the value of the *attestat zrelosti* meant different things in different parts of the country. As a result of this variability, the VUZy (universities and technical institutes) developed their own entrance examinations. Much like in the Japanese system, each university set its own questions, testing schedule and policy, cutoff score, and grading procedure. This diversified system placed a burden on students, who needed to negotiate a web of uncoordinated examinations, and travel great distances to sit for the necessary examinations at the university or institute of their choice. Much of the examination process involved oral examinations. The system was described as erratic, inconsistent, confusing, and subject to influence peddling and

Size	8,649,496 square miles, the largest country in the world, approximately 2.5 times the size of the United States
Population	290,939,000 (1990)
School enrollment	4.9 million (1988)
Age of compulsory schooling	7 to 17
Number of school days	September 1 to May 30—exact number of days not available
Selection points and major examinations	1. Secondary school-leaving examinations set by each republic, graded by local teachers 2. Each university and technical institute sets its own entrance examination
Curriculum control	National, central control

corruption. There were persistent reports of discrimination against ethnic and religious groups in the examination process.[50]

Controlling the flow of students into the university system was part of the overall regional and national planning that had been carried out through test quotas. During the revolution of 1917, university entrance examinations were abolished, and access was opened to all students. However, the examinations were reinstated in 1923.[51] The more recent balance between central planning and local flexibility was another example of the need for political compromise. Some maintained that the tradeoff for local flexibility had been an incoherent and inconsistent system. In part to find more objective and standardized forms of testing, Soviets had begun looking to ''American tests,'' machine-scorable multiple-choice tests, for possible use in the *attestat zrelosti*. It is not clear how the various republics will react to relinquishing some of their local discretion in developing and scoring tests. As noted above, it is yet to be seen how the independence of the Soviet republics will affect the examination systems that were developed to serve the centralized political system of the past.

---

[46]Eckstein and Noah, op. cit., footnote 6, p. 308.

[47]This snapshot refers to the period before the recent breakup of the U.S.S.R. into separate republics.

[48]Education and examination processes are undergoing radical changes and it is too soon to draw final conclusions. V. Nebyvaev, third secretary, Embassy of the Union of Soviet Socialist Republics, personal communication, July 31, 1991.

[49]Noah and Eckstein, op. cit., footnote 44, p. 23.

[50]Ibid.

[51]Ibid.

Japan

When the United States compares itself to Japan, it is common to bemoan the fact that our schools are not more like theirs. Interestingly, one of the few things the two education systems have in common is their reliance on machine-scorable multiple-choice examinations. In other ways our cultures and traditions are so different that many comparisons are superficial and, in some cases, potentially destructive.[52]

When Japan emerged from its feudal period in the mid-19th century, it began to look to the West for models to modernize aspects of Japanese life.[53] Among these models were the Western goals of compulsory primary education and of a high-quality university system. Japan also followed the French example of a centrally prescribed curriculum and textbooks, frequent testing during a school year, and end-of-year final tests. However, since Japanese students often finished the prescribed curriculum before the end of the school year, they began to focus on the use of entrance examinations for the higher level, rather than school-leaving examinations from the lower level. These entrance examinations became valued for several reasons. The first and most obvious was the need to select a few students from the many seeking higher levels of education. Another reason for devotion to examinations came from the uniquely Japanese cultural disposition known as *ie* psychology, "... the tendency to rigorously evaluate individuals before permitting them to join a family system or a corporate residential group, but once they are admitted, to accept and adjust to them as full members."[54] This concept of first passing rigorous scrutiny and then receiving what becomes lifetime acceptance into established groups can be seen in acceptance of spouses into a family unit or employees into membership in Japanese firms.[55]

Size	145,856 square miles, slightly smaller than California
Population	123,778,000 (1990)
School enrollment	21.2 million (1988)
Age of compulsory schooling	6 to 15
Number of school days	243
Selection points and major examinations	1. Examinations for entry to some junior high and high schools
	2. Joint First Stage Achievement Test: national preliminary qualifying examination for national local public universities (approximately 49 percent of all university candidates); abolished in 1989 and replaced with Test of the National Center for University Entrance Examinations for public universities (and some private universities)
	3. Each university sets own College Entrance Examinations
Curriculum control	National, central control

The second major reform in Japanese schooling was implemented by the American occupation following World War II.[56] The School Education Law of 1947 caused a massive reorganization of the existing school facilities that is the basis for today's educational system. Among these reforms were the establishment of a 6-year compulsory primary school and 3 additional years of a compulsory middle or lower secondary school. The first 9 years of compulsory education are free to all students. An additional 3 years of high school are modeled on the lines of the American comprehensive high school; however, all high schools charge tuition. While the law said that "... co-education shall be recognized in education," many private junior high or high schools and some national and public local high schools are for one gender.[57]

Higher education also was to be reformed, with the aim of broadening goals, leveling the traditional

---

[52]See, e.g., Fallows, op. cit., footnote 40.

[53]While the education system imported the "practical" disciplines (mathematics, science, and engineering) from the West, its moral content was strictly Japanese. The 1890 Imperial Rescript on Education made "the teachings of the ancestors of the Imperial Family" the basis for all instruction. "Education Reform in Japan: Will the Third Time be the Charm?" *Japan Economic Institute Report*, No. 45A, Nov. 30, 1990, p. 2.

[54]William K. Cummings, "Japan," in Murray (ed.), op. cit., footnote 43, p. 131.

[55]Ibid.

[56]"Education Reform in Japan," op. cit., footnote 53.

[57]Article 5 of the Fundamental Law of Education, Horie, op. cit., footnote 10.

hierarchy, expanding opportunities, and decentralizing control. While many of the reforms envisioned for changing higher education were not long-lived, opportunities were vastly expanded, and important powers devolved to universities, e.g., power over academic appointments, admissions, and so on. The postwar constitution formally guarantees academic freedom, and university autonomy is held sacred. Nevertheless, the government controls the purse strings for national universities, and ties between large employers and the national universities have led to a perpetuation of the hierarchy in Japanese education.[58]

Japanese education today is highly centralized, with a common curriculum and little choice in subjects. Test scores become important early and throughout the structured progression of students along a carefully defined path. Some suggest this has had the impact of transforming Japan from an aristocracy to a society where what counts is the university one attends.[59] There is a progression, based on examinations, that has provoked considerable competition among students and their parents. While primary schools are quite egalitarian, many students compete for the more elite national junior high schools that grant entrance based on test scores and, in some cases, a lottery. There are also many private junior high schools whose entrance examinations are very competitive. It is hoped that success in an elite junior high will help guarantee entrance to the best high schools. There is space for approximately 60 percent of all the students in public high schools; private schools receive the rest.[60]

Since there is now room for all students to attend high school of some sort, and since the curriculum is centralized, based on the university entrance examinations, today there is somewhat less competition for high school entry than in the past. But those high schools (public and private) with larger numbers of successful university applicants are still prized. Student selection to high school is based on prior grades and teacher recommendations as well as the high school entrance examination. With recent

education reforms, some of the pressure of this first stage of Japan's examination system has been reduced.

While the entrance examination system for Japanese universities has been in existence for over a century, the pendulum of common examinations v. university-developed examinations has swung back and forth. In the prewar period, an entrance examination was used only for those prestigious national universities that attracted large numbers of applicants. The private institutions did not require these examinations. With the postwar educational reforms, a single common examination, the Japanese National Scholastic Aptitude Test, was instituted for all universities. This examination was abolished in 1954 and replaced by a system whereby each university conducted its own entrance examination. School grades and recommendations from high school teachers were not given much weight, and eventually educators became concerned that the university entrance examinations did not adequately cover the scholastic ability of applicants.[61]

In 1979, therefore, a new system was put into place that eventually led to today's two-tiered examination system. The first stage required all applicants to national and local public universities (currently approximately 49 percent of all 4-year college applicants[62]) to take the Joint First Stage Achievement Test (JFSAT), a retrospective examination created by the Ministry of Education. This examination was offered once a year to test mastery of the five major subjects in secondary school curriculum. In 1990, the JFSAT was abolished and replaced by the Test of National Center for University Entrance Examinations (TNCUEE). The main difference between these two tests is use and content. The JFSAT was required of applicants to national and local public universities only, while the TNCUEE is taken by some applicants for some private universities as well. In addition, the TNCUEE requires applicants to take examinations only in those subjects required by the universities to which

[58]William Cummings, Harvard University, personal communication, August 1991.

[59]In the United States and Korea, having the credential or degree is what counts in terms of prestige and career possibilities. In Japan, though, the status stems from *attending* a university: it is more important to be ''Todai Man''—to attend Tokyo University, than to earn a Ph.D. James Fallows, personal communication, July 18, 1991.

[60]Cummings, op. cit., footnote 58.

[61]Ikuo Amano, ''Educational Crisis in Japan,'' in Cummings et al. (eds.), op. cit., footnote 7, pp. 38-39.

[62]Horie, op. cit., footnote 10.

they are applying.[63] The second tier of examinations is the College Entrance Examinations (CEE), individually developed, administered, and graded by the faculties of each of the prestigious and highly selective universities.

While 34 percent of high school graduates seek university entrance, only 58 percent of these applicants gain entrance.[64] One-third[65] of the applicants each year are *ronin,* "masterless samurai," who are repeating the examinations after attending special prep schools (*yobiko*) and *juku* (tutorial, enrichment, preparatory, and cram schools) in order to get higher scores, qualifying them for admission into the prestigious universities.

In fact, the *juku,* or cram school, and the yobiko have become almost a parallel school system to the public schools. The sole curriculum of these after-hours or additional schools is examination preparation. There are 36,000 *juku* in Japan. It is a $5-billion a year industry. More than 16 percent of the primary school children and 45 percent of junior high students attend *juku,*[66] even though the extra schooling costs several hundred dollars a month and represents a significant financial burden for many families.[67] In fact, with competition even to gain entry into some of the most successful cram schools, some of which give their own admission tests, there are jokes about going to *juku* for *juku.*

There has been a great deal of concern in Japan about the impacts of "exam hell" in two regards— the impact on students and the impact on curriculum. In Japan, high school is not the time of exploration and discovery, socialization and extracurricular activities, football games and dating that is found in the American high school. Instead, students spend almost every waking hour in school, in *juku,* or at home studying. The school day is long and after school children go to *juku;* the school week extends through Saturday morning, and the school year is approximately 240 days long. Pressure is great and continuous until a student makes the final cut—

entrance into a prestigious university. One popular saying is: "Sleep four hours, pass; sleep five hours, fail."[68]

Other impacts are more subtle, but of equal concern: students who memorize answers but cannot create ideas, and a curriculum that focuses everything on preparation for the examinations. When students view schooling as ". . . truly relevant when it promotes preparation for the CEE and as only marginally useful when it does not contribute directly to university admission,"[69] this has a major cognitive and motivational impact on students' approaches to education. It is not clear whether a love of learning for learning's sake can be inspired later, once the student jumps the final hurdle and makes it to the home stretch of the university. Indeed, once accepted into college, students can take it easy and relax, discover the joys of the opposite sex and perhaps begin to rediscover some of the pleasures forsaken in their "lost childhoods." In fact, the college period in Japan has often been referred to as a "4-year vacation," although a well earned one, since the average Japanese student ranks at the top of the list in mathematics, science, and a number of other subjects in international comparisons.[70]

France

The locus of control for education in France is the Ministry of Education (MOE). The curriculum, topics for examinations, and guidelines are set by MOE, with examination questions and overall administration coordinated by the 32 regionally dispersed academies. The Minister of Education sets a general program of what should be examined, but each academy is responsible for

[63]Ibid.

[64]Ibid.

[65]Ibid.

[66]Carol Simons, "They Get by With a Lot of Help From Their Kyoiku Mamas," *Smithsonian,* vol. 17, March 1987, p. 49.

[67]Fallows, op. cit., footnote 59.

[68]Simons, op. cit., footnote 66, p. 51.

[69]Nobuo Shimahara, "The College Entrance Examination Policy Issues in Japan," *Qualitative Studies in Education,* vol. 1, No. 1, 1988, p. 42.

[70]Ibid., p. 52.

Size	220,668 square miles, about twice the size of Colorado
Population	56,184,000 (1990)
School enrollment	9.6 million (1988)
Age of compulsory schooling	6 to 16
Number of school days	185
Selection points and major examinations	1. State-controlled *brevet* at end of comprehensive school (age 15)
	2. *Baccaulearet* at completion of *lycee* (age 18), 38 options, 3 types of diploma, set by each regional academy with Ministry of Education (MOE) oversight
	3. Admission to selective *grandes ecoles* via *concours* after 1 to 2 more years
Curriculum control	National, central MOE control

administering the curricula and testing within a region.[71]

French students spend 5 years in the *ecole primaire*, or primary school, and move to the secondary school without taking a graduation or selection examination. However, there has been a recent interest in examining students to see how well the schools are doing. At the beginning of the 1989 school year, MOE, concerned with reports showing a large proportion of students (30 percent) with reading problems on entering secondary school, set out on an ambitious national examination that could be compared with the U.S. NAEP.[72] Inspectors, teachers, and specialists from all across France gathered and created a matrix of national goals and achievement levels. Teachers submitted ideas for questions and, after a period of pretesting, the group developed a common standardized test for mathematics, reading, and writing at the third and sixth grade levels. All 1.7 million students in these grades were tested in their classrooms, and teachers administered and scored the tests using coded answer sheets. Since the goal was to diagnose individual problems, every student was tested and the results were sent to parents. Each teacher was given copies

of the exercises (a mixture of open-ended and multiple-choice questions) with discussion of the objectives, commentary on kinds of responses students made, and overall scoring results. Although summative national results were collected, there was to be no classification or comparison made between classrooms, schools, and regions. A followup to this examination was planned for September 1991, using a sampling of students rather than an every student census.[73]

Democratic reform implemented some 15 years ago has meant that almost all 11-year-olds begin sixth grade in comprehensive secondary schools (*college*) of mixed ability levels. At the completion of comprehensive school, examinations for the *brevet de college* (college certificate) are given in three subjects: French, mathematics, and history/ geography. The *brevet* examinations were abolished in 1977 and completely replaced by a school-based evaluation. However, because of concern with declining results and complaints about what it meant to complete secondary school, the *brevets* were reestablished in 1986. At present, graduation from secondary school is based on a combination of examinations controlled by the State and an evaluation by the school.[74]

A common curriculum has been an expression of the value placed on the ideal of a unitary, cohesive, clearly defined French culture. Some have suggested this unity was won at the price of official neglect of minority and regional cultures within the country.[75] But this is changing, and nowhere is this change better reflected than in the discussion of what subjects should be taught at the *lycee* (the third level of schooling) and for the *Baccalaureat* (*Bac*), taken at the completion of the *lycee*. While once the focus was to provide the French *culture generale*, a common French culture through a central curriculum for the few who could demonstrate a high level of formal academic ability in literature, philosophy, and mathematics, this attitude has changed dramatically in recent years.

---

[71]Henk P.J. Kreeft (ed.), ''Issues in Public Examinations,'' paper prepared for the International Association for Educational Assessment, 16th International Conference on Issues in Public Examinations, Maastricht, The Netherlands, June 18-22, 1990.

[72]Marten Le Guen and Catherine Lacronique, ''Evaluation CE-6eme. A Survey Report of Assessment Procedures in France on Mathematics, Reading and Writing,'' paper prepared for the International Association for Educational Assessment, 16th International Conference on Issues in Public Examinations, Maastricht, The Netherlands, June 18-22, 1990.

[73]Ibid., p. 4.

[74]Kreeft, op. cit., footnote 71, p. 16.

[75]Eckstein and Noah, op. cit., footnote 6, p. 312.

Current practice has been moving to reduce the uniformity and increase variety and options. Since 1950, the French have changed the *Bac* radically in order to meet demands for a more relevant set of curricula and to open access to a larger group of students. While in the period before 1950 there were 4 options, the *Bac* has diversified into some 53 options and 3 types of *Bac* diploma: secondary (general) education diploma, with 8 options; technician/vocational *Bac*, with 20 options; and, since 1985, a new vocational diploma with 25 options.[76] The vocational and technical programs have been strengthened and the numbers of students enrolled are also rising.

Indeed, one of the goals of education reform in France has been to democratize the *Bac*. Between ages 13 and 15, the proportion of children attending schools leading to the *Bac* drops from 95 to 67 percent. Among these, one-half actually passed the *Bac* in 1990, i.e., 38.5 percent of students in the relevant age group were eligible for admission to university.[77] In 1991, 46 percent of the examinees passed.[78] This represents a dramatic reform to the French pyramidal system: in 1955, only about 5.5 percent of French students qualified for university-level education.[79] The French Government has set a goal for the year 2000 to have 80 percent of students in the age group reach the *Bac* level.[80] Part of this process is the creation of a number of new technological, vocational, and professional *Bacs*, and better counselling for students concerning specialties, along with restructuring of the *Bac* to make all tracks as prestigious as the ''*Bac C*,'' the mathematically oriented track.[81]

Despite these changes, the *Bac* remains a revered institution in France. It is debated each year as questions and model answers are printed in newspapers after the examinations are given each spring. A central core of general education subjects (e.g., French literature, philosophy, history, and geography) is required of all candidates, but different weights are given in scoring them depending on the student's specialization. Examination formats are generally composed of four types of questions: the dissertation—an examination that consists of a question to be answered in the form of an essay; a commentary on documents; open-ended questions; and multiple-choice questions for modern foreign languages.[82] While MOE formulates the various *Bac* examinations, working from questions proposed each year by committees made up of *lycee* and university teachers, each academy provides its own version from centrally approved lists. Thus questions for each subject, though all of the same nature and level of difficulty, vary from one region to another. Teachers are given some latitude to set their own standards of grading, and there have been concerns regarding a lack of common standards and comparability in the various forms of the *Bac*.

Today the *Bac* can no longer be described as a single nationally comparable examination administered to all candidates. While success in the *Bac* remains the passport to university study, it has been suggested that today there is more than one class of travel in a two-speed university system.[83] Thus entry to the slower track remains automatic with the *Bac*, but entry into more remunerative and prestigious lines of study (*classes preparatoires* of *grandes ecoles* and faculties of medicine, dentistry, and some science departments) require high scores in a more difficult *Bac* series. Students who wish to seek admission to the highly selective *grandes ecoles*, which provide superior study conditions and enhanced career opportunities for higher ranks of government service, professions, and business, compete in another examination, the *concours*, usually taken after another year or two of intense preparation. This competition is rigorous; only 10 percent of the age cohort attends the *grandes ecoles*.[84] Thus, competition to enter a prestigious university or

---

[76]Sylvie Auvillain, cultural service, French Embassy, Washington DC, personal communication, August 1991.

[77]Embassy of France, Cultural Service, *Organisation of the French Educational System Leading to the French Baccalaureat* (Washington, DC: January 1991).

[78]Auvillian, op. cit., footnote 76.

[79]Eckstein and Noah, op. cit., footnote 6, p. 304.

[80]National Endowment for the Humanities, op. cit., footnote 37, p. 9.

[81]Ibid.

[82]Kreeft, op. cit., footnote 71, p. 16.

[83]Eckstein and Noah, op. cit., footnote 6, p. 309.

[84]Ibid., p. 304.

professional track has maintained the high value placed on examinations in France.

Germany

Germany is credited with pioneering the use of examinations in Europe. In 1748, candidates for the Prussian civil service were required to take an examination. Later, as a university education became a prerequisite for government service, the *Abitur* examination was introduced in 1788 as a means for determining completion of middle school and consequent eligibility for a university entrance.[85]

Today tracking into one of three lines of schooling begins at approximately age 10 in Germany. After completing 4 years of common schooling (*grundschule*), German students move into one of three lines of schooling. The *hauptschule* (main school) or lower general education extends for 5 years and leads to terminal vocational training at about age 16. The *realschule* or higher general education extends for 6 years and directs students to intermediate positions in occupations. The *gymnasium* is the university track and extends for 9 years. There is also a *gesamtschule*: 6 or 9 years of comprehensive schooling containing all three lines. During each of these levels of schooling there are relatively few examinations until their conclusion. There is a reasonable balance in the number of openings for the next level for each track, and examination pressure is not terribly intense at this level.[86] Because of a traditionally strong and well-respected vocational track, Germany's dual system means that students have several options available to them. Ironically, the traditional distinctions between these two career paths is becoming somewhat blurred and so, by the same token, is the function of the *Abitur*. Increasing numbers of *Abitur* holders are turning toward apprenticeship or technical training rather than

Size	137,743 square miles, slightly smaller than Montana
Population	77,555,000 (1990)
School enrollment	11.0 million (1988)
Age of compulsory schooling	6 to 16
Number of school days	160 to 170 (varies per State)
Selection points and major examinations	1. Tracking at end of common school (age 10) into three lines of schooling, but not via examination 2. *Abitur* at end of grade 13 for university entrance, determined by each State (*land*), with oversight by national government
Curriculum control	*Land* control

academic careers, changing the function of the examination process.[87]

At the conclusion of grade 13 in the *gymnasium*, students take the *Abitur*, which entitles them to study at their local university or any university in Germany.[88] The specific content of each *Abitur* is determined by the education ministries in the various *lander* (or States) in Germany, within a general framework established by the national Standing Conference of Ministers of Education and Cultural Affairs. It should be noted that the *Abitur*, like the French *Bac*, has changed over the years as the number of students in *gymnasium* has increased, and greater numbers of *Abitur* holders has meant restrictions on their constitutional right to enroll at a university in a chosen course of study. In 1986, 23.7 percent of the relevant age group held the *Abitur*.[89]

In the past, the *Abitur* required candidates to complete an extraordinarily demanding curriculum, but in recent years the breadth and depth of studies has been reduced as variety and options have added diversification to what was once a relatively uniform examination. Demands made on students have been subject to swings; in 1979, candidates could take selected subjects at lower levels of difficulty, but in the fall of 1987 the Council of Ministers reconsidered these changes and restored some of the older regulations and standards, especially limiting candi-

---

[85]Cummings, op. cit., footnote 43, p. 90.

[86]Ibid., p. 92.

[87]Eckstein and Noah, op. cit., footnote 6, p. 306.

[88]Quite a high number of students do not study at their local university, but at another elsewhere in Germany. Lack of places at the local university means that some students have to study at distant universities. Reinhard Wiemer, second secretary, German Embassy, Washington DC, personal communication, August 1991.

[89]National Endowment for the Humanities, op. cit., footnote 37, p. 29.

dates' freedom to select subjects at lower levels of difficulty. Students choose four subjects in which to be examined, across three categories of knowledge: languages, literature, and the arts; social science; and mathematics, natural sciences, and technology. Examinations are strongly school-bound, with much effort placed on tying questions to the training provided by a particular school. Even if questions are provided centrally across a *land*, different sets are provided from which teachers may choose. In virtually all *lander*, the assessment of the examination papers takes place entirely within the school, by the students' own teachers. Only Baden-Wurtenberg has a system of coassessment by teachers of other schools.[90]

Examinations always consist of open-ended questions, which usually require essay responses. Some examinations are oral, while others, in subjects such as art, music, and natural sciences, may involve performance or demonstration.[91]

Despite the open format of the *Abitur*, there has been more concern with comparability across the various *lander* than across individuals, since schooling is a *land* prerogative. There is a delicate balance between State ownership of examinations and national comparability. As a result, some *lander* regard *Abitur* earned in other *lander* with a certain degree of suspicion, limiting student ease of movement to universities across the country and comparability and transferability of credentials.[92]

Sweden

Swedish schooling has always been characterized by a blend of central control of curriculum and decentralized management and assessment. In seeking to offer equivalent education to all students, regardless of social background or geographic location, there has been a national curriculum,

Size	173,731 square miles, slightly larger than California
Population	8,407,000 (1990)
School enrollment	1.2 million (1987)
Age of compulsory schooling	7 to 16
Number of school days	180
Selection points and major examinations	1. After compulsory school (age 16) admission to upper secondary school (*gymnasieskolan*) by marks, not examinations.
	2. University entrance by grades or the Swedish Scholastic Aptitude Test (national tests).
Curriculum control	National, common curriculum with local flexibility

accompanied by detailed earmarking of grants to municipal authorities for the organization and administration of schools. Recent reforms have specified that the national government will indicate goals and guidelines, while municipalities are responsible for the achievement of targets set by the national education authority. Each municipality will receive financial support from the national authority, but without detailed spending regulations.[93]

Compulsory schooling for Swedish children begins at age 7 and extends through grade nine, to age 16. The elementary school (*Grundskol*) is divided into three levels: lower (1 to 3); middle (4 to 6); and upper (7 to 9). Students remain in common heterogeneous classes throughout the first 9 years, but at the upper school level (grades 7 to 9) they begin to choose from a number of elective courses. There is a common curriculum for all schools at each level; those studying any given subject at the same level follow the same curriculum, have the same number of weekly periods, and use common texts and materials. However, it is understood that within the general framework it is up to the teacher to develop his or her own approach to teaching the subject.[94]

After finishing compulsory schooling at age 16, the great majority of students continue on to the integrated upper secondary school or *gymnasieskolan*. At the upper secondary school, there are a variety of

[90]Kreeft, op. cit., footnote 71, p. 18.

[91]National Endowment for the Humanities, op. cit., footnote 37, p. 29.

[92]Eckstein and Noah, op. cit., footnote 6, p. 314.

[93]As of July 1, 1991, the National Board of Education and regional country education committees were abolished and a new central education authority was established. Karin Rydberg, *A Redistribution of Responsibilities in the Swedish School System* (Stockholm, Sweden: The Swedish National Board of Education, January 1991).

[94]National Swedish Board of Education, ''Assessment in Swedish Schools,'' informational document, February 1985, p. 1.

courses of study in 2-, 3-, and 4-year programs. Overall some 25 options or lines of study are available, each characterized by a combination of special subjects and a common core of compulsory subjects.[95] Admission to the integrated upper secondary school is based on teacher grades (referred to as marks) obtained in elementary school, with a certain minimum average required. All subjects (including music, drawing, and handicraft) are included in computing the marks, with none weighted more heavily than any other. In 1983, approximately 85 percent of the age cohort were admitted to the *gymnasieskolan*, with 10 percent applying and not admitted, and about 5 percent not applying to upper level schooling.[96]

Assessment in Swedish schools consists of both marks and standardized tests (*centralaprov*). The individual teacher is solely responsible for the marking, and no educational or legal authority can alter a given mark or force a teacher to do so. Marks are given at the end of each course as a means of providing information to the students and parents on the student's level of success in a course, and are the basis of selection of students for admission to the upper secondary school and to the university. Thus there is considerable effort to provide assurance that marks have the same value, despite the fact that marks are given by thousands of individual teachers across the country.

The main purpose of standardized achievement testing in Sweden is to enable the teachers to compare the performance of their own class with that of the total population and adjust their marking scale. While the *centralaprov* are developed by the national education authority, the tests correspond closely to the syllabi and are aimed at measuring achievement based on national standards. All standardized tests, which are short answer, fill in the blank, and short essay examinations, are centrally developed but administered and graded by the classroom teacher. Detailed instructions on scoring principles are issued by the national board. A sample of results representative of the total population of students tested is submitted to the national board, and marking norms are developed so that test results can be converted into one of the marks on the 5-point Swedish scale. These norms are then sent to all

schools, and teachers mark their tests based accordingly.

Although some tests are used for diagnosis at the classroom level, neither these nor *centralaprov* are used for selection or school accountability in the sense of ranking schools. A large number of standardized tests measuring skills and knowledge are used, along with diagnostic materials. Achievement testing is not conducted until grade eight (in English) and grade nine in Swedish and mathematics. All standardized tests at the elementary level are voluntary for the school and/or teacher; however, about 80 percent of all teachers use them. These tests are used repeatedly over a period of some years and are kept confidential.[97]

In the upper secondary school, the standardized achievement tests must be given in each subject. These, too, have been developed by the national board and are scored by teachers.

Final assessment of each student at the end of a term is a carefully orchestrated business. Teachers keep records of each student's performance on compulsory written tests (in addition to the standardized tests); these are filed and made available when the inspectors from the county education committees visit schools. On these visits, they check to see if the marking principles applied by the teacher are more lenient or severe than national norms. At the end of a term, the teacher surveys all evaluation data collected above (written tests, standardized tests, and observations based on running records) and ranks the pupils in the class from top to bottom on the same 5-point scale.

Here again the standardized tests play an important role. First the teacher calculates the mean of the preliminary marks and records their distribution over the 5-point scale, then compares these data with the mean and distribution of marks obtained by the class in taking the standardized tests. These results are compared and the teacher adjusts the preliminary marks as he or she sees fit, depending on the circumstances surrounding the standardized test (the class may not have covered some part of the standardized test, or there may have been several of the best or the weakest pupils missing when the test was administered, thus skewing results.) The final

[95]Ibid., pp. 3-5.

[96]Ibid., p. 3.

[97]Ibid., p. 13.

judgment is the teacher's, although a meeting called the class conference, attended by the head, assistant head, and all teachers teaching the class for one or more subjects, is also held. At this meeting, comparisons are made between the standard achieved in different subjects and between the achievements of different classes in the same subject. "A teacher who wants to retain noticeable differences between test results and preliminary marks has to convince the class conference that there is a valid reason for doing so."[98]

Sweden abolished its school-leaving examination (for graduation) in the mid-1960s. From that point on, admission to universities and colleges for students coming directly from the upper secondary school has been based entirely on the marks given by teachers. Applicants 25 years or older and with more than 4 years of work experience were admitted based on the Swedish Scholastic Aptitude Test (SWESAT). This test consists of 6 subtests, for a total of 144 multiple-choice items, with a testing time of approximately 4 hours. The SWESAT is administered by the National Swedish Board of Universities and Colleges, with test construction placed in the hands of the department of education at Umea University. About 10,000 persons take the test each year. The selection procedure was part of an elaborate system of quota groups to ensure a fair distribution of openings for different groups of applicants. There are three groups: those submitting formal measures of academic ability—grades and SWESAT for those who have not completed upper secondary education; those relying on work experience—which for all groups of applicants may compensate for a low score on academic ability; and a small number of places for those accepted for special reasons, despite low scores.

In the 1970s and 1980s, the number of applicants to higher education greatly exceeded the number of available places, and this created debate. The existing system of quotas was criticized for being cumbersome, uniform, and complex. Furthermore, the use of work experience was criticized on the grounds that it delays the transition to higher

education. In fact work experience has become almost compulsory for many programs in high demand. (Today the average age of a first-year freshman in Sweden is 23.) The fact that practically all experience is given credit, regardless of relevance to the study program in question, has also been debated. Some believe the system should give weight largely to academic ability as a better predictor of success in higher education.

As a result of this debate, the Swedish Parliament established a new scheme for selection to higher education that more strongly stresses the need for measures of academic ability and restricts the role of work experience. The new system, which went into effect in July 1991, uses several factors for determining admission. Average grades from upper secondary school will continue to constitute a major factor in the selection process. (Between one-half and two-thirds of all students will be selected on the basis of grades alone.) A general aptitude test (currently the SWESAT) is open to students leaving upper secondary school as well. This is seen as an alternative path to higher education for those who do not have sufficient grades. Between one-third and two-thirds of all students will be selected on the basis of the test results. Finally, flexibility is being added to ensure that a small number of students can be admitted on an individual basis.[99] It is not yet clear what the impact of these changes will have on school curriculum across Sweden.

England and Wales

The Education Reform Act (ERA) of 1988 set in motion a major overhaul of the education system of the United Kingdom (England, Wales, and Northern Ireland).[100] Although authority over the schools had been shifting from local to central government at least since the second World War, the 1988 reforms were seen by many as a watershed event. One analysis by comparative education re-

---

[98]Ibid., p. 17.

[99]Hans Jansson, "Swedish Admissions Policy on the Road From Uniformity and Central Planning to Flexibility and Local Influence?" paper prepared for the International Association of Educational Assessment, November 1989. See also Ingemar Wedman, Department of Education, University of Umea, Sweden, "The Swedish Scholastic Aptitude Test: Development, Use and Research," unpublished document, October 1990.

[100]There are actually three education systems in the United Kingdom: one for England and Wales, a second for Scotland, and a third for Northern Ireland. This report deals predominantly with England and Wales, but all three systems are reforming curriculum and assessment programs.

Size	94,226 square miles, slightly smaller than Oregon
Population	57,121,000 (1990)
School enrollment	10,089,000 (1983)
Age of compulsory schooling	5 to 16
Number of school days	192[a]
Selection points and major examinations	1. New national assessments at age 7, 11, 14, 16 (not for selection)
	2. Two-tiered school-leaving examinations: General Certificate of Secondary Education at age 16 or earlier; "A levels" at grades 11 or 12 (sixth form) at age 18 (all set by local boards, national oversight, considered for university entrance)
Curriculum control	National, central control (since 1988)

[a]Wayne Riddle, Congressional Research Service, personal communication, Nov. 26, 1991.

searchers concluded that the reforms "... represented an abrupt acceleration of the otherwise glacially slow process of transferring authority over the schools from local to central government."[101]

England always had a diverse and decentralized school system. The great universities and "public" schools,[102] which were closely tied to the Church of England, existed for the upper classes; there was no need for selective entrance examinations, given that student qualifications were not an issue for admissions.[103] In the middle of the 19th century, England's highly decentralized system distinguished it from other European countries, which already had strong central curricula and uniform school-leaving examinations. To bring some order to the system, the British Government instituted the "payment by results" system. Beginning in 1861, local governments whose students performed well on a special national test received extra subsidies. The goal of this policy was to promote quality in key subject areas. There was no attempt to create a central curriculum.[104] This testing program was eventually scuttled because of dissatisfaction with the inequalities it aggravated. Schools that had the most difficult

problems were those that suffered most under the system; essentially the rich got richer.

Following World War II, in an effort to democratize secondary school selection procedures, the 11+ examination was developed. These were local examinations, run by local education authorities (LEAs). The goal was to track students at age 11, according to ability, as measured on the examination and according to need. Roughly 20 percent of students were tracked into grammar school (i.e., the college preparatory track) and the rest into secondary "modern" schools. As LEAs introduced comprehensive schools in place of the grammar and secondary moderns, the 11+ was no longer needed. Although it is still in use in a small number of places in England and Wales, by and large the 11+ was dropped during the 1960s and 1970s.

The General Certificate of Secondary Education (GCSE) continues the tradition of local control of curriculum and testing. Although the concept of merging the prior "ordinary" examination ("O levels") and the GSCE examinations goes back to the early 1970s, the first GCSE examinations were administered in 1988. The GCSE became the single examination, mirroring the switch from the grammar and secondary moderns to one comprehensive school. The GCSE is taken by students at the age of 16 or earlier. Local groups of teachers and school administrators, through the examining boards, introduce examination topics related to their own syllabi. A central School Examinations and Assessment Council, established by Parliament, establishes national examination criteria to which all GCSE syllabi and examinations must conform. Recruitment into certain jobs and selection into advanced training are influenced by the number and quality of passing grades on the GCSE.

More advanced examinations, the "A levels" are also offered in the upper grades of comprehensive school (age 18). Success on at least three A levels has become an important criterion for advancement to university study. Thus the school-leaving examination system in the United Kingdom has evolved into a two-tiered examination system. A recent

---

[101]Noah and Eckstein, op. cit., footnote 44, p. 25. This characterization may be somewhat overstated, given that local management of schools remains an important component of the school system. Robert Ratcliffe, academic programs officer, The British Council, personal communication, Aug. 15, 1991.

[102]English "public" schools would be called "private" in the American idiom.

[103]Cummings, op. cit., footnote 43.

[104]Ibid., p. 93.

survey of 16-year-olds in England showed slightly over one-half planning to continue their education. About one-third of the country's 16-year-olds, who achieved grades of A, B, or C (on a scale of A to G) on five or more of their GCSE examinations, are most likely to continue. In 1988-89, 22 percent of all 18-year-olds in England passed one or more A-level examinations; 12 percent, three or more.[105] Students have, in the past, been able to select their own subjects for the GCSE and its predecessors and for the A levels.[106] There is some concern that early specialization in grades 11 and 12, to prepare for A levels, is one factor causing many students to abandon study in mathematics and the sciences at age 16 in favor of the humanities or social sciences.

The background for the 1988 reform was similar to the push for educational changes in the United States: business people were complaining that students arrived at the workplace lacking basic skills, while others were troubled by inequalities in teaching, resources, and by an education system out of sync with technology. The Conservative Government under Margaret Thatcher put into place a reform bill that forced the issue. As the chief executive of the newly established National Curriculum Council noted: "The educational establishment, left to its own, will take a hundred years to buy a new stick of chalk. . . . In the end, to say: 'It's time you guys got on with it; here's an act and a crisp timetable' was probably necessary."[107]

First and foremost, the ERA defined a comprehensive national curriculum for all public school students ages 5 to 16. These students are to take foundation subjects: core subjects are English (Welsh, in Wales), mathematics, and science, plus, for 11- to 16-year-olds, technology (including design), history, geography, music, art, physical education, and modern foreign language. Attainment targets set general objectives and standards for 10 levels covering the full range of pupils of different abilities in compulsory education. Average pupils will reach level two by age 7; each new level represents, on average, 2 years of progress. The statements of attainment provide the basis for the assessment

arrangements. Assessment is to take place by classroom teachers throughout the year, with special soundings via national tests known as standard assessment tasks (SATs) given at or near the completion of each of four "key stages" of teaching (ages 7, 11, 14, 16).

The assessments are meant to serve multiple purposes:

>. . . *formative*, providing information teachers can use in deciding how a pupil's learning should be taken forward, and in giving the pupils themselves clear and understandable targets and feedback about their achievements; *summative*, providing overall evidence of the achievements of a pupil and of what he or she knows, understands and can do; *evaluative*, providing comparative aggregated information about pupils' achievements as an indicator of where there needs to be further effort, resources, changes in the curriculum; and *informative*, helping communication with parents about how their child is doing and with governing bodies, LEAs and the wider community about the achievements of a school.[108]

The objective is to keep the schools working within a national framework but with local discretion in implementing the curriculum. As parents can now send children to any school they choose, it is anticipated that parents will compare published examination results of schools, and thus schools will try to raise standards to attract more pupils.[109] But there is concern that comparisons may mask differing social and economic levels of students, and that problems associated with the "payment by results" approach of 100 years ago could return. Teachers also feel overwhelmed by the requirements of the program: the double system of assessment at key stages—with the SATs as well as continuous assessment in the classroom—means that British school children will soon be the most assessed in Europe.

The program is being implemented at the primary level in the spring of 1991 and will be phased in over the next 3 years. Secondary students may be assessed through GCSEs or according to National Curriculum assessments at age 16. GCSE criteria

[105]National Endowment for the Humanities, op. cit., footnote 37, p. 45.

[106]Few schools allowed students to omit mathematics and English for the General Certificate of Secondary Education and its predecessors, but rules about what must be studied at this level will become tighter under the national curriculum assessment. Nuttal, op. cit., footnote 14.

[107]Tim Brookes, "A Lesson to Us All," *The Atlantic*, vol. 267, No. 5, May 1991, p. 28.

[108]Department of Education and Science, *National Curriculum: From Policy to Practice* (Stanmore, England: 1989), p. 6.

[109]Brookes, op. cit., footnote 107.

and syllabi will be brought into line with the statutory requirements for attainment targets, programs of study, and assessment strategies, but the relationship between National Curriculum's 10 levels of attainment and the GCSE grades has yet to be determined.[110] In early 1991, plans were announced to require all students to take GCSEs in the three core subjects of English (or Welsh), mathematics, and science. The study of either history or geography, technology, and a modern foreign language is also compulsory to age 16. Students can choose whether to have their competence in these and other subjects assessed by GCSE examinations.[111]

The SATs are one of the most interesting features of the program, and the feature most likely to influence curriculum. As in most European testing programs, the SATs have only open-ended questions. Many innovative testing approaches were developed for an earlier comprehensive assessment England embarked on in 1975.[112] These innovative test items and formats are the basis for many of the performance testing items that are to become the backbone of the SATs and classroom assessment procedures under the new program.

A nationally representative sample of students at ages 11, 13, and 15 were tested in a survey similar to NAEP. The 1975 goal was to assess the achieve-ment and knowledge of student performance in four areas: mathematics, language, science, and foreign languages.

Mathematical abilities were tested in several formats, including 50 short-response items drawn from a total of 700 test items in each survey. A subsample of students in each age group were given written tests of problem-solving skills; another subsample of 1,200 students in each age group were given oral tests of problem-solving tasks. The mother language survey assessed reading, writing, and "oracy," a term coined for its analogy to literacy as a measure of the ability to communicate effectively in a spoken as opposed to written medium. The science assessments were made up of individual and small group tasks emphasizing practical skills performed at a number of "stations." Foreign language testing used oral and written testing formats.

The program led to the evolution and application of innovative techniques to assess student performance, such as mathematical skills in a practical context, especially those whose mathematical abilities were masked by reading difficulties; written and spoken skills in the mother tongue and in foreign languages; and practical assessments in science.

---

[110]Department of Education and Science, op. cit., footnote 108, paragraph 6.7.

[111]National Endowment for the Humanities, op. cit., footnote 37, p. 45.

[112]Clare Burstall, ''Innovative Forms of Assessment: A United Kingdom Perspective,'' *Educational Measurement: Issues and Practice*, vol. 5, No. 1, spring 1986.

CHAPTER 6

Standardized Tests in Schools: A Primer

Contents

Boxes

Figures

Tables

Standardized Tests in Schools: A Primer

Highlights

A test is an objective and standardized method for estimating behavior, based on a sample of that behavior. A standardized test is one that uses uniform procedures for administration and scoring in order to assure that results from different people are comparable. Any kind of test—from multiple choice to essays to oral examinations—can be standardized if uniform scoring and administration are used.

Achievement tests are the most widely used tests in schools. Achievement tests are designed to assess what a student knows and can do as a result of schooling. Among standardized achievement tests, multiple-choice formats predominate because they are efficient, easily administered, broad in their coverage, and can be machine scored.

Advances in test design and technology have made American standardized achievement tests remarkably sophisticated, reliable, and precise. However, misuse of tests and misconceptions about what test scores mean are common.

Tests are often used for purposes for which they have not been designed. Tests must be designed and validated for a specific function and use of a test should be limited to only those functions. Once tests are in the public domain, misuse or misinterpretation of test results is not easy to control or change.

Because test scores are estimates and can vary for reasons that have nothing to do with student achievement, the results of a single test should never be used as the sole criterion for making important decisions about individuals. A test must meet high standards of reliability and validity before it is used for any "high-stakes" decisions.

The kind of information policymakers and school authorities need to monitor school systems is very different from the kind teachers need to guide instruction. Relatively few standardized tests fulfill the classroom needs of teachers.

Existing standardized norm-referenced tests primarily test basic skills. This is because they are "generic" tests designed to be used in schools throughout the Nation, and basic skills are most common to all curricula.

Current disaffection with existing standardized achievement tests rests largely on three features of these tests: 1) most are norm-referenced and thus compare students to one another, 2) most are multiple choice, and 3) their content does not adequately represent local curricula, especially thinking and reasoning skills. This disaffection is driving efforts among educators and test developers to broaden the format of standardized tests. They seek to design tests more closely matched to local curricula, and to design tests that best serve the various functions of educational testing.

Changing the format of tests will not, by itself, ensure that tests are better measures of desired goals nor will it eliminate problems of bias, reliability, and validity. In part because of these technical and administrative concerns, test developers are exploring ways to improve multiple-choice formats to measure complex thinking skills better. As new tests are designed, new safeguards will be needed to ensure they are not misused.

How Do Schools Test?

Nearly every type of available test designed for use with children is used in schools. Tests of personality, intelligence, aptitude, speech, sensory acuity, and perceptual motor skill, all of which have applications in nonschool settings as well, are used by trained personnel such as guidance counselors, speech-language specialists, and school psychologists. Certain tests, however, have been designed specifically for use in educational settings. These

Figure 6-1—Tests Used With Children

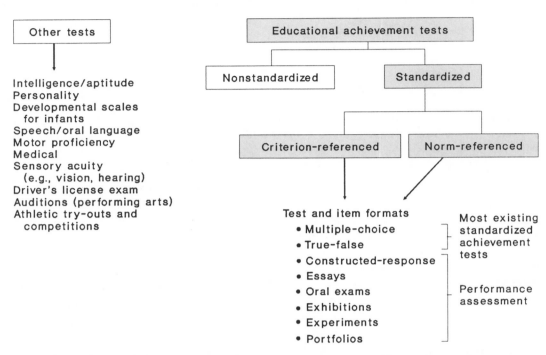

SOURCE: Office of Technology Assessment, 1992; adapted from F.L. Finch, "Toward a Definition for Educational Performance Assessment," paper presented at the ERIC/PDK Symposium, August 1990.

tests, commonly referred to as achievement tests, are designed to assess student learning in school subject areas. They are also the most frequently used tests in elementary and secondary school settings; with few exceptions all students take achievement tests at multiple points in their educational careers. Educational achievement tests are the primary focus of this report.

Figure 6-1 shows the distinction between educational achievement tests and the other kinds of tests. Achievement tests are designed to assess what a student knows and can do in a specific subject area as a result of instruction or schooling. Achievement test results are designed to indicate a student's degree of success in past learning activity. Achievement tests are sometimes contrasted with aptitude tests, which are designed to predict what a person can be expected to accomplish with training (see box 6-A).

Achievement tests include a wide range of types of tests, from those designed by individual teachers

to those designed by commercial test publishing companies. Examples of the kinds of tests teachers design and use include a weekly spelling test, a final essay examination in history, or a laboratory examination in biology. At the other end of the achievement test spectrum are tests designed outside the school system itself and administered only once or twice a year; examples of this include the familiar multiple-choice, paper-and-pencil tests that might cover reading, language arts, mathematics, and social studies (see box 6-B).

The first important distinction when talking about achievement tests is between standardized and nonstandardized tests (see figure 6-1 again).[1] A standardized test uses uniform procedures for administering and scoring. This assures that scores obtained by different people are comparable to one another. Because of this, tests that are not standardized have limited practical usefulness outside of the classroom. Most teacher-developed tests or "back-of-the-book" tests found in textbooks would be consid-

---

[1]Fredrick L. Finch, The Riverside Publishing Co., "Toward a Definition for Educational Performance Assessment," paper presented at the ERIC/PDK Symposium, 1990.

Photo credit: Dennis Galloway

Standardized achievement tests are often administered to many students at the same sitting. Standardization means that tests are administered and scored under the same conditions for all students and ensures that results are comparable across classrooms and schools.

Box 6-A—Achievement and Aptitude Tests: What is the Difference?

Attempts to measure learning as a result of schooling (achievement) and attempts to measure aptitude (including intelligence) each have different, yet intertwined, histories (see ch. 4). Intelligence testing, with its strong psychometric and scientific emphasis, has influenced the design of achievement tests in this country. Achievement tests are generally distinguished from aptitude tests in the degree to which they are explicitly tied to a course of schooling. In the absence of common national educational goals, the need for achievement tests that can be taken by any student has resulted in tests more remote from specific curricula than tests developed close to the classroom. The degree of difference can be subtle and the test's title is not always a reliable guide.

> A test producer's claims for an achievement test or an aptitude test do not mean that it will function as such in all circumstances with all pupils.[1]

> There clearly is overlap between a pupil's measured ability and achievement, and perhaps the final answer to the question of whether any test assesses a pupil's achievement or a more general underlying trait such as verbal ability rests with the local user, who knows the student and the curriculum he or she has followed.[2]

The farther removed a test is from the specific educational curricula that has been delivered to the test taker, the more that test is likely to resemble a measure of aptitude instead of achievement for that student.

Whenever tests are going to be used for policy decisions about the effectiveness of education, it is important to assure that those tests are measuring achievement, not ability; inferences about school effectiveness must be directly tied to what the school actually delivers in the classroom—not to what children already bring to the classroom. Accordingly, tests designated for accountability should be shown to be sensitive to the effects of school-related instruction.[3]

To understand better the distinctions currently made between achievement and aptitude tests, it is helpful to turn to one of the "pillars of assessment development,"[4] Anne Anastasi:

> Surpassing all other types of standardized tests in sheer number, achievement tests are designed to measure the effects of a specific program of instruction or training. It has been customary to contrast achievement tests with

---

[1]Eric Gardner, "Some Aspects of the Use and Misuse of Standardized Aptitude and Achievement Tests," *Ability Testing: Uses, Consequences, and Controversies*, part 2, Alexandra K. Wigdor and Wendell R. Garner (eds.) (Washington, DC: National Academy Press, 1982), p. 325.

[2]Peter W. Airasian, "Review of Iowa Tests of Basic Skills, Forms 7 and 8," *The Ninth Mental Measurements Yearbook*, vol. I, James V. Mitchell, Jr. (ed.) (Lincoln, NE: The University of Nebraska Press, 1985), p. 720.

[3]No achievement test, though, will measure *only* school-related learning. For any child, learning takes place daily and as a result of all his or her cumulative experiences. "No test reveals how or why the individual reached that level." Anne Anastasi, *Psychological Testing* (New York, NY: MacMillian Publishing Co, 1988), p. 413.

[4]Carol Schneider Lidz, "Historical Perspectives," *Dynamic Assessment: An Interactional Approach to Evaluating Learning Potential* C.S. Lidz (ed.) (New York, NY: Guilford, 1987), pp. 3-32.

---

ered nonstandardized. Although these tests may be useful to the individual teacher, scores obtained by students on these tests would not be comparable—across classrooms, schools, or different points in time—because the administration and scoring are not standardized.

Thus, contrary to popular understanding, "standardized" does not mean norm-referenced nor does it mean multiple choice. As the tree diagram in figure 6-1 illustrates, standardized tests can take many different forms. All achievement tests intended for widespread use in decisions comparing children, schools, and districts should be standardized. Lack of standardization severely limits the inferences and

conclusions that can be made on the basis of test results. A test can be more or less standardized (there is no absolute criterion or yardstick to denote when a test has "achieved" standardization); as a result, teacher-developed tests can incorporate features of standardization that will permit inferences to be made with more confidence.

Most existing standardized tests can be divided into two primary types based on the reference point for score comparison: norm-referenced and criterion-referenced.

Norm-referenced tests help compare one student's performance with the performances of a large group of students. Norm-referenced tests are de-

aptitude tests, the latter including general intelligence tests, multiple aptitude batteries, and special aptitude tests. From one point of view, the difference between achievement and aptitude testing is a difference in the degree of uniformity of relevant antecedent experience. Thus achievement tests measure the effects of relatively standardized sets of experiences, such as a course in elementary French, trigonometry, or computer programming. In contrast, aptitude test performance reflects the cumulative influence of a multiplicity of experiences in daily living. We might say that aptitude tests measure the effects of learning under relatively uncontrolled and unknown conditions, while achievement tests measure the effects of learning that occurred under partially known and controlled conditions.

A second distinction between aptitude and achievement tests pertains to their respective uses. Aptitude tests serve to predict subsequent performance. They are employed to estimate the extent to which the individual will profit from a specified course of training, or to forecast the quality of his or her achievement in a new situation. Achievement tests, on the other hand, generally represent a terminal evaluation of the individual's status on the completion of training. The emphasis on such tests is on what the individual can do at the time.[5]

Although in the early days of psychological testing aptitude tests were thought to measure "innate capacity" (unrelated to schooling, experience, or background), while achievement tests were thought to measure learning, this is now considered a misconception.[6] Any test score will reflect a combination of school learning, prior experience, ability, individual characteristics (e.g., motivation), and opportunities to learn outside of school. Aptitude and achievement tests differ primarily in the extent to which the test content is directly affected by school experiences.

In the 1970s, aptitude tests, particularly IQ tests, came under increasing scrutiny and criticism. A highly political debate, set off by Arthur Jensen's controversial analysis of the heritability of racial differences in intelligence, thrust IQ tests into the limelight. Similarly, the late 1960s and early 1970s saw several significant court challenges to the use of IQ tests in ability tracking. Probably because of these controversies, as well as increased understanding of the limitations of intelligence tests, many large school systems have moved away from using aptitude tests as components of their basic testing programs.[7] These tests are still widely marketed, however, and their use in combination with achievement tests is often promoted.

Achievement and aptitude tests differ, but the distinctions between the two in terms of design and use are often blurred. For policy purposes, the essential point is this: even though a test may be defined as an achievement test, the more it moves away from items tied to specific curriculum content and toward items that assess broader concepts and skills, the more the test will function as an aptitude test. Should a national test be constructed in the absence of national standards or curriculum, it is therefore likely to be essentially an aptitude test. Such a test will not effectively reflect the results of schooling.

---

[5]Anastasi, op. cit., footnote 3, pp. 411-414.

[6]Ibid.

[7]C. Dimengo, *Basic Testing Programs Used in Major School Systems Throughout the United States in the School Year 1977-78* (Akron, OH: Akron Public Schools Division of Personnel and Administration, 1978).

---

signed to make fine distinctions between students' performances and accurately pinpoint where a student stands in relation to a large group of students.[2]

These tests are designed to rank students along a continuum.

Because of the complexities involved in obtaining nationally representative norms, norm-referenced tests (NRTs) are usually developed by commercial test-publishing companies who administer the test to large numbers of school children representative of the Nation's student population (see box 6-C). The score of each student who takes that test can be compared to the performance of other children in the standardization sample. Typically a single NRT is used by many schools and districts throughout the country.[3]

Criterion-referenced tests (CRTs) are focused on "... what test takers can do and what they know, not

---

[2]Lawrence Rudner, Jane Close Conoley, and Barbara S. Plake (eds.), *Understanding Achievement Tests* (Washington, DC: ERIC Clearinghouse on Tests, Measurement, and Evaluation, 1989), p. 10.

[3]Many publishers offer district-level norms as well. Several publishers now create custom-developed norm-referenced tests that are based on local curricular objectives, yet come with national norms. These norms, however, are only valid under certain circumstances. See ibid.

Box 6-B—Types of Standardized Achievement Tests

Currently available standardized achievement tests are likely to be one of four types.[1] The best known and most widely used type is the broad general survey achievement battery. These tests are used across the entire age range from kindergarten through adult, but are most widely used in elementary school. They provide scores in the major academic areas such as reading, language, mathematics, and sometimes science and social studies. They are usually commercially developed, norm-referenced, multiple-choice tests. Examples include the Comprehensive Test of Basic Skills, the Metropolitan Achievement Test, and the Iowa Tests of Basic Skills (ITBS). In addition, many test publishers now offer essay tests of writing that can accompany a survey achievement test.

In the 1989-90 school year, commercially published, off-the-shelf, achievement battery tests were a mandated feature of testing programs in about two-thirds of the States and the District of Columbia (see figure 6-B1). Five of those States required districts to select a commercial achievement test from a list of approved tests, while 27 specified a particular test to be administered. In addition, many districts require a norm-referenced test (NRT), even if the State does not. A survey of all districts in Pennsylvania, which does not mandate use of an NRT, found that 91 percent of the districts used a commercial off-the-shelf NRT.[2]

The second type of test is the test of minimum competency in basic skills. These tests are usually criterion-referenced and are used for certifying attainment and/or awarding a high school diploma. They are most often used in secondary school and are usually developed by the State or district.[3]

Far less frequently available as commercially published, standardized tests, the third category includes achievement tests in separate content areas. The best known examples of these are the Advanced Placement examinations administered by the College Board, used to test mastery of specific subjects such as history or biology at the end of high school for the purpose of obtaining college credit.

The final type of achievement test is the diagnostic battery. These tests differ from the survey achievement battery primarily in their specificity and depth; diagnostic tests have a more narrowly defined focus and concentrate on specific content knowledge and skills. They are generally designed to describe an individual's strengths and weaknesses within a subject matter area and to suggest reasons for difficulties. Most published diagnostic tests cover either reading or mathematics. Many of the diagnostic achievement tests need to be individually administered by a trained examiner and are used in special education screening and diagnosis.

---

[1]This discussion of the four types of achievement tests is drawn from Anne Anastasi, *Psychological Testing* (New York, NY: Macmillian Publishing Co., 1988).

[2]Ross S. Blust and Richard L. Kohr, Pennsylvania Department of Education, ''Pennsylvania School District Testing Programs,'' ERIC Document ED 269 409, TM 840-300, January 1984.

[3]See ch. 2 for a discussion of uses of minimum competency tests.

---

how they compare to others.''[4] CRTs usually report how a student is doing relative to specified educational goals or objectives. For example, a CRT score might describe which arithmetic operations a student can perform or the level of reading difficulty he or she can comprehend. Some of the earliest criterion-referenced scales were attempts to judge a student's mastery of school-related skills such as penmanship. Figure 6-2 illustrates one such scale, developed in 1910 by E.L. Thorndike to measure handwriting. The figure shows some of the sample specimens against which a student's handwriting could be judged and scored.

Most certification examinations are criterion-referenced. The skills one needs to know to be certified as a pilot, for example, are clearly spelled out and criteria by which mastery is achieved are described. Aspiring pilots then know which skills to work on. Eventually a pilot will be certified to fly not because she or he can perform these skills better than most classmates, but because knowledge and mastery of all important skills have been demonstrated.

---

[4]Anne Anastasi, *Psychological Testing* (New York, NY: MacMillan Publishing Co., 1988), p. 102. The term ''criterion-referenced test'' is being used here in its broadest sense and includes other terms such as content-, domain-, and objective-referenced tests.

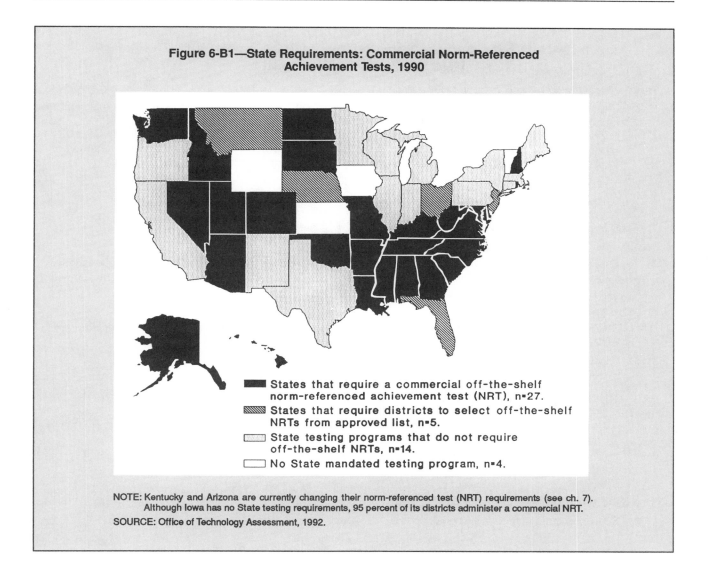

Figure 6-B1—State Requirements: Commercial Norm-Referenced Achievement Tests, 1990

■ States that require a commercial off-the-shelf norm-referenced achievement test (NRT), n=27.

▧ States that require districts to select off-the-shelf NRTs from approved list, n=5.

▨ State testing programs that do not require off-the-shelf NRTs, n=14.

□ No State mandated testing program, n=4.

NOTE: Kentucky and Arizona are currently changing their norm-referenced test (NRT) requirements (see ch. 7). Although Iowa has no State testing requirements, 95 percent of its districts administer a commercial NRT.

SOURCE: Office of Technology Assessment, 1992.

Such tests will usually have designated "cutoff" scores or proficiency levels above which a student must score to pass the test.

Another component of a standardized achievement test that warrants careful scrutiny is the format of the test, the kind of items or tasks used to demonstrate student skills and knowledge. The final level in figure 6-1 depicts the range of testing formats. Almost all group-administered standardized achievement tests are now made up of multiple-choice items[5] (see box 6-D). Currently, educators and test developers are examining ways to use a broader range of formats in standardized achieve-

ment tests. Most of these tasks, which range from essays to portfolios to oral examinations, are labelled "performance assessment" and are described in the next chapter.

Creating a Standardized Test: Concern for Consistency and Accuracy

The construction of a good test is an attempt to make a set of systematic observations in an accurate and equitable manner. In the time period since Binet's pioneering efforts in the empirical design of

---

[5]A number of commercially developed achievement tests have added optional direct sample writing tasks.

Box 6-C—How a Standardized Norm-Referenced Achievement Test is Developed[1]

Step 1—Specify general purpose of the test

Step 2—Develop test specifications or blueprint

- Identify the content that the test will cover: for achievement tests this means specifying both the subject matter and the behavioral objectives.
- Conduct a curriculum analysis by reviewing current texts, curricular guidelines, and research and by consulting experts in the subject areas and skills selected. Through this process a consensus definition of important content and skills is established, ensuring that the content is valid.

Step 3—Write items

- Often done by teams of professional item writers and subject matter experts.
- Many more items are written than will appear on the test.
- Items are reviewed for racial, ethnic, and sex bias by outside teams of professionals.

Step 4—Pretest items

- Preliminary versions of the items are tried out on large, representative samples of children. These samples must include children of all ages, geographic regions, ethnic groups, and so forth with whom the test will eventually be used.

Step 5—Analyze items

- Statistical information collected for each item includes measures of item difficulty, item discrimination, age differences in easiness, and analysis of incorrect responses.

Step 6—Locate standardization sample and conduct testing

- To obtain a nationally representative sample, publishers select students according to a number of relevant characteristics, including those for individual pupils (e.g., age and sex), school systems (e.g., public, parochial, or private) and communities (e.g., geographical regions or urban-rural-suburban).
- Most publishers administer two forms of a test at two different times of the year (fall and spring) during standardization.

Step 7—Analyze standardization data, produce norms, analyze reliability and validity evidence

- Alternate forms are statistically equated to one another.
- Special norms (e.g., for urban or rural schools) are often prepared as well.

Step 8—Publish test and test manuals

- Score reporting materials and guidelines are designed.

---

[1]Adapted from Anthony J. Nitko, *Educational Tests and Measurement: An Introduction* (New York, NY: Harcourt Brace Jovanovich, 1983), pp. 468-476.

tests,[6] considerable research effort has been expended to develop theories of measurement and statistical procedures for test construction. The science of test design, called psychometrics, has contributed important principles of test design and use. However, a test can be designed by anyone with a theory or a view to promote—witness the large number of "tests" of personality type, social IQ, attitude preference, health habits, and so forth that appear in popular magazines. Few mechanisms currently exist for monitoring the quality, accuracy, or credibility of tests. (See ch. 2 for further discussion of the issues of standards for tests, mechanisms for monitoring test use, and protections for test takers.)

How good is a test? Does it do the things it promises? What inferences and conclusions can be drawn from the scores? Does the test really work? These are difficult questions to answer and should not be determined by impressions, judgment, or appearances. Empirical information about the performance of large numbers of students on any given test is needed to evaluate its effectiveness and merits. This section addresses the principal methods used to evaluate the technical quality of tests. It

---

[6]See ch. 4.

Figure 6-2—Thorndike's Scale for Measuring Handwriting

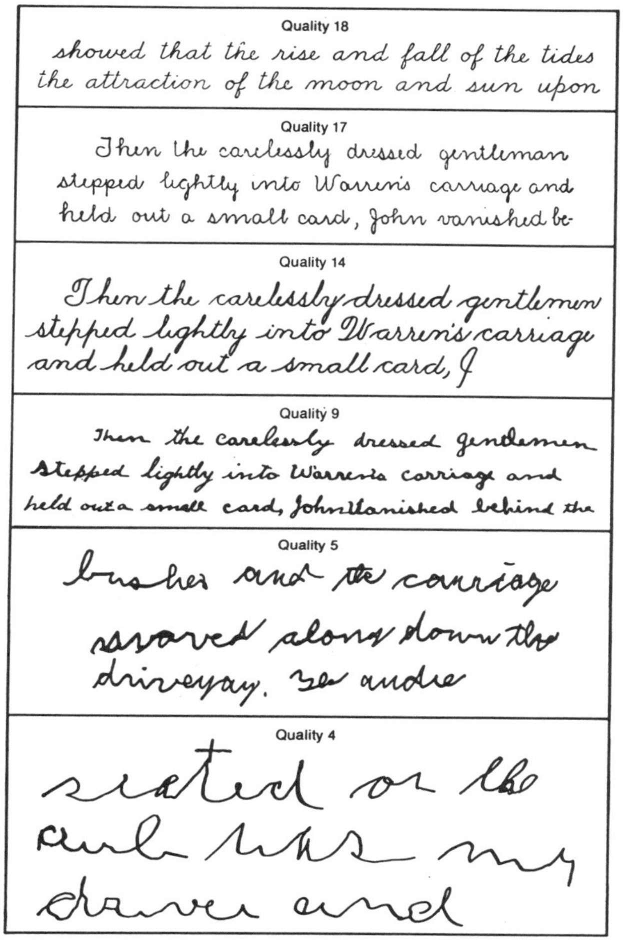

NOTE: A series of handwriting specimens were scaled on a numerical "quality" scale. To use the scale, a student's sample of writing is matched to the quality of one of the specimens and assigned the given numerical value. This figure shows only some of the specimens.

SOURCE: Anthony J. Nitko, *Educational Tests and Measurement: An Introduction* (New York, NY: Harcourt Brace Jovanovich, 1983), p. 450.

begins by dissecting the basic definition of a test and then examines concepts of reliability and validity.

What is a Standardized Test?

This type of test is an objective and standardized method for estimating behavior based on obtaining a sample of that behavior.[7] There are four key elements of this definition.

Sample of Behavior

Not all of an individual's behavior relevant to a given topic can be observed. Just as a biochemist must take representative samples of the water supply to assess its overall quality, a test obtains samples of behavior in order to estimate something about an individual's overall proficiency or skill level with respect to that behavior. Thus, to estimate a student's skill at arithmetic computations, a test might provide a number of problems of varying complexity drawn from each of the areas of addition, subtraction, multiplication, and division. The samples chosen must be sufficiently broad to represent the skill being tested. For example, performance on five long division problems would not provide an adequate estimate of overall computational skill. Similarly, a behind-the-wheel driving test that consists only of parking skills (parallel parking, backing into a space) would hardly constitute a valid indicator of a driver's overall competence.

Estimation

Precisely because much of human behavior is variable and because a person's knowledge and thinking cannot be directly observed, scores obtained on any educational test should always be viewed as estimates of an individual's competence. In general, the accuracy of estimates generated by tests will be enhanced when technical procedures are used to design, field test, and modify tests during development.

Standardization

Standardization refers to the use of a uniform procedure for administering and scoring the test. Controlling the conditions under which a test is given and scored is necessary to ensure comparability of scores across test takers. Each student is given identical instructions, materials, practice items, and amount of time to complete the test. This procedure can reduce the effects of extraneous variables on a student's score. Similarly, procedures for scoring need to be uniform for all students.

Objectivity

Objectivity in test construction is achieved by eliminating, or reducing as much as possible, the amount of subjective judgment involved in develop-

---

[7]The word "behavior" is used here in its broadest sense and includes more specific constructs such as knowledge, skills, traits, and abilities. This discussion of the components of the definition of a test is drawn from Anastasi, op. cit., footnote 4.

Box 6-D—Large-Scale Testing Programs: Constraints on the Design of Tests

The demand for standardized tests of achievement is driven by the need to collect comparable achievement data about large numbers of students, schools, and districts. Tests are required that can be given to a large number of students simultaneously and in many school districts. Because of this, and more so than for most other kinds of tests, the technology of standardized achievement testing reflects the practical considerations of economy, efficiency, and limits on the amount of time that can be devoted to test taking. The need for efficiency and economy has affected the design of standardized achievement testing in at least three important ways, each of which requires some tradeoffs in the information obtained.

Group administration—Most standardized achievement tests are group administered; large numbers of students take the test at the same sitting with no guidance by an examiner. Many other types of standardized tests (e.g., personality, speech, and visual-motor skills) are individually administered by trained examiners who can ensure systematic administration and scoring of results. While far more labor intensive and time consuming, individual examiners can make observations of the student that provide a rich source of supplementary information. Individually administered tests can also be tailored to the level of knowledge demonstrated by the child and thus can cover a number of content areas in some detail without becoming too long or frustrating for the child.

Machine scored—Most standardized achievement tests are scored by machine, because of the numbers of tests to be scored quickly and economically. This need restricts the format for student answers. Most machine-scored tests are made up of items on which students recognize or select a correct response (e.g., multiple choice or true-false) rather than create an answer of their own.

Broad, general content—The content of tests designed to be administered to all students will be broad and general when testing time is limited. The requirement that an achievement test can be taken by students of all skill levels in a given age group means that for every content area covered by the test, many items must be administered, ranging from low to high levels of difficulty. Most students will spend time answering extra items—some too difficult, some too easy—in order to accommodate all test takers.

Constraints

The design of standardized achievement tests for use with all students in a school system is therefore constrained by three factors: 1) the amount of testing time available which constrains test length, 2) the costs of test administration and scoring, and 3) the logistical constraints imposed by the large numbers of tests that must be administered and scored quickly. However, the tension between the economy and efficiency needs, and the desire for rich, individualized information, underlies much of the current testing debate.

Three major areas of technological development offer promise for expanding the range of possibilities for large-scale standardized achievement tests.

Machine scoring—As the technology advances, machines and computers may be able to score more complex and sophisticated responses by students (see ch. 7).

Individual administration via computer—The computer has considerable potential as a method for harnessing many of the important advantages of individualized test administration. These include the capability to adapt test items to match the proficiency of the student (allowing more detailed assessments in short time periods), and to record steps taken by the test taker. In essence, the computer may be able to replicate some of the important but expensive functions previously served by a trained testing examiner (see ch. 8).

Sampling designs—The technology of sampling, by which generalizable conclusions can be made based on testing of far fewer numbers of students, is an important development as well. The effectiveness of testing subgroups of children, or testing all children on a portion of the test, has been well demonstrated. This sampling methodology offers a practical avenue for trying some more expensive and logistically complex testing procedures, as every student in a system does not need to take the whole test.

SOURCE: Office of Technology Assessment, 1992.

ing, administering, and scoring the test. The goal of these procedures is to ensure that an individual receives a score that reflects his or her level of understanding and not the particular views or attitudes of persons administering or scoring the test. Thus, in theory an objective test is one on which the test taker will receive the same score regardless of who is involved in administering that test.[8]

Reliability of Test Scores[9]

As used with respect to testing, reliability refers to the *consistency* of scores. If the goal is to estimate a child's level of mathematics achievement then the test should produce consistent results, no matter who gives the test or when it is given. If, at the end of 3rd grade, a student scores at the 90th percentile on Monday in mathematics achievement, but the 40th percentile when retested on Friday, neither score would instill much confidence. Scores can be inconsistent for a number of reasons: behavior varies from moment to moment, the content of a test varies, or the persons or procedures involved in scoring are variable.

The theoretical ideal for score reliability is 100 percent. In practice, though, it is impossible for an instrument that is calibrating human behavior to achieve this level of consistency. Any data from tests of human behavior contain some ''noise'' or error component that is irrelevant to the purpose of the test. The control of testing conditions through specification of procedures can reduce the variance in scores due to these irrelevant factors, and make the test a more reliable indicator. However, because no test is perfectly accurate and consistent, it should be accompanied by evidence of reliability. (When public opinion polls are reported, for example, they are usually accompanied by statements that indicate how much the given figures might be expected to vary, e.g., ''this number might be expected to vary 4 points up or down.'' This statement provides information about the reliability of the poll estimates.)

As tests are currently designed, there are three principal ways to conceptualize the reliability of test scores. Estimates of reliability can be obtained by examining the consistency of a test administered across different occasions. To what extent do scores obtained on one day agree with those obtained on a different day? This form of reliability is called stability. Secondly, consistency across content, either of different groups of items or forms of a test, can be examined. To what extent does performance on one group of subtraction items agree with performance on a second group of subtraction items intended to assess the same set of skills? This form of reliability can be assessed by alternate test forms or by indices of internal consistency. Finally, the extent to which consistent test scores will be produced by different raters can be assessed. To what extent do the scores assigned by one judge reading an essay test and using a set of designated rating criteria agree with those given by another judge using the same criteria? Indices of inter-rater reliability are used to assess such agreement.

Reliability is partly a function of test length. As a rule, the more items a test contains, the more reliable that test will be. As the number of items, or samples, incorporated in a score increases, the stability of that score will also increase. The effect of chance differences among items, as well as the impact of a single item on the total score, is reduced as a test gets longer. This is one of the reasons that multiple-choice and other short answer tests tend to be very reliable and consistent—many items can be answered in a short amount of testing time. As will be discussed in chapter 7, reliability of scores based on fewer and longer tasks is one of the important challenges faced by the developers of new performance assessments.

Reliability is particularly important when test scores are used to make significant decisions about individual students. Recall that any one test score is considered to be only an estimate of the person's ''true'' proficiency; this score is expected to vary somewhat from day to day. Reliability coefficients,

---

[8]While scoring of certain tests can be made almost perfectly objective by use of machine-scoring technologies (see ch. 8), the writing of test questions, as well as the specification of what will be on the test and which is the right answer, remains a fundamentally subjective activity requiring a great deal of human judgment.

[9]The discussion of reliability and validity draw on Anastasi, op. cit., footnote 4; Anthony J. Nitko, *Educational Tests and Measurement: An Introduction* (New York, NY: Harcourt Brace Jovanovich, 1983); William A. Mehrens and Irvin J. Lehmann, *Measurement and Evaluation in Education and Psychology*, 3rd ed. (New York, NY: CBS College Publishing, 1984); and American Educational Research Association, American Psychological Association, and National Council on Measurement in Education, *Standards for Educational and Psychological Testing* (Washington, DC: American Psychological Association, Inc., 1985).

Box 6-E—Test Score Reliability: How Accurate is the Estimate?

All test scores are estimates of proficiency. "Reliability" is a statistical indicator of the accuracy of those estimates: tests with higher reliability are, by definition, more accurate instruments. For example, if a test has a reliability coefficient of 0.85, this means that 85 percent of the variance in scores depends on true differences and 15 percent is attributable to other factors.

Scores therefore need to be accompanied with information about the test's reliability. Suppose, for example, students took a test of arithmetic proficiency with high reliability, e.g., 0.95. As shown in figure 6-E1, the range of error around scores on this test is relatively narrow: a score of 100 reflects a proficiency level of somewhere between 93 and 107. On a test with very low reliability, e.g., 0.40, the proficiency of a student who scores 100 may be anywhere from 77 to 123.

This information is particularly important when test scores are the basis of decisions about students. The likelihood of incorrect decisions increases when a test's reliability is low: e.g., students could be denied remedial services based on an erroneously high score or retained in a special program because of erroneously low scores.

SOURCE: Office of Technology Assessment, 1992.

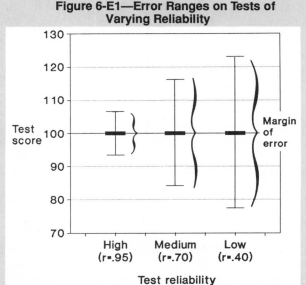

Figure 6-E1—Error Ranges on Tests of Varying Reliability

NOTE: Error ranges in this figure are based on the following statistical parameters: mean=100, standard deviation =15, p≤0.05 for all tests.

SOURCE: Office of Technology Assessment, 1992.

which estimate error, allow one to set a range of likely variation or "uncertainty" around that estimated score. Box 6-E illustrates how great the variation around a score can get as the reliability of a test decreases.[10] Interpretation of individual scores should always take into account this variability. Small differences between the test scores of individual students are often meaningless, once error estimates are considered. When test scores are used for classification of people errors will be greatest for those whose scores are at or near the cutoff point.[11]

This suggests two important implications for the interpretation of individual scores in educational settings: 1) if a test score is used to make decisions about individual students, a very high standard of reliability is necessary,[12] and 2) using test scores alone to make decisions about individuals is likely to result in higher rates of misclassification or

incorrect decisions. With respect to educational decisions about individuals, test scores should always be used in combination with other sources of information about the child's behavior, progress, and achievement levels.

Validity Evidence for Tests

"It is a useful oversimplification to think of validity as truthfulness: Does the test measure what it purports to measure?... Validity can best be defined as the extent to which certain inferences can be made from test scores."[13] Validity is judged on a wide array of evidence and is directly related to the purposes of the test.

Every test needs a clear specification of what it is supposed to be assessing. So, for example, for a test of reading proficiency, test designers first need to

---

[10]Reliability coefficients are based on the degree of relationship between two sets of scores. Correlation coefficients, generally signified with an "r," range from 0.00 indicating a complete absence of relation to +1.00 and −1.00 indicating a perfect positive or negative relationship. The closer a reliability coefficient is to +1.00, the better.

[11]Nitko, op. cit., footnote 9, p. 405.

[12]John Salvia and James E. Ysseldyke, *Assessment in Special and Remedial Education* (Boston, MA: Houghton Mifflin Co., 1985), p. 127.

[13]Mehrens and Lehmann, op. cit., footnote 9, p. 288.

Photo credit: American Guidance Services

Some standardized tests, such as those used in special education evaluations, are individually administered by a trained examiner.

specify clearly what is meant by reading proficiency. Similarly, a test of diving skill needs to make clear what proficient dives look like. Before any testing can be done, a clear definition of the skills and competencies covered by the test must be made. There must be a definition of what the skill of interest looks like before anyone can decide how to test it. Once a method and a metric for assessing the skill has been chosen, validity evidence is gathered to support or refute the definition and the method chosen.

EXAMPLE: A geometry teacher, who knows nothing about diving, is drafted to take over as coach of a high school diving team when the regular coach is taken ill. While watching the varsity and the junior varsity (JV) teams practice, he tries to develop his own definition of a skilled dive; noticing that highly ranked divers enter the pool with only a slight splash while JV team members tend to make lots of waves, he designs a 1-10 rating scale to measure diving

proficiency by judging the height of the splash as the diver enters the pool. While his criterion for measuring skill may be *related* to "true diving skill," it is not valid as the primary indicator of diving skill (as will be proven when he attempts to send his divers into statewide competition). In this case he has failed to define the trait of interest (diving skill) but rather jumped ahead to find an easy-to-measure indicator/correlate of diving skill. To carry this example farther, as the practice dives are rated on this scale, his divers begin to modify their dives in the attempt to increase their scores so that they might go to the State competition. They develop inventive ways to enter the water so that splashing is minimized. Slowly, their relative ranks (to each other) change and some JV members move up onto the varsity team. Finally, the best eight divers (judged on the 1-10 splash scale) are sent to statewide competition. Their scores are the lowest of any team and their awkward, gyrating dives send the spectators into an uproar. The most "truly" skilled divers from the team, who stayed home, never had a chance to compete.[14]

This example illustrates what can happen when an invalid measure is used. Often it is hard to define excellence or competence, and far easier to chose an easy-to-measure and readily available indicator of it. While many of these easy-to-measure characteristics may be correlated with excellence, *they do not represent the universe of characteristics that define competence in the skill of interest*. What can happen (as in this case) is that students practice to gain more skill in the measurable characteristic, often to the exclusion of other equally valid—but less readily measured—aspects of the skills. In this example, the coach should have first developed a definition of a skilled dive. Since statewide competition is a goal, he would do well to adopt the consensus definition and rating scale that is used by judges in the competition. This scale has developed validity over many years of use through a process of diving experts defining and describing: first, what skill in diving is and second, what level of skill one needs to get each score on a scale of 1 to 10.

The most often cited form of validity needed for achievement tests is called **content** validity. Establishing content validity is necessary in order to generalize from a sample to a whole domain—for example, a sample of science questions is used to

[14]Office of Technology Assessment, 1992.

generalize about overall science achievement. Does the content sampled by the test adequately represent the whole domain to which the test is intended to generalize? The tasks and knowledge included on a test of writing proficiency, for example, should represent the whole domain of skills and knowledge that educators believe to be important in defining writing proficiency. Since the whole domain can never be described definitively, the assessment of content validity rests largely on the judgment of experts. First the domain must be defined, then the test constructed to provide a representative sample across the domain.

There is no commonly used statistic or numerical value to express content validity. The traditional process for providing content-related validity evidence is a multifaceted one that includes review of textbooks and instructional materials, judgments of curriculum experts, and analysis of vocabulary. In addition, professionals from varying cultural and ethnic backgrounds are asked to review test content for appropriateness and fairness. The selection of test items is also influenced by studies of student errors, item characteristics, and evidence of differential performance by gender and racial-ethnic groups.

The content validity of an achievement test finally rests, however, on the match between the test content and the local curriculum.[15] Thus a school system selecting a test must pay careful attention to the extent to which test learning outcomes match the desired learning outcomes of the school system. "A published test may provide more valid results for one school program than for another. It all depends on how closely the set of test tasks matches the achievement to be measured."[16]

Another kind of validity evidence, called **criterion-related**, concerns the extent to which information from a test score generalizes to how well a person will do on a different task. In this case, validity is established by examining the test's relation with another criterion of importance. For example, the Scholastic Aptitude Test (SAT), which is used to help make decisions about college admissions, is designed to predict a specific criterion, i.e., freshman grade point average (GPA). One kind of validity evidence required for any selection test is a demonstrated relation to the outcomes being predicted.[17]

A third kind of validity evidence, **construct-related**, has to do with providing evidence that the test actually measures the trait or skill it attempts to measure. Is a test of science achievement actually measuring knowledge of science and not some other skill such as reading achievement? Do scores on a mathematics achievement test really reflect the amount of mathematics a child has learned in school and not some other characteristic such as ability to work quickly under time pressure? Evidence for construct validity is gathered in multiple ways.

One common form of construct validity for achievement tests relates to whether or not performance on the test is affected by instruction. Since an achievement test is, by definition, intended to gauge the effects of a specific form of instruction, then scores should increase as a result of instruction. As the kinds of tests and tasks required of children on tests change, it will be important to conduct validity studies to make sure tests are sensitive to instruction. Care needs to be taken to assure that new tests designed to assess thinking skills or complex reasoning actually do assess the skills that can be taught in classrooms and learned by students.

Evidence that tests of specific skills such as reading comprehension, spelling, and vocabulary[18] are actually assessing the skills they are designed to measure is particularly important if those scores are going to be used to diagnose a child's strengths and

---

[15]Ibid.

[16]Norman E. Gronlund and Robert L. Linn, *Measurement and Evaluation in Teaching*, 6th ed. (New York, NY: MacMillan Publishing Co., 1990), p. 55.

[17]The Scholastic Aptitude Test (SAT) is not considered an achievement test, but rather a test of "developed abilities" which consist of ". . . broadly applicable intellectual skills and knowledge that develop over time through the individual's experiences both in and out of school." (Anastasi, op. cit., footnote 4, p. 330.) The SAT is not intended to serve as a substitute for high school grades in the prediction of college achievement; in fact, high school grades predict college grades as well, or slightly better than does the SAT. However, when test scores are combined with high school grades, prediction of college grades is enhanced slightly. This "third view" of college-bound candidates (supplementing grades and personal information from applications, interviews, and reference letters) was seen originally as a way to offset potential inequities of the traditional system; see also James Crouse and Dale Trusheim, "The Case Against the SAT," *Ability Testing: Uses, Consequences, and Controversies*, part I, Alexandra K. Wigdor and Wendell R. Garner (eds.) (Washington, DC: National Academy Press, 1982).

[18]The subtests that typically appear on survey achievement batteries include vocabulary, word recognition skills, reading comprehension, language mechanics (e.g., capitalization and punctuation), language usage, mathematics problem solving, mathematics computation, mathematics concepts, spelling, language, science, social studies, research skills, and reference materials.

weaknesses. Similarly, scores designed to assess "higher order thinking" need validity evidence to support the assumption that they are capturing something distinctly different from other scores assumed to include only "basic skills." These other forms of construct validity have often been neglected by developers of standardized achievement tests.[19] Results of a recent survey of the technical characteristics of 37 published educational achievement tests indicate that while 73 percent of the tests presented information about content validity, only 14 percent presented criterion-related validity, and 11 percent construct validity evidence.[20]

Sometimes the argument is made that if a test *resembles* the construct or skill of interest, then it is valid. This is commonly referred to as face validity because the test looks like the construct it is supposed to be assessing. Because, for example, a test item seems to require complex reasoning, it is assumed to be an indicator of such reasoning. However, face validity is very impressionistic and is not considered sufficient kind of evidence for serious assessment purposes.[21]

The kinds of evidence discussed above constitute empirical or evidential bases for evaluating the validity of a test. Recently, however, some investigators have drawn attention to the importance of considering the **consequential** basis for evaluating the validity of test use. The questions posed by this form of validity are ethical and relate to the justification of the proposed use in terms of social values: ". . . should the test be used for the proposed purpose in the proposed way?"[22]

For example:

. . . tests used in the schools ought to encourage sound distribution of instructional and study time. . . . The worth of an instructional test lies in its contribution to the learning of students working up to the test or to next year's quality of instruction. . . . The bottom line is that validators have an obligation to review whether a practice has appropriate consequences for individuals and institutions, and especially to guard against adverse consequences.[23]

How are Achievement Tests Used?[24]

A precise description about how schools actually use achievement tests is difficult to obtain. Although there are many testing requirements imposed on children on their journey through elementary and secondary schools, it is difficult to say with any certainty how results are actually used, or by whom. Once a test is needed for a specific purpose such as determining eligibility for a compensatory education program, cost and time constraints often dictate that the test information is used for other purposes as well. In addition, the results of a test administration, once received by a school, are available to many people unfamiliar with the specific test administered. Test scores often remain part of a child's permanent record and it is unclear how they might be used, and by whom, at some future point. It is difficult to prevent use of the test information for other purposes once it has been collected.

The multiple uses of achievement tests in school systems can be broadly grouped into three major categories.[25] (See table 6-1 for a summary of these functions.)

---

[19]James L. Waldrop, "Review of the California Achievement Tests, Forms E and F," *The Tenth Mental Measurements Yearbook*, Jane Close Conoley and Jack J. Kramer (eds.) (Lincoln, NE: The University of Nebraska Press, 1989), p. 131.

[20]Bruce Hall, "Survey of the Technical Characteristics of Published Educational Achievement Tests," *Educational Measurement: Issues and Practice*, spring 1985, pp. 6-14.

[21]Mehrens and Lehmann, op. cit., footnote 9; Roger Farr and Beverly Farr, *Integrated Assessment System: Language Arts Performance Assessment, Reading/Writing*, technical report (San Antonio, TX: The Psychological Corp., 1991); Anastasi, op. cit., footnote 4.

[22]Samuel Messick, "Test Validity and the Ethics of Assessment," *American Psychologist*, vol. 35, No. 11, 1980, pp. 1012-1027. See also Samuel Messick, "Validity," *Educational Measurement*, 3rd ed., Robert Linn (ed.) (New York, NY: MacMillan Publishing Co., 1989).

[23]Lee J. Cronbach, "Five Perspectives on the Validity Argument," *Test Validity*, Howard Wainer and Henry I. Braun (eds.) (Hillsdale, NJ: Lawrence Erlbaum, 1988), pp. 5-6.

[24]This discussion of purposes draws on Jason Millman and Jennifer Greene, "The Specification and Development of Tests of Achievement and Ability" in Linn (ed.), op. cit., footnote 22, pp. 335-367; C.V. Bunderson, J.B. Olsen, and A. Greenberg, "Computers in Educational Assessment," OTA contractor report, Dec. 21, 1990; J.A. Frechtling, "Administrative Uses of School Testing Programs," in Linn (ed.), op. cit., footnote 22, pp. 475-485; and R. Darrell Bock and Robert J. Mislevy, "Comprehensive Educational Assessment for the States: The Duplex Design," *CRESST Evaluation Comment*, November 1987.

[25]Although many authors have discussed these three major categories, these distinctions are drawn most directly from Lauren B. Resnick and Daniel P. Resnick, "Assessing the Thinking Curriculum: New Tools for Educational Reform," *Future Assessments: Changing Views of Aptitude, Achievement, and Instruction*, B.R. Gifford and M.C. O'Connor (eds.) (Boston, MA: Kluwer Academic Publishers, 1989).

Table 6-1—Three Major Functions of Educational Tests

Functions	Examples
1. Classroom instructional guidance Used to monitor and provide feedback about the progress of each student and to inform teaching decisions about *individuals* on a day-to-day basis	• Diagnose each student's strengths and weaknesses • Monitor the effects of a lesson or unit of study • Monitor mastery and understanding of new material • Motivate and organize students' study time • Adapt curriculum to progress as indicated by tests • Monitor progress toward curricular goals • Plan lessons that build on students' level of current understanding • Assign students to learning groups (e.g., reading group)
2. System monitoring Used for monitoring and making administrative decisions about aggregated *groups* of students (e.g., a school, instructional programs, curricula, district)	• Report to parents and school board about a school or district's performance • Make decisions about instructional programs and curriculum changes • Evaluate Chapter 1 programs • Evaluate experimental or innovative programs • Allocate funds • Evaluate teacher performance/school effectiveness • Provide general information about performance of the overall educational system
3. Selection, placement, and certification of students ("gatekeeping") Used to allocate educational resources and opportunities among *individuals*	Selection: • Admission to college or private schools Placement: • Place students in remedial programs (e.g., Chapter 1) • Place students in gifted and talented programs Certification: • Certify minimum competency for receipt of high school diploma • Certify mastery of a course of study (e.g., Advanced Placement examinations) • Make decisions about grade promotion

SOURCE: Office of Technology Assessment, 1992.

The first broad category encompasses the kind of tests that can support and guide the learning process of each individual student in the classroom. These tests can be used to monitor and provide feedback about the educational progress of each student in the classroom, to diagnose areas of strength and weakness, and to inform teacher decisions about how and what to teach based on how well students are learning the material.

The second major function—system monitoring—encompasses the many managerial uses of tests to monitor the educational system and report to the public. In these uses, what is needed is aggregated information about the achievement of groups of students—from classrooms to schools, from districts to States. School administrators use this data to make decisions among competing curricula or instructional programs and to report to the public about student achievement. In addition, test scores are increasingly being used as accountability tools to judge the quality of the educational system and those who work for it. Tests used as accountability tools are often intended to allow a public evaluation of whether or not standards are being met.[26]

The third broad category of uses is also managerial, called here selection, placement, and certification. Included in this broad category are tests used to make institutional decisions affecting the progress of individual students through the educational system. Comparable information is needed for each

---

[26]Frechtling, op. cit., footnote 24.

Table 6-2—Consumers and Uses of Standardized Test Information

Consumer	Unit of analysis
National level	
Allocation of resources to programs and priorities	Nation, State
Federal program evaluation (e.g., Chapter 1)	State, program
State legislature/State department of education	
Evaluate State's status and progress relevant to standards	State
State program evaluation	State, program
Allocation of resources	District, school
Public (lay persons, press, school board members, parents)	
Evaluate State's status and progress relevant to standards	District
Diagnose achievement deficits	Individual, school
Develop expectations for future success in school	Individual
School districts—central administrators	
Evaluate districts	District
Evaluate schools	Schools
Evaluate teachers	Classroom
Evaluate curriculum	District
Evaluate instructional programs	Program
Determine areas for revision of curriculum and instruction	District
School districts—building administrators	
Evaluate school	School
Evaluate teacher	Classroom
Group students for instruction	Individual
Place students into special programs	Individual
School districts—teachers	
Group students for instruction	Individual
Evaluate and plan curriculum	Classroom
Evaluate and plan instruction	Classroom
Evaluate teaching	Classroom
Diagnose achievement deficits	Classroom, individual
Promotion and graduation	Individual
Place into special programs (e.g., gifted, handicapped)	Individual
Educational laboratories, centers, universities	
Policy analysis	All units
Evaluation studies	All units
Other applied research	All units
Basic research	All units

SOURCE: Thomas M. Haladyna, Susan Bobbit Nolen, and Nancy S. Haas, "Raising Standardized Achievement Test Scores and the Origins of Test Score Pollution," *Educational Researcher*, vol. 20, No. 5, June–July 1991, p. 3.

individual student so that managerial decisions can be made about the allocation of additional resources, placement in instructional programs, and certification of mastery. Increasingly test scores have been used to make such decisions because they are perceived to provide clear, objective criteria. Thus, eligibility for a compensatory education program (e.g., Chapter 1) might be determined by a district policy that states a cutoff score below which children must score to qualify. Qualifying for an enrichment program might be contingent on scoring above some designated level on a standardized test.

The results of these tests clearly have significant implications for a student's progress through the school system.[27]

Consumers of Achievement Tests

In addition to the many *uses* for achievement test-based information, there are many different consumers or *users* who need that information. The kind of information needed is often very different depending on who wants it. Table 6-2 summarizes the major consumers of test-based information as

---

[27]Ironically, while most of the supplementary resources allocated by schools are likely to be targeted to children scoring either quite low or quite high on these tests, the norm-referenced achievement tests routinely used by most school districts are designed to measure most accurately in the middle of the achievement distribution rather than at either the highest or the lowest ends.

well as the most common uses of each consumer.[28] Within the educational system there are multiple levels of need for test-based information including Federal, State, district, school, and classroom information. Policymakers and legislators need the information, as well as education departments. Teachers, parents, students, and the public also require test-based information about achievement.

Mandatory schoolwide testing programs, in which each child in a given grade takes the same test, have become routine. Some tests are required at the Federal level, e.g., for Chapter 1 accountability,[29] some mandated by the States, and others implemented by local school districts. Because most school districts want to keep testing requirements to a minimum, a test is often chosen that can serve as many uses and consumers as possible.

Figure 6-3 illustrates the mandated schoolwide tests given in grades 1 through 12 for three large school districts. State-mandated testing requirements, which have increased in overall numbers in recent years, account for only a fraction of the total testing burden. Additional tests (not listed in the table) are also administered to some subgroups of children who need to be screened for special services. For example, although some districts may use schoolwide tests to satisfy Federal-level Chapter 1 accountability requirements (Philadelphia uses the City Wide Test for this purpose), many children who receive Chapter 1 services will take tests in addition to those listed in the table.

Although the specifics of who actually uses test results and for what purposes remain difficult to document, evidence suggests that requirements regarding standardized achievement tests are imposed largely to serve the two broad managerial purposes—system monitoring; and selection, placement, and certification. There are few standardized tests designed explicitly to help teachers assess ongoing classroom learning and inform classroom practice. Furthermore, evidence also suggests that teachers find the results of existing standardized achievement tests only generally useful for classroom practice. In

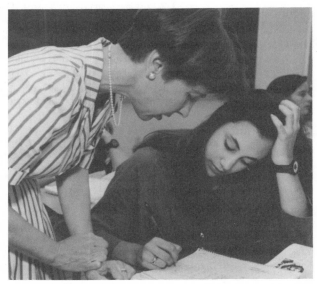

Photo credit: Arana Sonnier

Teachers need tests that are closely matched to instruction and that provide detailed information about student progress on a frequent basis. This kind of information, which can help teachers influence learning and guide instruction, is very different from the kind of information school administrators need to monitor school systems.

one study that interviewed teachers, 61 percent reported that standardized tests have little effect on their instructional decisionmaking.[30]

Current achievement tests do a good job of assessing a student's general level of knowledge in a particular content domain.... A low score relative to a student's grade placement on, say, a reading comprehension test is apt to be a valid indicator that a student will have difficulty reading and understanding assignments in the typical textbooks used at the grade level. Such global information, however, is more likely to confirm what the teachers already know about the student than to provide them with new insights or clear indications of how best to help the student. The global score simply does not reveal anything about the causes of the problem or provide any direct indications of what instructional strategies would be most effective.[31]

---

[28]See also Bock and Mislevy, op. cit., footnote 24, for a similar list and analysis of test consumers.

[29]Chapter 1 is a Federal compensatory education program serving low-achieving students from low-income schools. See ch. 3 for a fuller discussion of the testing and evaluation requirements under Chapter 1.

[30]Robert B. Ruddell, ''Knowledge and Attitudes Toward Testing: Field Educators and Legislators,'' *The Reading Teacher*, vol. 389, 1985, pp. 538-543.

[31]Robert L. Linn, ''Barriers to New Test Designs,'' *The Redesign of Testing for the 21st Century* (Princeton, NJ: Educational Testing Service, Oct. 26, 1985), p. 72.

Figure 6-3—Testing Requirements: Three District Examples

A child going to school in these districts would take each test listed.

Philadelphia, PA

Grade	1	2	3	4	5	6	7	8	9	10	11	12
			TELLS		TELLS			TELLS				
	PMET	PMET	PMET	PMET	PMET	PMET	PMET	PMET				
	CWT	CWT	CWT	CWT	CWT	CWT	CWT	CWT	CWT	CWT	CWT	CWT

Springfield, MO

Grade	1	2	3	4	5	6	7	8	9	10	11	12
	FGRMT											
	MMAT	MMAT	MMAT	MMAT	MMAT	MMAT	MMAT	MMAT	DAT	MMAT	......	TAP

Milwaukee, WI

Grade	1	2	3	4	5	6	7	8	9	10	11	12
			MPS ORT					Comp M Comp W				
			DPI-RT					Comp R Comp L TAP				
	......	ITBS		......	ITBS	......	ITBS DAT		TAP	PACT+	TAP	......

Comp L	Competency language
Comp M	Competency mathematics
Comp R	Competency reading
Comp W	Competency writing
CWT	Philadelphia City-Wide Test
DAT	Differential Aptitude Test
DPI-RT	DPI Reading Test
FGRMT	First Grade Reading and Math Test
ITBS	Iowa Tests of Basic Skills
MMAT	Missouri Mastery and Achievement Test
MPS ORT	Milwaukee Public Schools ORT Language Test
PMET	Philadelphia Mathematical Evaluation Test
TAP	Test of Achievement and Proficiency
TELLS	Test of Essential Learning and Literacy Skills (PA State test)

NOTE: If students have special needs or are in supplementary programs (e.g., Chapter 1 or gifted programs) they will usually take additional tests.

SOURCES: Milwaukee Public Schools, "Summary Report and Recommendations of the Assessment Task Force," unpublished report, June 2, 1989; Springfield Public Schools, 1990; Nancy Kober, "The Federal Framework for Evaluation and Assessment in Chapter 1, ESEA," OTA contractor report, May 1991.

Teachers desire diagnostic tests that are precise, closely matched to curricula and instruction and timely. Achievement tests of the kind now widely used do not match these criteria.[32]

Part of the reason that few existing standardized tests are applicable for classroom use, however, has to do with local control of curriculum. Achievement tests are designed to match the goals and objectives of the content being taught; the validity of an achievement test rests largely on the degree to which it mirrors the content being taught in the classroom. A test that contains a great deal of content not covered by the curriculum in a particular school is said to be "content invalid" for that school. Teachers, because they know what they are teaching, can design tests that are well aligned with the curriculum. If an examination is designed at a great distance from the local classroom (as commercially produced and published tests are bound to be) it is less likely to reflect the specific curricular content of the classroom; these tests will largely reflect only those broad content areas and skills that are common across school settings and on which there is implicit consensus.[33] Thus, tests that are precise and closely matched to curricula, and therefore useful to teachers, will need to be designed at the local level, close to where specific curricular goals and objectives are set. *"Generic" standardized achievement tests as currently designed cannot be both specific enough to assist teachers on an ongoing basis and generic enough to be useful to large numbers of school systems.*

Most mandated, standardized testing is put in place for managerial purposes and not for purposes related to shaping directly day-to-day learning processes in classrooms. Since such tests are generally given once a year, they can offer teachers a "snapshot" of a child's achievement at one particu-lar point in time, but offer little information about the ongoing, ever-changing *process* of a child's learning and development.[34]

The social success of testing in many ways is a product of the bureaucratization of education. Testing seems not so important in the stuff of teaching and learning, where surely there must be much personal contact, but rather in the interstices of our educational institutions—entry into elementary school, placement in special classes, the transition from elementary to secondary school, high school leaving and college going.[35]

Test Misuse

It is difficult to make general statements about the misuses of tests, because each test has to be evaluated with respect to its own specifications and technical evidence regarding the validity of its use for specific purposes.[36] Many different tests are used by school systems, some commercially designed, some designed by districts or States. However, results of one survey of mathematics teachers shed some light on the uses of well-known commercial achievement tests. In this survey, three commercial tests were found to account for 44 percent of district testing requirements. In districts where these three tests were used about two-thirds of the teachers reported their use by the district to group students by ability and to assign students to special programs. However, technical reviews of these three tests have suggested that evidence is lacking regarding inferences about student diagnosis and placement for these tests.[37] One reviewer cautioned about one of these tests that: ". . . although useful as an indicator of general performance, the usefulness of the test for diagnosis, placement, remediation or instructional planning has not been validated."[38]

[32]Leslie Salmon-Cox, "Teachers and Standardized Achievement Tests: What's Really Happening?" *Phi Delta Kappan*, vol. 62, No. 9, 1981, p. 634.

[33]See, e.g., Roger Farr and Robert F. Carey, *Reading: What Can be Measured?* 2nd ed. (Newark, DE: International Reading Association, Inc., 1986), p. 149.

[34]The majority of districts test at the end of the school year and the results are often received too late to be of help to that year's classroom teacher. Some districts test more than once a year.

[35]Walter Haney, "Testing Reasoning and Reasoning About Testing," *Review of Educational Research*, vol. 54, No. 4, 1984, p. 641.

[36]See also Robert L. Linn, Center for Research on Evaluation, Standards and Student Testing, University of Colorado at Boulder, "Test Misuse: Why Is It So Prevalent?" OTA contractor report, September 1991; Larry Cuban, Stanford University, "The Misuse of Tests in Education," OTA contractor report, Sept. 9, 1991; and Nelson Noggle, "The Misuse of Educational Achievement Tests for Grades K-12: A Perspective," OTA contractor report, October 1991.

[37]T. Romberg, E.A. Zarinnia, and S.R. Williams, *The Influence of Mandated Testing on Mathematics Instruction: Grade 8 Teachers' Perceptions* (Madison WI: National Center for Research in Mathematical Sciences Education, March 1989).

[38]Peter W. Airasian, "Review of the California Achievement Tests, Forms E and F," Jane Close Conoley and Jack J. Kramer (eds.), *The Tenth Mental Measurements Yearbook* (Lincoln, NE: The University of Nebraska Press, 1989), pp. 719-720.

Although most standardized achievement tests are not designed to be used as selection or placement instruments on which to base judgments about future proficiency or capability, there are few mechanisms to prevent such uses. Tests that are going to be used for selection should be designed and validated for that purpose. **Tests designed to be used as feedback mechanisms to inform the learning process should not be used to make significant decisions about an individual's educational career unless additional evidence can be provided substantiating this use.** However, there are few safeguards available to make sure this does not happen.

One of the most consistent recommendations of testing experts is that a test score should never be used as the single criterion on which to make decisions about individuals. Significant legal challenges to the over-reliance on IQ test scores in special education placements led to an exemplary federally mandated policy on test use in special education decisions. In Public Law 94-142, Congress included several provisions designed to protect students and ensure fair, equitable, and non-discriminatory assessment procedures. Among these were:

- decisions about students are to be based on more than performance on a single test,
- tests must be validated for the purpose for which they are used,
- children must be assessed in all areas related to a specific or suspected disability, and
- evaluations should be made by a multidisciplinary team.[39]

This legislation provides, then, a number of significant safeguards against the simplistic or capricious use of test scores in making educational decisions. Similar safeguards are needed to prevent over-reliance on single test scores to make educational decisions about all students, not just those in special education programs.[40]

Other examples of test misuse arise when results of available tests are used in the aggregate to make unsupportable inferences about educational effectiveness. The use of college admissions tests (SAT and the American College Testing program—ACT)

Photo credit: Educational Testing Service

Some standardized tests are used to make significant decisions about the progress of individual students through the educational system. These tests must meet very high technical standards and are most subject to scrutiny and legal challenge.

to compare the quality of education in various States, as in the "Wall Charts" produced by the U.S. Department of Education, is one prominent example. The SAT is taken by different numbers and samples of students (none of them randomly selected) in each State. Further, inferences about the achievement levels of high school seniors should be made only from a test designed to sample what high school seniors have been taught. The SAT is not designed for this purpose—it is designed to predict success (grade point average) in the freshman year of college. College admissions tests are designed for a distinctly different purpose than informing policy-makers interested in educational quality.[41] In some respects it is similar to using a test of reading achievement to draw conclusions about mathematics achievement; although the two are likely to show some relation to one another, it would be erroneous to draw conclusions and make decisions about mathematics based on test scores in reading.

Changing Needs and Uses for Standardized Tests

Current disaffection with the widely used existing standardized tests rests largely on three features of those tests: 1) most are norm-referenced and thus

---

[39]Salvia and Ysseldyke, op. cit., footnote 12.

[40]See ch. 2 for further discussion of test misuse and mechanisms for enforcing appropriate testing practices.

[41]See Robert L. Linn, "Accountability: The Comparison of Educational Systems and the Quality of Test Results," *Educational Policy*, vol. 1, No. 2, June 1987, pp. 181-198, for further discussion of the problems involved in using test scores to compare educational quality across States.

scores are based on comparing students to one another; 2) most are exclusively made up of multiple-choice items; and 3) their content does not adequately represent local curricula, especially those parts associated with thinking and reasoning skills. Most of the new developments in test design and alternative forms of assessment reflect a move away from this one dominant testing technology. What features do innovators seek in other designs?

What Should the Yardstick Be?

Traditional test theory and techniques of test construction have been developed on the assumption that the purpose of a test is to discriminate among individuals. If the purpose of a test is to compare each individual to a standard, then it is irrelevant whether or not the individuals differ from each other.[42]

Recent attempts to develop alternative tests represent a move away from the traditional testing model built on comparing individuals to one another. Instead, new testing developments represent attempts to extend the criterion-referenced model of testing and design ways to assess students against criteria and goals for achievement.

There are two main reasons that existing norm-referenced tests tend to provide broad coverage of a limited number of content areas. First, these tests are designed to be taken by students of all skill levels in a given grade; this means that for every content area covered by the test, many items must be administered, ranging from low to high levels of difficulty. Most students will spend scarce testing time answering extra items—some too difficult, some too easy—included in order to accommodate all test takers. This means that fewer content areas can be covered in a limited amount of testing time. Second, NRTs must concentrate on those content areas that are common to most schools throughout the country. In essence, the content areas represented on NRTs represent broad and generally implicit national consensus about the core skills that children should know at each grade level. If these tests are primarily tests of basic skills, as many have argued, it may be because it is these skills that are common to the

majority of curriculum frameworks throughout the country. Because of the way NRTs are developed, the content areas included can only represent a subset of the content areas covered in any particular school. Arizona, for example, found that only 26 percent of their curriculum goals were covered in the NRT they had been using. Thus, existing NRTs will only assess a limited set of content areas and only in a very general way. However, they can provide a basis for comparing children across the Nation on that common general content.

Comparing children across the Nation on what they have been taught, without setting any standards or goals as to what they should have been taught, entails testing only those skills for which there is an implicit national consensus—which is also likely to be the "least common denominator" of academic content. Local control over curricula means that each district can decide what skills and knowledge fourth graders should have, for example. To compare them fairly, one can only use a test that represents content all children have been taught. However, if one is willing to arrive at some kind of consensus about what children should know at various age levels, then tests can be designed to represent those areas.[43]

Criterion-referenced tests (CRTs) can provide specific information that is directly tied to the curricula being delivered in the classroom. Most tests need to be developed locally to achieve this level of specificity. Many States have, in recent years, implemented a CRT statewide program in order to assess progress on State-mandated goals and skills. However, many people, from policymakers to parents, also want a method for referencing how students are doing with respect to the education of the whole Nation. Parents and policymakers want assurance that children are not just getting the set of skills and knowledge that would make them successful in Wyoming, for example, but rather that the received education is preparing children for the national workplace and postsecondary educational institutions. Because States and districts continually need to evaluate their own goals and curriculum, data comparing their students to students across the

---

[42]Mehrens and Lehmann, op. cit., footnote 9, p. 21.

[43]Another important aspect of the design of norm-referenced tests has to do with the way items are finally selected to appear on the test. "One of the most important criteria for deciding whether to retain a test item is how well that item contributes to the variability of test scores." Rudner et al. (eds.), op. cit., footnote 2, p. 12. In this model, items that are too easy or too difficult may be eliminated from the test *even if those items are related to important learning goals*. For example, information that has been mastered by all children of a given age may not appear on the test because this information does not describe the differences in what they know.

Nation can provide an important perspective on the relative success of their educational efforts. At the present time, nationally norm-referenced standardized achievement tests are the only mechanism available for achieving this type of "national calibration."[44] Thus many States and districts will adopt an overall testing program that uses both an NRT and a CRT. One testing program (CRT) can describe how the State is doing with respect to its own curricular goals, the other (NRT) program can describe how children in the State are achieving relative to all children in the country.[45]

How Much is Enough? Setting Standards

It can be difficult to evaluate what either a CRT or NRT score *means* without reference to some standard or decision about how much is enough. If a child has mastered 70 percent of a given skill, how is she doing? This score means something different to her teacher if most other children in her class know 100 percent than if most know 50 percent. Or if the school district expects 100 percent mastery of this skill in first grade or fifth grade. Often, therefore, cutoff scores are set to establish mastery levels.

In discussions of testing, this represents the more technical meaning of the word "standard."[46] In this case:

. . . a standard is an answer to the question "How much is enough?" There are standards for many kinds of things, including the purity of food products, the effectiveness of fire extinguishers and the cleanliness of auto exhaust fumes. When you choose a passing score, you are setting a standard for performance on a test.[47]

The most familiar testing example comes from minimum competency testing; a passing score is set, based on some criteria for competency, above which students are certified and below which they are not.

The answer to "how much is enough?" is almost always "it depends." How safe is safe enough and how clean is clean enough are issues that have occupied consumer safety and environmental protection advocates and policymakers for years. Choosing a passing score on a test is rarely clear-cut. Any standard is based on some type of judgment. In testing, the choice of a passing score or scores indicating levels of proficiency will be largely reliant on judgments. In testing, ". . . it is important that these judgments be:

1. made by persons who are qualified to make them;
2. meaningful to the persons who are making them; and
3. made in a way that takes into account the purpose of the test."[48]

Because of the error inherent in any individual test score, however, it is virtually impossible to choose a passing score that will eliminate mistakes or wrong decisions. Some test takers will pass when they should have failed and some will fail when they should have passed. When setting passing scores or standards it is important to consider the relative likelihood, importance, and social value of making both of these kinds of wrong decisions.[49]

A second, more general use of the term standard is also being employed in many of the current discussions about testing.

As the history of the word reminds us, a "standard" is a set of values around which we rally; we "defend" standards. (The "standard" was the flag held aloft in battle, used to identify and orient the troops of a particular king.). . . Standards represent . . . desirable behaviors, not the best typical behavior.[50]

This meaning of standard draws more from the dictionary definition of a standard as ". . . something established by authority, custom, or general

---

[44]See Linn, op. cit., footnote 41, pp. 181-198, for further discussion of various options by which State and national comparisons might be made.

[45]See also the profiles of Arizona and Kentucky State testing programs in ch. 7.

[46]Webster's defines this meaning as ". . . something set up and established by authority as a rule for the measure of quantity, weight, extent, value or quality." *Webster's Ninth New Collegiate Dictionary* (Springfield, MA: Merriam Webster, 1988), p. 1148.

[47]Samuel A. Livingston and Michael J. Zieky, *Passing Scores: A Manual for Setting Standards of Performance on Educational and Occupational Tests* (Princeton, NJ: Educational Testing Service, 1982), p. 10.

[48]Ibid., p. 12.

[49]For analysis and discussion of technical problems in the setting of cutoff scores see, e.g., Robert Guion, "Personnel Assessment, Selection, and Placement," *Handbook of Industrial and Organizational Psychology*, vol. 2, M. Dunnette and L. Hough (eds.) (Palo Alto, CA: Consulting Psychologists Press, 1991), pp. 327-397.

[50]Grant Wiggins," 'Standards' Should Mean 'Qualities,' Not Quantities," *Education Week*, vol. 9, No. 18, Jan. 24, 1990, p. 36.

consent as a **model or example.**"[51] A standard, in this sense, is an exemplar—"... whether few, many, or all students can meet or choose to meet it is an independent issue. ..."[52]

An example of this kind of standard that is now widely cited is the *Curriculum and Evaluation Standards for School Mathematics* prepared by the National Council of Teachers of Mathematics (NCTM). This document contains a series of standards intended to be criteria against which schools can judge their own curricular and evaluation efforts. For example, the first standard reads as follows:

Standard 1: Mathematics as Problem Solving
In grades K-4, the study of mathematics should emphasize problem solving so that students can—

* use problem-solving approaches to investigate and understand mathematical content;
* formulate problems from everyday and mathematical situations;
* develop and apply strategies to solve a wide variety of problems;
* verify and interpret results with respect to the original problem;
* acquire confidence in using mathematics meaningfully.[53]

The specifics about how to test or assess this standard or about "how much is enough?" are not specified in the NCTM document. Instead it provides a common framework and a set of exemplars toward which educators and students can work— such standards describe what optimal performance looks like and what is desirable for students to know. Without clear standards for performance, many students are left struggling to understand the criteria on which they are being evaluated. Box 6-F, excerpted from a contemporary play, highlights one aspiring athlete's struggle to ascertain the criteria or standards by which his performance as an athlete is being judged. Box 6-G describes some of the issues involved in setting and maintaining standards.

What Should the Tests Look Like?

Currently almost all group-administered standardized achievement tests are made up of multiple-choice items; increasing dissatisfaction with multiple-choice technology as the single method for assessing

Box 6-F—Helping the Student Understand Expectations: The Need for Clear Criteria

The need for explicit standards and criteria in learning is aptly described in this letter excerpted from the play *Love Letters*. The letter is written by a teen-age boy about his performance in crew.

I'm stroking the 4th crew now. Yesterday, I rowed number 2 on the 3rd. Tomorrow I may row number 6 on the 2nd or number 4 on the 4th. Who knows? You get out there and work your butt off, and the launch comes alongside and looks you over, and the next day they post a list on the bulletin board saying who will row what. They never tell you what you did right or wrong, whether you're shooting your slide or bending your back or what. They just post the latest results for all to see. Some days I think I'm doing really well, and I get sent down two crews. One day I was obviously hacking around, and they moved me UP. There's no rhyme or reason. I went to Mr. Clark who is the head of rowing and I said, "Look, Mr. Clark. There's something wrong about this system. People are constantly moving up and down and no one knows why. It doesn't seem to have anything to do with whether you're good or bad, strong or weak, coordinated or uncoordinated. It all seems random, *sir*." And Mr. Clark said "That's life, Andy." And walked away. Well maybe that's life, but it doesn't *have* to be life. You could easily make rules which made sense, so the good ones moved up and the bad ones moved down, and people *knew* what was going on. I'm serious.[1]

[1]From *Love Letters*, a play by A.R. Gurney.

achievement has led to considerable current experimentation with other item types and testing formats. Although the pros and cons of multiple-choice items are being widely and hotly debated, this testing format has many valuable characteristics.

The multiple-choice item has achieved virtual dominance of the large-scale testing market primarily because of its psychometric and administrative properties. Although expensive and difficult to develop, multiple-choice items are efficient to administer and score, particularly when items and answers are kept secure. Large numbers of students can be tested simultaneously and their tests scored and returned within a relatively short period of

[51]*Webster's Ninth New Collegiate Dictionary*, op. cit., footnote 46.

[52]Wiggins, op. cit., footnote 50, p. 25.

[53]National Council of Teachers of Mathematics, *Curriculum and Evaluation Standards for School Mathematics* (Reston, VA: 1989), p. 23.

[54]A typical standardized achievement test battery can be scored and reported back to schools in about 6 weeks.

time.[54] These tests can also be administered without any special training or equipment. The answers can be objectively scored—thus seeming to avoid any judgment or subjectivity in scoring and potential controversy that might result.

The measurement properties of multiple-choice items also make them very efficient. Many items can be administered in a relatively short amount of testing time, providing much information and making composite scores highly stable and reliable. The large number of items also allows each content domain assessed to be represented by multiple questions, which increases both the reliability and validity of the test. Because large numbers of items can be pretested efficiently, a large pool of good items with empirical description of their difficulty levels (and other item parameters of concern in the design of tests) can be developed. Items in this pool can also be tested for statistical evidence of bias. Finally, multiple-choice items have been found to perform as well as other, less efficient kinds of items (e.g., essays) for specific functions such as predicting freshman college grades.[55] The dominant testing technology of the present—multiple-choice items in a norm-referenced test—has been shown to be a very efficient technology for some specific purposes, in particular those purposes that require ranking individuals along a continuum. However, this is only one of many educational uses for achievement tests.

The educational advantages of multiple-choice items, the ways in which they enrich or enhance learning, are harder to articulate. Historically, educational examinations consisted of oral or written questions used to demonstrate mastery of content taught. Most other industrialized countries do not use multiple-choice examinations in education.[56] Multiple-choice items were pressed into service in this country when more efficient methods of testing large numbers of students were needed (see ch. 4). Each step in the historical process of examining—from oral to written examinations, then from written to multiple-choice—has taken us farther away from the actual skills, such as oral and written expression, that we want children to develop. Critics of multiple-choice items argue that we spend considerable time

Photo credit: Bob Daemmrich

These elementary school students are taking a multiple-choice achievement test that requires filling in the correct "bubble" on a separate answer sheet. Although such tests have certain advantages, many educators believe that negative effects on classroom practice indicate a need for new testing approaches.

training students in a skill not required in life, namely answering multiple-choice questions. As one analyst has observed: "... most of the important problems one faces in real life are ill-structured, as are all the really important social, political, and scientific problems in the world today. But ill-structured problems are not found in standardized achievement tests."[57] Many educators are now arguing that achievement tests need to consist of items and tasks that are more "authentic"—i.e., are made up of skills that we actually want children to practice and master, such as producing and explaining how they reached the answer, writing a logical argument, drawing a graph, or designing a scientific experiment. These efforts are described at length in the next chapter.

One of the consistent themes of the debate throughout the last 70 years has been to ask whether more open-ended items (e.g., essays) really measure

[55]See, e.g., Brent Bridgeman and Charles Lewis, "Predictive Validity of Advanced Placement Essay and Multiple-Choice Examinations," paper presented at the annual meeting of the National Council on Measurement in Education, Chicago, IL, April 1991.

[56]A major exception is Japan, which does as much (if not more) multiple-choice testing than does the United States. See ch. 5 for discussion.

[57]Norman Fredericksen, "The Real Test Bias: Influences of Testing on Teaching and Learning," American Psychologist, vol. 39, No. 3, March 1984, p. 199.

Box 6-G—Setting and Maintaining Standards

Few tests in this country have attempted to provide interpretations of scores with respect to broad standards of performance. Most judgments about how well a child or school is doing have been made through the use of norms—essentially a standard based on average performance. The current effort by the National Assessment of Educational Progress to establish national proficiency levels of performance—basic, proficient, and advanced—in mathematics is one such attempt.[1]

Consider two different methods that could be used by a teacher to grade the tests of his students. He could decide to grade them all relative to one another; in this method he looks over all the answers that have been provided and assigns the highest grade to those students with the highest scores and the lowest grade to the lowest scores. This is a norm-referenced scoring system. Several problems arise with this system. First, there is no objective referent—all of his students' answers may still be better than the best answer given in the class next door. Second, all of his students may have mastered the material of interest; if all have mastered it the actual differences that underlie a high and a low score mean very little, and will reflect very fine-grained and perhaps unimportant distinctions in their understanding. Thus, the drawback of this procedure is that a student's performance is evaluated solely with respect to the performance of others.

The second method would be to judge the work against some standard reflecting what his students should be able to do. The teacher determines what an excellent, an average, and a poor answer would look like. All students are then judged relative to that standard. This is how many teachers assign letter grades. The most widely cited problem with a standard-based scoring system is that it is hard to equate standards across teachers. Different teachers hold different expectations for what their students should be able to do and what excellence looks like. However, reference to some absolute standard of proficiency is in many ways the most meaningful kind of score, particularly if one wants to compare progress across time or to raise the absolute level of achievement among students.

Some educational examinations, particularly in European countries, have attempted to set central standards and have used various mechanisms to maintain the consistency of the standards. In Great Britain, for example, the new national assessment involves a system of moderation of teacher judgments; initially, teachers are trained to make judgments about student performance on a number of standardized tasks. During the administration of these tasks at the end of the year, a moderator is sent to the schools to observe teachers, rate a subsample of students with the teacher, discuss discrepancies in judgments, and in various other ways maintain the consistency with which the standards are being applied by teachers in the school.[2]

---

[1]See ch. 3 for a further discussion of standard setting by the National Assessment of Educational Progress (NAEP).

[2]Clare Burstall, National Foundation for Educational Research, London, personal communication, February 1991. See also Department of Education and Science and the Welsh Office, *National Curriculum Task Group on Assessment and Testing: A Report* (London, England: 1987).

---

different traits, skills, or abilities than multiple-choice items. As one reviewer states:

> The enduring question for the [multiple] choice type items is whether or not these seemingly artificial contrivances measure the same thing as the more ''natural and direct'' free-response types of item. Popular opinion on this question is rather well formulated and almost universally negative, i.e., the two types of items do *not* measure the same thing. One can hear multiple-choice and true-false questions castigated in nearly any teachers' lounge in the country on a daily basis, and they are lampooned with regular frequency in cartoon strips. . . . But at

the root of the question of whether free-response and choice-type tests are measuring the same thing (trait, ability, level of knowledge) is an empirical one, not a philosophical or polemical one.[58]

Few data are available comparing the extent to which tests in different formats provide the same information or different information. Results of a few studies that shed light on this topic are somewhat mixed. In some areas, the research evidence suggests that multiple-choice and open-ended items measure essentially the same skills.[59] However, other research suggests that the extent to which open-ended or multiple-choice tests get at different

---

[58]Thomas P. Hogan, University of Wisconsin, Green Bay, ''Relationship Between Free-Response and Choice-Type Tests of Achievement: A Review of the Literature,'' paper prepared for the National Assessment of Educational Progress, 1981.

[59]Ibid.; and Millman and Greene, op. cit., footnote 24.

Similarly, the International Baccalaureate Program has been developed to confer a degree on high schools students worldwide. This program can be adopted by all high schools and is used at a number of schools in the United States. In order to maintain the comparability of the credential across schools, teachers, and countries, the program has a very detailed set of curricular requirements for various courses. Teachers are carefully trained in the criteria for grading and judging performance of students in each discipline. Teachers must have their examinations approved by the central administrative program. After an examination has been given and graded, the teacher sends several student examinations—one receiving the highest score, one the middle score, and one the lowest score—to the central administrative program where standards for grading are carefully matched. Feedback is provided to the teacher if his grading standards are not in line with the central program standard.[3]

Recent developments in psychometric theory and its application to large-scale achievement testing also provide some encouraging evidence of the possibility of calibrating test items designed at the State or local level to a common scale. Group-level item-response theory may provide the technical model by which a shared pool of items could be created for different States or districts. A State or district would not be limited to those items but would include a sufficient number of these items so that the rest of their test could be calibrated to national norms or standards.[4] Such a model still requires, however, some degree of consensus about the content and curricular areas to be tested.

"Trustworthy comparative data . . . demands a degree of agreement about the curriculum that many may consider to be a threat to local control. It is one thing to agree that arithmetic should be assessed, or even that the assessment should include applications of concepts such as ratios and percents. It may be something else to agree on the grade in which the assessment of specific skills such as these should take place or on the appropriate items.[5]

For subjects such as literature—what books should students read and at what age?—or social studies, these issues become even more thorny.

---

[3]Carol M. Dahlberg, coordinator, International Baccalaureate Program, Montgomery High School, Rockville, MD, remarks at OTA Workshop on Examination Systems in Other Countries and Lessons for the U.S., Mar. 27-28, 1991.

[4]Robert L. Linn, "Accountability: The Comparison of Educational Systems and the Quality of Test Results," *Educational Policy*, vol. 1, No. 2, June 1987, pp. 181-198; and R. Darrell Bock and Robert J. Mislevy, "Comprehensive Educational Assessment for the States: The Duplex Design," *CRESST Evaluation Comment*, November 1987.

[5]Linn, op. cit., footnote 4, p. 196.

---

skills will depend on the subject matter being tested. Evidence is strong, for example, that essay tests of writing provide different information than do multiple-choice tests of writing.[60] In part, the potential usefulness of open-ended items will depend on the purpose of the particular test and the kind of information needed.

Multiple Choice: A Renewable Technology?

Because of concerns related to efficiency, reliability, and economy, many researchers and test developers think that the multiple-choice test will probably always have some role to play in the assessment of achievement. Therefore, educators and psychometricians have become interested in exploring ways to improve the multiple-choice items that currently dominate standardized achievement tests. A number of State assessment programs have put efforts into developing multiple-choice items that seem to require more complex thinking skills and are more consistent with their changing educational goals.

For example, Michigan recently decided to move away from an exclusively skill-based approach to reading. New statewide reading objectives were developed consonant with a redefinition of reading as a process that involves constructing meaning through a dynamic interaction between the reader, the text, and the context of the reading situation. A new approach to assessing these goals was also needed, so the State embarked on developing new

---

[60]R.E. Traub, "On the Equivalence of the Traits Assessed by Multiple-Choice and Constructed-Response Tests," *Construction Versus Choice in Cognitive Measurement*, R.E. Bennett and W.C. Ward (eds.) (Hillsdale, NJ: L. Erlbaum Associates, in press); and Edys S. Quellmalz, "Designing Writing Assessments: Balancing Fairness, Utility and Cost," *Educational Evaluation and Policy Analysis*, vol. 6, No. 1, spring 1984, pp. 63-72. It should also be noted that much of the research that does exist about item differences has been based on college or college-bound students and ". . . hence those of (a) above average ability, (b) beyond the years of rapid cognitive development, and (c) from predominantly middle-class, White, Western cultural background." Hogan, op. cit., footnote 58, p. 46. Some of the field studies conducted as part of the National Assessment of Educational Progress can and will provide much needed data about the performance of a diverse population of elementary and secondary students.

tests to be used with grades 4, 7, and 10. Michigan's innovative reading assessment program involves many changes in the tests—including the use of stories drawn from children's literature and other primary sources instead of short excerpted passages or ones written for the test—while still employing a multiple-choice format for answering the questions. Such questions are designed to assess "constructing meaning" and "knowledge about reading" as well as factors typically not tested such as a child's familiarity with the topic of the story and his or her effort and interest in the testing questions.[61]

A point that is consistently made by those who design educational tests is that multiple-choice items are not restricted to assessing only basic skills or the memorization of facts.[62] Multiple-choice items, if carefully crafted, can be used to assess very high levels of expertise—for example in admissions tests for graduate education (Law School Admission Test, Graduate Record Exam) and board certification examinations for physicians. The ACT Science Reasoning Test, which is part of the ACT used for college admissions, uses multiple-choice items to assess interpretation, analysis, evaluation, reasoning, and problem-solving skills required in the natural sciences. Each unit on the test presents scientific information—in the form of graphs, results of experiments, or descriptions of conflicting scientific theories—that the student must interpret. According to the test designers, advanced knowledge in the subjects covered by the test (biology, chemistry, physics, and the physical sciences) is not required; instead the test emphasizes scientific reasoning skills.[63] The National Assessment of Educational Progress (NAEP) has also put considerable effort into developing multiple-choice items to measure thinking skills such as solving problems and conducting inquiries in science, conceptual understanding and problem-solving in mathematics,

and evaluating information and constructing meaning in reading. See figure 6-4 for examples of items drawn from these and other multiple-choice tests designed to assess more complex thinking skills.

Recent research and development efforts have suggested additional ways that multiple-choice tests might be designed to reflect complex processes of learning and development:

- One effort to assess science understanding has focused on trying to describe the various "mental models" that children hold before they master the correct understanding of basic scientific principles. Multiple-choice items, such as the one in figure 6-5, are then designed to represent these various mental models; each distractor (or incorrect choice) represents a commonly held misconception about a scientific principle. Wrong answers can be examined by the teacher to discern what misconceptions each child may hold and better focus instruction.[64]

- Similarly, if free-response answers given by children to all kinds of open-ended tasks can be analyzed, then the kinds of misunderstandings and errors commonly made by children can be described. This information can be used to write distractors that reflect these errors (not just to "trick" students) and may then be useful in diagnosing mistakes and error patterns.

- Researchers for some time have explored ways of giving partial credit for partial understanding on multiple-choice questions. One method of doing this involves giving different weights or points to different answers that are written to reflect incorrect, partial, and complete understanding of the solution. Partial credit scoring procedures are particularly relevant for diag-

[61]For more information on the new Michigan reading tests see Edward Roeber and Peggy Dutcher, "Michigan's Innovative Assessment of Reading," *Educational Leadership,* vol. 46, No. 7, April 1989, pp. 64-69; and Edward D. Roeber, Caroline S. Kirby, Geraldine J. Coleman, Peggy A. Dutcher, and Robert L.C. Smith, *Essential Skills Reading Test Blueprint,* 5th ed. (Lansing, MI: Michigan Department of Education, Michigan Educational Assessment Program, July 1989).

[62]William A. Mehrens, "Using Performance Assessment for Accountability Purposes: Some Problems," paper presented at the annual meeting of the American Educational Research Association, Chicago, IL, 1991; Anastasi, op. cit., footnote 4; Thomas M. Haladyna, "Context-Dependent Item Sets," *Educational Measurement: Issues and Practice,* in press; Millman and Greene, op. cit., footnote 24; and Lewis R. Aiken, "Writing Multiple-Choice Items to Measure Higher Order Educational Objectives," *Educational and Psychological Measurement,* vol. 42, No. 3, autumn 1982, pp. 803-806.

[63]The American College Testing Program, *The ACT Assessment Test Preparation Reference Manual for Teachers and Counselors* (Iowa City, IA: December 1990).

[64]Richard J. Shavelson, Neil B. Cary, and Noreen M. Webb, "Indicators of Science Achievement: Options for a Powerful Policy Instrument," *Phi Delta Kappan,* vol. 71, No. 9, May 1990, pp. 692-697.

Figure 6-4—Sample Multiple-Choice Items Designed To Measure Complex Thinking Skills

Thinking Skill:[a]
Knowing Science

Grade Levels: 4, 8, 12

	Always True	Sometimes True	Never True
Scientists should report exactly what they observe	*		
Belief is the main basis for scientific knowledge			*
Knowledge is the goal of scientific work	*		
Scientific knowledge can be questioned and changed	*		
Knowledge discovered in the past is used in current scientific work	*		
Scientists who do experiments find answers to their questions		*	

Grade Level: 4

The methods of science can be used to answer all of the following questions EXCEPT:

*(A) Are puppies more beautiful than spiders?
(B) How many oak trees grow in Pennsylvania?
(C) Which laundry detergent cleans best?
(D) What are the effects of lead pollution on trout?

Thinking Skill:[b]
Applying Principles

Grade 8

If the law of supply and demand works, the farmer will obtain the highest price for crops when

A. both supply and demand are great.
B. both supply and demand are low.
C. supply is great and demand is low.
*D. supply is low and demand is great.

Thinking Skill:[c]
Summarizing Ideas

Read the sentence. Then choose the essential phrase that should be included in research notes for a paper on the subject.

Despite the fact that Puritan forces in England objected to plays and tried to interfere with performances, theatrical entertainment enjoyed great popularity in Shakespeare's time, both with the public and with the members of the royal court.

A royal court enjoyed plays during Shakespeare's time

* B plays popular despite objection and interference by Puritans

C theatrical entertainment very popular with the public

D Puritans object to public performances

Thinking Skill:[c]
Comprehension

Read the question and then choose the best answer.

Which of these is most like an excerpt from a myth?

* A And so the turbulent sea suddenly grew calm as Father Neptune urged his steeds forward and flew off toward the setting sun.

B Gold coins were reported to have come from an ancient Phoenician ship that sank off the island during Homeric times.

C We lowered the sails but the *Moon Goddess* still lurched violently on the crashing waves as we prepared to ride out the storm.

D Retrace the voyage of Ulysses in a 21-day adventure that takes you from Asia Minor to the islands and mainland of Greece.

* Correct answers for multiple-choice items are indicated by an asterisk (*).

[a]SOURCE: National Assessment of Educational Progress, *Science Objectives: 1990 Assessment*, booklet No. 21-S-10 (Princeton, NJ: 1989), pp. 45-46.

[b]SOURCE: Connecticut State Department of Education, *Connecticut Assessment of Educational Progress 1982-83: Social Studies Summary and Interpretations Report* (Hartford, CT: 1984).

[c]SOURCE: CTB/McGraw-Hill, *Comprehensive Test of Basic Skills (CTBS) Class Management Guide: Using Test Results* (Monterey, CA: 1990), pp. 68, 70. These are sample items that do not appear on an actual test.

Figure 6-5—Sample Multiple-Choice Item With Alternative Answers Representing Common Student Misconceptions

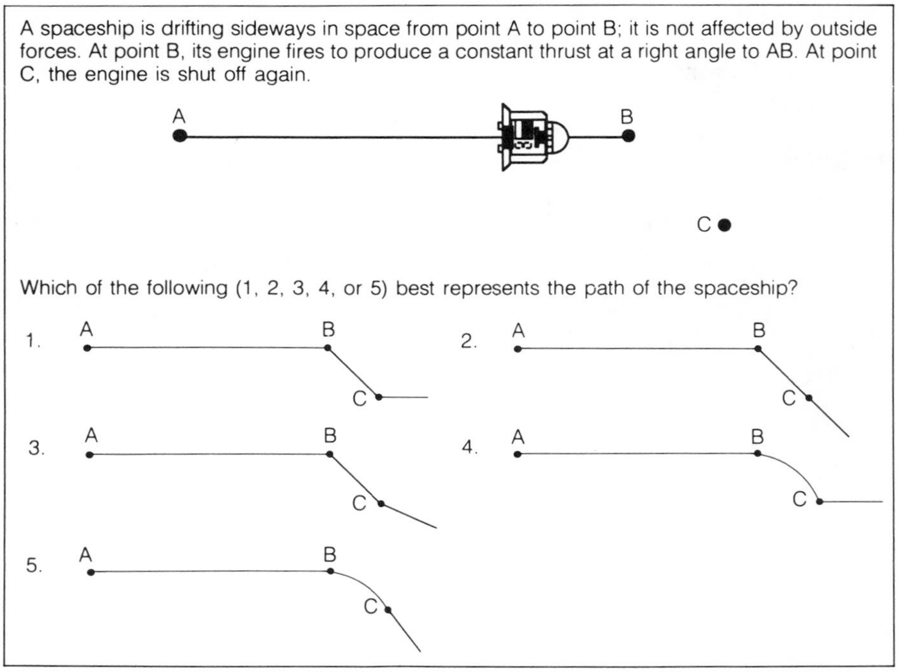

A spaceship is drifting sideways in space from point A to point B; it is not affected by outside forces. At point B, its engine fires to produce a constant thrust at a right angle to AB. At point C, the engine is shut off again.

Which of the following (1, 2, 3, 4, or 5) best represents the path of the spaceship?

The correct answer is __5__.

NOTE: The alternatives presented represent both the correct mental model of the effect of forces on a spaceship and a variety of possible answers based on known, erroneous mental models that children hold.

SOURCE: R.J. Shavelson, N.B. Carey, and N.M. Webb, "Indicators of Science Achievement: Options for a Powerful Policy Instruments," *Phi Delta Kappan*, vol. 71, No. 9, May 1990, p. 697.

nostic tests designed to describe a student's strengths and weaknesses.[65]

- The complex multiple-choice item is a widely used format in medical and health professions' testing programs where many questions have more than one right answer. In this item type, four or five answers are presented and the student can select any number of correct responses from none to all.[66]

- Another way that multiple-choice items can be used to measure more complex understandings is to group a series of them together based on a common set of data. The data may be in the form of charts, graphs, results of experiments, maps, or written materials. Students can be asked "... to identify relationships in data, to recognize valid conclusions, to appraise assumptions and inferences, to detect proper applications of data, and the like."[67]

Redesigning Tests: Function Before Form

Test use in schools has been increasing. Much of the increase in the volume of school-based testing in the last decade has come from its rising popularity as

---

[65]Millman and Green, op. cit., footnote 24; Thomas M. Haladyna, "The Effectiveness of Several Multiple-Choice Formats," *Applied Measurement in Education*, in press. For a discussion of ways in which test theory will have to develop and change in order to accommodate the measurement of problem-solving strategies and misconceptions see Robert J. Mislevy, *Foundations of a New Test Theory*, ETS Research Report RR 89-52-ONR (Princeton, NJ: Educational Testing Service, October 1989).

[66]Haladyna, op. cit., footnote 65. This item type has been found to have a number of technical problems. Haladyna recommends the related five-option "multiple true-false" item.

[67]Gronlund and Linn, op. cit., footnote 16, p. 193.

Table 6-3—Functions of Tests: What Designs Are Needed?

	Classroom instructional guidance	System monitoring	Selection, placement, and certification
Who needs to be described	Individuals	Groups of students	Individuals
"Stakes" or consequences attached	Low	High or low	High
Characteristics of the test needed			
Comparability of information	Low	High	High
Impartial scoring (not teachers)	No	Yes	Yes
Standardized administration...................	No	Yes	Yes
Type of information needed			
Detailed v. general	Detailed	General	General
Frequency	Frequently during a single school year	Once a year or less	Once a year or less
Results needed quickly	Yes	No	No
Technical requirements			
Need for high test reliability (internal consistency and stability)	Can vary	Depends on size of group	Very high
Type of validity evidence	Content	If low stakes: content If high stakes: content and construct	Content Additional validity evidence must be demonstrated for the specific purpose (e.g., certification = criterion validity, selection = predictive validity)

SOURCE: Office of Technology Assessment, 1992; adapted from Lauren B. Resnick and Daniel P. Resnick, "Assessing the Thinking Curriculum: New Tools for Educational Reform," paper prepared for the National Commission on Testing and Public Policy, August 1989. (To appear in B.R. Gifford and M.C. Connor (eds.), *Future Assessments: Changing Views of Aptitude, Achievement, and Instruction* (Boston, MA: Kluwer Academic Publishers, in press).)

an accountability tool for policymakers interested in a measure of system effectiveness (see ch. 2). The available testing technology—norm-referenced multiple-choice tests—has been pressed into service even when the properties of this technology were not well matched to the needs of the users. Similarly, there has been increasing interest in the role that tests can play in fostering learning and knowledge acquisition in the classroom. For tests to have educational value to the student in the classroom, educators argue, the tests must be frequent, provide feedback in a timely fashion, and make clear the expectations and standards for learning. A single testing technology no longer seems enough for the needs of multiple users. How, then, should we redesign achievement tests to better serve multiple testing needs?

Table 6-3 summarizes the characteristics of tests required for each of the three main functions of testing. Consider first the system monitoring function of tests. In this case only groups of students need to be described, that is classrooms, schools, districts, or States. Individual scores are not needed. This means that sampling methodologies can be used—a representative subset of students can be tested and accurate information obtained. One of the advan-

tages of a sampling methodology is that no individual scores are available, thus preventing their use for unintended purposes such as selecting students for special programs or grouping students according to ability. One of the drawbacks sometimes cited for sampling, however, is that students may not be particularly motivated to give their best performance when they are not going to receive personal scores (see ch. 3).

In system monitoring, managerial uses can include information that has both high and low stakes. Purely informational uses (without consequences) may include program evaluation and curricular evaluation. Similarly, some administrators may want information about how their system is doing but may not attach any particular rewards, sanctions, or expectations to the test scores; test results would have a "temperature taking" function. NAEP is an example of a test designed to provide nationally representative information of this type. However, increasingly tests are being used for accountability purposes—rewards and consequences are attached to the results of those tests and they are being used as a lever to motivate improvement. When this happens, the informational value of the test can be compromised. Attention is readily focused on test performance as a goal of instruction; in this case improvement in test scores may or may not signal growth in real achievement.[68]

Many of the characteristics of tests designed for monitoring systems are those expected from standardized achievement tests. It is very important that the results obtained from these tests be comparable across students and that they can be aggregated in a meaningful way. This means that the tests must be standardized in administration and scoring. Impartial scoring is very important. The monitoring of systems requires general information at occasional intervals (usually once a year or less). The results are not needed immediately.

Tests used for selection, placement, or certification differ from tests used for system monitoring in several major ways. First, each student must receive a score. Second, the kinds of decisions these tests are used to make are almost always high stakes—they can have significant consequences for an individual's educational career. Tests used for selection, placement, and certification must meet exceptionally high standards of comparability, reliability, and validity. As with tests used for monitoring systems, impartial scoring and standardized administration are required; similarly the information required is general, needed infrequently (once a year or less) and not required quickly.

The third major difference is in the kind of validity evidence required. Tests for selection, placement, or certification must be validated for each of those specific uses. Thus certification tests need criterion-related validity evidence particularly related to the "cutoff scores" that are established to certify mastery. Selection tests need predictive validity evidence demonstrating that test results relate to future performance or ability to benefit from a particular resource or intervention. In the current debate about redesigning tests, there is little discussion by educators or measurement specialists about needing or using various new test designs for selection. In part, this may be due to a fairly widespread and entrenched belief that selection tests are not appropriate for elementary school and, for the most part, not within secondary school either.[69]

Tests designed for classroom use are the most divergent in their design requirements (see table 6-3), differing significantly both from existing and new tests designed to serve managerial functions. Tests used by teachers to monitor learning and provide feedback need to provide detailed information on a frequent basis, as quickly as possible. Because classroom tests are very closely related to the goals of instruction, time spent on testing need not be considered "wasted time." As testing at the classroom level becomes more integrated with instruction, the time constraints so often imposed on tests can be relaxed considerably because time spent on tests is also time spent learning. Because these tests do not carry high stakes and because they are not going to be used to make comparisons among students or schools, they are free of many of the stringent requirements of standardization, impartial scoring, and need for comparability. However, the more that teachers or school systems want these classroom level tests to be useful for other purposes, i.e., to make high-stakes decisions about individuals or to aggregate the information across classrooms or schools, the more that these classroom tests will need to incorporate features that provide comparability and standardization. **It is difficult to prevent the misuse of information once that information has been collected. One of the dangers, therefore, in relaxing technical standards for classroom tests is that the use of the scores cannot be restricted or monitored appropriately once they are obtained.**

How can the various functions of testing and design requirements be coordinated with one another? Most investigators working in test design today believe that one test cannot successfully serve all testing functions.

Many of the features of tests that can effectively influence classroom learning are very different from the requirements of large-scale managerial testing. Many testing experts believe that we need two distinct types of tests to serve these two functions

---

[68]For a discussion of the "Lake Wobegon Effect" and other evidence about how gains in test scores can be attained without affecting "real achievement," see ch. 2.

[69]Haney, op. cit., footnote 35.

because the requirements are so divergent.[70] The Pittsburgh school district, for example, has developed a diagnostic testing system, called Monitoring Achievement in Pittsburgh (MAP), which is characterized by tests closely aligned with curricula, brief and frequent administration of those tests, and rapid turnaround of results. These test results are then used to inform instruction, as teachers can see whether an objective that has been covered has, in fact, been learned by the class and tailor instruction accordingly. Pittsburgh uses a different test for system monitoring; analyses have suggested that recent gains on this traditional norm-referenced test are largely due to the effects of MAP.[71]

Conclusions

No testing program operates in a void. The effects of any testing program on the school system as a whole, or of different tests on one another, need to be continually monitored. The effect of other testing requirements, imposed by the State or a special program such as Chapter 1, may also affect the impact of a new test or new reform program. The consequences of a given test—to the individual student, the teacher, the school—will heavily influence the effects of that test on learning and instruction. A beautifully designed and educationally relevant test may have no impact if no one looks at its scores; the poorest quality test available could conceivably influence much of a school's educational climate if the stakes attached to it are high.

What a test looks like—the kinds of tasks and questions it includes—should depend on the intended purpose of the test. As the next chapter will illustrate, test formats can vary widely from multiple-choice to essays to portfolios. Different types of testing tasks will be more or less useful depending on the purpose of the test and the type of information needed. The purpose of a test and a definition of what it is intended to assess need to be carefully determined *before* test formats are chosen. Moreover, critical issues such as bias, reliability, and validity will not be resolved by changing the format of the test.

---

[70]Paul G. LeMahieu and Richard C. Wallace, Jr., ''Up Against the Wall: Psychometrics Meets Praxis,'' *Educational Measurement: Issues and Practice*, vol. 5, No. 1, spring 1986, pp. 12-16; and Educational Testing Service, ''Instructional and Accountability Testing in American Education: Different Purposes, Different Needs,'' brochure, 1990.

[71]LeMahieu and Wallace, op. cit., footnote 70; and Paul G. LeMahieu, ''The Effects on Achievement and Instructional Content of a Program of Student Monitoring Through Frequent Testing,'' *Educational Evaluation and Policy Analysis*, vol. 6, No. 2, summer 1984, pp. 175-187.

CHAPTER 7

Performance Assessment: Methods and Characteristics

Contents

Boxes

Figures

Table

Performance Assessment: Methods and Characteristics

Highlights

- Many school districts and States are turning to performance assessment—testing that requires students to create answers or products that demonstrate what they know and can do—as a complement to their traditional testing programs. Thirty-six States now use direct writing samples, and 21 States use other types of performance assessment (in addition to writing samples) on a mandatory, voluntary, or experimental basis.

- Writing samples and constructed-response items, which require test takers to produce an answer rather than select from a number of options, are the most common forms of performance assessment; other methods, such as portfolios of student work, exhibitions and simulations, science experiments, and oral interviews, are still in their infancy.

- Although performance assessment methods vary, they share certain key features. They involve direct observation of student behavior on tasks resembling those considered necessary in the real world, and they shed light on students' learning and thinking processes in addition to the correctness of their answers.

- Performance assessment methods must meet the challenge of producing reliable and valid estimates of student achievement before they can be used for high-stakes decisions involved in system monitoring or selection, placement, and certification. Procedures to reduce subjectivity and eliminate error in human scoring have been developed and used with some success in scoring essays and student writing samples.

- Researchers are developing methods for machine scoring of constructed-response items. Test taking by computer is one approach. Others include having students fill in grids to answer mathematics problems or draw responses on a graph or diagram.

- Advanced information technologies could significantly enhance performance assessment methods: tracking student progress, standardizing scoring, presenting simulations and problems, video recording performance for later analysis, and training teachers are among the most promising possibilities.

- Performance assessment is usually more expensive in dollar outlays than conventional multiple-choice testing because it requires more time and labor to administer and score. However, these high costs might be balanced by the added instructional benefits of teacher participation in developing and scoring tests, and by the closer integration of testing and instruction in the classroom.

- For performance assessment to become a meaningful complement or substitute for conventional testing, educating teachers and the general public will be critical. Teachers need to learn how to use, score, and interpret performance assessments. The public, accustomed to data ranking students on norm-referenced, multiple-choice tests, needs to understand the goals and products of performance assessment.

- Changing the format of tests will not by itself ensure that the tests better meet educational goals. However, since what is tested often drives what is taught, testing should be designed to reflect outcomes that are desired as a result of schooling.

Introduction

Springdale High School, Springdale, Arkansas. Spring 1990. Instead of end-of-year examinations, seniors receive the following assignment for a required "Final Performance Across the Disciplines":

Discuss behavior patterns as reflected in the insect world, in animals, in human beings, and in literature. Be sure to include references to your course work over the term in Inquiry and Expression, Literature and the Arts, Social Studies, and Science. This may draw upon works we have studied, including *Macbeth*, Stephen Crane's poetry, Swift's "A Modest Proposal'' and other essays, Mark Twain's fiction, materials from the drug prevention and communication workshop, or behaviors you have observed in school. You may also add references to what you have read about in the news recently. On day 1 of the examination you will be given 4 periods in which to brainstorm, make an outline, write a rough draft, and write a final copy in standard composition form. You will be graded not only on how well you assimilate the material but also how well you reflect our ''student as worker'' metaphor and how responsibly you act during the testing period. On day 2 of the examination, you will assemble in villages of three, evaluate anonymous papers according to a set of criteria, and come to a consensus about a grade. Each paper will be evaluated by at least two groups and two instructors. Part of your overall semester grade will reflect how responsibly you act as a member of a team in this task.[1]

Constable Elementary School, South Brunswick, New Jersey. Fall 1990.[2] Every morning, between 10:30 and 11:50, first grade teacher Sharon Suskin settles her class down to a quiet activity supervised by an aide while she calls one student at a time up to her table. With Manuel she says: ''I'm going to read you this story but I want you to help me. Where do I start to read? ''As the shy 6-year-old holds the book right side up and points to the print on the first page, she smiles and continues: ''Show me where to start.'' She puts a check on her list if he begins at the top left, another if he moves his finger from left to right, another for going page by page. When it is Joanna's turn, she asks her to spell some words: ''truck,'' ''dress,'' ''feet.'' Mrs. Suskin makes a note that, while last month Joanna was stringing together random letters, she now has moved into a more advanced phonetic spelling—''t-r-k'', ''j-r-s'' and ''f-e-t''—representing the sounds in a word. Mrs. Suskin spends anywhere from 2 to 10 minutes with each child, covering about one-half the class each morning, and files the results in each child's portfolio later in the day. When parents come in for conferences, out comes the portfolio. Mrs. Suskin shows Manuel's parents how far he has come in reading skills; Joanna's parents see records of progress rather than grades or test scores. Mrs. Suskin refers to the portfolio regularly, when group-

ing students having similar difficulties, or when she wishes to check on special areas where an individual child needs help. It's a lot of work, she admits, but she says it gives her a picture of each child's emerging literacy. She laughs: ''It makes me put on paper all those things I used to keep in my head.''

All Over California, Spring 1990.[3] All 1.1 million fifth, seventh, and ninth grade students in California were huffing and puffing, running and reaching. They were being tested in five measures of fitness: muscular strength (pull ups); muscular endurance (sit ups); cardiovascular fitness (a mile run); flexibility (sit and reach); and body fat composition (skin fold measurements). Results were tabulated by age and sex, along with self-reported data of other behavior, such as the amount of time spent watching television or engaging in physical activity. The tasks and standards were known in advance, and local physical education teachers had been trained to conduct the scoring themselves. The results were distressing: only 20 percent of the students could complete four or five tasks at the ''acceptable'' level. The bad news sent a signal to the physical education programs all over the State. Teaching to this test is encouraged as schools work to get better results on the next test administration. The overall goal is more ambitious—to focus awareness on the need for increasing attention to physical fitness for all students, and to change their fitness level for the better.

Why Performance Assessment?

These vignettes are examples of performance assessment, a broad set of testing methods being developed and applied in schools, districts, and sometimes statewide. This concept is based on the premise that testing should be more closely related to the kinds of tasks and skills children are striving to learn. Emotionally charged terms have been applied to this vision of testing. ''Authentic,'' ''appropriate,'' ''direct,'' and even ''intelligent'' assessment imply something pejorative about multiple-choice tests. This rhetoric tends to ignore that certain multiple-choice tests can provide valuable information about student achievement. OTA uses the more

---

[1]Brown University, The Coalition of Essential Schools, *Horace*, vol. 1, No. 6, March 1990, p. 4.

[2]From Ruth Mitchell and Amy Stempel, Council for Basic Education, ''Six Case Studies of Performance Assessment,'' OTA contractor report, March 1991.

[3]Dale Carlson, ''What's New in Large-Scale Performance Testing,'' paper presented at the Boulder Conference of State Testing Directors, Boulder, CO, June 10-12, 1990.

neutral and descriptive term "performance assessment" to refer to testing that requires a student to create an answer or a product that demonstrates his or her knowledge or skills.

The act of creating an answer or a product on a test can take many forms. Performance assessment covers a range of methods on a continuum, from short-answer questions to open-ended questions requiring students to write essays or otherwise demonstrate understanding of multiple facts and issues. Performance assessment could involve an experiment demonstrating understanding of scientific principles and procedures, or the creation and defense of a position in oral argument or comprehensive performance. Or it may mean assembling a portfolio of materials over a course of study, to illustrate the development and growth of a student in a particular domain or skill (see ch. 1, box 1-D).

Whatever the specific tasks involved, this move toward testing based on direct observation of performance has been described by some educators as "nothing short of a revolution" in assessment.[4] **Given that performance assessment has been used in businesses and military training for many years, and by teachers in their classrooms as one mechanism to assess student progress, the real revolution is in using performance assessment as a part of large-scale testing programs in elementary and secondary schools.**

The move toward alternative forms of testing students has been motivated by new understandings of how children learn as well as changing views of curriculum. Recent research suggests that complex thinking and learning involves processes that cannot be reduced to a routine,[5] that knowledge is a complex network of information and abilities rather than a series of isolated facts and skills. According to this research, students need to be able to successfully engage in tasks that have multiple solutions and require interpretive and nuanced judgments. This kind of performance in real-world settings is inextricably supported and enriched by

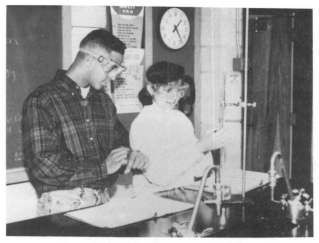

Photo credit: Norwalk High School, Norwalk, CT

Performance assessment often involves direct observation of students engaged in classroom tasks. For example, examinations that require students to plan, conduct, and describe experiments reinforce instruction that emphasizes scientific understanding through hands-on activities.

other people and by knowledge-extending artifacts like computers, calculators, and texts.[6]

This view of learning challenges traditional views of how to structure curricula and teach, and therefore also how to evaluate students' competence. If knowledge is linked in complex ways to situations in which it is used, then testing should assign students tasks that require interpretation and application of knowledge. If instruction is increasingly individualized, adaptive, and interactive, assessment should share these characteristics. However, educators trying to implement curricular innovations based on this more complex view of learning outcomes have found their new programs judged by traditional tests that do not cover the skills and goals central to their innovations. Many say that school reform without testing reform is impossible. For example, the National Council of Teachers of English recently warned that: ". . . school restructuring may be doomed unless it helps schools move beyond the limitations of standardized tests."[7]

---

[4]Jack Foster, secretary for Education and Humanities, State of Kentucky, personal communication, Mar. 11, 1991.

[5]See also ch. 2; and Center for Children and Technology, Bank Street College, "Applications in Educational Assessment: Future Technologies," OTA contractor report, February 1990.

[6]Additional interest in increased teaching of more complex thinking skills comes not only because of disappointing evidence about students' abilities, but also because of the belief that all workers will require these adaptive capabilities, i.e., the ability to apply knowledge to new situations.

[7]New York State United Teachers Task Force on Student Assessment, "Multiple Choices: Reforming Student Testing in New York State," unpublished report, January 1991, p. 12: citing the 1990 National Council of Teachers of English, *Report on Trends and Issues*.

Educators advocating performance assessment are also interested in the possibility of making good assessment a more integral and effective part of the learning process. These advocates hope that standardized performance-based testing can become a helpful part of classroom learning rather than a distraction or a derailment of classroom practices. In this view, time spent studying or practicing for tests, or even going through the tests themselves, is no longer seen as time away from valuable classroom learning but rather an integral learning experience.[8]

Indeed, some proponents of performance assessment suggest that its strongest value lies in how it can influence curriculum and instruction by modeling desired educational outcomes. Although "teaching to the test" is disparaged when a test calls for selection of isolated facts from a multiple-choice format, it becomes the modus operandi in performance assessment. Perhaps the prime reason for the popularity of performance assessment today stems from the idea that student learning should be guided by clear, understandable, and authentic examples that demonstrate the desired *use* of knowledge and skills. Assessment is then defined as the tool to judge how close the student has come to replicating the level of expertise modeled in the examples. The theory is that performance assessment is an effective method for clarifying standards, building consensus about goals, and delivering a more cohesive curriculum throughout a school system.

As States and districts begin to change their educational goals and curricula, student assessments are also being revised to meet these changing standards and goals. Educators have always recognized that traditional multiple-choice tests do not capture all the objectives valued in the curricula. Some testing programs have attempted to overcome this problem by incorporating some open-ended tasks. However, the increasing stakes attached to traditional test scores has given the tested objectives a great deal of attention and weight in classrooms, often at the expense of objectives that are valued but not directly tested. Policymakers have become interested in tests covering a much wider range of

skills and educational objectives, and in various forms of performance assessment that can broaden educational outcomes.

The real policy issue is not a choice between performance assessment and multiple choice, but using tests to enrich learning and understand student progress. Embracing performance assessment does not imply throwing out multiple-choice tests; most States are looking to performance assessment as a means of filling in the gaps. The skills that are not usually evaluated on multiple-choice tests—writing, oral skills, ability to organize material, or perform experiments—have been the first candidates for performance assessments. New York's position is illustrative:

> Student performance assessments should be developed as a significant component of the state's system of assessment. These assessments would include improved multiple-choice tests and incorporate authentic "real-life" measures of student knowledge. Student performance, judged against clearly defined standards of excellence, would better measure the skills of critical thinking, reasoning, information retrieval and problem solving. Such performance assessments could include portfolios, hands-on problem-solving projects, and demonstrations of ability and knowledge.[9]

State Activities in Performance Assessment

State and local districts have rapidly adopted performance assessment for a range of grade levels and testing objectives. OTA estimates that, as of 1991, 36 States were assessing writing using direct writing samples (see figure 7-1); in addition, 21 States had implemented other types of performance assessment on a mandatory, voluntary, or experimental basis[10] (see figure 7-2). At the present time, most performance assessments are on a pilot or voluntary basis at the State level. When mandated statewide, performance assessments tend to be administered in one or two subjects at selected grade levels.

---

[8]This issue has important implications for the estimation of costs associated with alternative testing programs. See discussion in ch. 1.

[9]New York State United Teachers Task Force on Student Assessment, op. cit., footnote 7, p. 4.

[10]Office of Technology Assessment data, 1991. The category of writing assessments includes just those tests that evaluate student writing skills by asking them to write at some length (paragraphs or essays); other performance assessments reported by States included portfolios, exhibitions or activities, and open-ended paper-and-pencil tests that include student-created answers. This last category includes student essays designed to test knowledge on a particular subject, not testing writing skills per se.

Figure 7-1—State Testing Programs: Direct Sample Writing Assessments, 1991

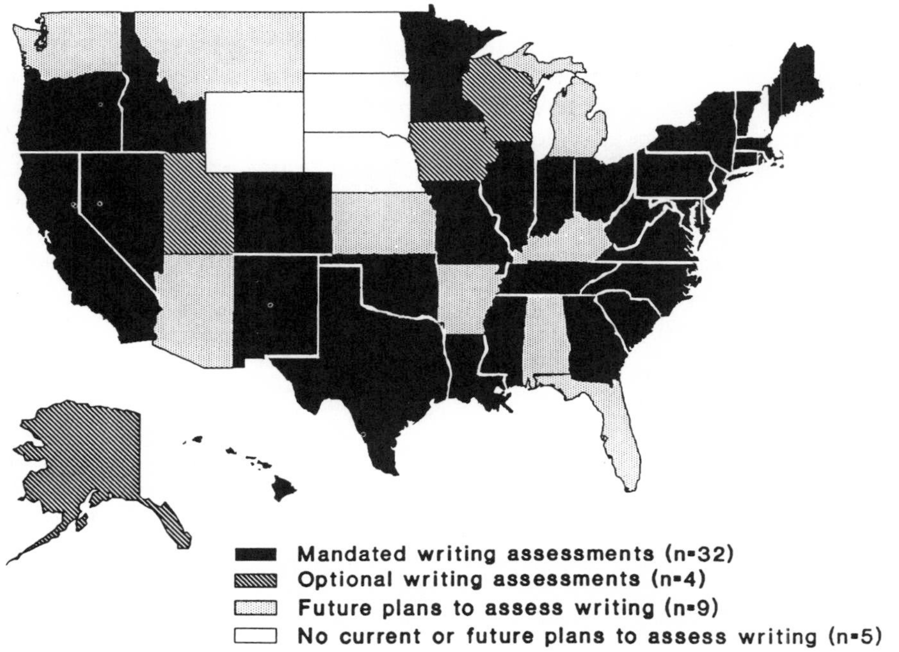

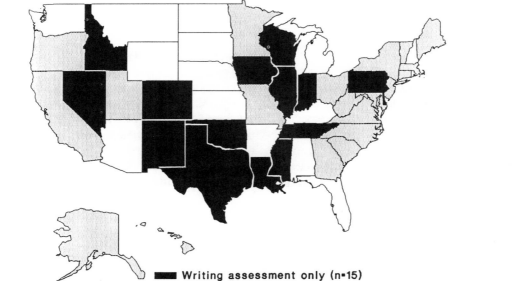

■ Mandated writing assessments (n=32)
▨ Optional writing assessments (n=4)
▤ Future plans to assess writing (n=9)
□ No current or future plans to assess writing (n=5)

NOTE: "Future plans" includes current pilot programs.
SOURCE: Office of Technology Assessment, 1992.

Figure 7-2—Statewide Performance Assessments, 1991

■ Writing assessment only (n=15)
▤ Writing and other types of performance assessments (n=21)
□ None (n=14)

NOTE: Map includes optional programs.
SOURCE: Office of Technology Assessment, 1992.

Seven States (Arizona, California, Connecticut, Kentucky, Maryland, New York, and Vermont[11]) are moving their educational evaluation systems toward performance assessment, gradually reducing reliance on norm-referenced multiple-choice testing. Each State has approached the change differently, but they view performance assessment as a tool not only for understanding the progress of individual students, but also for school, district, or State accountability. These State efforts will exert a tremendous influence as comparisons and rankings between schools develop, and policy decisions are made as a result of these new testing results.

The variety of approaches in State testing policies stands in contrast to the traditional State processes for test selection. Historically, State departments of education selected tests with little or no input from teachers or the public. The testing division would invite publishers to bid on the development of a norm-referenced or criterion-referenced test based on the State's curriculum, or, more commonly, shop around and then purchase "off-the-shelf" tests such as the Iowa Tests of Basic Skills, Stanford Achievement Tests, California Achievement Tests, or other popular norm-referenced achievement tests.[12] This process is changing.

The State profiles in boxes 7-A, 7-B, and 7-C provide a picture of how some States are moving toward greater use of performance assessment in their statewide testing programs. They illustrate the motivation behind these changes, as well as problems and barriers States face in implementing these changes.

The Many Faces of Performance Assessment: Forms and Functions

Performance assessment can take many forms. The central defining element in all performance assessment methods is that the test taker creates an answer or product to demonstrate knowledge or skills in a particular field. From paper-and-pencil, short-answer questions to essays requiring use of knowledge in context, oral interviews, experiments, exhibitions, and comprehensive portfolios with multiple examples of a student's work over a period of an entire year or longer, each type has its own characteristics. Nonetheless, many characteristics are shared. This section describes some of the common *forms* of performance assessment used in K-12 schools today. It is followed by a section that summarizes the common *characteristics* of performance assessment.

Constructed-Response Items

Paper-and-pencil tests designed by teachers have long been a regular feature of the classroom; teachers typically employ a range of item types that include mathematics calculations, geometry proofs, drawing graphs, fill-in-the-blank, matching, definitions, short written answers, and essays. Except for multiple choice and essays, few of these item types have been used for large-scale standardized testing programs, but test developers and educators have begun to consider this possibility.

The term **constructed-response (CR) item** is commonly used to distinguish these items from items such as multiple choice that require selecting a response among the several options presented. CR items require students to produce or construct their own answers.[13]

Several educational advantages might be gained by expanding the use of CR items.[14] First, they have higher face validities: they look more like the kinds of tasks we want children to be able to do. Second, these item types may do a better job of reflecting the complexity of knowledge, because they can allow partial credit for partial understanding. Third, these item types may enhance the reliability and validity of scores because they eliminate guessing and other

---

[11]Vermont did not require statewide testing prior to 1990. The introduction of performance assessment through portfolios in mathematics and writing is the first mandated statewide testing.

[12]See ch. 6 for further discussion of norm-referenced testing.

[13]A group of researchers at the Educational Testing Service has attempted to describe a framework for categorizing some of these item types. These researchers have ordered a number of such item types along an "openness" continuum that includes selection/identification, reordering/rearrangement, substitution/correction, completion, and construction. See Randy E. Bennett, William C. Ward, Donald A. Rock, and Colleen LaHart, "Toward a Framework for Constructed-Response Items," ETS research report RR 90-7, 1990.

[14]Ibid.; and James Braswell and J. Kupin, "Item Formats in Mathematics," *Construction Versus Choice in Cognitive Measurement*, R.E. Bennett and W.C. Ward (eds.) (Hillsdale, NJ: L. Erlbaum Associates, in press).

Box 7-A—The Arizona Student Assessment Program[1]

Arizona revised its curriculum substantially and then discovered that existing State-mandated tests were no longer appropriate. Teachers carried a heavy annual testing burden, but remained unsure how the various tests corresponded to what they were expected to teach. Describing the old State-mandated testing required in grades 1 through 12 every spring, using the Iowa Tests of Basic Skills (ITBS), Tests of Achievement and Proficiency (TAP), and district testing under the Continuous Uniform Evaluation System (CUES), one teacher expressed frustration:

> We have these CUES tests, pre- and post-test. . . . In one grade we have 135 little skills tests in all of those forms, pre- and post-test. We teach what we think is important to teach . . . until right before our CUES tests. Then we teach students how to do well on the CUES tests. We also give the Iowa Tests of Basic Skills and it takes about a week. We teach what we think is important all year long . . . until right before the ITBS. Then we teach students how to take the ITBS. . . . We get the scores back on the ITBS right before students leave for the summer, and I usually have to follow students out the door on the last day with a stapler in one hand and the test scores in the other so I can staple the score reports onto their report cards. We have an entirely different group of students over the next year so that it doesn't do much good to analyze the test scores over the summer. . . . I feel confused. What are we supposed to teach? What is valued? It seems to me we are spending a great deal of time getting ready for two measures that are at odds with what we have agreed in my district is important to teach.[2]

Statewide curriculum frameworks, known as Essential Skills Documents (ESDs), were developed starting in 1986, to outline broad competencies and goals at the elementary, middle, and high school levels across the State.[3] Most teachers enthusiastically embraced the documents but some lamented: "That's the way I'd like to teach . . . if it weren't for the way we test."[4] Reflecting this concern, the State legislature set up a joint committee in 1987 to review the overall teaching and assessment program in the State, looking especially to see if the skills and processes identified in the Essential Skills curriculum frameworks were being successfully acquired by Arizona students.

An independent committee analyzed whether the skills required in the ESDs were being assessed in the ITBS and TAP. Results for mathematics, reading, and writing indicated that only 20 to 40 percent (with an average of 26 percent) of the Essential Skills were assessed by the ITBS and TAP. Thus, even with annual testing for all grades, Arizona was only receiving information on how well students were mastering one-quarter of the content of the new curriculum. As one teacher said:

> The teachers in Arizona can't serve two masters. If they want the teachers to do a good job of teaching math they can use the Essential Skills Documents . . . and throw out the ITBS tests, or teach the ITBS tests and throw out the Essential Skills Documents.[5]

With the support of teachers, school boards, administrators, and the business community, the legislature passed State Law 1442 by a landslide. The act required the Arizona Department of Education to create an assessment plan that would do a better job of testing the Essential Skills. Thus the Arizona Student Assessment Program (ASAP) was born in the spring of 1990, setting a new approach to State testing.

ASAP is an umbrella program composed of new performance measures, continuing but reduced emphasis on norm-referenced testing, and extensive school, district, and State report cards. Riverside Publishing Co., the same company that produces the TAP and ITBS, was selected to produce the new assessments at the benchmark grades of 3, 8, and 12 in each of the three subject areas. To best match the goals of the ESDs, the new tests were to be performance- and curriculum-based assessments. The language arts assessment is an interesting example. Paralleling the way writing is taught under the language arts framework, the assessment is a two-step process. On the first day of testing, students engage in the steps that make up the "prewriting" process (e.g., brainstorming, listing, mapping, or "webbing" ideas) and creating a first draft; on the second day of testing, they reread the draft,

---

[1]Much of this discussion is taken from Ruth Mitchell and Amy Stempel, Council for Basic Education, "Six Case Studies of Performance Assessment," OTA contractor report, March 1991.

[2]Lois Brown Easton, "Developing Educational Performance Tests for a Statewide Program," *Educational Performance Assessment*, Fred L. Finch (ed.) (Chicago, IL: Riverside Publishing Co., 1991), p. 47.

[3]The language arts framework was published in 1986 and the mathematics framework in 1987; by the end of 1990, Essential Skills Documents were available in 12 subjects including, in addition to the above, frameworks in science, health, social studies, and the arts. Mitchell and Stempel, op. cit., footnote 1.

[4]Easton, op. cit., footnote 2.

[5]Arizona Department of Education, *Arizona Essential Skills for Mathematics* (Phoenix, AZ: July 1987), p. i.

Continued on next page

Box 7-A—The Arizona Student Assessment Program[1]—Continued

revise, and write a second draft. Similar performance-based assessments have been created for mathematics and reading, with science and social studies assessments also under development.

The first official assessment will be implemented in March 1992 and scored by teachers at regional scoring sites, none more than an hour's drive from any district. Classroom teachers are being trained and certified as scorers, and will receive a small stipend and graduate credit for their work. In pilot scoring sessions, scoring was found to be reliable between readers as well as consistent when a reader was given the same paper to score more than once. Scoring also took less time than expected.[6] Having the classroom teachers score the examinations is seen as a positive staff development activity, as teachers become involved in setting common quality standards and in sharing the review process with their colleagues from around the State.

Norm-referenced tests (NRTs) are being continued as a way to compare Arizona's student achievement against a national testing reference. However, their influence is being reduced. Students will take only a part of the ITBS and TAP each year (i.e., subtests, rather than the full test battery), reducing test-taking time overall by one-half to two-thirds.[7] The norm-referenced testing will be moved from spring to fall, further reducing their impact. Scores derived from spring testing had been considered a reflection of what the teachers taught over the past year, even if the test content did not always correspond to what was actually taught. Teachers often felt pressured to spend considerable time preparing students for the spring tests. With fall testing, both teachers and students should face the tests with more equanimity, and there will be less pressure to "prep" students. Fall testing also means that scores will be returned in time to be used for that year's instructional planning.

The third component of ASAP changes the way school and district achievement will be reported. Previously, each July things got "hot" in Arizona, as newspaper stories listed every school in a district alongside their test scores on the TAP and ITBS. Little interpretative information was provided and the message was implicit—the higher the score, the better the school. The new reporting system will try to paint a more realistic picture of achievement at the school, district, and State level. These annual "Arizona Report Cards" will report Essential Skills scores, NRT scores, and other factors that *reflect* achievement (e.g., numbers of students in advanced courses, science fair winners, and special award winners). However, to set these in context, factors that *affect* achievement are also reported, such as student socioeconomic status, mobility rate, percentage of students with limited English proficiency, and faculty turnover rates. Although it is assumed that school and district comparisons will continue to be made, it is hoped that these comparisons will be made on a more meaningful and realistic cluster of factors.

When the new program was introduced to teams of 850 teachers from across the State at a 3-day conference in October 1990, teacher reaction was mixed. Although many were pleased with the new approach, they were concerned with the difficulty of putting the new system into place. As one said: "The staff development needs are incredible. We need staff development on pedagogy, on writing, on logic, everything. To do this in the timeframe we have, we need big bucks."

Assessment costs are difficult to determine because the change in assessment is aligned to changes across the system—especially curriculum development and professional development. Money saved from less ITBS and TAP testing will be used for all three parts of the ASAP in coming years—the NRTs, performance assessments, and nontest indicators. Nevertheless, costs for the program (the request for proposal for developing the new performance-based assessments, the statewide teacher conference, preparing teacher scorers, and training all teachers in the new system) will be substantial. While perhaps an expensive gamble, the State commitment to move forward indicates the priority Arizona legislators and educators have placed on introducing a new approach to assessment throughout the State.

---

[6]Easton, op. cit., footnote 2, p. 56.

[7]Ibid., p. 57.

"back door" approaches, such as strategies of elimination or getting cues from incorrect choices. Fourth, some of these items can use scoring methods that recognize the correctness of a variety of different answers, representing the complexity of understanding and knowledge. (This suggests the potential diagnostic value of CR items. These items can reveal the processes used by the learner; e.g., a scorer can examine the student's problem-solving steps and detect errors in reasoning or misconceptions). And, finally, one of the most often cited (but least documented) assumptions is that these items

Box 7-B—Kentucky's Performance Assessments and Valued Outcomes[1]

Kentucky is fundamentally redesigning its State educational system. When the 1990 Kentucky Education Reform Act is fully implemented, the State will have the first system that measures student achievement entirely by performance-based testing. It will also be unique in the emphasis placed on these tests: schools will be rewarded and punished based on test results.[2]

In rethinking basic educational practices and premises, Kentucky educators hope to give classroom teachers a larger voice and improved ability to report on what they believe a student has achieved. They hope to move away from the common model that values the results of State-administered norm-referenced tests more highly than classroom-based testing and teacher's grade cards. The goal is to integrate teaching with assessment so it is almost invisible to the student, minimizing the use of external instruments as much as possible. The Kentucky approach will require extensive training of teachers as well as a backup system to ensure quality control.

Under the guidance of a Council on School Performance Standards, 11 task forces involving some 1,000 educators are working to identify the activities needed to define expected student outcomes and set the level of proficiency desired at three "anchor points": the 4th, 8th, and 12th grades. Teachers will continually evaluate students on a less formal basis in the interim grades to be sure progress is being made by all students as they prepare for the benchmark performance levels. Additionally, as younger children watch the performance of older peers, they will be encouraged to model themselves on the older students and see how close they are to that level of proficiency. This approach is based on a sports metaphor, with the students participating in "scrimmages" that involve practice tests at earlier grade levels. Younger students are similar to the "junior varsity" as they become motivated by and learn from watching the "varsity," older students at higher levels of performance.

Benchmark grades will be tested each year but reported every other year for accountability purposes. Successful schools will receive monetary rewards from the State; unsuccessful schools will be required to develop plans for improvement. If a school is particularly unsuccessful, it may be declared a "school in crisis" and its students may be permitted to transfer to more successful schools or administrators may be replaced and "distinguished educators" may be brought in to help.[3]

In the summer of 1991, a contractor was selected to create the 1995-96 performance assessments in language arts, science and technology, mathematics, social studies, arts and humanities, practical living, and vocational studies. Development costs over the first 18 months are estimated to be approximately $3.5 million. An interim testing program administered to a sample of students during the 1991-92 school year will provide baseline data for school success during 1993-94. The interim test has been controversial because of its traditional nature; some fear it could sidetrack implementation of the full program of performance-based measures.

---

[1]Much of this box is taken from Kentucky Department of Education, "Request for Proposals to Implement an Interim and Full-Scale Student Assessment Program for the Commonwealth of Kentucky," March 1991; and Jack Foster, secretary of Education, Kentucky, personal communication, June 1991.

[2]"Update," *Education Week*, vol. 10, No. 40, July 31, 1991, p. 33.

[3]Mary Helen Miller, Kevin Noland, and John Schaff, *A Guide to the Kentucky Education Reform Act of 1990* (Frankfort, KY: Legislative Research Commission, April 1990), p. 5.

---

tap more sophisticated reasoning and thinking processes than do multiple-choice items.

California has been a pioneer in the effort to use open-ended CR items. In 1987-88, the State piloted a number of open-ended mathematics problems as part of the 12th grade State test. Some of the questions were intentionally structured to be broad to allow ". . . students to respond creatively, demonstrate the full extent of their mathematical under-

standing, and display the elegance and originality of their thought processes."[15] One such question, along with representative answers, is pictured in figure 7-3. As the sample answers suggest, some students demonstrated a high degree of competence in mathematical reasoning while others displayed misconceptions or lack of mathematical understanding. Sixty-five percent of the answers to this question were judged to be inadequate, leading the developers to surmise that: ". . . the inadequate

---

[15]California State Department of Education, "A Question of Thinking: A First Look at Students' Performance on Open-Ended Questions in Mathematics," unpublished report, 1989, p. 3.

Box 7-C—The California Assessment Program: Testing That Goes "Beyond the Bubble"[1]

The California Assessment Program (CAP) was created in 1974-75 as part of an early school reform program. It has evolved over the years to reflect changes in curricula, student population, and pressures for accountability, but CAP continues to be seen as a model for other States, primarily due to two factors: the State carefully defined curricular objectives as the starting point for assessment, and devoted considerable research and support to the development of new forms of assessment.

Bringing education reform to a State as large as California, larger in population than many European countries, has been a monumental task. The main vehicle for change has come with the creation of statewide curriculum frameworks—documents developed starting in 1983 in response to a major school reform bill. These curriculum guidelines and frameworks have been modified over time and now center on developing students' ability to think, to apply concepts, and to take responsibility for their own learning. The frameworks mandate a curricula that is "... literature-based, value-laden, culturally rich, and integrated across content areas."[2] Writing across the curriculum, cooperative learning, experiential learning, and problem solving are emphasized. Although the frameworks are not mandated, they are the basis for the mandated CAP assessments, creating indirect pressure on districts to align the curriculum and instruction.

It became clear that much of what was to be taught with the new frameworks would not be taught or assessed appropriately if student achievement was evaluated with existing multiple-choice tests. A shift to performance assessment was sought to bring curriculum and instruction in line with the frameworks. The first performance assessment component, a direct writing assessment, was developed by teachers and put into place in 1987. Each year several hundred teachers gather over a 4- to 6-day period at four sites across the State to score the essays. Teacher scoring is emphasized to enhance the connection between instruction and assessment.

The success of the effort seems to validate this connection and meet expectations. One report suggests that: "... educators throughout California have expressed the belief that no single program has ever had statewide impact on instruction equal to that of the writing assessment."[3] A study at the completion of the first year of the writing assessment found that 78 percent of the teachers surveyed reported they assigned more writing, and almost all (94 percent) assigned a greater variety of writing tasks.[4] The percentage of students who reported that they wrote 11 or more papers in a 6-week period jumped from 22 to 33 percent. The writing assessment has also motivated a huge increase in staff development, with the California Writing Project training over 10,000 teachers in support of improved instruction in writing.[5]

In December 1989, California held an Education Summit, in response to the National Education Summit of the Nation's Governors in Charlottesville, Virginia. In seeking areas most likely to produce significant change ("targets of opportunity"), and building on the strengths of the California system, the educators called for statewide performance goals that would be measured through a strengthened assessment system. The report stated:

> The fundamental objectives of educational testing in California schools are far from fulfilled. *The dominant testing methods and formats not only fail to support the kind of teaching and learning that the state and national curriculum reform movement calls for, but actually retard that movement in California.* Students, teachers, and parents are not getting the necessary information to gauge the educational system's progress, detect strengths and weaknesses, improve instruction, and judge overall effectiveness. . . . The current approach to assessment of student achievement which relies on multiple choice student response must be abandoned because of its deleterious effect on the educational process. An assessment system which measures student achievement on performance-based measures is essential for driving the needed reform toward a thinking curriculum in which students are actively engaged and successful in achieving goals in and beyond high school.[6]

---

[1]Ruth Mitchell and Amy Stempel, Council for Basic Education, "Six Case Studies of Performance Assessment," OTA contractor report, March 1991.

[2]North Central Regional Educational Laboratory and Public Broadcasting Service, "Multidimensional Assessment: Strategies for Schools," Video Conference 4, 1990, p. 27.

[3]California Assessment Program, "California: The State of Assessment," draft report, Apr. 3, 1990, p. 8.

[4]An evaluation of the grade eight writing assessment by the National Center for the Study of Writing at the University of California, Berkeley, cited in ibid.

[5]Ibid., p. 8.

[6]California Department of Education, *California Education Summit: Meeting the Challenge, the Schools Respond*, final report (Sacramento, CA: February 1990).

The direct writing assessment was cited as an example of the kind of assessment needed to drive program improvements. The summit thus gave support and further stimulus for continuing research and piloting of new methods.

In the past, statewide testing used matrix sampling, in which each student takes only a portion of the test and scores are reported on the school or district level, but not for individual students. However, recent legislation[7] mandates that beginning in 1992-93 individual testing will be conducted statewide in grades 4, 5, 8, and 10 in basic skills and content courses. The use of direct writing assessment and other performance-based assessments is encouraged. Districts can also choose their own student tests at other grade levels. All testing is to be aligned to the California curriculum frameworks, with reporting based on common performance standards. The new program gives special emphasis to end-of-course examinations for secondary school subjects. These will be based on the existing Golden State Examinations, which students now take on a voluntary basis at the completion of Algebra, Geometry, Biology, Chemistry, U.S. History, and Economics. Districts may require that all students take one or more Golden State Examination. Finally, the integrated student assessment system will also include a portfolio for all students graduating from high school. The portfolio will contain documentation of performance standards attained on the grade 10 test (or other forms of the test taken in grades 11 and 12), on end-of-course Golden State Examinations, and on vocational certification examinations, as well as evidence of job experience and other valued accomplishments.[8]

This represents a big jump in required testing. Performance-based components are defined as building blocks for all the tests, both CAP and district-administered. CAP has indirectly influenced the testing done at the district level by "... opening the door ... giving permission to go ahead with performance assessment."[9] CAP also has pilot projects for portfolios in writing and mathematics, and research studying the impact on instruction of open-ended mathematics questions.

Developing performance-based assessments is not a simple task. At the 1987 "Beyond the Bubble" conference on testing, educators grappled with the issue of developing new ways to produce alternative assessments that more directly reflect student performance. A suggestion to support grassroots efforts by teachers with assistance from assessment experts eventually led to the Alternative Assessment Pilot Project. In 1991, the Governor authorized $1 million to implement its provisions, and two consortia of California school districts (one in the north and one in the south of the State) have been given grants totaling over $965,000 to begin the project. Each consortium will develop, field test, and disseminate alternatives to standardized multiple-choice tests for assessment of student achievement. At the school level, teachers will develop their own materials and strategies and pilot them with their own classrooms and schools, sharing information with other teachers across the State. A cost-benefit analysis of the local use of current performance-based assessment systems will also be conducted.[10]

Because of the scope of these endeavors, many other States are looking to the California experiment as a guide to their own efforts to realign testing and curriculum.

---

[7]Chapter 760, California Statutes of 1991 (SB 662; Hart).

[8]Superintendent Honig, California State Department of Education, "New Integrated Assessment System," testimony before the State Assembly Education Committee, background information, Aug. 21, 1991.

[9]Ruben Carriedo, director of Planning, Research and Evaluation Division, San Diego City Schools, cited in Mitchell and Stempel, op. cit., footnote 1, p. 17.

[10]California Department of Education News Release, Aug. 2, 1991.

responses of a large number of students occurred primarily because students are not accustomed to writing about mathematics."[16]

The National Assessment of Educational Progress (NAEP) has also successfully utilized a variety of open-ended items. In the 1990 NAEP mathematics assessment, about one-third of the items included open-ended questions that required students to use calculators, produce the solution to a question, or explain their answers. The 1990 reading test, which also employed text passages drawn from primary sources, including literary text, informational text, and documents, used a number of short essays to assess the student's ability to construct meaning and provide interpretations of text. The 1985-86 NAEP assessment of computer competence included some

---

[16]Ibid., p. 6.

Figure 7-3—Open-Ended Mathematics Item With Sample Student Answers

QUESTION: James knows that half of the students from his school are accepted at the public university nearby. Also, half are accepted at the local private college. James thinks that this adds up to 100 percent, so he will surely be accepted at one or the other institution. Explain why James may be wrong. If possible, use a diagram in your explanation.

Good Mathematical Reasoning: Sample Answers

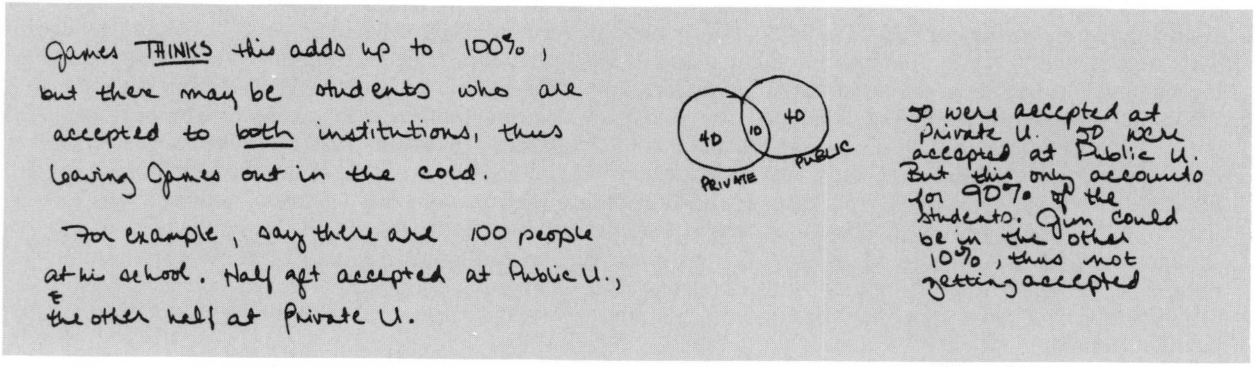

James THINKS this adds up to 100%, but there may be students who are accepted to both institutions, thus leaving James out in the cold.

For example, say there are 100 people at his school. Half get accepted at Public U., & the other half at Private U.

45 were accepted at Private U. 45 were accepted at Public U. But this only accounts for 90% of the students. Jim could be in the other 10%, thus not getting accepted

Some of the people accepted may have been accepted to both schools.

I got accepted to the public University

I got accepted to the private local college

I got accepted to both

I ain't be goin' to school

Misconceptions: Sample Answers

If 175 students apply, and ½ are accepted to the public university and ½ are accepted to the local private college.

½ of 175 is 87.

87 go to the university
87 go to the college
leaving one student out, which can be James

(175)

87 × 2 = 174

Thats wrong because everyone doesn't go to college I think its

15% doesn't go
45 That goes to local college
40 That goes to private college

NOTE: Used in the 1987-88 version of the 12th grade California Assessment Program test, this logic problem assesses a student's ability to detect and explain faulty reasoning. Answers are scored on a 0 to 6 point scale. The student must give a clear and mathematically correct explanation of the faulty reasoning. For the highest score, responses must be complete, contain examples and/or counter examples of overlapping sets, or have elegantly expressed mathematics. A diagram is expected.

SOURCE: California State Department of Education, *A Question of Thinking: A First Look at Students' Performance on Open-Ended Questions in Mathematics* (Sacramento, CA: 1989), pp. 21-28.

open-ended items asking students to write short computer programs or indicate how the "turtle" would move in response to a set of computer commands; students were given partial credit for elements of a correct response.

Scoring: Machines and Judges

Researchers and test developers are now considering ways to streamline available methods for scoring the more open-ended CR items. One promising area involves new types of CR items that can be entered on paper-and-pencil answer sheets and scanned by machines.[17] One such item type for mathematics problems is the grid-in format. Students solve the problem, write their solution at the top of a grid, and then fill in a bubble corresponding to each number in the column under that number (see figure 7-4). Questions that have more than one correct answer are possible, and the format allows for the possibility of answering in either fractions, decimals, or integers.[18]

"Figural response" items, which require drawing in a response on a graph, illustration, or diagram, were field tested in the 1989-90 NAEP science assessment (see figure 7-5). The feasibility of machine scoring of these items was also tested by using high-resolution image processors to score the penciled-in answers. Some initial technological difficulties were encountered with the scanning process—many student answers were too light to be read and the ink created some interference. However, the researchers express optimism that the scanning mechanism can be made to work.[19]

Researchers are working on technologies of handwriting recognition that will eventually result in printed letters and numbers that can be machine scanned from answer sheets, but these technologies

Figure 7-4—Machine-Scorable Formats: Grid-In and Multiple-Choice Versions of a Mathematics Item

The Question:

Section I of a certain theater contains 12 rows of 15 seats each. Section II contains 10 rows, but has the same total number of seats as Section I. If each row in Section II contains the same number of seats, how many seats are in each row?

Test 1, Multiple Choice Version

(A) 16
(B) 17
(C) 18*
(D) 19
(E) 20

Test 2, Grid Version

NOTE: This item was designed for high school juniors and seniors.

SOURCE: Educational Testing Service, Policy Information Center, *ETS Policy Notes*, vol. 2, No. 3, August 1990, p. 5.

are still far from reliable except under optimal conditions—the letters must be cleanly printed and properly aligned. Systems that can read cursive handwriting are in a more experimental stage; whether the ". . . scrawl likely to be produced under the pressure of examinations . . ." could ever be read by a computer is questionable.[20]

CR items vary considerably in the extent to which they can be scored objectively. More objective items will have scoring rules that are very clear and involve little or no judgment. Other responses, such as short written descriptions or writing the steps to a geometry proof, are more complicated to score—in part because there are multiple possibilities for

---

[17]Many of the problems involved in machine scanning are solved if constructed-response items can be delivered via computer. If the students take a mathematics computation test via computer, they can simply type in the correct numbers; a short essay can be written on the keyboard. As a result, the computer is in many ways a more "friendly" system for the delivery of many constructed-response type items, because problems related to scanning in the answer are solved. The machine-scanning problem is much less tractable for items delivered via paper-and-pencil tests. See ch. 8 for further discussion of the issues involved in administering tests via computers.

[18]James Braswell, "An Alternative to Multiple-Choice Testing in Mathematics for Large-Volume Examination Programs," paper presented at the annual meeting of the American Educational Research Association, Boston, MA, April 1990. Grid-in items for mathematics are currently under development for both the SAT and the ACT college admissions examinations. Preliminary results with college-bound students are encouraging:
   Guessing and back door approaches to solving mathematics questions are virtually eliminated and the range of answers that students offer to individual questions is great and frequently does not match well with the distractors provided in multiple-choice versions of the same items. As one would expect, the grid-in format requires more time. (p. 1)

[19]Michael Martinez, John J. Ferris, William Kraft, and Winton H. Manning, "Automated Scoring of Paper-and-Pencil Figural Responses," ETS research report RR-90-23, October 1990.

[20]Leslie Kitchen, "What Computers Can See: A Sketch of Accomplishments in Computer Vision, With Speculations on Its Use in Educational Testing," *Artificial Intelligence and the Future of Testing*, Roy Freedle (ed.) (Hillsdale, NJ: L. Erlbaum Associates, 1990), p. 134.

Figure 7-5—Figural Response Item Used in 1990 NAEP Science Assessment

The map below shows a high-pressure area centered over North Dakota and a low-pressure area centered over Massachusetts. Draw an arrow (——►) over Lake Michigan that shows the direction in which the winds will blow.

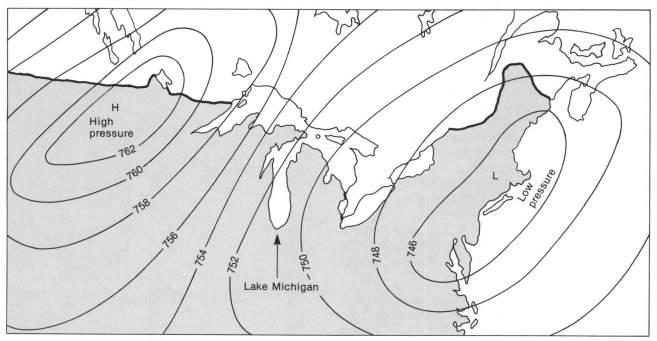

KEY: NAEP = National Assessment of Educational Progress.
NOTE: This item was used with 8th and 12th graders.
SOURCE: Michael E. Martinez, "A Comparison of Multiple-Choice and Constructed Figural Response Items," paper presented at the annual meeting of the American Educational Research Association, Boston, MA, April 1990.

correct or partially correct answers. Machine scoring of even more complex products, such as the steps in the solution of algebra word problems or computer programming, proves to be much more complicated; preliminary work drawing on artificial intelligence research suggests that automated scoring can eventually be developed. However, the time and cost required to develop such a program is very high. "In both instances, the underlying scoring mechanism is an expert system—a computer program that emulates one or more aspects of the behavior of a master judge."[21]

One of the more difficult and long-term problems of developing artificial intelligence models to score constructed responses is building their capacity for error detection. Programming machines to recognize correct answers is far easier than programming them to detect errors, grade partial solutions, and provide evaluation of error patterns.[22] When questions that allow for more than one right answer are used, programming of the scoring can get quite complicated.[23] Yet one of the highly desirable features of CR items is their potential for diagnosis of misconceptions, errors, and incorrect strategies.[24]

Although most CR items still require human scoring, procedures exist that can eliminate error and make this scoring more reliable. Development of clear standards for judging student answers and

[21]Randy Bennett, "Toward Intelligent Assessment: An Integration of Constructed Response Testing, Artificial Intelligence, and Model-Based Measurement," ETS research report RR-90-5, 1990, p. 5. For a description of artificial intelligence applied to a constructed-response computer programming problem, see Henry I. Braun, Randy E. Bennett, Douglas Frye, and Elliot Soloway, "Scoring Constructed Responses Using Expert Systems," *Journal of Educational Measurement*, vol. 27, No. 2, summer 1990, pp. 93-108.

[22]Roy Freedle, "Artificial Intelligence and Its Implications for the Future of ETS's Tests," in Freedle (ed.), op. cit., footnote 20.

[23]Braswell and Kupin, op. cit., footnote 14.

[24]See Menucha Birenbaum and Kikumi Tatsuoka, "Open-Ended Versus Multiple-Choice Response Formats—It Does Make a Difference for Diagnostic Purposes," *Applied Psychological Measurement*, vol. 11, No. 4, 1987, pp. 385-395.

intensive training of judges until they reach acceptable levels of agreement are important components of establishing high *inter-rater reliability* (see discussion in ch. 6). Preliminary indications are that most CR items can be scored with inter-rater reliability equal to or better than that achieved by judges grading essays. The process of training judges to grade essays reliably has been successfully developed in some large-scale testing programs; in addition, many commercial publishers and other companies now offer commercial grading services to schools that want independent and technically supervised rating procedures.

The feasibility of scoring geometry proofs on a large scale has recently been demonstrated by the State of North Carolina. Because an important objective of the high school geometry curriculum in North Carolina was for students to learn to develop complete proofs, the State assessment program included such proofs in the new assessment. All 43,000 geometry students in the State were given two geometry proof questions in the spring of 1989. Over 400 teachers from throughout the State were trained to score the proofs. Drawing on the lessons from the scoring of writing assessments (e.g., the importance of developing scoring criteria and training), high levels of scorer agreement were achieved. Actual time devoted to training was less than 3 hours.[25]

Constructed-Response Items as Diagnostic Tools

One of the features of CR items that makes them attractive to educators is that they allow closer examination of learners' thinking processes. When students write out the steps taken in solving a proof, or a list of how they reached their conclusions, the students' thinking processes can be examined and scored. Results of one study have suggested that CR-type items may be more effective than multiple-choice items for diagnostic purposes; i.e., for uncovering the processes of learners in ways that might help a teacher better understand students' errors or misconceptions.[26]

Not only might errors and misconceptions be more readily uncovered, but students' abilities to generate and construct meaning in complex tasks can also be assessed. The methods for developing these more complex scoring systems are not yet well established or understood. Cognitive research methods (see ch. 2) are beginning to be applied to the development of scoring rubrics for CR-type items. "Think aloud" methods, where children are closely observed and interviewed while solving open-ended problems, can provide a rich source of information to help build scoring rubrics. Early efforts to generate scoring criteria based on comparing the performance of experts and novices also have been encouraging.[27] One of the challenges for researchers in this area is to develop scoring criteria that have general utility across a number of tasks, instead of being specific to a particular test question or essay prompt.[28]

Although the relative virtues of multiple-choice and CR items have been debated in the educational literature since early in this century, there are few comprehensive empirical studies on the topic. Thus, although there is considerable "textbook" lore about the differences between the two types of items, few generalizations can be made with confidence about differences in student performance.[29] CR items have not been widely field tested in large-scale testing programs. Very few researchers have collected data that allows direct comparison of CR with multiple-choice items.

It is fair to say that no one has yet conclusively demonstrated that CR items measure more "higher order" thinking skills than do multiple-choice items. "All the same, there are often sound educa-

---

[25]Zollie Stevenson, Jr., Chris P. Averett, and Daisy Vickers, "The Reliability of Using a Focused-Holistic Scoring Approach to Measure Student Performance on a Geometry Proof," paper presented at the annual meeting of the American Educational Research Association, Boston, MA, April 1990.

[26]Birenbaum and Tatsuoka, op. cit., footnote 24.

[27]See, for example, Kevin Collis and Thomas A. Romberg, "Assessment of Mathematical Performance: An Analysis of Open-Ended Test Items," and Eva L. Baker, Marie Freeman, and Serena Clayton, "Cognitive Assessment of History for Large-Scale Testing," *Testing and Cognition*, Merlin C. Wittrock and Eva L. Baker (eds.) (Englewood Cliffs, NJ: Prentice Hall, 1991).

[28]Baker et al., op. cit., footnote 27.

[29]See R.E. Traub and K. MacRury, "Multiple-Choice vs. Free-Response in the Testing of Scholastic Achievement," *Tests and Trends 8: Jahrbuch der Padagogischen Diagnostik*, K. Ingenkamp and R.S. Jager (eds.) (Weinheim and Basel, Germany: Beltz Verlag, 1990), pp. 128-159; Ross Traub, "On the Equivalence of the Traits Assessed by Multiple-Choice and Constructed-Response Tests," in Bennett and Ward (eds.), op. cit., footnote 14; and Thomas P. Hogan, "Relationship Between Free-Response and Choice-Type Tests of Achievement: A Review of the Literature," ERIC document ED 224 811 (Green Bay, WI: University of Wisconsin, 1991).

tional reasons for employing the less efficient format, as some large-scale testing programs, such as AP [Advanced Placement], have chosen to do.''[30]

Essays and Writing Assessment

Essays, particularly when used to assess writing proficiency, are the most common form of performance assessment. In fact, the noun ''essay'' is defined as ''trial, test'' and the verb as ''. . . to make an often tentative or experimental effort to perform.''[31] Essays are a relatively well understood testing format, in part because they have been used for many years. An essay is an excellent example of performance assessment when used to assess students' ability to write. Essay questions for assessing content mastery are also a form of performance assessment, because they require student-created products that demonstrate understanding. The problem arises in scoring subject matter essays—are students' understanding of content being masked by a difficulty in written expression? In that case, writing skill can confound scoring for content knowledge.

Essays as Assessments of Content Mastery

Student understanding of a subject has long been assessed by requiring the student to write an essay that uses facts in context. Essay questions have been central to some large-scale testing programs overseas (see ch. 5); they also make up approximately 60 percent of the questions on the Advanced Placement examinations administered by the College Board. The essay to show content mastery is in fact the hallmark of classical education; student writing about a subject reveals how fully the student has grasped not only the obvious information but the relationships, subtleties, and implications of the topic. The use of writing as an instructional and testing device is familiar to scholars, and its use by all students is increasingly understood to help develop thinking skills as well as communications skills.

Students have different expectations about different types of tests. For example, one study found that students report a preference for multiple-choice over essay tests ''. . . on the grounds that these tests are easier to prepare for, are easier to take, and hold forth hope for higher relative scores.''[32] Other studies have suggested that students study differently for essay tests than they do for multiple-choice tests. For example, one study found that students ''. . . consider open questions a more demanding test than a multiple-choice test . . .'' and use more study time to prepare for it.[33] However almost no data exist about what students actually do differently when studying for different kinds of tests and evidence is ambiguous regarding whether these different study strategies affect actual achievement.[34]

Essays as Tests of Writing Skill

Many large-scale testing programs have begun the move toward performance assessment by adding a direct writing sample to their tests. One reason for this shift is a concern that the wrong message is sent to students and teachers when writing is not directly tested. According to one researcher of writing ability:

A test that requires actual writing is sending a clear message to the students, teachers, parents, and the general public that writing should be taught and tested by having students write. Although it may be that a test that includes a writing sample will gain little in psychometric terms over an all-multiple-choice test, the educational gains may be enormous. The English Composition Test, administered as part of the College Board Achievement Tests, contains one 20-minute essay section in the December administration only. At that administration approximately 85,000 students write in response to a set topic, and each of the 85,000 papers must be scored twice. That scoring may cost in the neighborhood of $500,000. The increase in predictive validity for the test is minimal. Admissions officers and others who use the scores are probably not seeing a dramatic increase in the usefulness of scores despite the expenditure of the half million dollars. *However,*

---

[30]R.E. Bennett, Donald A. Rock, and Minhwei Wang, ''Free-Response and Multiple-Choice Items: Measures of the Same Ability?'' ETS research report RR-90-8, 1990, p. 19.

[31]*Webster's Ninth New Collegiate Dictionary* (Springfield, MA: Miriam Webster, Inc., 1983), p. 425.

[32]Traub and MacRury, op. cit., footnote 29, p. 42.

[33]Gery D'Ydewalle, Anne Swerts, and Erik De Corte, ''Study Time and Test Performance as a Function of Test Expectations,'' *Contemporary Educational Psychology*, vol. 8, January 1983, p. 55. See also Gordon Warren, ''Essay Versus Multiple Choice Tests,'' *Journal of Research in Science Teaching*, vol. 16, No. 6, January 1979, pp. 563-567.

[34]Mary A. Lundeberg and Paul W. Fox, ''Do Laboratory Findings on Test Expectancy Generalize to Classroom Outcomes?'' *Review of Educational Research*, vol. 61, No. 1, spring 1991, pp. 94-106; and Traub and MacRury, op. cit., footnote 29.

thousands of English teachers in the United States consider the money well spent. The political clout that a writing sample provides for teaching writing and for emphasizing writing across the curriculum has no monetary equivalent.[35]

Of 38 States that currently assess student writing skills, 36 use direct writing samples in which students are given one or more "prompts" or questions requiring them to write in various formats. An additional nine States have plans to add a direct writing assessment. Many districts also use writing assessments (see figure 7-1). These tests are used for a variety of purposes: some are required to certify students for graduation or to identify students who need further instruction, while others are used for district accountability measures.

For example, in order to identify students who need extra help in writing instruction prior to graduation, all ninth graders in the Milwaukee, Wisconsin public schools write two pieces each spring—a business letter and an essay describing a solution to a problem in their own life. The assessment helps reveal strengths and weakness in writing instruction among the district's schools and teachers. It is a standardized procedure, with all students given the same set of instructions and a set time limit for completing both pieces. Scoring is done by the English teachers during a week in June. The training process and the discussions that follow the scoring are valued by the teachers as an important professional activity, guiding them to reflect on educational goals, standards, and the evaluation of writing. The central office staff finds this one of the best forms of staff development; by clarifying the standards and building a consensus among teachers, the writing program can be more cohesively delivered throughout the district.[36]

The testimony of practitioners like the Milwaukee teachers supports the positive effects of tests using writing samples on writing instruction. It also appears that the positive effects of direct writing assessments on instruction are enhanced when teachers do the scoring themselves. In 19 of the 36 States currently assessing writing with direct writing samples, teachers from the home State score the assessments.[37]

A recent survey of the teachers involved in the California Assessment Program's (CAP) direct assessment of student writing found that, as a result of the direct writing assessment, over 90 percent of them made changes in their own teaching—either the amount of writing assigned, variety of writing assigned, or other changes.[38] Most report that they believe the CAP writing assessment will increase teachers' expectations for students' writing achievement at their school and that the new assessment will strengthen their school's English curriculum. Finally, there was almost unanimous agreement with the position that: ". . . this test is a big improvement over multiple choice tests that really don't measure writing skills."[39] (See also box 7-C.)

An informal survey of practitioners using direct writing samples found these effects: increased quality and quantity of classroom writing instruction, changed attitudes of administrators, increased inservice training focused on teaching writing, use of test results to help less able pupils get "real help," and improvement in workload for English teachers.[40] However, some practitioners noted possible negative effects as well, including the increased pressure on good writing programs to narrow their focus to the test, tendencies of some teachers to teach formulas for passing, and fears that the study of literature may be neglected due to intense focus on composition.

Because essays and direct writing assessments have been used in large-scale testing programs, they provide a rich source of information and experience

---

[35]Gertrude Conlan, " 'Objective' Measures of Writing Ability," *Writing Assessment: Issues and Strategies*, Karen L. Greenberg, Harvey S. Wiener, and Richard A. Donovan (eds.) (New York, NY: Longman, 1986), pp. 110-111, emphasis added.

[36]Doug A. Archbald and Fred M. Newmann, *Beyond Standardized Testing* (Reston, VA: National Association of Secondary School Principals, 1988).

[37]The 19 States in which teachers participate as scorers are: Arkansas (voluntary), California, Connecticut, Georgia, Hawaii, Idaho, Indiana (voluntary), Maine, Maryland, Massachusetts, Minnesota, Missouri, Nevada, New York, Oregon, Pennsylvania, Rhode Island, Utah (voluntary), and West Virginia. In two-thirds of these States, teachers are trained by State assessment personnel. In the other one-third, they are trained by the contractor.

[38]California Assessment Program, "Impact of the CAP Writing Assessment on Instruction and Curriculum: A Preliminary Summary of Results of a Statewide Study by the National Center for the Study of Writing," draft report, n.d. The study sampled 600 teachers at California's 1,500 junior or middle schools in May 1988, just after the second statewide administration of the California Assessment Program's grade eight writing test.

[39]Ibid.

[40]Charles Suhor, "Objective Tests and Writing Samples: How Do They Affect Instruction in Composition?" *Phi Delta Kappan*, vol. 66, No. 9, May 1985, pp. 635-639.

for new attempts at performance assessment. Many practical issues, such as scoring and cost, are often raised as barriers to the large-scale implementation of performance assessment. The lessons drawn from the history of essays and direct writing assessments are illustrative—both for their demonstrations of feasibility and promise as well as their illumination of issues that will require further attention and care. These issues are discussed further at the end of this chapter.

Interviews and Direct Observations

Oral examinations were the earliest form of performance assessment. The example best known among scholars is the oral defense of the dissertation at the Master's and Ph.D. levels. There are many varieties and uses of oral examinations at all school levels. University entrance examinations in a few countries are still conducted through oral examinations. Foreign language examinations often contain a portion assessing oral fluency. Other related methods allow teachers or other evaluators to observe children performing desired tasks, such as reading aloud.

The systematic evaluation of speaking skills has been incorporated into the College Outcome Measures Program (COMP) for the American College Testing Program (ACT). This test was designed to help postsecondary institutions assess general education outcomes. For the speaking skills portion of the assessment, students are given three topics and told to prepare a 3-minute speech on each. At an appointed time they report to a test site where they tape record each speech, using only a note card as a speaking aid. At some later time, trained judges listen to the tapes and score each speech on attributes related to both content and delivery.

Methods that use interviews and direct observations are particularly appropriate for use with young children. Young children have not yet mastered the symbolic skills involved in communicating through reading and writing; thus most paper-and-pencil-type tests are inappropriate because they cannot accurately represent what young children have learned. The best window into learning for the very young may come from observing them directly, listening to them talk, asking them to perform tasks they have been taught, and collecting samples of their work. This approach uses adults' observations to record and evaluate children's progress in lan-

Photo credit: Educational Testing Service

Paper-and-pencil tests are often inappropriate for young children. This teacher, in South Brunswick, New Jersey, keeps a portfolio of her observations as she records each child's developing literacy skills.

guage acquisition, emphasizing growth over time rather than single-point testing.

Several States (i.e., Georgia, North Carolina, and Missouri) have developed statewide early-childhood assessments designed to complement developmentally appropriate instruction for young children. Most of these developmentally appropriate assessments are based on an English model, the Primary Language Record (PLR) developed at the Center for Language in Primary Education in London. The PLR is a systematic method of organizing the observations teachers routinely make. It consists of two parts, a continuous working record and a summary form, completed several times a year. The working record includes observations of the child's literacy behavior, such as "running records" of reading aloud, and writing samples, as well as a list of books the child can read either in

English or the language spoken at home. The summary record includes an interview with the parents about what the child likes to read and do at home and an interview with the child about his or her interests. The interviews take place at the beginning and end of each school year. The summary record goes with the child to the next grade, throughout primary school. The South Brunswick (New Jersey) schools have recently incorporated this approach into a teacher portfolio for assessing each student's learning in kindergarten through second grade (see box 7-D).

One assessment technique, used in South Brunswick as well as many other schools, is known as "reading miscue analysis." The teacher sits with an individual student, listens to him read aloud, and systematically records the errors he makes while reading. From this analysis, which requires training, teachers can determine what strategies each child uses while reading. This can be a very useful assessment technique for all children, and especially in programs focused on improving reading skills in disadvantaged children.

The Georgia Department of Education has recently developed a new kindergarten assessment program (see box 7-E). One important component of this assessment is repeated and systematic observations of each child by the kindergarten teacher in many skill areas throughout the year. In addition, each kindergarten teacher receives a kit containing a number of structured activities that resemble classroom tasks. A teacher spends individual time with each student conducting these activities, which assess the child's skills in a number of areas. For example, one of the identified skills in the logical-mathematical area is the child's ability to recognize and extend patterns. The teacher presents the child with a task consisting of small cut-out dinosaurs in a variety of colors. Following a standardized set of instructions, the teacher places the dinosaurs in a sequenced pattern and asks the child to add to the sequence. Several different patterns are presented so that the teacher can assess whether the child has mastered this skill. If the child does not successfully complete the task, the teacher will know to work on related skills in the classroom; later in the year the teacher can use another task in the kit, this time using cut-out trucks or flowers, to reassess the child's skill in understanding patterns. Through this process, in

which the teacher works directly with the child in a structured situation, the teacher is able to obtain valuable diagnostic information to adjust instruction for the individual child.

Exhibitions

Exhibitions are designed as inclusive, comprehensive means for students to demonstrate competence. They often involve production of comprehensive products, presentations, or performances before the public. They usually require a broad range of competencies and student initiative in design and implementation. The term has become popularized as a central assessment feature in the Coalition of Essential Schools (CES), a loose confederation of over 100 schools (generally middle and high schools) that share a set of principles reflecting a philosophy of learning and school reform that emphasizes student-centered learning and rigorous performance standards.

The term exhibition has two meanings as used in the Essential Schools. The most specific is the "senior exhibition," a comprehensive interdisciplinary activity each senior must complete in order to receive a diploma. In this regard they are similar to the "Rite of Passage Experience" initiated by the Walden III Senior High School in Racine, Wisconsin. In order to graduate from Walden III, all seniors must demonstrate mastery in 15 areas of knowledge and competence by completing a portfolio, project, and 15 presentations before a committee consisting of staff members, a student, and an adult from the community.[41]

The CES senior exhibitions mirror some of these requirements, and typically fall into two main categories: the recital mode, which is a public performance or series of performances; and the "comprehensive portfolio" or "exhibition portfolio," a detailed series of activities, projects, or demonstrations over the school year that are cumulatively assembled and provide an aggregate picture of a student's grasp of the central skills and knowledge of the school's program.

There is also a general use of the term "exhibition" to mean a more discrete performance assessment when the student must demonstrate that he or she understands a rich core of subject matter and can apply this knowledge in a resourceful, persuasive,

---

[41]Archbald and Newmann, op. cit., footnote 36, p. 23.

Box 7-D—South Brunswick Teacher Portfolios: Records of Progress in Early Childhood Learning[1]

How do you know if young children are developing critical language skills (reading, writing, and speaking) if you do not give them tests? This is the predicament facing many schools as educators become increasingly disenchanted with giving standarized paper-and-pencil tests to young children. When the South Brunswick, New Jersey schools adopted a new, more developmentally appropriate curriculum it became necessary to develop a new method of assessment consistent with this teaching approach. Teachers worked with district personnel to create a teacher portfolio that drew on several models, including the Primary Learning Record used in England and Wales. Teachers piloted the portfolios over the 1989-90 school year, and revised them in the summer of 1990 for use the following school year.

The purpose of the portfolio is to focus on language acquisition in young students, grades K through 2. Teachers view the portfolio as a tool to promote instruction. It gives them a picture of the learning strategies of each child, which can be the basis of developing activities that will stress students' strengths while providing practice and help with weaknesses.

Each portfolio consists of 10 parts, plus one optional part:

- Self portrait—The child is asked to ''draw a picture of yourself'' at the beginning and the end of the school year. The portraits are generally placed on the front and back covers of a manila folder.
- Interview—This may be conducted several times during the year and includes the child's answers to such questions as: What is your favorite thing to do at home? Do you watch TV? Sesame Street? Do you have books at home? What is your favorite book? Do other people at home like to read? What do they read? Does someone read to you at home?
- Parent questionnaire—Parents complete this before their first conference with the teacher. It includes questions about the child's reading interests as well as any concerns the parent has about the child's language or reading development.
- Concepts about print test—This check list measures the child's understanding of significant concepts about printed language, such as the front of the book, that print (not the picture) tells the story, what a letter is, what a word is, where a word begins and ends, and big and little letters. This is a nationally normed test and is also used to identify children in need of compensatory education.
- Word awareness writing activity—This records the level at which children begin to comprehend the rules of forming words in their writing. Progress is recorded along a five-stage scale: precommunicative (random spelling or scribbling); semiphonetic (some sounds represented by letters, e.g., the word ''feet'' might be rendered as ''ft''); phonetic (letters used appropriately for sounds, e.g., ''fet''); transitional (some awareness of spelling patterns, e.g., ''fete''); or mostly correct (10 out of 13 words correctly spelled).
- Reading sample—This is taken three or more times a year. The teacher may use a ''running record'' or ''miscue analysis.'' The running record is used with emergent readers, children who mimic the act of reading but do not yet know how to read. It records what a young child is thinking and doing while ''reading.''
- Writing sample—This is a sample of the student's free writing, ''translated'' by the student for the teacher if invented spelling and syntax make it difficult to read easily.
- Student observation forms (optional).
- Story retelling form.
- Diagnostic form.
- Class record—This class profile helps the teacher identify those children who may need extra attention in certain areas. It is a one-page matrix with yes-no answers to the following five questions: Does the child pay attention in large and small groups? Interact in groups? Retell a story? Choose to read? Write willingly? This is the only element of the portfolio not a part of the child's individual record.

Because of Federal requirements for determining eligibility for compensatory education, the South Brunswick schools also use norm-referenced, multiple-choice tests. However, teachers report that these tests are not useful because they do not assess development in the instructional approach adopted by the South Brunswick schools.

---

[1]Much of the material in this box comes from Ruth Mitchell and Amy Stempel, Council for Basic Education, ''Six Case Studies of Performance Assessment,'' OTA contractor report, March 1991.

The tests go from part to whole, and our programs go from whole to part. Those tests are basically for basals [i.e., reading textbooks], and to assess kids that have learned a whole language by basals (when the South Brunswick students used children's literature as texts)—it makes no sense at all.[2]

The portfolios provide a different approach to the question of student retention. While a student may have been held in grade before because of low test scores, research has suggested that having a child repeat a year in grade may in fact cause more harm than good.[3] In South Brunswick, when there is a question about retention or special education labeling in the early grades, the portfolio record is consulted to see if the child has made progress. If progress can be shown, then the student is promoted on the assumption that every child develops at his or her own rate and can be monitored closely until he or she reaches the third grade. If no progress is apparent at that point, the child is promoted but is identified for compensatory education.

One of the purposes of the portfolio is to help the teacher provide a clearer picture of student progress to parents than is possible from standardized test scores. Yet a tension remains between the old and the new. The numbers that are derived from norm-referenced, multiple-choice tests are familiar and understandable. The new developmentally appropriate methods of teaching and testing do not have the perceived rigor or precision of the old tests. Some parents assume that only norm-referenced tests can be objective, and worry about subjectivity in recording progress on the portfolios. Some want traditional test scores that assure that their children are learning what everyone else in the country is learning—or can be measured against children in other communities. Until this tension is resolved, full acceptance of a portfolio system may be slow. As one teacher said:

> The next step is to educate the parents. We need workshops for parents. That is the big issue, after we get all the teachers settled in using the portfolio. This is basically not going to be acceptable until these children get older and everyone can see that we're graduating literate kids and that's not going to be until many, many years from now.[4]

Standardization of the portfolio assessment was not an issue for the teachers, because of its primary role as an instructional information tool. Since the teachers were involved in the initial design and remain involved in modifications, and as they have attended workshops on its use, there is implicit standardization. Although the South Brunswick portfolio is primarily meant as a feedback mechanism to improve instruction, it also is being used as an accountability instrument. The Educational Testing Service (ETS), working with the teachers, has produced a numerical literacy scale based on the portfolio. The scale provides a means of aggregating data from the portfolios. Central office staff, working with a consultant from ETS, examined literacy scales and will rank children's literacy as evidenced by the portfolio on these scales. Teachers in one school rank the portfolios based on these scales, in order to evaluate how well the system communicates standards. The "South Brunswick-Educational Testing Service scale" for evaluating children's progress in literacy is now being used in all district schools. The literacy scales replace the first grade standardized reading test. The existence of aggregatable data will clearly enhance the scoring and the overall value of the portfolio in the South Brunswick public schools.

There are additional approaches to standardizing the portfolio. Some of the contents, such as the Concepts of Print test and the Word Awareness Writing Activity, can be scored using a key. Running record and miscue analysis can also be scored consistently. Those aspects that cannot be scored using a key—e.g., the writing sample—can be graded by a group of teachers developing a rubric from each set of papers. These could also be standardized by exchanging a sample of portfolios among teachers, so that each reads about 10 percent from each class and discusses common standards. This is the method used by the New York State Department of Education to ensure standardization of the results of their grade four science manipulative skills test. It is also used in several European school systems.

The issue of bias has not been raised, since the teachers record each student's growth against himself or herself, not in comparison with other students in the class or school. However, this issue will be more prominent if achievement levels are set and there are differing success rates in meeting these standards, or if the portfolio is used for school accountability or for student selection, two goals not currently planned.

---

[2]Willa Spicer, director of Instruction, South Brunswick Public Schools, New Jersey, personal communication, December 1991.

[3]Lorrie Shepard and Mary Lee Smith, *Flunking Grades: Research and Policies on Retention* (London, England: The Falmer Press, 1989).

[4]Mitchell and Stempel, op. cit., footnote 1, p. 17.

Box 7-E—Testing in Early Childhood: Georgia's Kindergarten Assessment Program

In recent years, many educators and policymakers have been reducing or eliminating the use of standardized paper-and-pencil tests in the early grades. Many of these tests were being used to make decisions about kindergarten retention and whether children were ready to begin first grade. The issue of retention in the early grades, as well as the role of tests in making such decisions, is receiving increasing scrutiny and many policies are changing. The Texas State Board of Education recently barred the retention of any pupils in prekindergarten and kindergarten.[1] The legislatures in both Mississippi and North Carolina have eliminated State-mandated testing in the early grades.[2] At least two States, Kentucky and Florida, are encouraging ungraded primaries (K-3) which loosen the rigid boundaries between the early grades and allow children to move according to individual progress.

In a policy running somewhat counter to these trends, the Georgia Legislature in 1985 mandated that all 6-year-olds must pass a test in order to enter first grade. During the first 2 years of this policy, a standardized paper-and-pencil test was used. However, the use of such a test quickly brought to public attention concerns about this approach to readiness assessment, including:

1. the appropriateness of a paper-and-pencil test for children who are five to six years of age.
2. the concern that a focus on tests narrows the curriculum . . .
3. the need to consider not just the child's cognitive skills, but the development of social, emotional, and physical capacities as well.
4. the need to consider the teacher's observations of the child throughout the course of the school year.[3]

In response to these concerns the Georgia Department of Education embarked on a large project to design a developmentally appropriate model of assessment. The Georgia Kindergarten Assessment Program (GKAP), piloted during 1989-90, uses two methods of assessment—observations by kindergarten teachers and individually administered standardized tasks that resemble classroom activities. GKAP assesses a child's capabilities in five areas: communicative, logical-mathematical, physical, personal, and social. This assessment program is designed to help teachers make multiple, repeated, and systematic observations about each child's progress during the year. Behavioral observations in all five areas are made in three time periods throughout the year. In addition, a set of structured activities have been designed to assess each child's communicative and logical-mathematical capabilities. The teacher conducts each of these activities individually with a child. If a child cannot successfully complete the task, teachers can plan activities to help the child work on that skill in the classroom; a second activity, assessing that same skill, can be given by the teacher later in the year. These tasks involve toys, manipulatives, and colorful pictures.

Each kindergarten teacher in Georgia receives a GKAP kit that contains manuals for administration, manipulatives, and reporting forms. Training and practice are required prior to the use of GKAP. A self-contained video training program developed for this purpose has been provided to each school.

The education department anticipates that this assessment program will serve a number of important functions:

A significant use of GKAP results is to provide instructionally relevant diagnostic information for kindergarten teachers. In the process of collecting GKAP information, teachers gain insights regarding their students' developmental status and subsequent modifications which may be needed in their instructional programs. In addition, when forwarded, this information will also be useful to the child's teacher at the beginning of the first grade year. Another use of GKAP results is communication with parents about their child's progress throughout the kindergarten year.

The results of the GKAP are also to serve, along with other information about the child, as a factor in the decision regarding whether to promote the child to the first grade. GKAP results, by themselves, should not be used as the sole criterion for promotion/retention (placement) decisions.[4]

---

[1]Deborah L. Cohen, "Texas Board Votes to Forbid Retention Before the 1st Grade," *Education Week*, vol. 90, No. 1, Aug. 1, 1990.

[2]Mississippi stopped testing kindergarten children and North Carolina banned testing of first and second graders. See Adria Steinberg, "Kindergarten: Producing Early Failure?" *Principal*, vol. 69, May 1990, pp. 6-9.

[3]Werner Rogers and Joy E. Blount, "Georgia's First Grade Readiness Assessment: The Historical Perspective," paper presented at the annual meeting of the American Educational Research Association, Boston, MA, April 1990, p. 3.

[4]Susan P. Tyson and Joy E. Blount, "The Georgia Kindergarten Assessment Program: A State's Emphasis on a Developmentally Appropriate Assessment," paper presented at the American Educational Research Association, Boston, MA, April 1990, p. 7.

and imaginative way. It is a creative and difficult concept to put into place, however, and requires that the teacher create assignments that take students beyond the surface of a subject. For example, one history teacher suggested: "Under the old system, the question would be 'Who was the King of France in 800?' Today, it is 'How is Charlemagne important to your life?' "[42] While the exhibition format could be an essay or research paper, it might also call for a Socratic dialog between student and teacher, an oral interview, debate, group project, dramatic presentation, or combination of multiple elements, partly in preparation for the more comprehensive senior exhibitions. Clearly, developing and evaluating successful exhibitions can be as big a challenge to the teachers as it can be for the students to perform well on them.

Exhibitions can also be competitions, some at the individual level, like the Westinghouse Science Talent Search, or in groups, like the Odyssey of the Mind, a national competition requiring groups of students to solve problems crossing academic disciplines. Group competitions add group cooperation skills to the mix of desirable outcomes.

One interesting group competition is the Center for Civic Education's "We the People . . ." program on Congress and the Constitution. It is a national program, sponsored by the Commission on the Bicentennial of the U.S. Constitution and funded by Congress. Students in participating schools study a specially developed curriculum and compete with teams from around the country. In the competition they serve as panels of "experts" testifying before a mock congressional committee. The curriculum can be used as a supplement to American history or civics classes and has materials that are appropriate for three levels (upper elementary, middle school, and high school). The text centers on the history and principles of the U.S. Constitution. When students have completed the curriculum the entire class is divided into groups, each responsible for one unit of the curriculum. Each group presents statements and answers questions on its unit before a panel of community representatives who act as the mock congressional committee members. Winning teams from each school compete at district, State, and finally a national-level competition. Training for judges at each level is conducted through videotapes and training sessions in which the judges evaluate each group on a scale of 1 to 10, on the criteria shown in figure 7-6.

Experiments

Science educators who suggest that students can best understand science by doing science have promoted hands-on science all across the science curriculum. Similarly, they maintain that students' understanding of science can best be measured by how they do science—the process of planning, conducting, and writing up experiments. Thus, science educators are seeking ways to assess and measure hands-on science. A number of States, including New York, California, and Connecticut, have pioneering efforts under way to conduct large-scale hands-on assessments in science.

In 1986, NAEP conducted a pilot project to examine the feasibility of conducting innovative hands-on assessments in mathematics and science. Working closely with the staff of Great Britain's Assessment of Performance Unit, 30 pilot tasks using group activities, work station activities, and complete experiments were field tested. School administrators, teachers, and students were enthusiastic and encouraging about these efforts. As part of the pilot project, NAEP has made available detailed descriptions of these 30 tasks so that other educators can adapt the ideas.[43] A sample experiment used with third graders and scoring criteria are pictured in figure 7-7.

New York Elementary Science Program Evaluation Test

In 1989, the New York State Department of Education, building on the NAEP tasks, included five hands-on manipulative skills tasks as an important component of their Elementary Science Program Evaluation Test (ESPET). Used with fourth graders, the test also included a content-oriented, paper-and-pencil component. It was the intent of the

---

[42]James Charleson, Hope High School, Providence, RI, quoted in Thomas Toch and Matthew Cooper, "Lessons From the Trenches," *U.S. News & World Report*, vol. 108, No. 8, Feb. 26, 1990, p. 54.

[43]See Educational Testing Service, *Learning by Doing: A Manual for Teaching and Assessing Higher Order Thinking in Science and Mathematics* (Princeton, NJ: May 1987); or the full-report, Fran Blumberg, Marion Epstein, Walter MacDonald, and Ina Mullis, *A Pilot Study of Higher Order Thinking Skills: Assessment Techniques in Science and Mathematics, Final Report* (Princeton, NJ: Educational Testing Service, November 1986).

Figure 7-6—Scoring Sheet for the "We the People" Competition

Student teams act as witnesses before a "Congressional Committee" and answer questions on the U.S. Constitution (history, law, and current applications). Each group is scored on a scale of 1-10 on the criteria listed below.

1-2 = poor 3-4 = fair 5-6 = average 7-8 = above average 9-10 = excellent

	Score	Notes
1. Understanding: To what extent did participants demonstrate a clear understanding of the basic issues involved in the questions?		
2. Constitutional Application: To what extent did participants appropriately apply knowledge of constitutional history and principles?		
3. Reasoning: To what extent did participants support positions with sound reasoning?		
4. Supporting Evidence: To what extent did participants support positions with historical or contemporary evidence, examples, and/or illustrations?		
5. Responsiveness: To what extent did participants' answers address the questions asked?		
6. Participation: To what extent did most group members contribute to the group's presentation?		
Group total		

Judge: _____ Date: _____

Congressional District: _____

Tie breaker*

*Please award up to 100 points for this group's overall performance. (Bonus points will only be used in the event of a tie.)

SOURCE: Center for Civic Education, Calabasas, CA.

test designers to align classroom practices with the State objectives reflected in the syllabus.[44]

The manipulative test consists of five tasks, and each student is given 7 minutes to work on each of the tasks. At the end of each timed segment, the teacher organizes a swift exchange of desks, or stations, moving the front row children to the back of the column and the others each moving up one desk, somewhat like a volleyball rotation. Test stations are separated by cardboard dividers and are arranged so that adjacent stations do not have the same apparatus. Four classes of about 25 children each can be tested comfortably in a school day. The skills assessed by the five stations include measure-ment (of volume, length, mass, and temperature), prediction from observations, classification, hypothesis formation, and observation.

The examinations were scored by their teachers, but student scores were not reported above the school level. School scores were reported in terms of the items on which students had difficulty. The ESPET is currently being evaluated for use in other grades.

Connecticut Common Core Science and Mathematics Assessments

Connecticut has been a leader in the development of a set of mathematics and science assessments that

---

[44]Sally Bauer, Sandra Mathison, Eileen Merriam, and Kathleen Toms, ''Controlling Curricular Change Through State-Mandated Testing: Teacher's Views and Perceptions,'' paper presented at the annual meeting of the American Educational Research Association, Boston, MA, Apr. 17, 1990, p. 7.

call on group skills and performance activities.[45] Under a 45-month grant from the National Science Foundation, Connecticut has assembled teams of high school science and mathematics teachers working jointly on Connecticut Multi-State Performance Assessment Collaborative Teams (CoMPACT). CoMPACT is made up of seven State Departments of Education (Connecticut, Michigan, Minnesota, New York, Texas, Vermont, and Wisconsin), CES, The Urban District Leadership Consortium of the American Federation of Teachers, and Project Re:Learning.

The CoMPACT group has designed and developed 50 performance assessment tasks, 31 across 8 areas of high school science (biology, chemistry, Earth science, and physics) and 19 in mathematics (general or applied mathematics, algebra, geometry, and advanced mathematics). After pulling together the experiences of CoMPACT teachers trying out these tasks, Connecticut will convene committees of expert judges to establish ''marker papers'' and common scoring standards. These scoring standards will be used during 1991-92 on the first administration of the Connecticut Common Core of Learning Assessments in high school science and mathematics across the State. A key element of the entire endeavor will be the assessment of student attitudes toward science and mathematics, and the demonstration of teamwork and interpersonal skills in these real-life testing contexts.

Each task has three parts that require individual work at the beginning and end, and group work in the middle (see figure 7-8). First, each student is presented with the task and asked to formulate a hunch, an estimate of the solution, and a preliminary design for a study. This portion of the task has several goals—it focuses the student's preliminary thinking, becomes a springboard for student group discussion, gives the teacher a feel for where the students are in their thinking, and serves as a record that the student can revisit throughout the assessment.

The middle section involves the longest phase. Here students plan and work together to produce a group product; teamwork is emphasized throughout. Evidence of deepening understanding is recorded through a variety of assessment tools such as written checklists, journals, logs, or portfolios. Oral or visual records such as videotapes of group discussions and oral presentations are also maintained. Teachers can rate individual performance on a subset of objectives in the group task. The ability to infer levels of individual contribution on collective work is one of the largest assessment challenges.

The third part of the task consists of individual performance on a related task. These tasks consist of similar activities that attempt to assess some of the same content and processes as the group task. The transfer task provides each student with an opportunity to synthesize and integrate the learning that occurred in the group experience and apply it in a new context. It also provides teachers, parents, and policymakers with a summative view of what each student knows and can do at the end of a rich set of learning and assessment opportunities.

Several evaluations of the project have been completed to date. Teacher perceptions are quite positive. Through the participation of the Urban District's Leadership Consortium, students in 16 large urban school systems tried out the performance tasks during the 1990-91 school year, demonstrating the feasibility of this type of assessment in schools with large populations of African-American and Hispanic students.[46]

Portfolios

Portfolios are typically files or folders that contain a variety of information documenting a student's experiences and accomplishments. They furnish a broad portrait of individual performance, collected over time. The components can vary and can offer multiple indicators of growth as well as cumulative achievement. As students assemble their own portfolios, they evaluate their own work, a key feature in performance assessment. Proponents suggest that this process also provides students a different understanding of testing, with the following positive effects:

---

[45]See Pascal D. Forgione, Jr. and Joan Boykoff Baron, Connecticut State Department of Education, ''Assessment of Student Performance in High School Science and Mathematics: The Connecticut Study,'' paper presented at the Seminar on Student Assessment and Its Impact on School Curriculum, Washington, DC, May 23, 1990.

[46]Joan Boykoff Baron, Connecticut Department of Education, personal communication, November 1991.

Figure 7-7—"Sugar Cubes": A NAEP Hands-On Science Experiment for 3rd Graders

NAME: _____
CODE: _____
SCHOOL DISTRICT: _____

Sugar Cubes Behavioral Checklist

NOT STIRRING
1. Loose sugar tested
2. Cube sugar tested

SET-UP
3. Volume of water measured—by eye
4. by ruler
5. by cylinder
6. Volume used < 10 cc
7. Volume used >10 cc
8. Volume same for both types
9. Mass same for both types

MEASUREMENT
10. No apparent measurement
11. Qualitative measurement
12. Clock used
13. within +- 3 secs. of start point
14. within +- 3 secs. of end point
15. Timed—until all dissolved
16. until partially dissolved
17. no clear end point
18. Fixed time—notes amount remaining

RESPONSE SHEET
*19. Reports results consistent with evidence

STIRRING
20. Stirring not tested—sugar type not controlled
21. Loose sugar tested
22. Cube sugar tested
23. Stirring tested—by counting number of stirs
24. by timing
25. Stirring at regular intervals
26. Stirring rate—constant
27. random

SET-UP
28. Volume of water measured—by eye
29. by ruler
30. by cylinder
31. Volume used < 10 cc
32. Volume used >10 cc
33. Volume same for both types
34. Mass same for both types

MEASUREMENT
35. No apparent measurement
36. Qualitative measurement
37. Clock used
38. within +- 3 specs. of start point
39. within +- 3 secs. of end point
40. Timed—until all dissolved

... nount remaining
... istent with evidence

... both trials
... ck findings
... er minimal)

*48. Acknowledges that procedures could be improved if experiment repeated—aware that certain variables

The Experiment

Students are given laboratory equipment and asked to determine which type of sugar, granulated or cubed, dissolves faster when placed in warm water that is stirred and not stirred, respectively. To complete this investigation, students need to identify the variables to be manipulated, controlled, and measured. They also need to make reliable and accurate measurements, record their findings, and draw conclusions. Examples of written conclusions are presented on the next page.

The Observation

Using detailed checklists, NAEP administrators recorded students' strategies for determining—with accurate and reliable measurements—whether loose sugar or sugar cubes dissolved at a faster rate.

FIND OUT IF STIRRING MAKES ANY DIFFERENCE IN HOW
FAST THE SUGAR CUBES AND LOOSE SUGAR DISSOLVE.

Score received _____

B) Use the space below to answer the question in the box.

5 point answer

> It makes a difference when you stir
> the loose sugar cause it dissapers
> faster than the cubes so if you stir
> the cubes they will make a tiny
> difference.

3 point answer

> I think that stirring helps dissolving
> because it faster contact with the
> water.

1 point answer

> It will make the sugar and
> it will make little spots on
> the the bottom of the glass.

Scoring of Written Answers

5 points = response states that both types of sugar dissolves the fastest.
4 points = response states that the loose sugar dissolves faster than the cube and that stirring is the cause of it.
3 points = response states that stirring makes a difference only or how or why an effect upon the sugar is found only.
2 points = response states that one type of sugar dissolves faster than another only.
1 point = incorrect response.
0 points = no response.

KEY: NAEP = National Assessment of Educational Progress.
SOURCE: Educational Testing Service, *Learning by Doing: A Manual for Teaching and Assessing Higher Order Thinking in Science and Mathematics* (Princeton, NJ: May 1987); and Fran Blumberg, Marion Epstein, Walter MacDonald, and Ina Mullis, *A Pilot Study of Higher Order Thinking Skills: Assessment Techniques in Science and Mathematics, Final Report* (Princeton, NJ: Educational Testing Service, November 1986).

Figure 7-8—Connecticut Science Performance Assessment Task: "Exploring the Maplecopter"

OVERVIEW: This task was designed for high school physics classes, and includes both individual and group work. Students study the motion of maple seeds and design experiments to explain their spinning flight patterns. Curriculum topics include laws of motion, aerodynamics, air resistance, and the use of models in explaining scientific phenomena. Equipment needed: maple seeds, paperboard, stopwatches, and scissors. The suggested length of time for the task is 3 to 5 class periods.

Part I: Getting Started by Yourself

1. Throw a maple winged seed up in the air and watch it "float" down to the floor. Describe as many aspects of the motion of the pod as you can. You may add diagrams if you wish.

2. One of the things you probably noticed is that the seed spins at it falls, like a little helicopter. Try to explain how and why the seed spins as it falls.

Part II: Group Work

The criteria that will be used to assess your work are found on the Objectives Rating Form - Group. Each member of your group will also fill out the Group Performance Rating Form.

1. Discuss the motion of the winged maple seed with the members of your group. Write a description of the motion, using the observations of the entire group. You may add diagrams if you wish.

2. Write down the variables that might affect the motion of the maple seed.

3. Design a series of experiments to test the effect of each of these variables. Carry out as many experiments as necessary in order to come up with a complete explanation for the spinning motion of the winged seed.

Using Models in Science

4. Sometimes using a simplified model (or a simulation) might help one to understand more complex phenomena. A paper helicopter, in this case, might serve as a simplified model of the seed.

    a. Construct a paper helicopter following the general instructions in figures 1 and 2.

    b. Throw the paper helicopter in the air and observe its motion.

    c. Try changing various aspects of the paper helicopter to test the effect of the variables your group chose.

    d. Experiment with different types of paper helicopters until you feel that you have a complete understanding of how the variables you identified affect the motion.

    e. Summarize your results with the help of a chart or a graph.

5. Based on what you've learned from the paper helicopters, design and perform additional experiments with the maple seeds.

6. Describe your group's findings from all your experiments. Raw data should be presented in charts or graphs, as appropriate and summarized by a short written statement.

7. Now, after you have completed all the necessary experiments, try to explain again the motion of the maple seed. Try to include in your explanation the effect of all the variables that you observed in your experiments. You may add diagrams if you wish.

8. In this activity you used simplified models to help explain a more complicated phenomenon. Describe the advantages and disadvantages of your paper helicopter as a model of a winged maple seed.

9. What are the biological advantage(s) of the structure of the maple seed? Explain fully.

Part III: Finishing by Yourself

THE GRAND MAPLECOPTER COMPETITION

Your goal is to design a helicopter, from a 4″ X 8″ piece of paperboard, that will remain in the air for the longest time when dropped from the same height.

    a. Design the "helicopter."
    b. Write down factors related to your design.
    c. Cut out the "helicopter."
    d. Mark the helicopter with your name.
    e. Good luck and have fun!

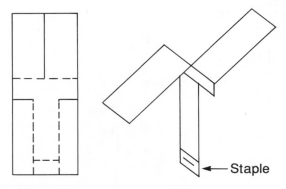

Figure 1   Figure 2

←— Staple

SOURCE: Connecticut State Department of Education, 1991.

GROUP PERFORMANCE RATING FORM

Student Name _____

Student ID # _____

	Almost always	Often	Some-times	Rarely

A. GROUP PARTICIPATION
1. Participation in group discussion without prom
2. Did his or her fair share of the work
3. Tried to dominate the group - interrupted oth
4. *Participated in the group's activities*

B. STAYING ON THE TOPIC
5. Paid attention, listened to what was being
6. Made comments aimed at getting the gro
7. Got off the topic or changed the subject
8. *Stayed of the topic*

C. OFFERING USEFUL IDEAS
9. Gave ideas and suggestions that help
10. Offered helpful criticism and comme
11. Influenced the group's decisions a
12. *Offered useful ideas*

D. CONSIDERATION
13. Made positive, encouraging rem
14. Gace recognition and credit to
15. Made inconsiderate or hostile
16. *Was considerate of others*

E. INVOLVING OTHERS
17. Got others involved by askir
18. Tried to get the group worki
19. Seriously considered the id
20. *Involved others*

F. COMMUNICATING
21. Spoke clearly, was easy to hea
22. Expressed ideas clearly and effectively
23. *Communicated clearly*

Part II: OBJECTIVES RATING FORM (GROUP)

Title of the tasks _____

Student ID numbers (1)_____

(2)_____ Teacher ID#_____

(3)_____

The group should be able to:	E	G	N.I.	U
1. describe the flight of a maple seed pod based on observation				
2. describe the variables that might affect the motion of a maple pod				
3. design and perform experiments to help explain the motion of a maple pod				
4. design and perform experiments to help explain the motion of a paper helicopter				
5. design and perform new experiments based on transfer from the model				
6. describe findings from experiments in words, charts, and graphs				
7. explain the motion of a maple pod based on experimental data				
8. describe the advantages and disadvantages of paper helicopters as models of maple pods				
9. explain the biological advantage of the design of the maple pod				
10. communicate effectively through written means				
11. collaborate effectively				

E= excellent   G= good   N.I.=needs improvement   U=unacceptable

A Sample of Other Science Performance Tasks Under Development

BOILING POINT LABORATORY: Students are asked to design and carry out a controlled experiment to determine the mixture of antifreeze and water that has the highest boiling point and is thus the most effective in keeping cars running smoothly in extreme temperatures.

OUTCROP ANALYSIS: Students are given a variety of information, including videotapes, pictures, and rock samples, from a site in Connecticut and are asked to determine if it is a good site on which to build a nuclear power facility. Students may be asked to investigate other factors, such as population, waste disposal, weather, politics, etc. in determining if it is a good site.

WEATHER PREDICTION: Students asre asked to predict the weather based on their knowledge of meteorology, data thay collect, and observations that they are able to make. Students may be asked to make simple weather instruments or create a weather forecasting segment as it would appear on a television newscast.

- testing becomes a personal responsibility;

- students realize that they need to demonstrate a full range of knowledge and accomplishments, rather than a one-shot performance;

- they begin to learn that first draft work is never good enough; and

- they appreciate that development is as important as achievement.[47]

A small but growing number of States have embraced portfolios as an educational assessment tool. As of 1991, five States (Alaska, California, North Carolina, Rhode Island, and Vermont) had implemented portfolios as a mandatory, voluntary, or experimental component of the statewide educational assessment program. Four additional States (Delaware, Georgia, South Carolina, and Texas) are considering implementing portfolios for this purpose. At the State level, portfolios have been implemented mostly in mathematics and writing at grade levels ranging from 1st to 12th but concentrated in the early grades.[48] The Vermont experience with portfolios is noteworthy (see box 7-F). Michigan's portfolio project, begun on a pilot basis in 22 districts during 1990-91, focuses on the skills that high school graduates are expected to have in order to be productive workers. As described in box 7-G, this use of portfolios aims at providing both students and prospective employers with information on workplace skill competencies.

Research on effectiveness of portfolios is being assembled by the project Arts PROPEL, a 5-year cooperative effort involving artists, researchers from Harvard University's Project Zero, the Educational Testing Service (ETS), and teachers, students, and administrators from the Pittsburgh and Boston public school systems. Supported by a grant from the Rockefeller Foundation, Arts PROPEL seeks to create a closer link between instruction and assessment in three areas of the middle and secondary school curriculum: visual arts, music, and imaginative writing.[49] The primary purpose of the assessment is not for selection, prediction, or as an institutional measure of achievement. Instead, it is focused on understanding individual student learning as a way of improving classroom instruction. The goal is to create assessments that provide a learning profile of the individual on as many dimensions as possible, as well as showing student change over time.[50] The two sources of assessment are portfolios and what is called the "domain project," an instructional sequence that focuses on central aspects of a domain and provides opportunities for multiple observations of the student. Domain projects function as self-contained instructional units central to the arts curriculum, and are graded by the classroom teacher.

The portfolio is the central defining element in Arts PROPEL. It is intended to be a complete process-tracking record of each student's attempts to realize a work of art, music, or writing. It also serves as a basis for students' reflection about their work, a means for them to identify what they value in selecting pieces for inclusion, and a vehicle for conversations about that work with teachers. A typical portfolio might contain initial sketches, drafts, or audiotapes; self criticisms and those of teachers and other students; successive drafts and reflections; and examples of works of others that have influenced the student. A final evaluation by the student and others is included, along with plans for successive work. Researchers and school district personnel are attempting to find methods of assessing artistic growth and of conveying this information effectively—through scores or other summary indicators—to administrators, college admissions officers, and others.

Like writing assessments, the use of portfolios is not new. For 19 years it has been the major component of the Advanced Placement (AP) studio art examination, administered by ETS[51] (see box 7-H).

---

[47]From Dennie Palmer Wolf, "Portfolio Assessment: Sampling Student Work," *Educational Leadership*, vol. 46, No. 7, April 1989, pp. 35-36.

[48]OTA data, 1991.

[49]Roberta Camp, "Presentation on Arts PROPEL Portfolio Explorations," paper presented at the Educational Testing Seminar on Alternatives to Multiple-Choice Assessment, Washington, DC, Mar. 30, 1990, p. 1.

[50]Drew H. Gitomer, "Assessing Artistic Learning Using Domain Projects," paper presented at the annual meeting of the American Educational Research Association, New Orleans, LA, April 1988, p. 4.

[51]Mitchell and Stempel, op. cit., footnote 2.

Art credit: Dennis Biggs, grade 8, Pittsburgh Public Schools

Portfolios of student work provide an ongoing record of progress and the development of skills. These pictures were drawn by a student in Pittsburgh's Arts PROPEL program. Each portrait was completed in 3 minutes using a black felt-tip pen. The first is a contour drawing of a classmate, the second is a portrait of the same student using all circular lines, and the third is the same student using only lines drawn with a ruler.

Common Characteristics of Performance Assessment

Although there is great variety in the kinds of measures that fall under the umbrella of performance assessment, certain common characteristics distinguish their use and implementation in school systems.

Performance tests require *student-constructed* responses as opposed to student-selected responses. While it is not certain that these two responses involve different cognitive processes, creating a

Box 7-F—"This is My Best": Vermont's Portfolio Assessment Project

Prior to 1990, Vermont was one of the few States with no mandated statewide testing program. Districts could conduct standardized norm-referenced testing for their own purposes. However, change came to Vermont when the legislature approved funds for a statewide assessment program to be integrated with classroom instruction. The first piece of the plan, piloted in the 1990-91 school year in one-quarter of the schools across the State, focused on writing and mathematics in grades four and eight. Eventually all the major academic disciplines will be covered. Each assessment has three parts: a uniform test, "best pieces" exemplifying the student's highest achievement in the judgment of the student and teacher, and a portfolio showing development throughout the year.

The mathematics assessment includes a standardized test that contains multiple-choice, open-ended, and longer computational problems. Each student is also responsible for assembling a mathematics portfolio, a collection of some 10 to 20 entries of problems and projects completed. Five to seven of these are pieces the student and teachers have chosen as best pieces, accompanied by a letter the student writes to the evaluator, explaining why these were selected. All this conferring, questioning, reviewing, and writing about mathematics is aimed at better understanding and communication about mathematical reasoning, logic, and problem solving. The mathematics portfolios are designed to foster an attitude of responsibility for learning on the part of the student, reveal the student's feelings about mathematics, and provide a means of showing growth in areas not well suited to standardized tests[1] (see figure 7-F1).

The writing assessment is made up of a uniform writing prompt and an interdisciplinary writing portfolio.[2] The writing assessment is similar to that used in other States, with students given a uniform prompt and 90 minutes to respond. The students are encouraged to think through ideas first and write rough drafts, using dictionaries and thesauruses provided in the testing room, and then produce a finished product. The prompt used for the 1990-91 pilot was:

> Most people have strong feelings about something that happened to them in the past. Think about a time when you felt happy, scared, surprised, or proud. Tell about this time so that the reader will understand what happened, who was involved, how the experience made you feel, and why it was important to you.[3]

Students also answered 12 general information questions that accompanied the writing assessment. Their responses were correlated to levels of writing performance and illuminated several issues the State found important. These included: the negative impacts of television viewing, positive effects of reading, and support for teaching of writing as a process and writing across the curriculum. The analysis was conducted by an outside contractor, also responsible for scoring the uniform writing assessments.

The writing portfolio can contain pieces from grades prior to the fourth and eighth grade "snapshot" years; works in various stages of revision; several other writing samples, including a poem, short story, play, or personal narration; a personal response to an event, exhibit, book, issue, mathematics problem, or scientific phenomenon; and prose pieces from any curricular area outside of English. As in the mathematics portfolio, the student also chooses one best piece, and writes a letter to the evaluators explaining why the piece was selected and the process of its composition.

The writing portfolios are scored by teachers. In the pilot year, approximately 150 fourth and eighth grade teachers from the sample schools did this scoring. Each portfolio and best piece was assessed by two teachers (using the writing benchmarks shown in table 7-F1) and the process took 2 days. Although it was an intense experience, the teachers' reactions were generally positive:

> . . . despite the work load, this was an invigorating and inspiring couple of days. A few things impressed me: the uniformity of the grading; the joy of discovering various "nuggets" of good stuff; the variety and the quality of eighth grade writing.

> I learned a hell of a lot. The experience confirmed the prevailing sense among the writing community that language can be the close, personal ally of every self, regardless of ability, age, or station.

> What was most useful about this process was that teachers from all over the state saw the variety and talked about it.[4]

---

[1]Vermont Department of Education, *Looking Beyond "The Answer": Vermont's Mathematics Portfolio Assessment Program, Pilot Year Report 1990-91* (Montpelier, VT: 1991).

[2]See Vermont Department of Education, *"This is My Best": Vermont's Writing Assessment Program, Pilot Year Report 1990-91* (Montpelier, VT: 1991), p. 7.

[3]Ibid., p. 19.

[4]Ibid., pp. 13-14.

Figure 7-F1—Portfolios as a "Window" on Student Feelings About Mathematics

Students keep copies of their mathematics problems as well as their feelings and opinions about mathematics in their portfolios. This student's current frustration is reflected in his entry:

> as you can see in this problem, and every problem in Stupid idiotic math class! I really stink in math. I have no stupid brain for it. Math is the dumbest, studidest class ever. The person who invented it should be drug out into the street and shot! I don't ever plan on be a High-Tech mathmatitian, or an Engineer. That all Bull crud. Sorry I am in such a bad mood but I just got a 45 on my math test. I studied hard, I want in for extra help but you know what? That all didn't do a thing for me!

Later in the year, he was faced with the following problem:

In a group of cows and chickens, the number of legs is four more than three times the number of heads. What is the least number of cows and chickens in the group?

What follows is his solution, and his reaction, in what he called his "opinion corner":

heads $3x$

legs $3x+4$

$3x + 3x + 4 = 6x + 4 =$

(8 cows | 4 chickens)

Opinion Corner

> This problem in a way was sort of a tough. I thought however that is was pretty fun. I don't really enjoy math, but though that this problem was kinda fun. I don't think I got the right answer but I put alot of thoughts and methods for solving it. I would recommend this problem for any one who enjoys math and thinking
>
> Sincerely From the president of Opinion Corner

SOURCE: Vermont Department of Education, *Looking Beyond "The Answer": Vermont's Mathematics Portfolio Assessment Program, Pilot Year Report 1990-91* (Montpelier VT: 1991), p. 31.

Continued on next page

Box 7-F—"This is My Best": Vermont's Portfolio Assessment Project—Continued

In 1991-92, all Vermont schools are required to use the assessments in the target grades. Local teachers will assess the writing portfolios in their own schools, after a series of professional development sessions. They have the option of working alone, assessing only their own students' portfolios, or working cooperatively with other teachers in their schools. In late spring they will bring a sample of five portfolios to a regional meeting, where teachers from others schools will score their sample portfolios to determine a rate of reliability. A sample of portfolios from each regional meeting will be assessed at a statewide meeting to ensure that common standards are applied statewide.[5] Aware of the importance of training teachers to use new assessment tools as levers for instructional change, the State has committed 40 percent of the assessment budget to professional development.[6]

The reporting system has also been carefully considered. Building on Vermont's tradition of town meetings, each district declares an annual Vermont School Report Day each spring. At this time community members and the press go to their schools for an analysis of assessment results and to discuss the district's response to a list of questions prepared by the State board to encourage discussion about local schooling goals and successes.

---

[5]Ibid., p. 8.

[6]Ross Brewer, presentation at "Educational Assessment for the Twenty-First Century: The National Agenda," sponsored by the National Center for Research on Evaluation, Standards and Student Testing, Manhattan Beach, CA, Mar. 9, 1991.

Table 7F-1—Vermont Writing Assessment Analytic Assessment Guide

Five dimensions of writing are rated on the following levels of performance: extensively, frequently, sometimes, rarely (criteria for each of these are listed)

Purpose	The degree to which the writer's response: • establishes and maintains a clear purpose; • demonstrates an awareness of audience and task; • exhibits clarity of ideas.
Organization	The degree to which the writer's response illustrates: • unity; • coherence.
Details	The degree to which the details are appropriate for the writer's purpose and support the main point(s) of the writer's response.
Voice/tone	The degree to which the writer's response reflects personal investment and expression.
Usage, mechanics, grammar	The degree to which the writer's response exhibits correct: • usage (e.g., tense formation, agreement, word choice); • mechanics—spelling, capitalization, punctuation; • grammar; • sentences; as appropriate to the piece and grade level.

SOURCE: Vermont State Board of Education, This is My Best": Vermont's Writing Assessment Program, Pilot Year Report 1990-91 (Montpelier, VT: 1991), p. 6.

---

response may more closely approximate the real-world process of solving problems. Most performance tasks require the student to engage in a complex group of judgments; the student must analyze the problem, define various options to solve the problem, and communicate the solution in written, oral, or other forms. Furthermore, often a solution requires balancing "tradeoffs" that can only be understood when the person making the choices explains or demonstrates the rationale for the choice. Performance assessment tasks make it possible to trace the path a student has taken in arriving at the chosen solution or decision.

Performance assessment attempts as much as possible to assess desired behavior directly, in the context in which this behavior is used. Tasks chosen for testing must sample representatively from the desirable skills and understandings: demonstrating ability to write a persuasive argument might be reflected in asking students to write a paragraph convincing the teacher why an extension is needed on an assignment; demonstrating an understanding of experimental design might involve designing and conducting an experiment to find out if sow bugs prefer light over dark environments; showing one's facility with the French written language might involve translating a French poem into English. In each of these cases, it is possible to conduct other kinds of tests that can accompany the performance task (e.g., vocabulary tests, lists of procedures,

---

Box 7-G—Michigan's Employability Skills Assessment Program

In an effort to ensure that Michigan's high school graduates acquire skills necessary to remain competitive in an increasingly technological workplace, the Governor's Commission on Jobs and Economic Development convened the Employability Skills Task Force in 1987. The Task Force, made up of leaders from business, labor, and education, was charged with identifying the skills Michigan employers believe important to succeed in the modern workplace. The Task Force concluded that Michigan workers need skills in three areas:

- *Academic skills*, such as the ability to read and understand written materials, charts, and graphs;
- *Teamwork skills*, such as the ability to express ideas to colleagues of a team and compromise to accomplish a goal; and
- *Personal Management skills*, such as the ability to meet deadlines and pay attention to details.[1]

The Task Force also served as a policy advisory group on the development of Michigan's Employability Skills Assessment Program for the State's high schools. The Task Force concluded that student portfolios would best describe the strengths and weaknesses of individual students in the skill groups, and could serve as the basis for planning an individual skills development program for each student.

The portfolio program was piloted during the 1990-91 school year in 22 school districts. Districts were encouraged to apply the program to a cross section of students in order to emphasize that the program was designed for everyone, not just noncollege-bound youth.

To help students, the State provided several tools including three portfolios (one in each skill area), a portfolio information guide for the student, a parent guide for the student's parents, a personal rating form to be filled out by students, teachers, and parents, and a work appraisal form for employers to complete.

Each of the three portfolios, Academic, Teamwork and Personal Management, stresses skills considered important in that particular area. Students are responsible for updating their portfolios with sample work and information about grades, awards, and recommendations. For example, the captain of the school track team might ask her coach for a letter of recommendation to place in her Teamwork portfolio as proof of her leadership ability. If students feel they are lacking in a particular skill category, they can seek out an activity designed to help them master that skill. In this way students are expected to *discover*, *develop*, and *document* their "employability skills." It is envisioned that the portfolios will serve as "resume builders."[2] When applying for jobs, students will use their portfolios to demonstrate employability skills.

It is difficult to assess the results of the Employability Skills Assessment since the program is so new. The few collected responses have been mixed. Schools that have taken the program to heart, contacting local businesses and informing them of the program, have been enthusiastic. Some schools have even invited local business managers to assess individual student's portfolios. Other schools, however, have been less satisfied. Some are resisting suggested changes because they appear incompatible with other reform efforts; others are hesitant to involve business in what is viewed primarily as the job of the schools. Michigan law now requires every school to design a portfolio system to assess ninth graders beginning in the 1992-93 school year. The State's Department of Education plans to continue piloting the Employability program.

---

[1]A similar emphasis on the blend of academic, cooperative, and personal skills underlies a recent U.S. Department of Labor report. See U.S. Department of Labor, Secretary's Commission on Achieving Necessary Skills (SCANS), *What Work Requires of Schools* (Washington, DC: June 1991).

[2]Edward D. Roeber, Michigan Department of Education, personal communication, Oct. 22, 1991.

---

questions about content), but in performance assessment direct performances of desired tasks are evaluated.

Performance assessments focus on the process and the quality of a product or a performance. Effectiveness and craftsmanship are important elements of the assessment; getting the "right answer" is not the only criterion.[52] The process as well as the results are examined in solving a geometric proof, improving one's programming skills, or formulating a scientific hypothesis and testing it.

---

[52]Grant Wiggins, "Authentic Assessment: Principles, Policy and Provocations," paper presented at the Boulder Conference of State Testing Directors, Boulder, CO, June 1990.

Box 7-H—Advanced Placement Studio Art Portfolios[1]

While the idea of portfolios for large-scale testing is considered a novel idea, portfolios have been the heart of the Advanced Placement (AP) examination for studio art for nearly 20 years.[2] The purpose of the AP Studio Art Portfolio Evaluation is to certify that a high school student has produced works that meet the achievement level expected of first year college students in studio art. The cost to the student is $65, the same as for other AP examinations. There are several points that make the assessment of particular interest:

- The assessment is conducted entirely through evaluation of the work contained in the student portfolio. There are no essays, no questions to answer, no standard paper-and-pencil examination.
- It is a considered a "high-stakes" assessment, for, like all AP examinations, students must receive a passing grade (a score of 3 or higher on a 1 to 5 ranking) to earn college level credit for the course.[3]
- Despite the fact that the topic is a "subjective" one like art, administration and scoring are standardized and conducted in an objective manner.
- There is no set curriculum; teachers have great flexibility in their choice of approach, organization, assignments, and so forth.
- A high degree of student initiative and motivation is required.
- The program has won the respect of teachers and students at both the high school and college level and there is little controversy surrounding it.

Standardization of Portfolio Submissions

Students submit a portfolio based on the work they have created during the year-long AP studio art course.[4] A student can choose one of two evaluations: the drawing portfolio or general portfolio evaluation. In the *drawing portfolio,* there must be six original works no larger than 16 inches by 20 inches, and from 14 to 20 slides on an area of special concentration. The concentration is a single theme (e.g., self portraiture) developed by the student. Some of the concentrations chosen as exemplary in recent years have included cubist still-life drawings, manipulated photographs, wood relief sculptures, still lifes transformed into surreal landscapes, and expressionist drawings that serve as social commentary.[5] Another 14 to 20 slides illustrate breadth. The *general portfolio* is set up in much the same format.[6] Film and videotapes may be submitted in the concentration section.

Standardizing Artistic Judgment

In June 1991, nearly 5,000 portfolios were submitted for the evaluation. These were graded by a panel of 21 *readers* (scorers) assembled at Trenton State College in Trenton, New Jersey. The readers all teach either AP studio art or analogous college courses; scoring took 6 days.

Each grading session began with a standard-setting session. A number of portfolios were presented to the assembled readers, roughly illustrating all the possible scores. These examples were chosen beforehand by the *chief reader* for the whole evaluation and the *table leader* for each section; their selection and judgment were guided by their experience of teaching. There was no general scoring rubric per se; no analytic scales of *primary traits* as there are in the evaluation of writing. As one former chief reader suggested:

---

[1]Much of this discussion comes from Ruth Mitchell and Amy Stempel, Council for Basic Education, "Six Case Studies of Performance Assessment," OTA contractor report, March 1991.

[2]Studio art was added to the Advanced Placement (AP) program in two stages—the general portfolio in 1972 and the drawing portfolio in 1980. A separate AP art history course is also offered; its examination has a more typical format of multiple-choice and free-response items.

[3]Colleges have varying polices regarding AP credits. Some grant exemption from freshman-level courses, while others require students to take the introductory courses, but grant a certain number of elective credits. In general, students can reduce the number of courses required to graduate from college by passing these AP college-level courses in high school. Thus there is a strong financial incentive to succeed on the AP examination.

[4]Not all schools offer a separate AP course. A separate AP studio art course is "almost a luxury"; in some schools, a small number of AP students work alongside other students in regular classes, while other students submit work done independently during the summer or in museum courses. Alice Sims-Gunzenhauser, Educational Testing Service consultant, AP studio art, personal communication, November 1991.

[5]Ibid.

[6]Only four works are required in the original work portion. The breadth section specifies that eight slides illustrate drawing skill, with four each in three other categories (color, design, and sculpture).

Factors that are included in assessing quality include imagination; freshness of conception and interpretation; mastery of concepts, composition, materials, and techniques; a distinct sense of order and form; evidence of a range of experience; and, finally, awareness of art-historical sources, including contemporary artists and art movements. It is not expected that every student's portfolio will reflect all of these considerations to the same degree. . . . What you're really after is a mind at work, an interested, live, thinking being. You want to see engagement. Recognition of it comes from long experience and you intuit it.[7]

In commenting on how this approach related to judgments in other disciplines, he noted:

There are more things that join us together than separate us. You can make those judgments as accurately as you can in mathematics or in writing or in any other subjects. These other subjects frequently have much more difficulty than we do in the visual arts in agreeing on standards. . . . You get a sense for copied work, a sense when there's engagement, when inspiration, belief, direct involvement are present or absent.[8]

The portfolios chosen to exemplify each grade remained on display throughout the scoring as references for comparison. The readers assigned scores to each part separately, on a scale from 1 to 4. Originality of work was scored independently by three readers; concentrations and breadth by two readers. The scores were manipulated by computer to arrive at a raw score (1 to approximately 100) to which the three sections (original work, concentration, and breadth) contribute equally. If discrepancies of 2 or more points between two readers' evaluations of the same section occurred, the chief reader reviewed the section and reconciled the scores. The chief reader might speak with a reader and use the models to reinforce the agreed standard.

After all portfolios had been evaluated, *cutoff scores* were determined and the total scores then converted to the AP grades on a scale of a high of 5 to a low of 1. Although assigning the cutoff scores (i.e., determining the lowest total score to receive an AP grade of 5 on down) is the chief reader's responsibility, there was input from a long debriefing meeting of all readers and from statistical information supplied by the computer, historical data regarding previous years' cutoff scores, composite and raw scores for present year's candidates, and tables showing the consequences of choosing certain cutoff scores, in terms of percentage of students receiving 5, 4, 3, and so on. The scores overall were roughly distributed in a bell curve, with most receiving a 3, but fewer 1s than 5s. (Colleges do not usually accept either 2 or 1 scores, so a 2 can perform the same function as a 1 (i.e., denying the awarding of college credit) without making such a negative judgment of a student's work.)

Impacts on Students

In the process of creating portfolios for AP studio art, students begin to develop artistic judgment about their own work and that of their fellow students. Students are taught to criticize each other's work constructively. As they learn how to select works for their own portfolios, they also learn to communicate with each another about areas that need improvement. This climate of reflection is an important byproduct of portfolio assembly.

Another key factor is motivation. As one teacher suggested, the course is a test of students' self motivation.[9] For example, students must have the ability to envision a concentration project and then work steadily toward completing it for 8 or 9 months, solving problems as they arise. The work on all three sections must be timed so that the entire portfolio is ready at the deadline. Pieces have to be photographed for slides and final selections made for the collection of original works.

Broad Public Acceptance

Another important point is the relative lack of controversy surrounding judgment of a subject traditionally considered subjective. This respect comes from the long history of the evaluation and the refinements the Educational Testing Service has made to the jury method of judging works of art, based on collective, but independent, judgments by teachers who are involved in the day-to-day teaching of students like those being assessed. These teachers are well trained in the objectives of the course as well as the performance standards for each level, and their judgment is valued and respected.

---

[7]Walter Askin, *Evaluating the Advanced Placement Portfolio in Studio Art* (Princeton, NJ: Advanced Placement Program, 1985), p. 25.
[8]Ibid.
[9]Raymond Campeau, AP studio art teacher in Bozeman, MT, in Mitchell and Stempel, op. cit., footnote 1.

The product or record of a performance assessment is scored by teachers or other qualified judges. In classroom testing this observation is done by the teacher, but in large-scale assessments, products, portfolios, or other records of work are scored by teams of readers. How much psychometric rigor is required in making these qualitative and complex judgments varies with the purpose of the assessment; less rigor is acceptable for use within the classroom for diagnostic purposes than would be acceptable in large-scale testing programs where comparability is essential. **What is important is that performance tests are not "beyond standardized testing"; they should be standardized whenever comparability is required.**[53]

The criteria for judging performance assessments are clear to those being judged. Criteria for judging successful performance must be available and understood by teachers and students. The tasks and standards must allow for thorough preparation and self-assessment by the student,[54] if the test is to be successful in motivating and directing learning, and in helping teachers to successfully guide practice.[55] The goal in performance assessment is to provide tasks that are known to the student— activities that not only can but should be practiced. Performance assessment tasks are intended to be "taught to," integrating curriculum and assessment into a seamless web. Practice required for good performance is understood to increase and stimulate learning.

Performance assessment may take place at one point or over time. Typically it examines patterns of student work and consistency of performance, looking at how an individual student progresses and develops. This is particularly true of portfolios, which are collections of student work over time.

While multiple-choice and other paper-and-pencil examinations are almost exclusively taken by an individual student, some performance assessments can be and are often conducted as group activities. This group activity reflects increasing interest in student team work and cooperation in solving tasks as a valued outcome of the educational process. Proponents suggest that, if teamwork is a valued

skill, it should be assessed. However, the problems associated with inferring individual effort, ability, and achievement from group performances are significant. Individual performance and performance as a member of a group are often scored as two separate pieces of the assessment.

Performance assessments are generally criterion-referenced, rather than norm-referenced. Although it is important to collect information on how a wide range of students respond to performance assessment tasks, the primary focus is on scoring students relative to standards of competence and mastery. Developers of performance assessment are seeking test-based indicators that portray individual performance with respect to specific educational goals rather than those that simply compare an individual's performance to a sample of other test takers.

Performance Assessment Abroad

The standardized, machine-scored, norm-referenced, multiple-choice tests so common in this country for large-scale testing are rarely used in other countries. In fact, these are often referred to generically as "American tests." Instead, examinations like the French *Bac*, the German *Abitur*, or the English General Certificate of Secondary Education or "A levels," generally require students to create rather than select answers, usually in the format of short-answer or longer essay questions or, in some cases, oral examinations. These examinations share several of the characteristics noted above regarding performance assessments in American schools: they are typically graded by teachers, the content is based on a common curriculum or syllabus for which students prepare and practice, and the questions are made public at the end of the examination period.

It is important to note, however, as discussed in chapter 4, that these tests are most commonly used for selection of students into postsecondary education rather than for classroom diagnosis or school accountability. Consequently, several of the characteristics noted in American performance assessments are not present in these examinations. That is, the examinations are usually individual assessments, with no opportunity for group activities; they

---

[53]Frederick L. Finch, "Toward a Definition for Educational Performance Assessment," paper presented at the ERIC/PDK Symposium, Alternative Assessment of Performance in the Language Arts, Bloomington, IN, Aug. 23, 1990.

[54]Wiggins, op. cit., footnote 52.

[55]Center for Children and Technology, op. cit., footnote 5, p. 3.

do not involve self assessment or student involvement in evaluation; the examinations are timed rather than open-ended; and, even when administered over several days, they do not involve tasks that take several testing periods or longer time periods to complete.

Nevertheless, European experience can be informative. For example, the national assessment in Holland structures performance-based assessments for students by designing comprehensive problems for the year-end examinations. A committee of teachers in art history, for example, selects a unifying subject (e.g., "revolution"). Students are provided with information packages to guide their study of art throughout the year in ways that help them to critically develop the theme (e.g., readings and lists of museums). Teachers are encouraged to work with students to help them develop individual interpretations and points of view. This assessment approach supports students in doing individualized in-depth work in a context of shared ideas, procedures, and problems.[56]

The United Kingdom is the furthest along of European countries using performance assessment for national testing. The Education Reform Act of 1988 set in place a national curriculum, which has at its core a set of attainment targets for each of the 10 foundation subjects to be taught to all students. These statements of attainment provide the basis for the criterion-referenced assessment system. Teachers have been given detailed, clearly defined Standard Assessment Tasks (SATs) to use with all students at or near the completion of four levels or "key stages" of schooling: ages 7, 11, 14, and 16. Each SAT carries with it levels of attainment and the tasks for determining levels, described in manuals provided to all teachers. The tasks involve one or more components of every aspect of performance: reading, writing, speaking, listening, investigating, demonstrating, drawing, experimenting, showing, and assembling. The tasks were developed through research conducted at schools across the United Kingdom by the National Foundation for Education Research in England and Wales.

Following a 2-day teacher training period, three sets of SATs were piloted in May 1990, testing 6,219 students in level one (age 7) in schools throughout England and Wales. Each was constructed around an overall theme hoped to engage the interest of 7-year-olds: Toys and Games, Myself, and The World About Me.

Evaluation data and recommendations reflect widespread concern with the extremely detailed and directive nature of the assessment system:

> In view of the issue of time and workload ... an inescapable conclusion must be that future SATs should be significantly shorter than those piloted. SEAC [School Examinations and Assessment Council] are likely to recommend that the SAT is to be carried out in a *three week period, and to take not more than half the teacher's time during those three weeks.* ... The number of activities that can be fitted in will need to be reduced to about six in order to be sure that these time constraints can be observed. ... The model of a SAT covering all or most, or even half of the ATs has now been proven to be unworkable in light of the number and nature of ATs included in the final statutory orders. ... The SAT should still offer teachers the opportunity to embed the assessments within a coherent cross-curricular theme.[57]

How far the United Kingdom will be able to move forward on this ambitious assessment plan that requires so much teacher time is still under debate. However, the close tie to the national curriculum strengthens the likelihood that the SATs will be maintained as centerpieces for assessment.

Finally, some countries are experimenting with the use of portfolios for large-scale testing activities, and many are looking to the United States for guidance in this field. Because the United States is widely respected as a leader in psychometric design, many other countries are watching with interest how we match psychometric rigor to the development of performance assessment techniques.

Policy Issues in Performance Assessment

Various direct methods of assessing performance have long been used by teachers as a basis for making judgments about student achievement within the classroom. Teachers often understand intuitively their own potential for errors in judgment and the

[56]Center for Children and Technology, op. cit., footnote 5, p. 8.

[57]National Foundation for Educational Research/Bishop Grosseteste College, Lincoln Consortium, *The Pilot Study of Standard Assessment Tasks for Key Stage 1—Part 1: Main Text & Comparability Studies* (Berkshire, England: March 1991), p. 10, emphasis added.

ways in which student performance can vary from day to day. As a result they use daily and repeated observations over time to formulate judgments and shape instruction. An error in judgment on one day can be corrected or supplanted by new observations the next.

The stakes are raised when testing is used for comparisons across children, classrooms, or schools, and when test results inform important decisions. As noted by several experts in test design and policy:

> . . . . when direct measures of performance take on an assessment role beyond the confines of the classroom—portfolios passed on to next year's teacher, district wide science laboratory tasks for program evaluation, or state-mandated writing assessments for accountability are just a few examples—whatever contextual understanding of their fallibility may have existed in the classroom is gone. In such situations, a performance assessment, like any other measurement device, requires enough consistency to justify the broader inferences about performance beyond the classroom that are likely to be based on it. Most large-scale performance assessments are being proposed today for fundamentally different purposes from those of classroom measurement, such as monitoring system performance, program and/or teacher evaluation, accountability and broadly defined educational reform. Even though none of these uses typically involves scores for and decisions about individual students, each is a high stakes application of an educational measurement to the extent that it can effect a wholesale change in a school program affecting all students.[58]

The feasibility and acceptance of the widespread use of performance assessment by policymakers must rest on consideration of a number of important issues. In addition, the purpose of a particular test will, in large part, determine the relative importance or weight that should be given to each of these issues.

Standardization of Scoring Judgments

One of the first concerns about the applicability of performance assessment to large-scale testing is the extent to which human judgment is required in scoring. Variability across judges and potential for bias in scoring could create impediments to using these methods for high-stakes testing. For scores to

yield meaningful inferences or comparisons, they must be consistent and comparable. A student's score should reflect his or her level of achievement, and should not vary as a function of who is doing the judging. A key feature of performance assessment is the complexity of judgment needed for scoring; however, this very complexity, some suggest, may be a barrier to its widespread implementation in situations where comparability matters.

For performance assessment to fulfill its promise, it must meet challenges regarding reasonable standards for reliable scoring, whether this scoring is done by individuals, teams, or by machines programmed to simulate human judgment. This is an area where test publishers have experience and expertise to offer school districts and States considering performance assessments. As noted above, Arizona has hired the Riverside Publishing Co., in part because of experience with the Arizona educators and their curriculum and past testing activities (the Iowa Tests of Basic Skills and the Tests of Achievement and Proficiency programs), but also because the publishers claim expertise in field testing items or tasks and providing scales that meet previous standards for reliability.

Because there has been considerable research by curriculum experts and the research community on developing and scoring essays and writing assessments, they present a model that students, teachers, and the general public can appreciate. Scoring has been made more systematic and reliable by a number of procedures. Scoring criteria are carefully written to indicate what constitutes good and poor performance; representative student papers are then selected to exemplify the different score levels. Panels of readers or scorers are carefully trained until they learn to apply the scoring criteria in a manner consistent with other readers. In most large-scale writing assessments, each essay is read by two readers. When significant scoring discrepencies occur, a third reader (often the ''team leader'') reads and scores the essay. Various scoring systems can be employed from holistic (a single score is given for the quality of the writing) to more fine-grained analytic scores (each essay is rated on multiple criteria). Table 7-1 presents an example of one analytic scoring system that focuses on rating five aspects of the student's writing: organization, sen-

---

[58]Stephen Dunbar, Daniel Koretz, and H.D. Hoover, ''Quality Control in the Development and Use of Performance Assessments,'' paper presented at the annual meeting of the National Council on Measurement in Education, Chicago, IL, April 1991, p. 1.

Table 7-1—Criteria for Analytical Scoring

Scale:	1	2	3	4	5
Organization:	Little or nothing is written. The essay is disorganized, incoherent, and poorly developed. The essay does not stay on the topic.		The essay is not complete. It lacks an introduction, well-developed body or conclusion. The coherence and sequence are attempted, but not adequate.		The essay is well-organized. It contains an introductory supporting and concluding paragraph. The essay is coherent, ordered logically, and fully developed.
Sentence structure:	The student writes frequent run-ons or fragments.		The student makes occasional errors in sentence structure. Little variety in sentence length or structure exists.		The sentences are complete and varied in length and structure.
Usage:	The student makes frequent errors in word choice and agreement.		The student makes occasional errors in word choice or agreement.		The usage is correct. Word choice is appropriate.
Mechanics:	The student makes frequent errors in spelling, punctuation, and capitalization.		The student makes an occasional error in mechanics.		The spelling, capitalization, and punctuation are correct.
Format:	The format is sloppy. There are no margins or indentations. Handwriting is inconsistent.		The handwriting, margins, and indentations have occasional inconsistencies—no title or inappropriate title.		The format is correct. The title is appropriate. The handwriting, margins, and indentations are consistent.

SOURCE: Adams County School District No. 12, Northglenn, CO.

tence structure, use of language, mechanics, and format.

In the California Assessment Program's writing assessments, essays and answers are read by a single reader, but there are a variety of techniques used to maintain consistency of grading. Marked papers already read are circulated back into the pile to see if they get the same grade again; the table leaders randomly reread papers to make sure that readers are consistent; examples of graded papers are kept available for comparison as "anchors." Using these techniques, the inter-rater reliability for the CAP writing assessment is about 90 percent in a single year, although less high for the same question across years. This remains an unsolved problem for CAP and other States and districts using group grading if they want to make longitudinal comparisons.[59]

Other scoring questions related to design have yet to be solved. One of these is the time allotted for producing a composition. A 15-minute essay, with no chance for revision, may not be a true test of the kind of writing that is valued. Thus, testing time affects how reliably the writing sample reflects writing skill. Additionally, specifying scoring criteria and rating scale format are no easy matters.

Although research has recently provided some empirical analysis of the features of writing that distinguish skilled from unskilled writing, some suggest that the criteria applied to a particular assessment may represent arbitrary preferences of the group designing the scale. It is difficult but necessary to come to a consensus on these issues.

Photo credit: Educational Testing Service

Essays and writing samples can be graded consistently if teachers are trained to apply scoring criteria based on common standards. In this example, the Educational Testing Service has assembled experienced teachers to read and score essays written by students across the country on their Advanced Placement examinations.

[59]Mitchell and Stempel, op. cit., footnote 2.

Policy Implication

Writing assessments, essays, and courses like AP studio art have a proven track record of assessing performance in a standardized and reliable fashion. Whether these same procedures for obtaining consistency in scoring can be applied to other forms of performance assessment (e.g., portfolios, exhibitions, oral examinations, and experiments) is as yet largely unexplored. Moreover, although inter-rater reliability is relatively high (for judging essays), it still contains some variation that may add error to scores. What degree of error in measurement is acceptable depends, in part, on the purposes of the test. **Careful development of scoring criteria and intensive training of judges are key to establishing consistency of judgment.**

Generalizability of Scores: Are the Tests Valid Estimates of What Students Know?

Most students, current and former, can remember taking an essay test and feeling "lucky" because the questions just happened to hit topics they knew well; a high score, perhaps higher than their study and knowledge actually deserved, was the result. More likely, they remember the time they "bombed" on a test, unjustly they felt, because the essays covered areas they had not understood or studied as well. One of the advantages of item-based tests is that a large number of items can be given in a limited amount of testing time, thereby reducing the effect of a single question on the overall score.

When only a few tasks are used there is a much higher risk that a child's score will be associated with that particular task and not generalize to the whole subject area that the test is meant to cover. Writing assessment provides a particularly good example of the problem of generalizing results from a single question. In many cases a 30-minute essay test is given to students in order to estimate something about their overall ability to write well. However, a number of different kinds of writing tasks can be given. The National Council of Teachers of English lists five methods of communication in writing—narrating, explaining, describing, reporting, and persuading—that provide the framework for much of the classroom instruction in writing.[60] When tests are given, the essay question (or prompt) can be in any of these modes of discourse.

Two kinds of information are needed to make essay test results generalizable. First, would two different essays drawn from the same mode of discourse result in the same score? Results of several studies cited in a recent review suggest that agreement between two essays written by the same child in the same writing mode is not very high (reliability scores range from 0.26 to 0.46).[61] Second, are scores for essay prompts from different modes of writing similar? For example, if a student is asked to write a narrative piece, will the score for this prompt be similar to a score the same child receives for writing a persuasive piece? Results of several investigations of writing assessments indicate that correlations across tasks are low to moderate.

Other factors such as the topic of the essay, the time limit, and handwriting quality have been shown to affect scores on essay tests.[62] Preliminary results suggest that a number of tasks would need to be administered to any given child (and scores aggregated across tasks) before a sufficiently high level of reliability could be achieved to use these tests for making decisions about individuals. One investigation of these issues has suggested that six essays, each scored by at least two readers, would be needed to achieve a level of score reliability comparable to that of a multiple-choice test.[63]

One of the particular problems faced by performance assessment is that of substantiating that similar generalizations to the whole domain can be made on the basis of a few tasks. Very little research exists that can shed light on the extent to which different performance assessment tasks intended to assess the

---

[60]A.N. Hieronymus and H.D. Hoover, University of Iowa, *Writing: Teachers Guide*, Iowa Tests of Basic Skills, Levels 9-14 (Chicago, IL: Riverside Publishing Co., 1987).

[61]Dunbar et al., op. cit., footnote 58. See also Peter L. Cooper, *The Assessment of Writing Ability: A Review of Research*," GRE Board research report GREB No. 82-15R (Princeton, NJ: Educational Testing Service, May 1984).

[62]Cooper, op. cit., footnote 61.

[63]H.M. Breland, R. Camp, R.J. Jones, M.M. Morris, and D.A. Rock, "Assessing Writing Skill," research monograph No. 11, prepared for the College Entrance Examination Board, 1987, cited in Wayne Patience and Joan Auchter, "Monitoring Score Scale Stability and Reading Reliability in Decentralized Large-Scale Essay Scoring Programs," paper presented at the annual meeting of the National Testing Network in Writing, Montreal, Canada, April 1989.

same set of skills produce similar scores. Data from writing assessments suggest, for example, that a child who produces a superior essay in one format may write only a mediocre one on a different day in a different format.

The issue of generalizability—whether a child's performance on one or two tasks can fairly represent what he or she knows in that area—is an important one that greatly influences the conclusions that can be made from tests. Establishing generalizability is particularly critical if a test is going to be used to make decisions about individual students. Again the experience of writing assessment offers important lessons for other forms of performance assessment:

> It has long been known that neither an objective test nor a writing sample is an adequate basis for evaluation of an *individual* student, whether for purposes of placement, promotion or graduation. [One author] ... noted that a reliable individual evaluation would require a minimum of four writing samples, rated blindly (i.e., without knowledge of the student's identity) by trained evaluators. It is a continuing scandal of school testing programs that patently inadequate data are used for placement and categorization.[64]

Policy Implications

Issues of task generalizability present an important challenge to policymakers and test developers interested in expanding the uses of performance assessment. If individual scores are not required, however, sampling techniques can mitigate these issues. For example, many large-scale assessments of writing administer multiple prompts in each mode but each individual child only answers one or two of a larger number of prompts. The large number of children answering any one prompt, however, allows generalizable inferences to be made within and across modes about levels of writing achievement for students as a whole. The use of sampling techniques can allow policymakers and administrators to make generalizable inferences about schools

or districts without having to administer prohibitively long or costly tests to every student (see box 7-I).

Costs

The costs of performance assessment represent a substantial barrier to expanded use. Performance assessment is a labor-intensive and therefore costly alternative unless it is integrated in the instructional process. Essays and other performance tasks may cost less to develop than do multiple-choice items, but are very costly to score. One estimate puts scoring a writing assessment as 5 to 10 times more expensive as scoring a multiple-choice examination,[65] while another estimate, based on a review of several testing programs administered by ETS, suggests that the cost of assessment via one 20- to 40-minute essay is between 3 to 5 times higher than assessment by means of a test of 150 to 200 machine-scored, multiple-choice items.[66] Among the factors that influence scoring costs are the length of time students are given to complete the essay, the number of readers scoring each essay, qualifications and location of readers (which affects how much they are paid, and travel and lodging costs for the scoring process), and the amount of pretesting conducted on each prompt or question. The higher these factors, the higher the ratio of essay to multiple-choice costs. The volume of essays read at each scoring session has a reverse impact on cost—the greater the volume, the lower the per item cost.[67]

Is performance-based assessment worth the significantly higher direct costs of scoring? First, it is important to recall that high direct costs may overestimate total costs if the indirect costs are not taken into account. As explained in chapter 1, comparison of two testing programs on the basis of direct costs alone is deceiving. Because performance assessment is intended to be integrated with instruction, its advocates argue that it is less costly than it

---

[64]Suhor, op. cit., footnote 40. The author referred to is Paul Diederich, *Measuring Growth in English* (Urbana, IL: National Council of Teachers of English, 1974).

[65]John Fremer, ''What Is So Real About Authentic Assessment?'' paper presented at the Boulder Conference of State Testing Directors, Boulder, CO, June 10-12, 1990.

[66]The testing programs reviewed included: ''. . . the Advanced Placement Program, several essay assessments we operate for the state of California, the College Level Examination Program, the Graduate Record Exam, NAEP, the National Teacher Examination Programs, and the English Composition Test with Essay of the Admissions Testing Program. . . .'' Penny Engle, Educational Testing Service, Washington, DC, personal communication, June 10 1991. Multiple-choice tests are scored for $1.20 per student; in contrast, scoring of the Iowa Tests of Basic Skills writing test costs $4.22 per student. Frederick L. Finch, vice president, The Riverside Publishing Co., personal communication, March 1991.

[67]Engle, op. cit., footnote 66.

Box 7-I—Assessing Hands-On Science Skills

The National Science Foundation has supported a research project that attempts to explore reliability, transferability, and validity issues affecting performance tasks for large-scale science assessments.[1] The researchers first developed three different hands-on laboratory tasks for children to solve. Each requires students to conduct an experiment and manipulate equipment. In the ''Paper Towels'' experiment, students had to determine which of three kinds of paper towels soaked up the most water. The second task required students to figure out the contents of a number of ''mystery boxes'' containing wires, batteries, and/or light bulbs. The third assessment had students determine what kinds of environments sow bugs prefer (e.g., dark or light, dry or damp). Students were observed by experts while they performed the experiments; the experts scored students according to the procedures they used as well as the findings of the investigation.

Evidence about the validity of these measures was obtained by giving the participating students a traditional multiple-choice standardized test of science achievement, in order to compare the scores they obtained on their hands-on experiments with the scores received on multiple-choice tests. In addition, the performance of students who had been taught using a hands-on approach to science was compared to those studying under a more traditional approach.

Results provide some encouragement and some warnings. Among the findings of these initial development efforts with fifth and sixth graders were the following:

- Hands-on investigations can be reliably scored by trained judges.
- Performance on any one of the tasks was not highly related to that on the others. A student could perform well on one hands-on task and quite poorly on another. This suggests that a substantial number of tasks will be needed unless matrix sampling can be used.
- Hands-on scores were only moderately related to student's scores on the traditional multiple-choice science test, suggesting that different skills are being tapped.
- Students who had been taught with a hands-on approach did better on these tasks than did students from a traditional science classroom, suggesting that the tests are sensitive to classroom instruction.

---

[1]Richard J. Shavelson, Gail P. Baxter, Jerome Pine, and Jennifer Yure, ''New Technologies for Large-Scale Science Assessments: Instruments of Educational Reform,'' symposium presented at the annual meeting of the American Educational Research Association, Chicago, IL, April 1991.

appears. Resolution of this issue requires agreement on the degree to which any given testing options under consideration are integrated with regular instruction.

Second, although a performance assessment may provide less data than a typical multiple-choice test, it can provide richer information that sheds light on student capacities not usually accessible from multiple-choice tests. Even in an externally scored writing assessment, for example, teachers can gain insight into students' writing difficulties by looking not just at the raw scores, but at the writing itself. Similarly, some outcomes that cannot be measured on multiple-choice tests (e.g., ability to work cooperatively in a group) can be assessed in performance tasks.

Finally, many educators maintain that the staff development that accompanies performance assessment is in itself a valuable byproduct. For example,

when teachers gather to discuss what distinguishes a weak piece of writing from an acceptable or an excellent piece of writing, they learn from one another and internalize the teaching standards.

The major problem in approaching an analysis of the costs of performance assessment is a lack of a common base for the information. When the Council of Chief State School Officers compiled a chart of performance assessments in the States in order to make comparisons, they asked for reporting under the category of ''costs.'' As the data came in, the numbers fluctuated dramatically, because different respondents thought of costs differently: some reported costs of development ($2 million in one case), some costs of administration ($5 per student), and some combined them. In the end, the researchers decided to eliminate the question altogether because it could provide no meaningful information and

Hands-on assessments like this are costly in time, equipment, and human resources. Because of this, these investigators also sought "surrogate tasks" that might provide much of the information obtained from hands-on tasks but at considerably lower cost. To this end they created the following surrogates for the three experiments, listed in order of "conceptual verisimilitude" (similarity to the hands-on experiments):

- laboratory notebooks students kept as a record of their experiments;
- computer simulations;
- short-answer, paper-and-pencil questions based on the experiments; and
- multiple-choice items based on the hands-on procedures.

The researchers then examined the extent to which these various surrogates were exchangeable for the hands-on benchmark tasks. If simpler, less costly methods can provide the same information, why not use them? Preliminary findings from these investigations suggest the following:

- Laboratory notebooks provide the best surrogate for the hands-on investigation and can acceptably be used in lieu of direct observation.
- In the computer simulations, the computer saved all the child's moves, so they could be replayed and scored by the evaluator. The average time required for grading was about one-tenth of that needed for observing hands-on investigations—suggesting that computer simulations can offer a big savings in skilled personnel time.
- Neither the computer simulation nor the paper-and-pencil measures appeared to be adequate substitutes for the benchmark hands-on procedure. The computer simulation showed considerable variability for individual students—some individuals appear to do very well on this type of test while others do not.
- The students enthusiastically participated in the hands-on procedures as well as the computer simulations.

As investigators throughout the country begin to develop new performance assessments, they will need to collect data like this in order to evaluate the technical quality of their new measures. As one of the investigators involved in the above study concludes: ". . . these assessments are delicate instruments that require a great deal of piloting to fine tune them."[2] Because so many investigators are experimenting in uncharted testing and statistical territories, research support will be needed to encourage the collection of test data and the dissemination of results so that others can learn from data that are innovative, instructive, and yet costly to obtain.

---

[2]Richard J. Shavelson, "Authentic Assessment: The Rhetoric and the Reality," paper presented at a symposium at the annual meeting

would require extensive explanation no matter what it included.[68]

In light of these uncertainties about the relative costs of testing programs, some school systems are striving for improved definitions and better cost data. In California, for example:

The lead consortium is required to develop a cost-benefit analysis of existing vs. various types of alternative assessment for consideration by the California Department of Education and the State Board of Education. The cost-benefit analysis should consider payoffs, tradeoffs and advantages or disadvantages of alternative vs. existing assessment practices. The testing costs of alternative assessments, especially the staff development component, should be considered as a part of overall curriculum costs. Teachers' renewed motivation and commitment to the Curriculum Frameworks should be viewed as a major element in the cost-benefit analysis.[69]

Policy Implications

In considering the costs of performance assessment, policymakers may wish to adopt a more inclusive cost-benefit model than has typically been considered for testing. Benefits in the areas of curriculum development and teacher enhancement (staff training) may offset the higher costs associated with performance assessment. However, little data has been collected to date; a broader and deeper analysis will be required before judgments can be made.

---

[68]Mitchell and Stempel, op. cit., footnote 2, p. 11.

[69]California Department of Education, California Assessment Program, "Request for Applications for the Alternative Assessment Pilot Project," unpublished document, 1991.

Fairness

There has long been a concern about the effect of background factors such as prior experience, gender, culture, and ethnicity on test results. Achievement tests, for example, need to eliminate the effect of background factors if they are to measure learning that has resulted from instruction. A combination of statistical and intuitive procedures have been developed for conventional norm-referenced tests to eliminate or reduce background factors that can confound their results. Little is known, however, about how background factors may affect scores on performance assessments.

In addition, judgments about fairness will depend a great deal on the purposes of the test and the interpretations that will be made of the scores. For example, on a test that has no significant personal impact on a student, such as the National Assessment of Educational Progress, it is reasonable to include problems that require the use of calculators even though student access to calculators may be quite inequitable. On the other hand, equitable access would be an important consideration if the assessment were one that determined student selection, teacher promotions, or other high-stakes outcomes.[70]

Performance assessments could theoretically lead to narrowing the gap in test scores across those who have traditionally scored lower on standardized multiple-choice achievement tests. By sampling more broadly across skill domains and relying less heavily on the verbal skills central to existing paper-and-pencil tests, proponents hope that these differences might be minimized. Performance assessments, by providing multiple measures, may be able to give a better and therefore fairer picture of student performance.

On the other hand, performance assessments could exacerbate existing differences between groups of test takers from different backgrounds.

Some minority group advocates, for example, fear that tests are being changed just when students from racially diverse backgrounds are beginning to succeed on them. They worry that the rules are being changed just as those who have been most hurt by testing are beginning to learn how to play the game.

The President of the San Diego City Schools Board of Education voiced the apprehensions of the minority community:

> We have a long way to go to convince the public that what we're doing is in the best interests of children. . . . When we talk about the issue of equity, the kind of assessments we're talking about require much more faith in individuals and the belief that people can actually apply equity in testing. Most of the time with a normed test you think of something that has some subjectivity in the development of the instrument, but then in the final result you know what the answer is. When you start talking about some of the assessments we're doing—portfolios—it's all subjective.[71]

Research on the effects of ethnicity, race, and gender on performance assessment is extremely limited. Most existing research has explored group differences on essay test scores only. Moreover, almost all the subjects in this research were college-bound students, limiting its generalizability considerably. Results of studies that examine the performance of women relative to men suggest that women perform somewhat better on essays than they do on multiple-choice examinations.[72]

Studies that report results for different minority groups are even more scarce. Results are mixed but tend to suggest that differences on multiple-choice tests do not disappear when essays are used. For example, data from NAEP indicate that black/white differences on essays assessing writing were about the same size as those observed on primarily multiple-choice tests of reading comprehension.[73] Similarly, adding a performance section to the California Bar Examination in 1984 did not reduce

---

[70]Robert Linn, Eva Baker, and Stephen Dunbar, "Complex, Performance-Based Assessment: Expectations and Validation Criteria," *Educational Researcher*, in press.

[71]Shirley Weber, remarks at Panasonic Partnerships Conference, Santa Fe, NM, June 1990, cited in Mitchell and Stempel, op. cit., footnote 2, California Assessment Program Case Study, p. 15.

[72]H.M. Breland and P.A. Griswold, *Group Comparison for Basic Skills Measures* (New York, NY: College Entrance Examination Board, 1981); Cooper, op. cit., footnote 61; S.B. Dunbar, "Comparability of Indirect Assessment of Writing Skill as Predictors of Writing Performance Across Demographic Groups," unpublished manuscript, July 1991; Brent Bridgeman and Charles Lewis, "Predictive Validity of Advanced Placement Essay and Multiple Choice Examinations," paper presented at the annual meeting of the National Council on Measurement in Education, Chicago, IL, April 1991; and Traub and MacRury, op. cit., footnote 29.

[73]Cited in Linn et al., op. cit., footnote 70.

the difference in passing rates between blacks and whites. On the contrary, some studies have suggested that ethnic group differences actually increase with essay examinations.[74]

On the other hand, another study showed that minority college students in California actually performed better on tests that were direct measures of writing ability (the California State University and Colleges English Placement Test Essay Test or EPT) than on a multiple-choice test of English usage and sentence correction (the 50-question, multiple-choice formatted Test of Standard Written English or TSWE). In this study, score distributions on the TSWE and the EPT were similar for white students. Among African-American, Mexican-American, and Asian-American students, however, the two tests generated different score distributions. For these groups, the TSWE rendered a much more negative judgment of their English proficiency than the EPT.[75]

Policy Implications

Because of the limited research on the differing subgroup performance on new assessment instruments, Congress and other policymakers should approach these changes with caution. Data on the impacts of performance assessment on varying groups is needed in considering extension to more high-stakes applications. Careful planning, including representatives of groups traditionally negatively affected by testing, will be required in developing, administering, and scoring performance assessments for school accountability, student certification, or other selection purposes.

Role of Teachers and Teacher Training

In performance assessment, the role of the teacher in administering and scoring tests is much greater than with multiple-choice tests. Although some performance assessments still rely on outsiders to conduct the scoring of papers, in the future, classroom teachers are likely to have greater responsibility.

Although teachers observe performance all day, most have not been involved in defining and determining standards of performance common to those of their colleagues. In Sweden and several other countries a process called ''moderation'' refers to the development of a standardized scoring approach among multiple teacher readers. The procedure is similar to scoring of the Advanced Placement tests and other examinations relying on panels of scorers. It requires an intensive effort to agree on standards of performance. How does excellent work vary from that which is only fair or is not acceptable at all? This process is based on a shared understanding of curriculum, respect for teacher judgment, compromise, shared values, and a strong dose of common sense. This may be easier to manage in those countries where there is a common curriculum and a more homogeneous teaching population that has been prepared under a central system of teacher training institutions. It is not clear that this can be adopted in the U.S. system. One educator suggested: ''If we can trust our teachers to teach, we should be able to trust them to assess students.''[76]

Teachers in this country receive little formal training in assessment. A recent survey found that fewer than one-third of the States require new teachers to have demonstrated competence in educational measurement.[77] A survey of the six States in the Pacific Northwest reported that only Oregon explicitly requires assessment training for certification.[78]

One reason for the neglect of assessment training may be the assumption on the part of educators that the quality of assessments in the classroom is assured from outside the classroom; that is, most assessment is ''teacher proof,'' beyond the control of the teacher.[79] Textbooks come with their own

---

[74]Breland and Griswold, op. cit., footnote 72; Dunbar, op. cit., footnote 72; Ina Mullis, ''Use of Alternative Assessment in National Assessments: The American Experience,'' paper presented at the Office of Educational Research and Instruction conference on the Promise and Peril of Alternative Assessment, Washington, DC, Oct. 30, 1990.

[75]Edward M. White and Leon L. Thomas, ''Racial Minorities and Writing Skills Assessment in the California State University and Colleges,'' *College English*, vol. 43, No. 3, March 1981, pp. 276-283.

[76]Jack Webber, teacher, Samantha Smith Elementary School, Redmond, WA, personal communication, 1991.

[77]''Testing,'' *Education Week*, vol. 10, No. 27, Mar. 27, 1991, p. 9.

[78]Richard J. Stiggins, ''Teacher Training in Assessment: Overcoming the Neglect,'' *Teacher Training in Assessment*, vol. 7 in the Buros Nebraska Symposium in Measurement and Testing, Steven Wise (ed.) (New York, NY: L. Erlbaum Associates, in press).

[79]Ibid., p. 6.

worksheets and quizzes, unit tests, and even computerized test items, so teachers feel little responsibility for developing their own. Yet many of these text-embedded tests and quizzes are in fact developed in the absence of quality control standards. Furthermore, the tests that teachers know will be the ultimate judge of student proficiency are seen as beyond the teacher's responsibility. Finally, the courses on testing are often seen as irrelevant to the classroom.[80] There is very little treatment of assessment as a teaching tool. Teachers regularly use assessments to communicate achievement expectations to students, using assignments both as practice and as assessments of achievement, involving students in self and peer evaluation to take stock of their own learning with practice tests. This important area is neglected in teacher training.[81]

The inservice training situation is not much different.[82] However, if standard teacher courses in measurement are irrelevant, there is no reason to try to get more teacher candidates or practicing teachers to take them. On the other hand, if teachers are trained in new curriculum frameworks that have been the basis for much of the move to performance assessment, the techniques of teaching and assessing should be taught as a whole. This is the approach being taken in California, Arizona, and Vermont, and envisioned for Kentucky.

Technology can be a means to fast and efficient delivery of teacher training, as in Kentucky, where the educational television network provides satellite downlinks to every school in the State, making it possible to get the word out to all teachers simultaneously. And, if administrators are to understand the role of assessment in curricular change, and be able to communicate with the public about school attainment of intended outcomes, they too need training in changing methods and goals of classroom and large-scale assessment.

Policy Implications

If performance assessment is given a larger role in testing programs around the country, **teachers will need to be involved in all aspects: designing tasks, administering and scoring tests, and placing test results into context.** Teacher training will need to accompany these efforts. Redesigning the tests will not change teaching unless teachers are informed and involved in the process. The tests themselves could block educational progress unless classroom teachers are given a larger sense of responsibility for them.

Research and Development: Sharing Experience and Research

Performance assessment has been spurred primarily by State Departments of Education as they endeavor to develop tests that better reflect their particular curricular goals. Yet there are many common goals and concerns that have led them to come together to share experience with each other. In an effort to encourage the development of alternative methods of assessment, the U.S. Department of Education has supported the development of a State Alternative Assessment Exchange. The goal is to create a database of new forms of assessment, develop guidelines for evaluating new measures, and help prevent States from making costly mistakes. This collaborative effort, led by the Department's Center for Research on Evaluation, Standards, and Student Testing (CRESST) and the Council of Chief State School Officers, is aimed at facilitating development work, not at creating a new test.

The National Science Foundation (NSF) has also played an important role in supporting research leading to new approaches to assessment in mathematics and the sciences. NSF supported NAEP in the development and pilot testing of hands-on assessment tasks in mathematics and science. Several of these tasks were adopted by the State of New York for their hands-on science skills test for fourth graders. More recently, NSF has committed $6 million for 3 years to support projects in alternative assessment approaches in mathematics and science.

---

[80]Ibid.

[81]Ibid., p. 8.

[82]There are some exceptions, however. For example, the Northwest Regional Educational Laboratory has created a video-based training program that places critical assessment competencies within reach of all teachers and administrators. They have also created ''trainer-of-trainer'' institutes that will make it possible for attendees to present to teachers and others a series of workshops on such topics as understanding the meaning and importance of high-quality classroom assessment; assessing writing proficiency, reading proficiency, and higher order thinking in the classroom; developing sound grading practices; understanding standardized tests; and designing paper-and-pencil assessments and assessments based on observation and judgment. Northwest Regional Educational Laboratory, *The Northwest Report* (Portland, OR: October 1990).

Assessment research remains a small part of the overall Department of Education research budget.

Greater effort should be directed toward monitoring the development of performance assessment and sharing information about models and techniques to facilitate implementation, prevent duplication of effort, and foster collaboration.[83]

Policy Implications

Because performance assessment is at a developmental stage, encouraging States and districts to pool experience and resources is an appropriate policy goal. Expanding research and comparing results requires a thoughtful atmosphere and adequate time. Although States are making progress in redesigning testing to serve educational goals, pressures for quick implementation of low-cost tests could present a barrier to this goal. Commitment to research projects and careful weighing of outcomes is essential to an improved testing environment.

Public Acceptance

One of the greatest problems with tests is the misuse of data derived from them. There is no reason to believe this would not also be true with performance assessment.

Because performance assessments aim to provide multiple measures of achievement, it may be difficult for parents, politicians, and school officials to understand its implications. The public has grown familiar with test results that rank and compare students and schools; it may be difficult to appreciate the information derived from tests that do not follow this model. Some attempts are being implemented to improve public understanding of the goals and products of performance assessment, through such vehicles as public meetings. But it is not easy. The press may be among the most difficult audiences to educate, since simple measures and statistics, ranking and ordering, and comparing and listing winners and losers makes news. Nevertheless, they may be the most important audience, since so much of the public's awareness of testing comes from press reports.

Policy Implications

Policymakers need to carefully consider the importance of keeping the public and press aware of the goals behind changing testing procedures and formats and the results that accrue from these tests. If not, there is a strong likelihood of misunderstanding and impatience that could affect the ability to proceed with long-term goals.

A Final Note

Writing assessment is up and running in many States. Although careful development is needed and issues of bias and fairness need attention, this technology is now workable for all three major testing functions.

Other methods of performance assessment (e.g., portfolios, exhibitions, experiments, and oral interviews) still represent relatively uncharted areas. Most educators who have worked with these techniques are optimistic about the potential they offer for at least two functions—testing in the classroom for monitoring and diagnosing student progress, and system monitoring through sampling. However, much research is needed before performance tasks can be used for high-stakes applications where students are selected for programs or opportunities, certified for competence, and placed in programs that may affect their educational or economic futures. Some of this research is now under way for tests used for professional certification (see ch. 8), but much more research support is needed for understanding the implications in elementary and secondary schooling. Finally, even the most enthusiastic advocates of performance assessment recognize the importance of policies to guard against inappropriate uses. Without safeguards, any form of testing can be misused; if this were to happen with performance assessment, it could doom a promising educational innovation.

---

[83]Joe B. Hansen and Walter E. Hathaway, ''A Survey of More Authentic Assessment Practices,'' paper presented at the National Council for Measurement in Education/National Association of Test Developers symposium, More Authentic Assessment: Theory and Practice, Chicago, IL, Apr. 4, 1991.

Information Technologies and Testing: Past, Present, Future

Contents

Boxes

Figures

Information Technologies and Testing: Past, Present, Future

Highlights

- Information and data processing technologies have played a critical role in making existing modes of testing more efficient. The combination of the multiple-choice item format and machine scoring technologies has made it possible for massive numbers of students to be tested all through their educational careers.
- By and large, computers and other information technologies have not been applied toward fundamentally new ways of testing. However, advances in computers, video, and related technologies could one day revolutionize testing.
- Computer-based testing and computer-adaptive testing can have several advantages over conventional paper-and-pencil tests. They are quicker to take and score, provide faster feedback, and reduce errors due to human scoring and administration. Some computerized tests can hone in on students' achievement levels much more quickly and accurately than conventional tests.
- Cutting-edge technology could push tests well beyond the existing paper-and-pencil formats. Structuring and presenting complex tasks, tracking student cognitive processes, and providing rapid feedback to learners and teachers are promising avenues for continued research and development.
- Computerized testing also has drawbacks. It may introduce new types of measurement errors, place students who lack familiarity with computers at a disadvantage, make it harder for students to skip or review questions, raise new privacy issues, and create questions of comparability when students take essentially ''personalized'' tests.
- Realizing the full potential of new testing technologies will require continued research, and better coordinated research, in the fields of learning theory, computer science, and test design.

Information and data processing technologies have had a powerful influence on educational testing. The invention of the multiple-choice item format, coupled with advances in machine scoring, made possible the efficient testing of millions of children at all stages of their education. But these efficiency attributes of machine-based scoring and reporting also raised serious concerns: from the earliest days of application of these technologies, critics lamented the loss of richness in detail that had been a feature of open-ended questions scored by human judges, and contended that machine-scored tests encouraged memorization of unrelated facts, guessing, and other distortions in teaching and learning.

Multiple-choice items and machine scoring of tests brought a revolution in student assessment. And, not surprisingly, once the technology became an entrenched feature of school life, there began a 70-year period of gradual evolution: as information and data processing technologies become more powerful and sophisticated, they continued to influence educational testing, but the applications have principally improved automation of the basic test designs initiated at the turn of the century. There has been relatively little exploration of how the technology might open altogether new approaches to student assessment. Today, however, some experts believe a new revolution is in the making: they contend that the increasing power and flexibility of personal computers, video, and telecommunications could move testing well beyond what paper-and-pencil testing can accomplish.

The purpose of this chapter is to examine the state of the art of information technologies in testing, consider policy initiatives that could foster better uses of current technology, and explore the possibilities for wholly new paradigms of student assessment. The chapter is divided into four sections. The first provides a brief historical synopsis of technology in testing, focusing on the combined effects of multiple-choice and electromechanical scoring.

The second section is concerned with applications of computers and video-related technologies to conventional models of educational assessment. It addresses issues such as test design and construction, scoring and analysis of test results, item banking, computer-adaptive testing, and new video and multimedia applications.

The third section of the chapter describes the gap between current and future models of testing, and explores ways in which computers or other technologies could advance the development and implementation of new models.

Finally, the fourth section examines key policy issues in developing new models of testing.

Historical Synopsis

Multiple choice made its debut in 1915 with the Kansas Silent Reading Test, produced by Frederick Kelly at the State Normal School in Emporia. With modifications by psychologist Arthur Otis, multiple choice ''. . . soon found its way . . . from reading tests to intelligence tests,'' and made possible the administration of the Army Alpha and Beta tests to millions of draftees during the First World War.[1] Clerks scored each test by hand, using stencils superimposed on answer sheets. This new method of testing transformed Alfred Binet's individually administered test format (called by some authors the ''methode de luxe''[2]) into a format amenable to group administration and the development of group norms. According to one chronicle of this technological change:

. . . the multiple choice question [was] . . . an invention ingenious in its simplicity . . . [an] indispensable vehicle for the dramatic growth of mass testing in this country in the span of a few years. It had not existed before 1914; by 1921 it had spawned a dozen group intelligence tests and provided close to two million soldiers and over three million schoolchildren with a numerical index of their intelligence; it was also about to transform achievement testing in the classroom.[3]

It was the Iowa testing program, under the leadership of E.F. Lindquist, that was instrumental in turning the twin concepts of group testing and the multiple-choice item format into a streamlined process for achievement testing of masses of school children.[4] Lindquist took the first hand-scored tests and designed a scoring key that could be cut into strips, each strip fitting a test page, with the answers positioned on the key to match the pupil's responses on the page. Later, Lindquist pursued his dream of mechanical, and later electronic, scoring. IBM's prototype photoelectric machine encouraged Lindquist, who built his own analog computer in the 1940s. During the 1950s, he embarked with Professor Phillip Rulon of Harvard in an effort to design an electronic scoring machine. Their basic innovation has since become a staple of the testing industry:

. . . a specially designed answer sheet would pass under a row of photo tubes in such a manner that each photo tube would sense a mark in one of the boxes on the answer sheet when illuminated by a light source, and the pulses from this sensing would trigger a counter cumulating a total raw score for each test on the answer sheet; the raw score would be converted to a standard score in a converter unit; the standard score would be recorded by an output printer geared to the scoring device.[5]

The first ''Iowa machine'' went into production in 1955, and cost close to $200,000 (nearly three times more than planned).[6] Continuing refinements through 1957 led Lindquist to boast that the machine was living up to virtually all expectations. It could now, in a single reading of an answer sheet, obtain up to 14 separate raw scores; convert these into 20 different standard scores, percentile ranks, or converted totals of the converted scores; obtain simultaneously as many totals and/or subtotals as the desired combinations of counters would permit; print and punch scores simultaneously; print or punch both names and scores simultaneously; and

---

[1]Franz Samelson, ''Was Early Mental Testing (a) Racist Inspired, (b) Objective Science, (c) A Technology for Democracy, (d) The Origin of Multiple Choice Exams, (e) None of the Above? Mark the RIGHT Answer,'' *Psychological Testing and American Society, 1890-1930*, M. Sokal (ed.) (New Brunswick, NJ: Rutgers University Press, 1987), pp. 113-127. See also ch. 3 of this report for discussion, and ch. 1 for a reproduction of the cover of the 1915 Kansas test.

[2]Rudolf Pintner, cited in Samelson, op. cit., footnote 1, p. 116.

[3]Samelson, op. cit., footnote 1.

[4]For a comprehensive discussion of the history of the Iowa program, see Julia J. Peterson, *The Iowa Testing Program* (Iowa City, IA: University of Iowa Press, 1983.) For discussion of the principal roles of Lewis Terman, Edward Thorndike, Robert Yerkes, and others in the birth of the group-administered intelligence and achievement testing movement, see, e.g., Paul Chapman, *Schools as Sorters: Lewis M. Terman, Applied Psychology, and the Intelligence Testing Movement, 1890-1930* (New York, NY: New York University Press, 1988); also see ch. 3 of this report.

[5]Peterson, op. cit., footnote 4, p. 91.

[6]Ibid., p. 89.

do a number of "interesting tricks" it was not originally intended to do.

A new era of testing in American schools had dawned. Here is how one test publisher, whose experiences date from the earliest days of this new era, describes the transition:

> . . . [before machine scoring] most standardized tests were hand-scored by the teachers. . . . Under that system, tests corrected and scored by the teacher provided opportunity for careful pupil analysis by the teachers. In turn that analysis, pupil by pupil and class by class, provided meaningful measures for individualizing pupil instruction, improving instruction, reassessing the curriculum, and making appropriate textbook selections. Furthermore, and by no means should this be overlooked, it gave the teacher support beyond his or her undocumented human judgment of pupils that by no means goes unchallenged by many parents and, for that matter, pupils. As the machine-scoring movement grew, the activities related to testing changed. Certainly, the scoring activity left the classroom and often as not the school system itself. Test results moved increasingly into the hands of the administrative staff. Test specialists were employed who were interested in an ever broader array of derived scores to be used for many purposes . . . the hands-on dimension for teachers receded and in due course disappeared almost entirely.[7]

Current Applications of Computers in Testing[8]

Design and Construction of Tests

Item Writing

Computers have many capabilities that can aid test publishers in the efficient design and construction of standardized tests. In addition, basic word processing, graphics, and spreadsheet programs make it possible for State and district school personnel, as well as individual teachers, to create their own items or to edit items developed by others. Editing the text of test items, selecting specific items from a collection stored in memory, and sequencing the test items are all substantially easier with basic desktop computers and generic tool software.

Increasingly, however, dedicated item writing and test construction packages have become available. These go beyond the capacity of generic word processing software and are intended specifically for writing tests. For example, they can contain item templates and special notations such as mathematical symbols not usually available with commercial word processing software. Once the test is created on the computer, it can then be printed out, reproduced, and administered to students who fill in the responses in the traditional paper-and-pencil format.

Using computers to construct items is not a new concept. Researchers in the 1960s had attempted to develop software to facilitate the construction of sentence completion and spelling items, but the software was not adopted by test constructors.[9] This is explained in part by the feeling among some experts that item writing for educational and psychological testing is more art than science, and that computer technology routinizes what ought to be a more fluid and creative process. Most item-writing efforts for standardized achievement tests involve an interplay between content specialists (teachers in the content areas) and psychometric experts who identify item-writing flaws and examine the match between items and objectives of the test.[10]

Item Banking

Increases in computer memory capacity have made "item banks" an important enhancement in test construction. Large collections of test items are organized, classified, and stored by their content and/or their statistical properties, allowing test developers or teachers to create customized tests. Item banks in use today consist almost exclusively of multiple-choice or true-false questions, although there is some research under way on the use of CD-ROM technology to store longer open-ended items.[11]

---

[7]Harold Miller, former Chairman of the Board, Houghton Mifflin Co., Inc., personal communication, Dec. 14, 1990.

[8]This section draws on C.V. Bunderson, J.B. Olsen, and A. Greenberg, "Computers in Educational Assessment," OTA contractor report, December 1990.

[9]Tse-chi Hsu and Shula F. Sadock, *Computer Assisted Test Construction: The State of the Art* (Washington, DC: ERIC Clearinghouse on Tests, Measurement, and Evaluation, American Institutes for Research, November 1985), p. 5.

[10]Gale H. Roid, "Item Writing and Item Banking by Microcomputer: An Update," *Educational Measurement Issues and Practice,* vol. 8, No. 3, fall 1989, p. 18.

[11]See, e.g., Judah Schwartz and Katherine A. Viator (eds.), *The Price of Secrecy: The Social, Intellectual, and Psychological Costs of Current Assessment Practice: A Report to the Ford Foundation* (Cambridge, MA: Harvard Graduate School of Education, September 1990).

A variant on the item-bank concept is one in which testing *objectives* are stored in the form of algorithms that can be used to create individual test items. The algorithm draws on stored data to produce a vast number of variations on an objective. Instructors choose the objective and specify the number of different problems, and the computer provides the appropriate test items (see figure 8-1). One item bank currently on the market covers mathematics objectives, from basic mathematics through calculus.[12] If the teacher wishes to test a student on adding two two-digit numbers, the objective is represented as $A + B$, where A and B are whole numbers greater than 9 and less than 100. The computer would then insert random numbers for A and B, so that literally thousands of different items sharing a similar measurement function can be produced. The system can be customized to meet the objectives of States, districts, or even specific textbook or curriculum objectives.

Constructing standardized tests to meet the elaborate and detailed test specifications of school districts and States is a complex and time-consuming task. Computers can help speed and streamline this task by selecting test questions for use in a test form to match detailed statistical and content specifications. After the computer selects test questions for the first draft of a test form, these items can be reviewed by test development staff, and possibly field tested.[13] Computing power greatly speeds up this process and makes it possible for States and local education authorities to create their own standardized tests as well as varying forms of the same test for multiple administrations.

Among the many applications of the item-bank concept, a large-scale effort begun in West Virginia in 1988 offers some useful lessons.[14] As part of a larger effort to restructure financing in the State and to assess learning outcomes for students, the State purchased 1,200 copies of the testing software, one for every school in the State. Reflecting a bottom-up strategy, the system allows teachers to select items, construct their own tests, print them out, copy them, and administer them in the traditional paper-and-

Figure 8-1—Three Questions Created by One Algorithm

1. What fraction of this figure is shaded?

A. 5/7   B. 5/12

C. 7/12   D. 5

2. What fraction of this figure is shaded?

A. 3/10   B. 3

C. 3/7   D. 7/10

3. What fraction of this figure is shaded?

A. 2/3   B. 3

C. 1/3   D. 1/2

SOURCE: ips Publishing, *Exam in a Can* (brochure) (West Lake Village, CA: 1990).

pencil format. Score results can be analyzed and student progress tracked through the use of instructional management software. A pilot test of the system highlighted the fact that teachers needed training on how to use the hardware and software and that the existing infrastructure of computers for teachers was inadequate. Among the benefits noted were the ease in generating tests for many uses and the advantages of relieving teachers of some of the "busy work" of test construction and administration.

The West Virginia system deals with traditional subject areas. Note, however, that in its request for proposals for a computer system, the State sought a system capable of storing item types other than multiple choice and true-false, with software available in both IBM and Apple formats.

[12]ips Publishing, *Exam in a Can* (computer software) (Westlake Village, CA: 1990).

[13]Mark D. Reckase, director, Development Division, Assessment Innovations, American College Testing Program, personal communication, September 1991. See also Dato N.M. de Gruijter, "Test Construction by Means of Linear Programming," *Applied Psychological Measurement*, vol. 14, No. 2, 1990, pp. 175-182; and Ellen Beokkooi-Timminga, "The Construction of Parallel Tests From IRT-Based Item Banks," *Journal of Educational Statistics*, vol. 15, No. 2, 1990, pp. 129-145.

[14]John A. Willis, "Learning Outcome Testing Program: Standardized Classroom Testing in West Virginia Through Item Banking, Test Generation, and Curricular Management Software," *Educational Measurement: Issues and Practice*, vol. 9, No. 2, summer 1990, pp. 11-14.

Scoring, Reporting, and Analyzing Test Results

Computers are now vital to large-scale testing programs. They allow for fast and efficient scanning and processing of answer sheets, computation of individual and group scores and subscores, and storage of score data for later analysis. Item analysis and item-response theory statistics can be calculated across large numbers of test takers, and the item and test statistic files can be automatically updated using only a few simple commands. Archival copies of test scores can also be easily made. Computers provide a wide range of individual and group reports that can be printed from the resulting test scores and profiles. Computerized interpretative reports are also prepared for an increasing number of educational and psychological tests.

Large mainframes or computers are used to process and analyze test data and to prepare printed reports for individual students or groups of students. These mainframes and computers are typically located at centralized test development, publication, and scoring service centers run by test publishers.

Taking Tests on the Computer

In addition to their role as workhorses to aid in test construction, recordkeeping, and analysis and reporting of results, computers can also be the medium on which tests are administered. This report defines computer-based testing (CBT) as applications in which students respond to questions directly on the computer, via keyboard, keypad, mouse, or other data-entry device. Test booklets, fill-in-the-bubble answer sheets, and other traditional paper-and-pencil testing techniques are not used.[15]

Classroom Testing With Networks and Integrated Learning Systems

Much of the available computer software designed for instruction includes questions throughout the program designed to check on a student's understanding of the material. Responses can be printed out for the teacher to gauge student progress and identify problem areas. Many schools have linked the computers they have in laboratories and

Photo credit: Courtesy of National Computer Systems, Inc.

Using machines like the National Computer Systems' Opscan 21, 10,000 tests can be scored in 1 hour.

classrooms; networks generally consist of 15 to 25 computers linked through a central file server. With these local area networks (LANs), the same software can be shared among many computers, easing the logistics of administration for the teacher. Through computers connected by a networked system, programs and data can be shared and then sent to common peripheral devices such as a printer, hard disk, or videodisc. Each computer on the LAN can operate independently, using different pieces of software for each student, or share software among several or all students, enhancing the teacher's ability to manage and individualize instruction and testing for each child.[16]

One of the greatest selling points of networks is the added tracking and reporting capabilities that become possible when all student data are stored on a single storage device such as a hard disk. Stand-alone computers with individual floppy disks do not have sufficient storage capacity for all of the student records in a class or school. In contrast, networked systems make it possible to collect extended reports on student progress. In large part because of the appeal of these assessment features, the number of districts with network installations has grown steadily over the past 3 years, from just over 1,500 in 1988-89 to over 2,800 in 1990-91.[17]

---

[15]Paper and pencils may be used as backup tools, such as scratch pads or worksheets, but they are not the form of entry of final answers to test questions.

[16]For further discussion of how school computers can be networked, see, e.g., U.S. Congress, Office of Technology Assessment, *Power On! New Tools for Teaching and Learning*, OTA-SET-379 (Washington, DC: U.S. Government Printing Office, September 1988).

[17]Quality Education Data, ''Technology in Schools: 1990-91 School Year,'' *Market Intelligence* (Denver, CO: 1991), p. T-7.

Photo credit: Steve Woit

Computers are a key feature at the Saturn School of Tomorrow. A Mac Lab is available at all times for students to do word processing and publishing.

Photo credit: Steve Woit

At the Saturn School of Tomorrow, students work independently on integrated learning systems.

Integrated learning systems (ILSs) are LANS with a comprehensive instructional management system. Courseware is typically published and sold by the ILS vendor, and spans part or all of a curriculum (e.g., K-6 language arts). It is possible to add additional software in some ILSs. As in other networked systems, instruction is controlled and managed through the central computer, which may be connected to printers, modems, videodiscs, or other peripheral devices.

Because of their close linkages between instruction and testing, both of which can be matched to district curricula, ILSs have become increasingly popular. Although fewer schools have ILSs than networks, their number has been growing rapidly (from about 3,300 in 1989-90 to almost 7,000 in 1990-91).[18] The vast majority of ILS use is at the elementary level, with more than 80 percent of ILS usage in reading/language arts and mathematics.[19]

With an ILS testing is an integral part of instruction. The testing part of the system highlights what to teach, and the instructional part is designed for easy assessment of student performance. Some critics fear this focus on test-based skills reinforces a linear and limited approach to learning. Others,

however, suggest it could help bridge assessment and instruction. The importance of networks/ILSs is heightened by the fact that continued demand for these technologies could create opportunities for testing-software developers to collaborate with suppliers of these products.

ILS vendors include Computer Curriculum Corp., Education Systems Corp., ICON, PLATO, Wasatch, WICAT, and the Jostens Learning Corp. For example, Jostens' Instructional Management System is intended to allow teachers to deliver a customized sequence of lessons to each student; direct and monitor student progress; adopt the sequence of the embedded curricula and prescribe lessons from third-party materials; branch students to appropriate remedial or enrichment activities; generate criterion-referenced pre- and post-tests; create, maintain, and update instructional records on each student; and electronically transfer records within and between schools.

Although networks and ILSs offer a promising way to bring computerized testing into the schools, their focus is primarily on classroom instruction. The growth in the installed base of networks and ILSs in schools suggests the potential for their expanded application in testing. It is important to note that these centralized systems place software and test items under the control of one person (usually the teacher).

---

[18]Ibid., p. T-4.

[19]Charles L. Blaschke, ''Integrated Learning Systems/Instructional Networks: Current Uses and Trends,'' *Educational Technology*, vol. 30, No. 11, November 1990, p. 21.

Computers and Testing: Beyond the Classroom

Computer-based testing is not commonly used for system monitoring or student selection, placement, and certification in elementary and secondary schools. Few schools have enough computers to implement a large-scale testing program via computer.[20] Even where adequate hardware exists, the demand for computerized standardized tests has, in the past, been low. Today's standardized paper-and-pencil tests are a well-entrenched technology and practice. Students, teachers, and the public are familiar with test books and "bubble" answer sheets and the technology is easy to use, score, and administer. There is also a well-developed and longstanding support system underpinning this type of testing.

In their most basic form, CBT takes existing paper-and-pencil tests and administers them on a computer: test items, format, and procedures remain the same as for paper-and-pencil, and the computer's role is that of an "automated answer sheet."[21] Computers offer capabilities that make even these limited applications more flexible, powerful, and efficient.

Tests other than those of academic achievement have also become the subject of research in CBT. Examples are various psychological tests and tests used for admissions, placement, and certification at the postsecondary level. The Educational Testing Service (ETS) has been pilot testing computer-based versions of the Graduate Record Examination (GRE); both ETS and the American College Testing Program (ACT) have developed computer testing packages for college placement testing and are currently conducting research to verify comparability of scores from the computerized and paper-and-pencil tests. Finally, there is growing interest in the use of computerized tests for professional certification, in the military, and in industry for selection and placement purposes.

To date, research on comparability between computer-based and conventional paper-and-pencil tests has had mixed results. Most studies have found that students score slightly, but not significantly, higher on paper-and-pencil tests than on computer-based tests. Although it was hypothesized that computer inexperience and computer anxiety might exacerbate score differences between testing models, this has not been found to be significant. It has been suggested, however, that earlier forms of CBT, which did not allow examinees to skip items and go back and answer them later in the test, or to review and change responses of items already answered, may have accounted for lower scores on computer-based tests.[22] Because of this concern, the American Psychological Association *Guidelines* recommends that test publishers perform separate equating and/or norming studies when computer-based versions of standardized tests are introduced.[23] It should be noted that current forms of CBT usually allow students to skip items, return to them later, and change their answers just as they would in a paper-and-pencil test.

Computerized Adaptive Testing

An innovation in testing that applies the computer's rapid processing capability to an advanced statistical model is called "computerized adaptive testing" or CAT. In conventional testing all examinees receive the same set of questions, usually in the same order. But with CAT the computer chooses items to administer to a given examinee based on that examinee's responses to previous test items. Thus, not all examinees receive the same set of test items.[24]

The advent of "item-response theory" in the 1960s led to the realization that relative performance of students could be assessed more efficiently if test items were selected and sequenced with specific reference to individual student ability. Instead of presenting a broad range of items to all students, some of which are too difficult and some too easy, item-response theory allows the range of difficulty

[20]James B. Olsen, Apryl Cox, Charles Price, Mike Strozeski, and Idolina Vela, "Development, Implementation, and Validation of a Computerized Test for Statewide Assessment," *Educational Measurement: Issues and Practice*, vol. 9, No. 2, summer 1990.

[21]Isaac I. Bejar, "Speculations on the Future of Test Design," *Test Design: Developments in Psychology and Psychometrics*, S.E. Embretson (ed.) (Orlando, FL: Academic Press, 1985), p. 280.

[22]Steven L. Wise and Barbara S. Plake, "Research on the Effects of Administering Tests Via Computers," *Educational Measurement: Issues and Practice*, vol. 8, No. 3, fall 1989, p. 7.

[23]Ibid.

[24]Ibid., p. 5.

of items to be determined by the test-taker's responses to previous items:

> Adaptive testing . . . seeks to present only items that are appropriate for the test taker's estimated level of skill or ability. Questions that are too easy or too difficult for the candidate contribute very little information about that person's ability. More specifically, each person's first item on an adaptive test generally has about medium difficulty for the total population. Those who answer correctly get a harder item; those who answer incorrectly get an easier item. After each response, the examinee's ability is estimated, along with an indication of the accuracy of the estimate. The next item to be posed is one that will be especially informative for a person of the estimated ability, which generally means that harder questions are posed after correct answers and easier questions after incorrect answers. The change in item difficulty from step to step is usually large early in the sequence, but becomes smaller as more is learned about the candidate's ability. The process continues until there is enough information to place the person on the ability scale with a specified level of accuracy, or until some more pragmatic criterion is achieved.[25]

The concept of adaptive testing is not new; most individually administered tests have some adaptive features, and in some group testing in a paper-and-pencil format there may be a form of pretest to determine student ability and to narrow the range of items presented on the main test. However, the enormous superiority of the computer in terms of storage capacity and processing speed has made adaptive testing much more efficient.

Computerized adaptive tests can be used for instructional feedback, system monitoring, or selection, placement, and certification functions. One example is the College Board Computerized Placement Tests, developed jointly by the College Entrance Examination Board and ETS, for use by 2- and 4-year colleges to assess the readiness of entering students for college-level work in English, reading, and mathematics, and to determine their need for additional preparatory courses. These tests have been used since the mid-1980s at approximately 80 colleges across the United States.[26]

The Portland (Oregon) school district has developed a CAT system linked to its districtwide testing program. The Portland Achievement Level Testing (PALT) program, a combined norm-referenced and criterion-referenced test battery developed by the district, has been the district's principal evaluation instrument since 1977. It has been expanded and refined regularly to keep up with changes in curricula and instructional priorities. All students in grades three to eight take the PALT paper-and-pencil tests in reading and mathematics twice yearly; eighth graders are expected to meet the district's minimum competency levels, and if they fail they must repeat the test periodically through high school in order to graduate with a standard diploma. Roughly 40,000 students (out of a total K-12 enrollment of 55,000) are tested twice yearly.

The CAT version of the test, known as Computerized Adaptive Reporting and Testing (CARAT), was initially developed over the 5-year period 1984 to 1989 with annual support from the Portland School Board of $250,000 or more. It is expected to be implemented districtwide by 1992 under a 3-year $1 million grant from the school board. It is available for students to work on any time during the year.

CARAT consists of items drawn from the PALT item banks. CARAT tests can count for placement in special programs (talented and gifted, or Chapter 1). However, at present students must take the paper-and-pencil test on its electronic equivalent—not the adaptive version—in order to be certified for graduation.

CARAT began on a pilot basis in six schools in 1985-86, and has since been implemented in all Chapter 1 schools in the district. Computer adaptive tests have been used for more than 5,000 students for Chapter 1 evaluation and for assessing competency in mathematics and reading, grades three through eight, since the program was begun.

District officials hope to have CARAT installed in every school by the 1992-93 school year, and eventually to shift the entire testing program to CARAT. They believe that CARAT:

- makes it possible to test students as soon as they enter the district, in order to place them in appropriate instructional programs;

[25]Bert F. Green, R. Darrell Bock, Lloyd G. Humphreys, Robert L. Linn, and Mark D. Reckase, ''Technical Guidelines for Assessing Computerized Adaptive Tests,'' *Journal of Educational Measurement*, vol. 21, No. 4, winter 1984, pp. 347-348.

[26]Bunderson et al., op. cit., footnote 8, p. 22.

- makes possible more continuous assessment of student progress during the school year than would be possible from the fall and spring testing alone;
- is available at all times, providing access to students alone or in groups at any time and at any site;
- provides ready access to longitudinal test data on any designated group of students in the school;
- allows for the shortest possible tests (a CARAT test takes about 20 minutes) with known measurement properties; and
- offers enhanced test security, since students rarely get the same questions and since test questions can be changed regularly.[27]

The Northwest Evaluation Association has marketed the Portland adaptive testing system, including the item banks and computerized software, to other districts in Oregon, at a cost of approximately $16,000. Currently about 15 districts, including some other large systems, use PALT-based paper-and-pencil tests and CAT.

Computerized Mastery Testing

One application of CAT, known as computerized mastery tests, includes cut scores (the decision point separating masters from nonmasters) to assess whether the test taker has achieved ''mastery'' in a field.[28] Students pass or fail the test depending on how many items they answer correctly. If the responses do not provide a clear enough picture, additional items of similar difficulty are presented until mastery is determined. These tests typically require only one-half of the questions administered in the conventional paper-and-pencil format to reach the same reliability levels. Reliability is high around the cut score. As in the case of Portland, computerized mastery testing can be used for minimum competency testing.

Occupational competency testing has also been a target of new technological applications. Although assessments such as the one designed for the National Board of Medical Examiners (see box 8-A) serve quite different functions than tests in the elementary and secondary school years, they offer some important lessons for the capability of computers and simulation software. (See also below, under ''New Models of Assessment and the Role of Technology.'')

Taking Tests on the Computer: Pros and Cons

Computer-based testing can improve the efficiency of standardized test administration and provide administrative benefits when compared to standardized paper-and-pencil testing. But like any new technology, benefits need to be weighed against potential drawbacks.

Advantages of CBT

Because questions are presented together with the response format (as opposed to a separate answer sheet), *it is faster to take a computer-administered test.* One study showed that CBTs and CATs are between 25 and 75 percent faster than paper-and-pencil tests in producing otherwise comparable results (see figure 8-2).[29]

A greater variety of questions can be included in the test-builder's tool kit.[30] Constructed response items and short answers involving words, phrases, or procedures can also be scored relatively easily by matching them to the correct answer (or answers) stored in the computer. Voice synthesizers can be used for spelling or foreign language examinations. Computer graphics and video can make possible other novel item types or simulations.

Computers allow new possibilities for items that require visualization of motion or complex interdependencies. For example, a conventional physics examination might require long and complex syntax or a series of static diagrams to depict motion. On a computerized test, motion can be more simply and clearly depicted using either a high-resolution graphic or video display. A computerized version of the item gives a purer measure of the examinee's understand-

---

[27]District officials note, however, that Computerized Adaptive Reporting and Testing test items can appear on the paper-and-pencil version of the test that counts. The extent of overlap, which could affect test validity, has not been measured.

[28]David J. Weiss and G. Gage Kingsbury, ''Applications of Computerized Adaptive Testing to Educational Problems,'' *Journal of Educational Measurement*, vol. 21, winter 1984, pp. 361-375.

[29]James B. Olsen, ''The Four Generations of Computerized Testing: Toward Increased Use of AI and Expert Systems,'' *Educational Technology*, vol. 30, No. 3, March 1990, p. 37.

[30]Howard Wainer, ''On Item Response Theory and Computerized Adaptive Tests,'' *The Journal of College Admissions*, vol. 27, No. 4, April 1983, p. 15.

Box 8-A—Certification Via Computer Simulations:
The National Board of Medical Examiners

A 65-year-old man arrives at the Emergency Department of a major teaching hospital, complaining of respiratory distress and sharp chest pains. He appears to be in acute distress, moaning and holding his hands over the left side of his chest. The emergency medical technician who brought the patient in says he has a history of asthma and emphysema. You are a medical student, and must diagnose and treat the patient. The entire spectrum of modern medicine is at your fingertips, but time is of the essence in this potentially life-threatening condition of respiratory or cardiovascular distress. What do you do?[1]

This is an example of 1 of 25 patient simulations in a Computer Based Exam (CBX) that has, since 1988, been used at 75 medical schools in the United States and Canada. The ultimate objective for these simulations is use in the certification examination of the National Board of Medical Examiners (NBME), required of physicians in training before they can become licensed.

Medical schools have long been concerned that the examinations used to test students are heavy on the recall of factual information, but may not adequately test other important indicators of a candidate's readiness to practice medicine. One of these characteristics is the ability to employ the skills needed in clinical care—evaluating patient symptoms, conducting the appropriate procedures, ordering and evaluating tests, bringing in other experts for consultation—in order to accurately and quickly diagnose patient problems and diseases. In the NBME's CBX, the examinee is provided a simulated clinical environment in which cases are presented for actual patient management. Through a blank entry screen that automatically processes free-text orders, the examiner can request more than 8,500 terms representing over 2,300 diagnostic studies, procedures, medications, and consultants, and can move the patient among the available health care facilities. As the examinee proceeds, the computer records the timing of all actions taken. These actions are compared with a codified description of optimal management based on the judgments of expert doctors, and scoring is based on how well the examinee follows appropriate practice.

An examinee's management of the case presented above might proceed as follows (see figure 8-A1):

The results suggest a diagnosis of spontaneous pneumothorax (a collapsed lung), a possibly life-threatening disease process. The patient's low blood pressure suggests some degree of cardiovascular difficulty, indicating immediate decompression of the patient's left hemithorax (one-half of the patient's chest cavity). Pressing F1 allows a review of tests on order. It is currently 16:03; the chest x-ray result will not be available until 16:20 and the examinee must decide whether to treat the patient now or wait until x-ray results are available. She decides to perform an immediate needle thoracostomy (insertion of a needle into the chest cavity to evacuate the air) and the computer simulates the process and results:

The rush of air confirms the diagnosis, but suddenly another message appears on the screen: "Nurses Note: The patient's pain is more severe." More action is required. The examinee orders placement of a chest tube; once the patient is stabilized, she orders blood to be drawn and additional medical history to be taken. The examination continues until, at 16:37, the examinee completes the workup, admits the patient to the ward, and leaves orders for followup procedures. At 16:50 the message appears on the screen: "Thank you for taking care of this patient."

In this example, the simulated case time was 50 minutes; it took the student 17 minutes in real time to complete the case simulation. Cases can last for months of simulated time; examinees typically are allowed about 40 minutes, but usually take 20 to 25 minutes.

NBME computer-based testing is being phased in in stages. In Phase I, results from a 1987 field study were reviewed by an external advisory panel of experts in medicine, medical education, medical informatics, and psychometrics; they concluded the following:[2]

- CBX succeeded in measuring a quality (reasonably assumed to be related to clinical competence) not measured by existing examination formats.
- NBME should continue its current level of developmental activity directed at the ultimate use of the CBX in the NBME examination sequence for certification.

---

[1]This example is excerpted from K. E. Cotton and D.M. Durinzi, *Computer Based Examination Software System: Phase I-Phase II Update* (Philadelphia, PA: National Board of Medical Examiners, 1990).

[2]S.G. Clyman and N.A. Orr, "Status Report of the NBME's Computer-Based Testing," *Academic Medicine*, vol. 65, No. 4, April 1990.

- Examinations should be delivered through a system that incorporates collaborations with medical schools.
- A phased approach should be taken: Phase I would entail distribution of software so that students and faculty could familiarize themselves with the format and participate in collaborative research; Phase II would entail formal field studies; Phase III would entail extended intramural testing services; Phase IV would entail introduction in the certification examination(s).

For the first phase of testing, the case simulations, an evaluation of each student's management of the case is offered in the form of qualitative ''case-end feedback,'' derived from a scoring key developed by interdisciplinary committees of expert clinicians. The record of action is preserved by the computer and becomes the basis for computer grading of performance. Actions are evaluated in several item categories:[3]

Benefit: considered appropriate and useful in the management of the patient;

Neutral: representing acceptable actions that do not necessarily differentiate one student from another;

Risk: not required and may result in morbidity;

Inappropriate: represent nonharmful actions that are not indicated in the management of the patient;

Flag: indicate that the student did not successfully fulfill the testing objective or subjected the patient to unacceptable risk or poor probable outcome, through errors of omission or commission.

Additional data provided include itemized charges for services and tests, and a transaction list of actions taken.

---

[3]Stephen G. Clyman, M.D., project director for Computer Based Exam, National Board of Medical Examiners, personal communication, November 1991.

Figure 8-A1—CBX Case Computer Screen

Day 1 (Wed) Time 16:03   Location: Emergency Department

Vital signs (MD-recorded)   **Day 1 @ 16:03**

Pulse rate (supine)   118 beats/min
Systolic (supine)   98 mm Hg
Diastolic (supine)   58 mm Hg
Respiratory rate   32/minute

Chest/lung examination   **Day 1 @ 16:03**

Thorax normal. Breath sounds absent on the left.
Hyperresonance to percussion on the left.

Cardiac examination   **Day 1 @ 16:03**

Heart sounds faint. Radial, brachial, femoral and popliteal
   pulses weak but equal bilaterally.

****
SELECT ANY FUNCTION KEY
****

F1-ORDER **F2**-H&P **F3**-REVIEW **F4**-CLOCK **F5**-PAUSE **F6**-HELP

SOURCE: K. E. Cotton and D.M. Durinzi, *Computer Based Examination Software System: Phase I-Phase II Update* (Philadelphia, PA: National Board of Medical Examiners, 1990).

Continued on next page

Box 8-A—Certification Via Computer Simulations: The National Board of Medical Examiners—Continued

Phase II entails formal field studies addressing the validity, reliability, utility, and practicality of the system and its derivative scores for use at the level of clinical clerkships. The testing software includes 8 CBX simulations and a 140-item multiple-choice examination. These examinations were administered at the completion of clerkships in surgery, pediatrics, internal medicine, and obstetrics-gynecology. Separate scores were generated for each measure in each discipline for over 1,700 students at 9 schools since 1989. Scores are generated by an automated scoring system that codifies criteria specified by expert clinicians and consist of an ability measure and flag score. The findings to date are as follows:[4]

- Student surveys indicated that students believed that CBX simulations were more representative of the materials in the clerkship and more effective in allowing demonstrations of what was learned in the clerkship than were the multiple-choice questions.
- Reliability of the CBX scores in which there were large samples ranged from 0.70 to 0.80. These findings have been consistent across subjects, time, examinee level of training, and machine interface changes.
- The validity of the scores in this context is supported by multiple studies in which independent evaluations of average case performance by clinicians show high correlations with the CBX scoring systems.
- Correlations between multiple-choice and CBX scores in the same discipline are more moderate (0.37 to 0.50 corrected for the unreliability of the measures). Assuming the CBX scores are valid, as supported by the above-mentioned rating studies, this indicated that unique measurement information of merit in the evaluation of medical students is provided by both CBX and the multiple-choice questions.
- Analysis of multiple-choice questions compared the computerized versus paper-and-pencil versions. Students were ranked similarly on both versions, although the computerized multiple-choice version appears to be more difficult than the paper-and-pencil version by about 25 standard score points ($p<0.01$), suggesting that use of norm data from the paper-and-pencil tests would be inappropriate for the computer-based version.

Several other research questions are being addressed. They include:[5]

1. Are the CBX scores valid as an interdisciplinary evaluation of senior medical students?
2. What are effective means for weighting the relative importance of items and defining pass-fail standards?
3. How comparable are different sets of simulations in providing equivalent challenges to examinees?
4. Can simulations be "disguised" and reused without jeopardizing test fairness and meaningfulness of scores?

In addition, the Nation Council of State Boards of Nursing has taken the CBX model and is in the process of adapting it to the model of nursing education, and researching its use for possible certification examination.

---

[4]Unpublished National Board of Medical Examiners data, cited in National Board of Medical Examiners, *Interim Report on CBT Phase II* (Philadelphia, PA: 1991).

[5]Clyman, op. cit., footnote 3.

ing of the physics concept because it is less confounded with other skills such as reading level.[31]

Alternate modes of response can be used on the computer. Keyboarding reduces problems in interpreting handwriting, and the use of tablets, mouse, touch screens, light pens, and voice entry can provide new data entry formats. These new sources for data input also open doors for testing students with physical disabilities who may be unable to use traditional paper-and-pencil testing methods.

CBTs allow for improved standardization of test administration. For example, time allowed for any given item can be controlled, and instructions to test takers are not affected by variations in presentation by human examiners.

Scheduling of CBTs is more flexible, since not all students have to be tested at the same time.[32]

CBTs are not affected by measurement error due to erasures or stray marks on answer sheets. Young

---

[31]Wise and Plake, op. cit., footnote 22, p. 6.

[32]See, for example, Gerald Bracey, "Computerized Testing: A Possible Alternative to Paper and Pencil?" *Electronic Learning*, vol. 9, No. 5, February 1990, p. 16.

Figure 8-2—Mean Testing Time for Different Testing Formats

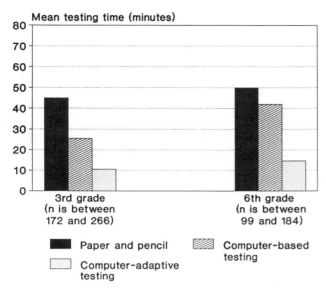

SOURCE: James B. Olsen et al., "Comparisons of Paper-Administered, Computer-Administered and Computer Adaptive Achievement Tests," *Journal of Educational Computer Research*, vol. 5, No. 3, 1989, pp. 311-326.

children, who may have difficulty connecting an answer with its associated letter on a separate answer sheet, may have less trouble supplying their answer directly on the computer.

Computerized adaptive tests provide greater measurement accuracy at all ability levels than either CBTs or paper-and-pencil tests,[33] because *they can more accurately discriminate using fewer items.*

CBTs allow for immediate scoring and reporting; responses entered directly on the computer can be scored and tabulated in seconds, and scores can be reported back to the examinee and the teacher virtually instantaneously. Rapid feedback of this sort can be particularly important for teachers and more useful than paper-and-pencil tests that can require 6 weeks or more to be scored.

CBT allows for greater integration between instruction and assessment. Students working through lessons on an ILS can be assessed as they progress. Assessment can take the form of pauses in the instructional sequence during which students respond to questions or other prompts; with more sophisticated tracking software the assessment can take place on a continuous basis, providing information to teachers about student strengths and weaknesses as they work.

CBTs can provide more detailed information than paper-and-pencil tests. For example, student response time for any or all items can offer clues to student strengths and weaknesses; tests equipped with this feature can keep track of skipped questions, item-response times, and other possibly relevant data. This information can be useful to test takers as well as teachers.

CBTs provide a more efficient means to pretest new items, which can be inserted unobtrusively into any sequence of questions; faulty items can be eliminated and the computer can adjust its scoring algorithm accordingly.[34]

CBTs are more secure than paper-and-pencil tests. There are no paper copies of tests to be misplaced or stolen, items can be presented in mixed sequences to different students, and the number of items stored in memory is too large for anyone to attempt to memorize. Computerized adaptive tests have a particular security advantage: each test taker gets essentially a unique test.

Finally, CBTs may offer a set of less tangible advantages over paper-and-pencil. Among the issues researchers are exploring are: whether successful handling of the technology itself raises self esteem of students, especially developmental or low-ability students; whether rapid feedback reduces test anxiety; whether students become less frustrated and bored with CBT than with paper-and-pencil tests; and whether students are less embarrassed when results are given by the computer rather than by a teacher.

Disadvantages of CBT

CBTs may introduce new kinds of measurement error or may introduce new factors that compromise the accuracy of the results. For example, results on a mathematics or science test could be skewed if poor screen resolution interferes with the student's decoding of graphs or images; long reading passages requiring the examinee to scroll through many screens could favor students with ability to manipulate computer keys rapidly rather than gauge relative

---

[33]Bunderson et al., op. cit., footnote 8, p. 385.

[34]Wainer, op. cit., footnote 30.

reading comprehension proficiency.[35] Input devices such as a mouse may be difficult for some students to operate, and current touch screens may not be accurate enough for sophisticated items requiring pointing and drawing. These issues suggest also that the lack of experience or familiarity with computers and keyboarding may put some students at a disadvantage compared to others.

Most CAT software, because of its branching algorithms, *prevents examinees from reviewing or changing an answer without changing all of the items following the changed ones*. The effects of this rigid sequencing on response patterns and cognition are not well understood.

Results of CATs are less obviously comparable to one another because each student's test is different in both the questions presented and the time allotted to finish. This may cause a perception on the part of students or others that test scores are somehow not a fair basis for comparisons.[36] These problems are aggravated by the general lack of familiarity with CAT on the part of test takers and the general public.

Ironically, *the computer might provide too much information*: teachers, parents, students, and administrators may be unable to digest the large amounts of data made available from CBTs.[37]

Reliability and validity of CBT generally and CAT specifically are important issues. Some studies have found that CAT can achieve reliability as high as conventional tests with far fewer items.[38] However, potential threats to validity and reliability warrant careful consideration: for example, issues related to content validity, effects of presentation mode on construct validity, potential negative effects on low-ability examinees, different contexts for item presentation, and the uses of data from conventional tests to set parameters of CATs.

Cost Considerations

Cost factors could pose formidable barriers to widespread adoption of CBT. Under current large-scale testing arrangements, when masses of students are tested at the same time, hardware requirements for CBT would be prohibitive. Scheduling students to be tested at different times could provide relief and would not necessarily create security risks, especially if a CAT model is used. But this approach would require drastic organizational changes from existing testing practice. Nevertheless, it may be possible to conduct some large-scale testing activities in shared facilities equipped with the appropriate testing hardware. Today's college entrance examinations are not offered in every school, but in selected sites on preselected dates; ETS is now considering setting up testing sites for administration of the GRE and professional certification examinations that are supplied with sufficient hardware to support CBT. These sites could be in schools or separate testing centers; in either event, the facility would be rented or leased by the test users (e.g., a professional association sponsoring certification examinations) for the time required to conduct the testing. Schools could adopt this shared facilities concept if it were necessary to conduct large-scale testing activities during a set time period.

Test Misuse and Privacy: A Further Caveat

Fully integrated instruction and assessment, hailed by some as the ideal approach to student testing, raises important questions related to test misuse and privacy. In a word, when testing is more closely linked to instruction it may become increasingly difficult if not impossible to prevent test results from being used inappropriately. It is precisely the tremendous recordkeeping and administrative efficiencies of CBT that pose this threat. To illustrate this concern, consider the ethical dilemmas that arise if students do not know they are being tested: as long as the information is used solely as feedback to teachers and students to improve learning, then there would be little objection. But if the results are used in high-stakes decisions such as graduation from grade school or placement into special classes (e.g., gifted or remedial) or made

---

[35]Research has shown that most people read 30 to 50 percent slower from a computer screen than from paper. Until screen resolution is improved significantly (e.g., 2,000 by 2,000 lines of resolution), this problem may not be resolved. Chris Dede, George Mason University, personal communication, Sept. 3, 1991.

[36]Green et al., op. cit., footnote 25.

[37]Olsen et al., op. cit., footnote 20, argue that too much information was provided to teachers on each child in the Texas pilot study. The solution was finally to print one page of analysis for each child accompanied by an order form for the teacher wanting additional information.

[38]For example, a study of the California version of the Armed Services Vocational Aptitude Battery found that the alternate forms reliability coefficient for a 15-item California test was equivalent to that of a 25-item conventional test. Similar findings have been found in other studies. Wise and Plake, op. cit., footnote 22, p. 8.

available to districts and States for accountability measures, the concept of seamless integration of instruction and assessment becomes less obviously attractive. And, in addition to the ethical problems of using data derived from tests that students did not know were tests, there is also the danger that in the long run students (and teachers) will figure out how their test results are being used, which would lead to distortions in test-taking practice and teaching. ''Teaching to the test'' and other unintended effects of high-stakes testing (see also ch. 2), could undermine the value of integrated teaching and testing.

Other New Tools for Testing: Video, Optical Storage, Multimedia

Video technologies are the newest tools of instruction. The near ubiquity of videocassette recorders (VCRs) in schools makes the use of video more feasible for testing as well.[39] Furthermore, videodiscs and digital video interactive also offer new possibilities for integrating video capabilities in item presentation for more realistic kinds of tasks. Often new technologies are combined with older formats for innovative testing arrangements. In the Oregon Statewide Assessment test of listening skills, for example, prerecorded videotapes set the scene for questions, which are presented on traditional paper-and-pencil multiple-choice tests. Developers believe that the visual stimuli presented on the tape is more realistic and better than having questions read aloud from text. The system was first used as an element of the statewide assessment in the spring of 1991.[40]

A more sophisticated optical storage device now also coming into use in some schools is the videodisc: a large silver platter (resembling a long-playing record) that uses analog technology to store text, data, sound, still images, and video. Computer branching algorithms can be used to manage and sequence the vast amounts of information stored on videodisc; this coupling of optical storage and computing technology has already resulted in some powerful instructional applications,

either in the form of enrichment materials or for courseware, some of which contain built-in testing and evaluation components. Researchers in this field anticipate new testing applications of videodisc in the future, given the capacity of the technology to store large amounts of multimedia items and integrate them with testing programs residing in the computer. Roughly one-fifth of American schools already own videodisc players.[41]

An application of videodisc to certification testing is the prototype developed by ETS to assess teaching and classroom management skills as part of the new National Teachers Examination. The experimental program presents filmed dramatizations of classroom management problems that typically occur in an elementary school classroom, and prompts the viewer to respond to each vignette. For example, after watching a scene the viewer may be asked to choose the teacher's next course of action; the choice activates a branch in the computer algorithm and displays the consequences of the choice.

Cost Considerations

As with many other instructional technologies, high costs of software development coupled with uncertainty and fragmentation on the demand side have slowed the development of innovative applications. However, if videodisc technology becomes a more common instructional tool in classrooms, software developers will face better prospects for return on their development investments. Without some sort of public intervention, it is unlikely the private market will produce the kinds of videodisc or other high-end technological innovations that could make a real difference in schools.[42] There is already some evidence that State education policies could stimulate growth in this market. For example, the decision of the Texas Board of Education to allow videodisc purchases with textbook funds is expected to lead to increased videodisc use in Texas schools, and, because of the large percentage of the school market that Texas represents, this policy is likely to spur increased videodisc development and use.[43]

---

[39]As of the 1990-91 school year, 94 percent of all schools have one or more videocassette recorders. Quality Education Data, op. cit., footnote 17, p. T-8.

[40]Evelyn Brezinski, Interwest (Oregon), personal communication, Jan. 3, 1991.

[41]Quality Education Data, op. cit., footnote 17, p. T-10.

[42]For analysis of the instructional software market and discussion of public policy options see Office of Technology Assessment, op. cit., footnote 16, especially ch. 4.

[43]Peter West, ''Tex. Videodisc Vote Called Boon to Electronic Media,'' *Education Week*, vol. 10, No. 13, Nov. 28, 1990, p. 5.

New Models of Assessment and the Role of Technology[44]

Most current uses of computer and information technology in large-scale testing make the conventional test format faster and more efficient than paper-and-pencil methods. The computer technologies have not, to date, created real alternatives to standardized multiple-choice tests.[45] Rather, the focus of computer applications has been on the familiar psychometric model, with enhancements that adapt the number, order, difficulty, and/or content of standard assessment items to the responses.[46]

There are two possible consequences that may spring from this replication. First, such a concentration may reinforce existing test and item formats by disguising them in the trappings of modern technology, creating a superficial air of advancement and sophistication. Moreover, these technical advances could make it even harder to break the mold of current testing practices, ignoring advances in test theory.

Using Information Technologies to Model Learning

How could computers and computer-related information technologies make possible enhancements to the current models of testing? How could these technologies be applied toward assessments of a broader range of human ability, cognition, and performance? Recent developments in cognitive psychology point to fruitful avenues for research and development (R&D).

First, human cognition and learning are now seen as *constructive processes*: seeing, hearing, and remembering are themselves acts of construction. Learners are viewed not as blank slates, passively recording and recalling bits of information, but as active participants who use the fragmentary cues permitted them by each of their senses to construct, verify, and modify their own mental models of the outside world.

Assessment procedures consistent with this view of cognition as an active, constructive activity are not limited to simply judging responses as correct or incorrect, but take into account the levels and types of understanding that a student has attained. Imaginative new types of test items are required to accomplish these ends, along with new techniques for scoring items that permit construction of dynamic models of the levels and types of learner understanding. Most if not all of these new techniques will require the use of computers. This work could lead to measures of human cognition and performance that are at present only dimly perceived, because of limited access and inexperience in measuring them.[47]

Second, some research on cognition holds that all learning is *situated* within "webs of distributed knowledge."[48] Cognitive performances in real-world settings are supported by other people and knowledge-extending artifacts (e.g., computers, calculators, texts, and so forth). This concept challenges traditional views of how to determine students' competence. If knowledge is tied in complex ways to situations of use and communities of knowers, then lists or matrices of abstracted concepts, facts, procedures, or ideas are not adequate descriptors of competence. Achievement needs to be determined by performances or products that interpret, apply, and make use of knowledge in situations. It follows from this view that estimates of learner competencies are inadequate if they are abstract or without context.

Computer-related technologies may be able to help integrate what is known about how children learn into new methods of assessment. This could include: diagnosing individualized and adaptive learning; requiring repeated practice and performance on complex tasks and on varying problems, with immediate feedback; recording and scoring multiple aspects of competence; and maintaining an

---

[44]Much of this discussion is based on Bank Street College, Center for Children and Technology, "Applications in Educational Assessment: Future Technologies," OTA contractor report, 1990.

[45]Walter Haney and George Madaus, "Searching for Alternatives to Standardized Tests: Whys, Whats, and Whithers," *Kappan*, vol. 70, No. 9, May 1989, p. 686.

[46]Dexter Fletcher, Institute for Defense Analyses, "Military Research and Development in Assessment Technology," unpublished report prepared for OTA, May 1991.

[47]Ibid., p. A-2.

[48]Bank Street College, op. cit., footnote 44.

efficient, detailed, and continuous history of performances. There are four specific areas in which computer technology has begun to demonstrate the potential for significant enrichments to assessment.

Tracking Thinking Processes

Computers enable certain kinds of process records to be kept about students' work on complex tasks as the work evolves and is revised. They allow the efficient capturing of views of students' problem-solving performances that would otherwise be invisible, evanescent, or cumbersome to record. For example, it is possible to keep records of whether students systematically control variables when testing a hypothesis, to look at their metacognitive strategies, to determine what they do when they are stuck, how long they pursue dead ends, and so forth.[49]

Learning With Immediate Feedback

Because students can be put into novel learning environments where the feedback is systematically controlled by the computer, it is possible to assess how well or how fast different students learn in such environments, how they use feedback, and how efficiently they revise.

Structuring and Constraining Complex Tasks

Computer environments can structure and constrain students' work on complex tasks in ways that are otherwise difficult to achieve. In simulations, dynamic problems that may have multiple outcomes can be designed, and student progress toward solutions can be automatically recorded, including time, strategy, use of resources, and the like. The tasks can be designed to record students' abilities to deal with realistic situations, like running a bank, repairing broken equipment, or solving practical problems that use mathematics. They can show how students sift, interpret, and apply information provided in the computer scenarios, making it possible to measure students abilities in understanding situations, integrating information from different sources, and reacting appropriately in real time.

Using Models of Expertise

In more advanced assessment systems, models of expertise can be programmed and used to guide and gauge students' development of understanding in a subject area or domain. In this case, learning and its monitoring occur simultaneously as the expert system diagnoses the student's level of competence. This makes it possible to record the problem-solving process and compare the student's process with that of experts in the field.

Hardware and Software

Many types of hardware and software configurations apply to these concepts of assessment. *Telecommunications*, for example, is an important tool for sharing information about alternative assessment tasks. Vermont is using a computer network to share information on student portfolios that are now used for statewide accountability in mathematics and writing. Teachers will be able to share examples of work to help develop common standards of grading the portfolios, as well as to discuss teaching strategies and other concerns over the statewide electronic bulletin board.[50] As shown in box 8-B, another example is the use of technology in support of the demonstrations of mastery (''exhibitions'') required of students in the Coalition of Essential Schools (see also ch. 6).

There are many examples of attempts to adapt *generic software tools* to assessment: word processors, database software, spreadsheets, and mathematics programs for statistical reasoning. These tools can be modified in order to record information in a sequence of work sessions and provide snapshots of students' processes in solving a problem or task. A word processor can record the stages of development of an essay; a spreadsheet program can record the steps taken in the solution of a multistage problem in mathematics. Because technology-based environments support accumulation and revision of products over time, they are well suited to portfolio models of assessment (see also ch. 6).

As teachers use these tools in teaching, it is appropriate that they be employed in testing situations as well. For example, when writing is taught as a process using a word processor, students develop

---

[49]This represents an extension of basic concepts such as the ''audit trail,'' already in use in some instructional software, to assessment. For discussion of intelligent tutoring and related concepts, see Office of Technology Assessment, op. cit., footnote 16, ch. 7.

[50]Harry Miller, New England Telephone, personal communication, September 1991.

Box 8-B—The IBM/Coalition of Essential Schools Project: Technology in Support of "Exhibitions of Mastery"[1]

"Planning backwards"—that is the term for how schools in the Coalition of Essential Schools determine what knowledge they want their students to possess, and what skills they want them to be able to demonstrate when they graduate. At Sullivan High School in Chicago, every member of the school community reads and participates in seminars discussing the works of great men and women, from Aristotle to Martin Luther King, in order to demonstrate their abilities to analyze and interpret works of original text. Seniors at Walbrook High School in Baltimore spend 1 year researching a specific question like "Is the city water safe to drink?" and must present findings, answer questions, and defend their positions before a panel of teachers and students, much like a Ph.D. student defending a dissertation. At Thayer High School in Winchester, New Hampshire, the faculty work in teams of four with a group of students for 3½ hours each day on a set of interdisciplinary "essential questions" chosen by the teaching team, allowing the students to show the connections among multiple disciplines.

These new teaching approaches require new assessment approaches. What is perhaps unique is how technology is being considered from the start as a tool for facilitating the restructuring that such "planning backwards" requires. IBM has committed $900,000 to the Coalition project at Brown University, along with equipment and technical

[1]Material for this box is from The Brown University News Bureau, "IBM and Brown University Select Five High Schools for National 'Exhibitions of Mastery' Project," news release, June 26, 1991, and David Niguidula, Coalition for Essential Schools, Providence, RI, personal communication, December 1991.

Figure 8-B1—Menu for Coalition of Essential Schools' Exit-Level Exhibitions

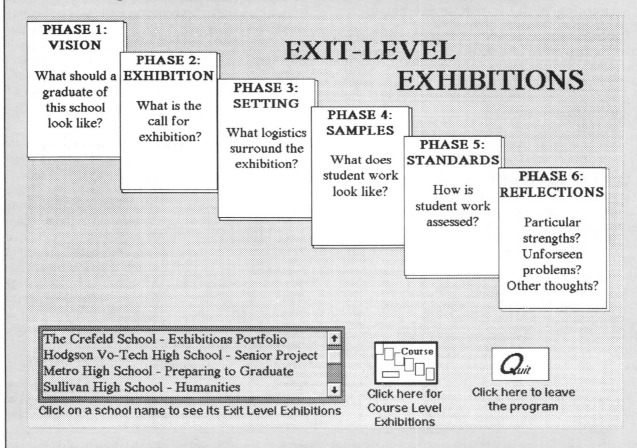

SOURCE: Coalition for Essential Schools, Brown University, Providence, RI.

support, to work with these schools and two others (Eastern High School, Louisville, and English High School, Boston) to examine how technology can facilitate the planning, development, and evaluation of the "exhibitions of mastery" assessment procedures at these schools. Technology is expected to be used in the following ways:

- Research: CD-ROM, videodiscs, computer databases, and telecommunications will be used for accessing and keeping track of information the teachers need for their teaching and the students need for their exhibitions.
- Student-Teacher Communications: Electronic mail will make it possible for information to be shared between students and their teachers both within a school and among sister exhibition schools. Project management will be tracked on the computer networks, and file transfers will be made so teachers can "red-pen" student drafts in progress.
- Performances: Tools such as word processing, desktop publishing, and multimedia will be used for creating student products.
- Assessment: Electronic portfolios of work in progress and records of student activity throughout the exhibition project will be created. Telecommunications will be used for assessing exhibitions within and among schools.

An electronic exhibitions resource center has been established by the 110+ member schools of the Coalition for Essential Schools. They are all contributing to this library of practical ideas, methods, and materials, which will be available on-line to help Coalition member schools create their own exhibitions. The exhibition resource center will provide a forum for discussing exhibitions and receiving updated information (see figures 8-B1 and 8-B2).

Figure 8-B2—Sample Screen When "Visions" is Selected From Menu

VISION — What should a graduate of this school know?

Central Park East Secondary School
Senior Institute

Graduating seniors will know that they have produced quality work in a broad range of intellectual areas. Their graduation, then, will be a meaningful celebration of achievement, not a perfunctory passage. These students will leave this school confident that they have developed the "habits of mind" necessary to meet the challenges of the world into which they enter.

These "habits" translate into a series of questions that should be applied to all learning experiences:

1. How do we know what we know? What is the evidence? Is it credible?
2. What viewpoint are we hearing, seeing,

To view more of this exhibition, click on a phase button

Phase 1: VISION

Phase 2: EXHIBITION

Phase 3: SETTING

Phase 4: SAMPLES

Phase 5: STANDARDS

Phase 6: REFLECTIONS

To return to the list of schools, click on the menu button.

Exit

SOURCE: Coalition for Essential Schools, Brown University, Providence, RI; example from Central Park East Secondary School, New York, NY.

the skills of freewriting, drafting ideas, writing a draft, revising, moving ideas around, editing—using all the tools of creation and revision provided by today's word processing software. To then test these writing skills using a paper-and-pencil examination would be as inappropriate as teaching a pilot to fly a jet and then testing his skills in a hang glider. Similarly, students taught to use calculators as mathematical tools should be tested on their ability to use these tools to carry out mathematical calculations.

The tests under development for certifying architects provide an interesting example of how advanced tools available on computers can enrich test design and scoring. Examinees use the computer tools that allow them to draw, measure, calculate, change the size and scale of objects, and extract information from databases embedded within the testing software (see box 8-C).

Another category of software includes *simulations and modeling programs* that create highly realistic problem-solving contexts. Examples can be found in most domains, both in and out of school, and are available for computers in the schools. They enable students to observe, control, and make decisions about scientific phenomena that would otherwise be difficult or impossible to observe. For example, with *Physics Explorer,* students can conduct and observe a series of experiments that simulate the behavior of objects and phenomena under different conditions.[51] For example, a student can compare the upward acceleration of an object under different conditions of gravity. The assessment includes onscreen records of various experiments that are conducted; printouts of steps taken by the student in the form of note cards, experimental parameters, and sequences of decisions; and video recordings of students interacting with software and explaining their work. Scoring is based on understanding of interactions among parameters, appropriateness of experiments conducted, systematic approach to testing of variables, use of different information sources, nature of predictions and hypotheses, interpretation of experiments, and quality of group collaboration.

Other computer simulations enable students to carry out complex actions by simulating decision-

Photo credit: MECC

Wagon Train 1848, created by MECC, is an example of an educational simulation program.

making activity in the sciences, social science, history, and literature. For example, *Rescue Mission* is a simulation that allows elementary school students to navigate a ship to rescue a whale trapped in a net by learning the mathematics and science required to read charts, plot a course, and control navigation instruments.[52]

One of the most promising aspects of simulation software for education is the fact that this software is already in use and popular in schools today, and can be supported on relatively inexpensive computers. Simulation and modeling programs can provide multiple complex tasks and record how students go about solving them. They provide opportunities for assessing students' skill in such problem-solving activities as formulating the relationships between variables, troubleshooting or diagnosing problems, and integrating multiple types of information in decisionmaking.

Video and multimedia systems are a third category of technology with applications to new concepts of student assessment. VCRs can record the interactions of students in groups, and the ways they use aspects of their social and physical environment in accomplishing tasks. Video technologies can record continuing activities, products at various stages of development, explanations, and presentations in rich detail. The video record can be analyzed in minute

---

[51]Bank Street College, op. cit., footnote 44.

[52]Ibid.

detail over time, much as one would review a written record of performance.

The electronic integration of different media (video, graphics, text, sound) has made possible new multimedia opportunities for instructional environments and new, but relatively unexplored opportunities for assessment. These developments allow multiple forms of media to be stored and orchestrated on a single disk, simplifying the ease of use.

Although the technology for some of these projects is currently too expensive for average classroom use, costs are expected to drop as more powerful computers enter classrooms.[53] Some schools have begun to experiment with multimedia applications. The *Jasper Woodbury Series*, for example, presents a story through dramatic video segments, and enlists the student in solving problems using information provided through multiple linked databases (see box 8-D). *Jasper*, which is still in R&D, is being integrated into the science and mathematics programs in a number of schools that have expressed their willingness to experiment.[54]

Performance assessments often call for student-created productions or projects over time as a basis for evaluation, and multimedia systems can provide rich composition tools to meet this goal. In some systems, students can make use of the information (in graphic, text, or video formats) available within a multimedia system as they compose their own projects or productions. This makes new kinds of student products available for assessment purposes. Since students create these productions from within these ''closed'' systems, traces of their creative composition process in choosing and composing information can be recorded.

Finally, *intelligent tutoring systems* (ITSs), originally conceived as instructional systems, have recently begun to be adapted to assessment. ITSs are based on principles of artificial intelligence and expert systems.[55] They combine models of what

Ulysses, created for IBM Corp. by And Communications Inc., is an example of an advanced interactive educational program combining video, graphics, text, and sound.

constitutes expertise within a field or domain with models of the learners' own technique—diagnosing, evaluating, and guiding student performance compared to expert performance. Responses of students throughout the learning process can be aggregated and interpreted in relation to representation of expert problem solving. The systems offer the opportunity to understand student performance not simply in terms of correct answers, but in sequences of responses that can reveal how a student learns.

There are very few ITSs available today and their focus is typically on instruction, not assessment. They are extremely expensive to develop and require a higher level of computer technology than most schools own. The few in place cover circumscribed parts of the curriculum, and concentrate on the domains where computational power has the most leverage and where skills and content are more narrowly defined (e.g., science, mathematics, and computer science). It is unclear how feasible they would be in other areas that are more open-ended, such as history or literature.

---

[53]The digitial video interactive product *Palenque*, which allows users to ''explore'' the Mayan archaeological site via computer and screen, and to consult a variety of visual databases to gather additional data along the way, requires a hardware/software system costing approximately $20,000. It is currently being used in several science museums around the United States. See ibid., p. 26; and Office of Technology Assessment, op. cit., footnote 16.

[54]Jasper and other similar systems attempt to capitalize on students' ever-increasing familiarity (and comfort) with television and video, and promotes the development of their skills in analyzing and using information provided via video format.

[55]''Artificial intelligence asks the questions: what is the fundamental nature of intelligence and how can we make computers do the things that we consider intelligent? . . . An expert system is an automated consultant. Given a problem, it requests data relevant to the solution. After analyzing the problem, it presents a solution and explains its reasoning. Expert systems are relevant to education because they can represent problem-solving expertise and explain to students how to use it.'' See Henry M. Halff, ''Instructional Applications of Artificial Intelligence,'' *Educational Leadership*, March 1986, pp. 24-26.

Box 8-C—Computer Technology for Professional Certification Testing: National Council of Architectural Registration Boards

It is not surprising that perhaps the most ambitious research on the use of computer technology for professional certification examinations is found in the field of architecture: architects often look for creative solutions and new ways to solve problems, using the most advanced technologies. At the same time, because only one-half the States require architects to have a college education and only 60 percent of the candidates who sit for the architectural boards have a professional degree in architecture, the examination has traditionally played an important gatekeeping role, i.e., assuring that candidates who receive national certification meet high standards of skills and knowledge. Furthermore, since the number of candidates who seek certification is relatively small (each year only 4,500 candidates begin the examination process), field testing is more manageable than in other professions.[1] Several other professional groups are following this research with great interest before developing their own technology-based testing for professional certification.

Since 1965, all architecture candidates have been required to pass a multipart uniform paper-and-pencil national examination developed by the National Council of Architectural Registration Boards (NCARB). This examination, which has been revised periodically based on task analyses of the profession, currently consists of nine parts, seven of which are traditional multiple-choice tests of discrete knowledge in various architectural fields. Two sections require candidates to draw solutions to design vignettes; one section involves solving six discrete site design problems, while the other entails a comprehensive building design. These sections are scored by juries of practicing architects, similar in process to the scoring of Advance Placement examinations (see ch. 6).

Since 1985, NCARB has been working with the Educational Testing Service (ETS) in a joint research project to develop computer-administered examinations. The first phase of the research entailed converting four of the seven multiple-choice sections to Computer Mastery Tests.[2]

The computer mastery model uses item-response theory to select questions from the full item bank, reorganizing them into "testlets," each of which provides a collection of questions, which offers precise measurement of a candidate's ability. The items within a testlet are presented on the computer. When the candidate answers enough questions to determine that a passing or failing score has been achieved, testing ceases. If the outcome is unclear, more questions are presented until a clear pass-fail determination has been made. The computer mastery tests were pilot tested between 1988 and 1990. They successfully met the desired psychometric standards; the computerized tests achieved the same or better accuracy of measurement at the pass-fail point as that provided by the current tests, using as few as one-third as many test items as are needed in the paper-and-pencil version. However, because the computer tests were offered as an option to paper-and-pencil testing but were more expensive ($75 per subject as compared to $35 per subject for the paper-and-pencil format), not enough candidates opted for the computer version to make it economically feasible. Since 1990, only the paper-and-pencil version has been offered.

NCARB plans to switch over to computer-administered testing for all seven of the discrete knowledge sections in 1997, dropping the paper-and-pencil option altogether. At that point, the second research activity will also be put into place. This project involves administering the test (examinees use a mouse or other pointing or drawing device to design directly on the computer screen), and scoring the discrete site design vignettes directly on the computer. Field testing has shown that design problems that take an average of 20 minutes on the paper-and-pencil version require only 5 minutes to complete on the computer, because of the ease of erasing, redrawing, and adjusting drawings. As a result of this research, NCARB expects to be able to present candidates with up to 15 vignettes to solve, compared to the existing 6, in the same period of time (see figure 8-C1).

Finally, the comprehensive building design problem is being converted to a computer-administered examination as well. In this case, each candidate will use two computers, one which presents and serves as the "answer sheet" for a candidate's design solutions to comprehensive, multistep design problems; the other monitor provides the "model architect's office," containing all the design tools, resources, and reference manuals needed

---

[1]Jeffrey F. Kenney, director of Examinations Development, National Council of Architectural Registration Boards, personal communication, October 1991.

[2]"Breakthrough Development in Computerized Testing Offers Shorter Test, More Precise Pass-Fail Decisions," *ETS Developments*, vol. 33, Nos. 3 and 4, winter/spring 1988, pp. 3-4.

Figure 8-C1—Example of an NCARB Site Design Vignette

A recreational center site plan must accommodate a club house in its present position, as well as tennis courts, pool, bleachers, and a service building. Prepare the site plan according to the following objectives: (1) Preserve all trees. (2) Bleachers shall serve the tennis courts. (3) Pool shall be adjacent to the clubhouse. (4) Service building shall relate to the club house and the parking lot.

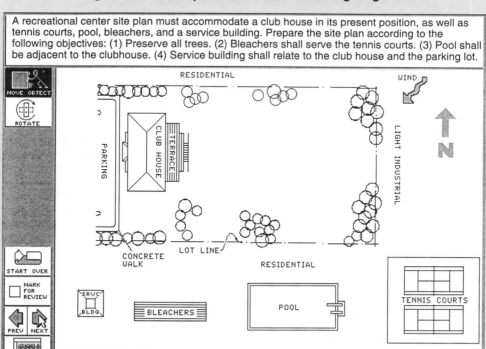

KEY: NCARB = National Council of Architectural Registration Boards.
SOURCE: Educational Testing Service, 1991.

to complete each task. Each of the substeps in the comprehensive design problems will be presented as separate sections and scored separately. For example, a candidate may be asked to design a library that meets certain site and client requirements. In the first step, the "bubble diagrams" that relate rooms to one another would be drawn. A second section would require taking a block diagram and relating it to the site requirements in terms of light, ground contours, zoning, and other constraints. Each of these individual predesign tasks will be scored separately, making it possible to give a candidate partial credit, instead of scoring the building problem as a whole, as is done in the existing paper-and-pencil format.

In 1989, six different item types were developed for the simulations and pilot tested at an architectural firm and the NCARB annual meeting. It is anticipated that the computer format will permit more reliable assessment of candidates' abilities. Whereas it now takes candidates up to 12 hours to complete 1 comprehensive problem (typically 4 hours to come up with a design and another 8 to put it down on paper), using the computer simulations broken down into subtasks, up to 10 design samples can be presented over a period of 5 to 6 hours. It is anticipated that perhaps 3 comprehensive building problems, with a total of some 20 to 30 subtasks can be administered for this portion of the examination over the same time period, giving the State board examination a fuller and more reliable picture of an architect's design skill and ability to meet the necessary health, safety, and environmental standards.

Researchers are encouraged by the progress made in the design of the computer interfaces; indeed, erasers, drafting tools, measuring tapes, calculators, and other design tools that make it possible to move and adjust drawings are available in many computers today, as are the appropriate data storage and retrieval capabilities. The hardware required is Windows-based 386 machines with approximately 4 megabytes of memory. Advances in object-oriented

Continued on next page

**Box 8-C—Computer Technology for Professional Certification Testing:
National Council of Architectural Registration Boards—Continued**

programming make it possible to use icons for frequently used architectural components (e.g., corridors, doors, walls, and windows). It is the development of scoring psychometrics that poses the largest research challenge. In order to develop scoring protocols, each solution must be decomposed or broken into component parts. Seasoned practitioners list the characteristics of an appropriate solution to a particular problem and these judgments are programmed into the computer. The computer, functioning as an expert system, evaluates the examinee's response. In cases where the expert system is unable to make a clear ''right or wrong'' judgment (similar to the case with live panels of judges when two scorers disagree), a master scorer will be brought in to make a final determination.

Although the original target goal was 1997,[3] the NCARB/ETS team has moved along further than originally anticipated and, if progress continues as the same rate, implementation of a fully computer-administered and scored examination system could be possible in 1996.[4]

---

[3]Richard DeVore, senior examiner, Center for Occupational and Professional Assessment, Educational Testing Service, personal communication, Oct. 15, 1991.

[4]William Wiese II, ''License Exams by Computer,'' *Architectural Record*, vol. 179, No. 7, July 1991, p. 80.

One of the greatest concerns with ITSs is that, like all testing activities, they may gravitate toward promoting the skills that they measure best. These skills tend to be algorithmic and routine. At the same time, educators are concerned that we may not be focusing our efforts on developing in students those thinking skills dependent on complex knowledge. The skills required for understanding a written passage, writing a composition, solving a problem that has many steps and approaches, interpreting the results of an experiment, or analyzing an argument are not so easily broken into discrete components. Furthermore, attempts to segment these skills may result in analysis that fails to capture the overall picture of what makes up true competence. Creativity may be neither recognized nor rewarded in existing ITS models.

Toward New Models of Assessment: Policy Issues

A main finding of this chapter is the gap that separates current applications of information technology in testing from a vision of fundamental reform in the assessment of human learning and educational achievement. In sum, computers and other data processing equipment that have made possible a ''mass production'' testing technology could become essential in the design and implementation of new testing paradigms.

Computers and related technologies have proven indispensable to research on human cognition, and lessons from this research are, in turn, being applied—also with the help of sophisticated computer-based systems—to the design of educational assessments that correspond to the growing body of research on learning. The research community, though still fragmented, has begun to coordinate the efforts of cognitive theorists, computer scientists, subject matter experts, and educators. These early efforts have led to particularly promising breakthroughs in the application of technology to improved classroom diagnosis and instructional feedback. Whether these efforts will eventually also contribute to the creation of tests that can be used for other functions, such as system monitoring or student placement and certification, remains to be seen. In any event, it is not clear that these latter functions of testing require the diagnostic specificity of computer-based learning and assessment tools. Overall, most experts would agree that applications of computer technology to new forms of assessment are still at a very rudimentary stage. The road ahead is a long one.

Research Support

Policymakers face a formidable dilemma: reaching the as-yet uncharted territory of *new* assessment models requires investments in technologies that have uses in the current paradigm of testing and that render that paradigm ever more efficient. Increased efficiency encourages reliance on old models of testing. This problem is manifest in the arena of funded research: much of the research on test theory and new technology is funded by commercial test companies, which face strong incentives to reinforce

Box 8-D—The Jasper Series: A Story is Worth a Thousand Questions

The National Council of Teachers of Mathematics has suggested that the mathematics curriculum should:

. . . engage students in problems that demand extended effort to solve. Some might be group projects that require students to use available technology and to engage in cooperative problem solving and discussion. For grades 5-8 an important criterion of problems is that they be interesting to students.[1]

The *Jasper Woodbury Problem Solving Series* is a video-based adventure series designed to help students develop their skills in solving mathematical problems.[2] Each of the six video segments is from 14 to 18 minutes long and presents a dramatic adventure featuring Jasper and his friends. Students are motivated to solve the problem posed at the end of each segment to see how the story ends. (There is a solution shown on the video that students see only after they have solved the problems themselves.) Although the problems are complex and require many steps, all the data needed to solve the problems are contained as a natural part of the story.

For example, the adventure "Rescue at Boone's Meadow" begins with Jasper's friend Larry flying his ultralight airplane. Larry teaches Emily the principles she needs to know in order to fly solo in the plane: fuel capacity, speed, payload limits, how the shape of the wing produces lift, and so on. After Emily's maiden solo flight, she, Larry, and Jasper celebrate at a local restaurant. They discuss Jasper's upcoming fishing trip, and his plan to hike 15 miles into the woods at Boone's Meadow. Details presented as a part of the unfolding adventure become important data that students will later need to use in solving the problem. The next scene shows Jasper alone in the deep woods, peacefully fishing, when a shot rings out. He runs in the direction of the sound, finds an eagle that has been seriously wounded, and radios for help on his CB radio. Emily receives his message, contacts a local veterinarian, and is told that time is of the essence in rescuing the eagle. The story ends with Emily posing the question: "What's the fastest way to rescue the eagle and how long will it take?" The students, no longer passive watchers, have to put themselves in the role of Emily and solve the problem using data contained in the video.[3]

Researchers, working with teachers and students in 9 States, have found that students become extremely engaged in the problem-solving tasks. Teaching strategies vary, but most teachers begin with large group activities and then move into smaller cooperative learning groups, guiding the students to consider a variety of solutions. In the episode summarized above, for example, if the students contemplate using the ultralight plane as a rescue vehicle, they must take into account landing area, fuel consumption, payload limitations, speed, and other information that can be reviewed by going back into the videodisc. Groups typically spend a minimum of two 1-hour class periods working out their solution, and then must present and defend their plan to the entire class.

One of the research goals has been to create new ways to assess the learning that occurs in solving problems presented in the series. One-on-one interviews with students were found to be much too time consuming. Paper-and-pencil tests were developed, asking students to list and explain the kinds of subproblems that Jasper and his friends needed to consider to solve each problem. Transfer problems, similar to the problems in the series but involving new settings and data, were also given. Although the paper-and-pencil assessments showed that learning occurred, there was one problem: teachers and students hated them! Teachers said: "My kids, as much as they liked Jasper, as much as they begged for Jasper, finally told me: 'If I have to take another test on Jasper I don't want to see another Jasper' "; or "it seems to me that we're really asking kids to do something strange when we've introduced this wonderful technology and we've gotten them involved in the video experience. . . . Then you give them this test that's on paper."[4]

How then should the students be tested? One approach has been to explore ways technology can be used in the assessment process. In May of 1991 the researchers produced an experimental teleconference, the *Challenge Series*, a game show format featuring three college students as contestants, each of whom claimed to be an expert

---

[1]National Council of Teachers of Mathematics, *Curriculum and Evaluation Standards for School Mathematics* (Reston, VA: March 1989).

[2]The series is a research and development project of the Cognition and Technology Group at Vanderbilt University, supported by the James S. McDonnell Foundation, the National Science Foundation, and Vanderbilt University.

[3]Cognition and Technology Group at Vanderbilt University, "The Jasper Experiment: An Exploration of Issues in Learning and Instructional Design," July 26, 1991, p. 7 (forthcoming in Michael Hannafin and Simon Hooper (eds.), *Education Technology Research and Development*, special issue).

[4]Cognition and Technology Group at Vanderbilt University, "The Jasper Series: A Generative Approach to Improving Mathematical Thinking," pp. 11-12 (forthcoming in American Association for the Advancement of Science, *This Year in School Science*).

Continued on next page

Box 8-D—The Jasper Series: A Story is Worth a Thousand Questions—Continued

on flight and on the Jasper adventure "Rescue at Boone's Meadow." While the contestants all answered questions correctly on the first round, by the fourth round everyone except the true expert had made some erroneous arguments. Would the students be fooled by actors, or could they identity the real expert? They called in their votes and 85 percent of the students correctly identified the true expert. Enthusiasm for this form of "testing" was sky high.

Other ideas building on the teleconference motif are being considered for each of the Jasper adventures. There are also plans to help teachers engage in formative evaluations of student learning following each Jasper adventure with video-based "what if" analogs like the ones used to prepare for the *Challenge Series* teleconference. Spinoff vignettes that connect with other parts of the curriculum (e.g., an exploration of Lindbergh's historic flight from New York to Paris) are also in progress. Finally, the researchers are designing a prototype set of computer-based "students" or "tutees." The students must teach the "tutees" how to solve Jasper problems, and their progress is tracked by the computer. This approach may be linked with the teleconferences. For example, the students could teach computer-based tutees, who would then compete in a game show where the tutees become game show contestants. The class that did the best job teaching its tutees wins.

The seven design principles underlying the Jasper Series, and their hypothesized benefits, are summarized in table 8-D1.

Table 8-D1—Seven Design Principles Underlying the Jasper Adventure Series

Design principle	Hypothesized benefits
1. Video-based format	a. More motivating. b. Easier to search. c. Supports complex comprehension. d. Especially helpful for poor readers yet it can also support reading.
2. Narrative with realistic problems (rather than a lecture on video)	a. Easier to remember. b. More engaging. c. Primes students to notice the relevance of mathematics and reasoning for everyday events.
3. Generative format (i.e., the stories end and students must generate the problems to be solved)	a. Motivates students to determine the ending. b. Teaches students to find and define problems to be solved. c. Provides enhanced opportunities for reasoning.
4. Embedded data design (i.e., all the data needed to solve the problems are in the video)	a. Permits reasoned decisionmaking. b. Motivates students to find. c. Puts students on an "even keel" with respect to relevant knowledge. d. Clarifies how relevance of data depends on specific goals.
5. Problem complexity (i.e., each adventure involves a problem of at least 14 steps)	a. Overcomes the tendency to try for a few minutes and then give up. b. Introduces levels of complexity characteristic of real problems. c. Helps students deal with complexity. d. Develops confidence in abilities.
6. Pairs of related adventures	a. Provides extra practice on core schema. b. Helps clarify what can be transferred and what cannot. c. Illustrates analogical thinking.
7. Links across the curriculum	a. Helps extend mathematical thinking to other areas (e.g., history, science). b. Encourages the integration of knowledge. c. Supports information finding and publishing.

SOURCE: Cognition and Technology Group at Vanderbilt University, "The Jasper Experiment: An Exploration of Issues in Learning and Instructional Design," July 26, 1991 (forthcoming in Michael Hannafin and Simon Hooper (eds.), *Education Technology Research and Development*, special issue).

the economic and educational advantages of the conventional test paradigm. This is in contrast to the test development process in other countries, which is usually undertaken or supported wholly by the government. Just how far the commercial research community will go in experimenting with nontraditional test designs, without external support, is uncertain.

It is important to recall, however, that Federal intervention frequently played a critical role in the history of research, development, and implementation of new testing technology: perhaps the best example is the Army testing program during World War I (see also ch. 3), which provided the most fertile ground imaginable for proving the feasibility of new forms of testing, such as group administration, as well as statistical models based on normative comparisons and rankings.

Indeed, the military has since then remained a major player in the development of personnel selection and placement tests, assessments of basic job skills, and experimentation with a variety of models of performance assessment. Some of these advances have spilled over into the civilian arena.[56] In addition, there is the more recent example of National Science Foundation (NSF) support for research leading to development of tasks used in the 1988 National Assessment of Educational Progress (NAEP) science assessment. Not only were these items viewed as important innovations in NAEP, but many of them were then adopted by New York State for its statewide fourth grade hands-on science assessment. Similarly, Department of Education funding for NAEP has supported research into constructed response items and innovative testing formats. Thus, while federally funded research on assessment has not been large, it has been an important complement to the large R&D projects financed privately—such as those by ETS, ACT, the National Council of Architectural Registration Boards, the National Board of Medical Examiners, and computer companies such as IBM and Apple— or financed by States and districts, such as in California and Portland, Oregon.

The history of testing in the United States teaches that the Federal Government can be a catalyst for reform, through support for expansion of existing technologies and through support for basic research leading to new technologies. The Federal Government could continue to support basic research and applied development of a wide range of new models of testing. Specific options include:

- earmarking resources in programs like Chapter 1 for research into how advanced technologies can improve testing;
- continuing to fund educational laboratories and centers for school-based research on assessment;
- providing grants to independent researchers, States, and school districts through NSF or other existing programs;
- coordinating the efforts of the many research players both within and outside the Federal Government's research network, i.e., Federal laboratories, the National Diffusion Network, NSF Net, and Star School Programs in support of improvements in testing; and
- supporting the exchange of data among the many States and districts involved in pioneering theoretical and practical research.

Infrastructure Support

If computers, video, and telecommunications technologies are to play a significant role in assessment, a combined ''technology-push/market-pull'' strategy will be necessary.[57] Technology-push in this context focuses on the technology of software, and is shorthand for software development support that could lead to increased demand for computer-based instructional and assessment systems in schools. The market-pull side of the equation refers to direct investments in hardware: increasing the installed base of technology in the schools could lead to increased demand for good software, which could in turn create improved economic incentives for software developers and entrepreneurs.

To make inroads in this interrelated system, the Federal Government could support investments in CBT facilities that could be shared among schools within and across districts. This could entail investments in communications technologies to link hardware already in place, along with software and training. Another approach would be for schools to

---

[56]The flow has gone in the other direction too: assessment techniques developed for educational institutions have been adopted by the military.

[57]See also Office of Technology Assessment, op. cit., footnote 16, for discussion of this approach to fostering improved instructional software development.

lease their computer facilities to the Federal Government for use in its large education and training programs, or to other outside users (adult education, business, professional groups). The idea is to utilize the capacity of the hardware that exists in schools now, or the hardware that could be installed in the schools, during nonschool hours, and to reinvest the revenues in testing-related hardware or software technologies. Federal support for purchase of multipurpose computer and video technologies for testing activities under existing Federal programs, such as Chapter 1, Magnet Schools, and Bilingual Education could build up the infrastructure of testing technologies.

Continuing Professional Development for Teachers

Teachers are the most important link between instructional or testing technologies and the students whose achievement and progress those technologies are intended to affect. The problem is that few teachers have adequate preparation in the theory and techniques of assessment. This gap in teacher education is not limited to the arcana of psychometrics, but extends even to the design and interpretation of classroom-based tests.[58] At the same time, many teachers have not yet come "online" with computer use.[59] While teachers may be learning about computers faster than about testing and assessment, most teachers have not been exposed to continuing professional development aimed at helping them master the implications of matching technology and new approaches to testing.

Federal support for teacher development could have two benefit streams: first, it could result in greater acceptance of new testing and assessment technologies, which would in turn lead to heightened demand for innovative software products; and

Photo credit: Educational Testing Service

Teachers need help in learning to use teaching technology for testing purposes.

second, it could involve teachers in the early stages of testing technology development, which could make the technologies that much more relevant.

Leadership

In 1990, the President and the Governors adopted ambitious education goals to be met by the year 2000, and there has been much discussion on developing new tests to measure success in meeting these goals. The Federal Government has the opportunity to provide guidance in a time that has been marked by many suggestions for improvement and much accompanying confusion. Congress could take a leadership position in guiding, shaping, and supporting a vision of education that links learning with assessment in a rich, meaningful, engaging, and equitable fashion.

---

[58]See, e.g., John R. Hills, "Apathy Concerning Grading and Testing," *Phi Delta Kappan*, vol. 72, No. 7, March 1991.

[59]See, e.g., Bank Street College, op. cit., footnote 44.

APPENDIXES

ACT —American College Testing Program
AERA —American Educational Research Association
AP —Advanced Placement
ASAP —Arizona Student Assessment Program
ASP —Accelerated Schools Program

CAP —California Assessment Program
CARAT —Computerized Adaptive Reporting and Testing
CAT —computerized adaptive testing
CBT —computer-based testing
CBX —Computer Based Exam

CEE —College Entrance Examinations
CES —Coalition of Essential Schools
COMP —College Outcome Measures Program
CoMPACT —Connecticut Multi-State Performance Assessment Collaborative Teams
CR —constructed response

CRESST —Center for Research on Evaluation, Standards, and Student Testing
CRT —criterion-referenced test
CUES —Continuous Uniform Evaluation System
EC —European Community
EPT —English Placement Test

ERA —Education Reform Act (United Kingdom)
ESDs —Essential Skills Documents
ESEA —Elementary and Secondary Education Act
ESPET —Elementary Science Program Evaluation Test
ETS —Educational Testing Service

FERPA —Family Education Rights and Privacy Act
GCSE —General Certificate of Secondary Education
GED —General Educational Development
GKAP —Georgia Kindergarten Assessment Program
GPA —grade point average

GRE —Graduate Record Examination
HOTS —Higher Order Thinking Skills
ILS —integrated learning system

ITBS —Iowa Tests of Basic Skills
ITS —intelligent tutoring system

JFSAT —Joint First Stage Achievement Test
LAN —local area network
LEA —local education authority
LSAT —Law School Admissions Test
MAP —Monitoring Achievement in Pittsburgh

MCT —minimum competency testing
MOE —Ministry of Education
NAEP —National Assessment of Educational Progress
NAGB —National Assessment Governing Board
NBME —National Board of Medical Examiners

NCARB —National Council of Architectural Registration Boards
NCE —Normal Curve Equivalent
NCTM —National Council of Teachers of Mathematics
NIMSY —not-in-my-school-yard
NRT —norm-referenced test

NSF —National Science Foundation
PALT —Portland (Oregon) Achievement Level Testing
PLR —Primary Language Record
R&D —research and development
SAT —Scholastic Aptitude Test

SAT —Standard Assessment Task
SEA —State education agency
SWESAT —Swedish Scholastic Aptitude Test
TAP —Tests of Achievement and Proficiency
TIERS —Title I/Chapter 1 Evaluation and Reporting System

TNCUEE —Test of the National Center for University Entrance Examinations
TSWE —Test of Standard Written English
VCR —video cassette recorder

APPENDIX B
Contractor Reports

Copies of contractor reports done for this project are available through the National Technical Information Service (NTIS), either by mail (U.S. Department of Commerce, National Technical Information Service, Springfield, VA 22161) or by calling NTIS directly at (703) 487-4650.

Douglas A. Archbald, University of Delaware, and Arnold C. Porter, University of Wisconsin, Madison, "A Retrospective and an Analysis of Roles of Mandated Testing in Education Reform," PB 92-127596.

C.V. Bunderson, J.B. Olson, and A. Greenberg, The Institute for Computer Uses in Education, "Computers in Educational Assessment: An Opportunity to Restructure Educational Practice," PB 92-127604.

Paul Burke, "You Can Lead Adolescents to a Test But You Can't Make Them Try," PB 92-127638.

Center for Children and Technology, Bank Street College, "Applications in Educational Assessment: Future Technologies," PB 92-127588.

Nancy Kober, "The Role and Impact of Chapter 1, ESEA, Evaluation and Assessment Practices," PB 92-127646.

George F. Madaus, Boston College, and Thomas Kellaghan, St. Patricks College, Dublin, "Examination Systems in the European Community: Implications for a National Examination System in the United States," PB 92-127570 (see also below).

Gail R. Meister, Research for Better Schools, "Assessment in Programs for Disadvantaged Students: Lessons From Accelerated Schools," PB 92-127612.

Ruth Mitchell and Amy Stempel, Council for Basic Education, "Six Case Studies of Performance Assessment," PB 92-127620.

Misuse of Tests, PB 92-127653

1. Larry Cuban, Stanford University, "The Misuse of Tests in Education."
2. Robert L. Linn, University of Colorado at Boulder, "Test Misuse: Why Is It So Prevalent?"
3. Nelson L. Noggle, Center for the Advancement of Educational Practices, "The Misuse of Educational Achievement Tests for Grades K-12: A Perspective."

* * *

A copy of the contractor report listed below may be obtained by writing to the SET Program, Office of Technology Assessment, U.S. Congress, Washington, DC 20510-8025; or by calling (202) 228-6920.

George F. Madaus, Boston College, and Thomas Kellaghan, St. Patricks College, Dublin, "Student Examination Systems in the European Community: Lessons for the United States" (abridged version of Madaus-Kellaghan paper listed above).

INDEX

Superintendent of Documents **Publications** Order Form

Order Processing Code:

* **6145**

P3

Charge your order.
It's Easy!

[MasterCard] [VISA]

To fax your orders (202) 512–2250

☐ **YES**, please send me the following:

_____ copies of *Testing in American Schools: Asking the Right Questions*
S/N 052-003-01275-8 at $14.00 each.

The total cost of my order is $_____. International customers please add 25%. Prices include regular domestic postage and handling and are subject to change.

_____ (Please type or print)
(Company or Personal Name)

_____
(Additional address/attention line)

_____
(Street address)

_____
(City, State, ZIP Code)

_____
(Daytime phone including area code)

_____
(Purchase Order No.)

                                                                    YES NO
May we make your name/address available to other mailers?   ☐   ☐

Please Choose Method of Payment:

☐ Check Payable to the Superintendent of Documents

☐ GPO Deposit Account ☐☐☐☐☐☐ – ☐

☐ VISA or MasterCard Account

☐☐☐☐☐☐☐☐☐☐☐☐☐☐☐☐☐☐☐☐☐☐☐☐

☐☐☐☐ (Credit card expiration date)   *Thank you for*
                                        your order!

_____
(Authorizing Signature)   2/92

Mail To: New Orders, Superintendent of Documents
          P.O. Box 371954, Pittsburgh, PA 15250–7954

ISBN 0-16-036161-3

90000

9 780160 361616